CW01337436

£18
27/11/24
£10
12/5/25

John Ruskin's Correspondence with Joan Severn
Sense and Nonsense Letters

LEGENDA

LEGENDA, founded in 1995 by the European Humanities Research Centre of the University of Oxford, is now a joint imprint of the Modern Humanities Research Association and Maney Publishing. Titles range from medieval texts to contemporary cinema and form a widely comparative view of the modern humanities, including works on Arabic, Catalan, English, French, German, Greek, Italian, Portuguese, Russian, Spanish, and Yiddish literature. An Editorial Board of distinguished academic specialists works in collaboration with leading scholarly bodies such as the Society for French Studies and the British Comparative Literature Association.

MHRA

The Modern Humanities Research Association (MHRA) encourages and promotes advanced study and research in the field of the modern humanities, especially modern European languages and literature, including English, and also cinema. It also aims to break down the barriers between scholars working in different disciplines and to maintain the unity of humanistic scholarship in the face of increasing specialization. The Association fulfils this purpose primarily through the publication of journals, bibliographies, monographs and other aids to research.

MANEY
publishing

Maney Publishing is one of the few remaining independent British academic publishers. Founded in 1900 the company has offices both in the UK, in Leeds and London, and in North America, in Boston. Since 1945 Maney Publishing has worked closely with learned societies, their editors, authors, and members, in publishing academic books and journals to the highest traditional standards of materials and production.

EDITORIAL BOARD

Chairman
Professor Martin McLaughlin, Magdalen College, Oxford

Professor John Batchelor, University of Newcastle (English)
Professor Malcolm Cook, University of Exeter (French)
Professor Colin Davis, Royal Holloway University of London
(Modern Literature, Film and Theory)
Professor Robin Fiddian, Wadham College, Oxford (Spanish)
Professor Paul Garner, University of Leeds (Spanish)
Professor Marian Hobson Jeanneret,
Queen Mary University of London (French)
Professor Catriona Kelly, New College, Oxford (Russian)
Professor Martin Maiden, Trinity College, Oxford (Linguistics)
Professor Peter Matthews, St John's College, Cambridge (Linguistics)
Dr Stephen Parkinson, Linacre College, Oxford (Portuguese)
Professor Ritchie Robertson, St John's College, Oxford (German)
Professor Lesley Sharpe, University of Exeter (German)
Professor David Shepherd, University of Sheffield (Russian)
Professor Alison Sinclair, Clare College, Cambridge (Spanish)
Professor David Treece, King's College London (Portuguese)
Professor Diego Zancani, Balliol College, Oxford (Italian)

Managing Editor
Dr Graham Nelson
41 Wellington Square, Oxford OX1 2JF, UK

legenda@mhra.org.uk
www.legenda.mhra.org.uk

John Ruskin's Correspondence with Joan Severn

Sense and Nonsense Letters

❖

Edited by Rachel Dickinson

LEGENDA

Modern Humanities Research Association and Maney Publishing
2009

Published by the
Modern Humanities Research Association and Maney Publishing
1 Carlton House Terrace
London SW1Y 5AF
United Kingdom

LEGENDA is an imprint of the
Modern Humanities Research Association and Maney Publishing

Maney Publishing is the trading name of W. S. Maney & Son Ltd,
whose registered office is at Suite 1C, Joseph's Well, Hanover Walk, Leeds LS3 1AB

ISBN 9-781-905981-90-8

First published 2009

All rights reserved. No part of this publication may be reproduced or disseminated or transmitted in any form or by any means, electronic, mechanical, photocopying, recording or otherwise, or stored in any retrieval system, or otherwise used in any manner whatsoever without the express permission of the copyright owner

© Modern Humanities Research Association and W. S. Maney & Son Ltd 2009

Printed in Great Britain

Cover: 875 Design

Copy-Editor: Richard Correll

CONTENTS

❖

Foreword	ix
Acknowledgements	x
Note on References	xi
Introduction	1
I. Relational Roles	5
II. The Evolution of Baby-Talk	19
III. Ruskin and Girls	33
Afterword	51
LETTERS	
Notes on Editorial Practice	69
Letters from John Ruskin, 1864–88	72
Letters from Joan Agnew (later Severn), 1868–88	254
Appendices	273
A. Idiolectical Glossary	274
B. Baby-talk Names	281
C. Chronology	283
D. Names Identified in the Edition	287
Works Cited	293
Index	296

TO MY BELOVED JOHN

FOREWORD

❖

This is an annotated edition of selected letters from the correspondence between John Ruskin and his cousin Joan (Agnew Ruskin) Severn. It offers an indicative cross-section of this, the key epistolary relationship of Ruskin's later years, represented by 260 of Ruskin's letters to her and 20 of her letters to him. The introductory essay defines the roles she occupied in Ruskin's life and home, comparing their epistolary relationship with those Ruskin shared with others. Exploring his letters to Joan in connection with their personal relationship, the essay considers the constructions of self and home enabled by this exchange, focusing on this epistolary relationship as a context through which Ruskin negotiated between notions of gender, power and identity. By disempowering himself within a private, domestic sphere of epistolary conversation and existence, he paradoxically empowered himself by achieving comfort and peace. This strategy implicitly reinforced his public persona.

For Ruskin scholars, the introduction proposes a new angle on some of his apparently more baffling behaviours and interests, entering into ongoing debates about Ruskin and gender, constructions of genius, and the composite nature of Ruskin's oeuvre. As a resource for research, it offers clear transcriptions of 280 personal letters, with annotations, a glossary, and a comprehensive index, making the letters easily accessible and searchable. The letters themselves present an important resource for studying Ruskin's views on a wide variety of topics including travel, botany, landscape, education, literary influences, and changes wrought by industry, to name but a few. For Victorian scholars, the introduction offers an approach to reconciling apparently paradoxical aspects of public and personal personae within the nineteenth century. It also contributes to epistolary, autobiographical and gender studies, particularly in relation to issues of self-sustaining, playful self-construction and the Victorian construction of childhood.

ACKNOWLEDGEMENTS

❖

This book began as doctoral thesis and has been in progress for a decade. Over the course of those years, I have benefited from the help of many individuals and organisations. First, I must thank the Committee of Vice-Chancellors and Principals of the Universities of the United Kingdom (now UUK) for an Overseas Research Studentship, 1999–2002, and the Social Sciences and Humanities Research Council of Canada for a Doctoral Fellowship, 2001–03, as well as the Arts and Humanities Research Council, through which I have been employed as the Research Associate on the 'John Ruskin, Cultural Travel and Popular Access' project while also preparing this manuscript for publication. Thanks are also due to various groups at Lancaster University: the Ruskin Centre; its Director and my doctoral supervisor, Keith Hanley; its administrators, most recently Lauren Proctor; and the members of the Ruskin Seminar, who are too many to name but whose feedback over the years has helped to shape this work; also, to the Department of English and Creative Writing, through which I did my doctorate. I am indebted to those involved in my Viva for their feedback and for encouraging me to prepare the thesis for publication: John Batchelor, Kate Newey and Jeffrey Richards. Special thanks are due to the staff of the Ruskin Library: Stephen Wildman, Rebecca Patterson, Diane Tyler, Jen Shepherd and Linda Moorhouse. My thanks, too, to the Ruskin Foundation for providing access to material in the Ruskin Library, as well as to the former Curator, James S. Dearden. I also owe much gratitude to Graham Nelson, Managing Editor, and Richard Correll, Copy Editor, and others behind the scenes at Legenda for helping in the production of this book.

Finally, I want to express appreciation for my family and their support, especially to my parents 'Dr. Bob' and Myrna Wilson, and my husband, John Dickinson.

NOTE ON REFERENCES
❖

Generally, I refer to Ruskin's letters in the present tense, but to their composition in the past tense.

Unless otherwise stated, references to Ruskin's published works are taken from *The Works of John Ruskin* ('Library Edition'), ed. by E.T. Cook and Alexander Wedderburn, 39 vols (London: George Allen, 1903–12). References are given by volume and page number, thus: 35.537.

References to Tim Hilton's two-volume biography of Ruskin are referred to as '*Early*' for vol. I, and '*Later*' for vol. II.

When referring to numbered letters published in other editions, the references appear thus: '*Winnington*, p. 620 (11 May 1868, L. 456)'; however, notes by the editors of those volumes appear as 'Burd, *Winnington*, p. 620n.'

Unpublished letters reproduced in the Appendix are referred to by date of composition followed by their numerical listing within the Appendix, thus: '31 October 1872 [189].' All manuscript letters and diaries in this work come from the Whitehouse Collection held in the Ruskin Library, Lancaster University and are reproduced here with the kind permission of the Ruskin Foundation.

A note on copyright: The Ruskin Foundation, which has care of these materials, has sought to establish the copyright for John Ruskin's unpublished literary manuscripts, but has been unable to do so on the basis of all the information currently known to it. It would therefore welcome contact from any person or persons who can show they hold this copyright.

FIG. 1. Photograph of John Ruskin, Joan Severn, family and friends on the ice of Coniston Water, with Brantwood behind, 14 February 1895. John McClelland, photographer. The Ruskin Foundation (Ruskin Library, Lancaster University).

INTRODUCTION

❖

The photograph is haunting.[1] It shares a curious quality with most such Victorian images: it suggests that those depicted have been captured in a real moment in time, yet a moment that appears staged. Despite this stiffly choreographed feeling, it is easy to imagine echoes of spontaneous laughter, which must have preceded the decision to capture this snow- and ice-filled moment for posterity. The skating party obviously enjoyed frolicking in the winter sun; yet, one figure is juxtaposed pathetically to the energy around him: the old man sits limply in his chaise, bundled in furs, his eyes peering out from behind a massive beard. Beside him sits the substantial figure of a woman. Apparently several decades his junior, her posture declares a sense of ownership and control. Although she shares the centre of the composition with another woman,[2] her size and the contrast of her pale scarf against dark clothing give her the pre-eminence. She dominates the scene, yet it is the man — his quiet, diminished presence — who somehow draws and captures the gaze. The woman is Joan (Agnew Ruskin) Severn and the man is her cousin, John Ruskin. They are on Coniston Lake, outside what had been Ruskin's Lake District home, Brantwood. By the time this photograph was taken, on Valentine's Day 1895, that home was really hers, not his.

Ruskin was a major and celebrated cultural figure, the author of the five-volume *Modern Painters* and the three-volume *Stones of Venice*, to name just two of the texts which made him famous. When his collected works were published as the 'Library Edition' at the beginning of the twentieth century, they filled 39 weighty tomes.[3] His writings expressed opinions on a variety of topics, ranging from art criticism, to educational theories, to political economy. His tone was often didactic, moralistic and prophetic. He was sensitive, though, and felt acutely the burden of expectations on him — imposed by his society, his family, and himself. As he aged, he was weighed down by a sense of powerlessness. Struck by the heartache and social injustice around him, he attempted to shape Victorian culture by rebuking and enticing his contemporaries to effect moral changes within society. Often, he felt that his voice was not heeded; commenting in 1886 on his political and social views, he said: 'I am silent at present because no one could understand a word I said'.[4]

Over the years, as he suffered from bouts of mental and physical illness, Ruskin withdrew from society. He lived out his later years in near seclusion at Brantwood under the guardianship of Joan Severn. Some three decades earlier, in the mid-1860s, she had entered his home as the teenaged Joanna Agnew and become his ward. In common with many parent–child relationships, Ruskin and his adopted daughter gradually underwent a role-reversal; the elder took on roles of the younger, while the younger succeeded to dominance. Joan Severn, his 'di ma' (dear mother), offered John Ruskin, her 'di pa' (dear father),[5] a controlled, protected world dominated by a parental figure — she was his conscience, imposing her views on such matters as who was an acceptable guest, how he should use his finances, and how he should interact appropriately with his preferred playmates — real girls. She also fulfilled more distinctly maternal roles: engaging in nursery letter correspondence, preparing his food, finding lost 'toys', physically grooming him, setting up 'governesses' to watch him when she could not, and playing games with him. Unlike many such relationships, Ruskin had actively infantilized and apparently disempowered himself in relation to his cousin long before this was necessitated by illness or old age.

The interaction between this Victorian cultural sage and his much younger cousin is intriguing because of its ambiguity. The story of their relationship can be told in many different ways. It can be approached like an historical artefact such as the photograph discussed above. The composite, textual artefact of almost 3,000 extant letters, which Ruskin wrote to Joan over three decades, presents a tangible, 'real' record of their relationship. Yet to view the correspondence and its underlying relationship as an artefact — a cold representation of something long dead — is to undermine much of what invests it with interest for modern readers. It is to strip it of its dynamic, shifting and interpersonal aspects. This edited collection offers a selection of their letters, preceded by this Introduction which explores identities portrayed and roles played within the extant letters, offering a reading of the impetus behind them. I am, in this project, ultimately interested in tracing how Ruskin's imaginary, epistolary construct of a fantasy nursery, where he was free to play under the guardianship of his 'di ma', became his reality — how he, at least partly of his own volition, ceased to be a 'Master' in the public sphere and became, as he expressed it, 'a wee baby'[6] and 'like a itie wee school*girl*'[7] within the private sphere.

Although there are disturbing aspects in these letters, taken as a whole the correspondence is delightfully conversational and appealingly honest. Like *Praeterita*, his autobiography, Ruskin's letters to his cousin are deeply concerned with memory and with (re-)constructing the remembered and present self. While he destroyed many of her letters to him,[8] his letters to her were sacrosanct and he berated her for losing any of them. On occasion, he demanded that she transcribe a letter and keep a clean copy of it for him.[9] Ruskin considered these letters to be an *aide-mémoire*. In other words, while even more fragmented than the official autobiography — and far less unified in purpose and constructed self — they functioned in part as a private autobiography and reference text, effectively an extension of his diaries. Within this composite text, Ruskin played with the roles allocated to him by culture — as professor and prophet — and often removed these masks, substituting selves with whom he felt more at ease. Take, for example, Ruskin's first extant letter to his cousin about his role as Slade Professor of Fine Art at Oxford: 'Poo Donie must go to p– p — pro — fess, tings at Oxford — Pease, mamie dee — tell wee Donie, what peepies mean by — pro-fess — ? Donie ike doin tings — : he don't know how to pro-fess tings.'[10] Here, the 'Poo Donie' persona expressed anxiety. By constructing his authoritative, professorial self as a humorous, stuttering figure who will inactively and haltingly 'pro– fess' and his expectant public as 'peepies',[11]

Ruskin created an imaginary, fantasy image that enabled him to feel more confident about this new, public role.

What he called the 'nonsense' aspects of his letters actually made a great deal of sense to him and his cousin. He articulated this repeatedly in the letters, but was most explicit in the late spring and early summer of 1869, the period when he experimented most with his 'play letters'. On 2 July 1869, he wrote of such 'teazing', 'nonsense' components and, several days later, on 13 July, he added: 'the nonsense letters [...] are the only relief I have for a moment in the day, from the infinite pain of seeing — and thinking.'[12] Similarly, he overtly expressed the comfort he found in the very act of writing such play letters: 'I must just say, I love my wee Pufsie and no more — but it does me good to say that'. He then elaborated on the comfort he generated within himself by writing to her: 'I do not write only to please Pufsie. I write to please myself — it is the only refreshing moment I have in the day. except when pussy's letter comes [...] pussie's make me laugh'.[13]

While the composite text formed by the letters to Joan offers a less self-consciously sculpted first-person life-story than does the crafted and censored autobiography presented in *Praeterita*, it is nevertheless a constructed and self-constructing story. It reveals a remarkable mind torn between a desire to find structure, pattern and harmony, and a deep longing for freedom, both from the self-imposed quest for structure and from the weight of (his perceptions of) society's expectations of him. The epistolary play of language helped to create a space where Ruskin literally could play, indulging his desire for freedom from responsibility. He orchestrated their epistolary conversations and identities.

Joan was the central playmate and colleague in this exercise of self-fashioning through which Ruskin attempted to construct for himself a life that never changed. Essentially, he needed to change, to grow up, to learn and to evolve. Yet, he had an innate drive to remain constant and unchanged, to be a beloved child comfortingly wrapped in a world of security. He was torn between these needs: he felt pressure to be a renowned public figure, but he could not sustain this externally empowered self within the private world of his own mind. In order to perform as the public, proactive genius and 'Master' figure, he needed to feel he was consistently nurtured like a domesticated infant. Ruskin's cousin provided just such a context for him, dominated by her feminine presence. She was a feminizing domesticator; and he wrote up this ideal, constructing it as he reflected it within their correspondence. As he expressed it in a letter of 1868, they might both find freedom from sadness and disturbing memories through a shared domestic haven:

> Are there not <u>some</u> things you would fain forget — & cannot? But it requires no memory to dust books, it requires no memory to dust books, to weed gardens — to plan furnishings — to paint flowers — to illuminate — to cook — to sew — or to write from Cuzzies dictation. All that we ought to do — we always can. What we can't — we ought'nt — Ever your loving Cuzzie Piggie, J R.[14]

The activities described here are all ones the cousins explored together. With the possible exception of writing from 'dictation', they were all feminized within Victorian culture. By indulging in them with his cousin, Ruskin hoped they would both achieve personal relaxation, then peace. There is an essential equality — almost a shared, common identity — implied in his phrasing here: the nicknames used in this letter — 'Cuzzie' and 'Piggie' — apply to both cousins within the correspondence. Through writing such letters to Joan, Ruskin refreshed and re-masculinized himself within a shared, degendered, ostensibly disempowered and infantilized world. From within this space he could make forays into the overwhelmingly stressful public world where he wielded social and intellectual power.

The letters reproduced here are chosen from those Ruskin wrote to Joan which are now part of the John Howard Whitehouse Collection, housed in the Ruskin Library, Lancaster University. While taking letters from across the whole correspondence, this volume concentrates on the most significant moments in their relationship. It first focuses on the extant letters of 1864–69, when their relationship was being cemented and their baby-talk idiolect emerged; it then deals mainly with two periods of transition in Ruskin's life and in his relationship with his cousin: 1871–73 and 1887. The former of these two time-frames encompasses Ruskin's first term as Slade Professor of Fine Art, his mother's death, his search for a home, and his cousin's marriage and first pregnancy; it also coincides with the first instalment of his public letters, *Fors Clavigera*. The latter period marks his complete withdrawal from public life, his banishment from Brantwood, his major falling out with his beloved cousin, and some of his most moving letters. Both periods use the infant persona extensively and are very much concerned with finding a home — and peace.

The main body of this volume comprises an annotated edition of 260 letters by Ruskin to Joan, followed 20 letters by Joan to Ruskin. Following a brief note on editorial practice, it offers the letters in chronological order. This presentation, rather than a thematic one, has been chosen since a given letter may speak to several arbitrary themes and because of the cumulative nature of the correspondence. Letters from Ruskin to Joan have only previously been published as excerpts and are not generally available for research. Seventeen of the selected letters previously have been published in the 'Library Edition', but warrant reprinting because of their inherent content as well as what they reveal about decisions Ruskin's previous editors have taken in representing this material; all were normalized in the 'Library Edition' and most were significantly shortened, often with no indication that anything had been excised. Because the letters are in Ruskin's often erratic handwriting, it is useful for readers to know precisely how I have read specific words, and where the script is unclear I try to offer alternate readings in notes; different transcriptions of the same letter can give rise to different interpretations — as I demonstrate when discussing other critics' approaches to parts of this correspondence.

The letters are followed by two appendices. Appendix A is an 'Idiolectical Glossary' listing the 'baby-talk' and 'Tottish' terms used in these letters. This glossary offers a standard English term for each of Ruskin's words and, because the terms evolve and increase over time, I list the date of first usage within the letters reproduced. Appendix B offers three name-specific glossaries: pet-names for Ruskin, pet-names for Joan and terms used to denote baby-talk.

I · RELATIONAL ROLES

'A Joanie to manage everything for me'

Ruskin's autobiography, *Praeterita*, ends with the chapter 'Joanna's Care', expressing gratitude to and love for Joan. This closing chapter describes their shared life from the moment he collected her from her uncle John Tweddale and was told 'This is Joan'.[15] In his account, he included his cousin's own memories of her early days with him; she claimed to have only 'stayed seven years' with Ruskin, referring to her wedding to Arthur Severn (1871) as the point when she left. But her marriage merely represented the official transferral of financial and legal responsibility for her from guardian to husband. Due in part to his willingness to support her financially and to his insistence on regular epistolary (if not physical) proximity to her,[16] this legal transition put no real emotional, physical or financial distance between the cousins. Admittedly, as the years passed, there were periods when Ruskin's moods and illnesses made it difficult for his cousin and her family to be in his company, and they certainly argued, but a bond of love and loyalty was early forged between them and their households were permanently joined.

Young Joanna Agnew came from a poor, Scottish branch of the family based in Wigtown. Her father had died when she was five years old. When she joined the Ruskin household in 1864 at the age of seventeen, her social and economic prospects improved markedly and she enjoyed possibilities she would not otherwise have known.[17] Both cousins recognized this, and in 1878 Ruskin wrote fondly to his cousin about 'the country girl' she had been when they met.[18] In his company, she befriended important cultural figures such as the writer Thomas Carlyle, the artist Edward Burne-Jones and the political family of the Gladstones. Her brief engagement to the wealthy Percy La Touche and subsequent marriage to the aspiring artist Arthur Severn would not have occurred without contacts derived from Ruskin. Not only did Ruskin provide her — and later her family — with food and shelter, he also showered her with gifts: their private letters are sprinkled with references to precious jewels and trinkets he acquired for her and *Praeterita* publicly states that he gave her gifts.[19] Over time, he ceded control of his homes, money and person to her.[20] While this furthered her interests, it also furthered Ruskin's. He was childless, but in making Joanna Agnew his ward he could experience fatherhood. Later, through the matronly Joan Severn, he could feel part of a family, and her offspring represented a potential dynasty.

Ruskin scholars have viewed the cousins' relationship in seemingly contradictory ways. She has been cast in the role of gold-digging manipulator of Ruskin, but also in the role of self-sacrificing, self-effacing saviour of Ruskin. His letters to her have been used to suggest that he was a paedophile, but also to demonstrate ways she used him. These letters have the potential to lend support to all of these claims.

Some of Ruskin's letters partially corroborate the view of Joan as a grasping, avaricious woman who manipulated her cousin for her own socio-economic ends, offering love in exchange for financial stability. One such narrative emerges in letters Ruskin wrote to her during spring 1882, when her husband was sent to sell paintings of which Ruskin had been fond.[21] These letters suggest this was done to raise money so the Severns could expand Brantwood, shaping it to accommodate their familial and social aspirations. Ruskin stated overtly that 'I have more Turners than I want', adding:

> you need not be the least anxious about your new building expenses — for it [selling paintings] is sure to cower cover much more than those. and — if Christie's people have a good water colour sale coming on — Ill clear off my light Turner sketches. and some of the drawings which I do not need — and get a Pot of money to potter on with at ease.'[22]

This may suggest Ruskin was blackmailed emotionally, forced to sell paintings in exchange for gratitude and affection; or, it may simply reflect the fact that, although a wealthy man who had inherited '£120,000, together with substantial property' — the 'cash inheritance' being 'about £6 million in today's terms'[23] — Ruskin was spending beyond his means. He recognized this and, in letters such as that of Christmas Day 1884, wrote that 'he wants his di ma to take care of his money for him'.[24] The Severns may have been well justified in pressuring him to free the domestic cash-flow by selling some paintings. The one reading sets Joan up as Ruskin's abuser, the other as his helper; both readings reflect aspects of the truth.

Early biographers tended to take a positive view of Joan. As M. H. Spielmann phrased it shortly after Ruskin's death, 'No memoir of Ruskin, however brief, can omit mention of the influence for good that Mrs. Severn exercised upon her cousin's life'.[25] This is certainly part of the story: Ruskin relied on her — perhaps too much — as a centre-point on which to fix his affection and sanity. He undeniably found strength in her, yet his letters to her suggest there may have been disquieting aspects to the relationship. And Spielmann's glowing praise of 'Mrs. Severn' may have been coloured by his own need for her help. As he aged, Ruskin had used his cousin as a buffer between his private sphere and the public world. From Sandgate in 1887, he wrote: 'I'm beginning to be curious to know what [drawing for Cassell's Magazine of Art] you'll send to SPielmann.'[26] She exercised control over material offered to Spielmann, and Ruskin forwarded material to her for Spielmann.[27] These letters suggest Spielmann was indebted to Joan for what access he had enjoyed to 'the Master'.

Joan may have manipulated Ruskin to achieve her own and her family's socio-economic ends, but it is clear in these letters that she cared deeply for him; and, although sometimes perhaps misguided in her attempts to protect him, she felt a real affection for her cousin. He, in turn, trusted her. This trust included not only confiding in her about a variety of topics (such as his interest in girls, his mental health and his financial worries), it extended to empowering her with control over his material self. This manifested itself in several ways. For example, he established the Guild of St George over which he was keen to be 'Master'. Yet in 1887, from Sandgate where he was living in self-banishment from Brantwood because Joan found it difficult to cope with his mental and physical instability, he wrote to her, saying, '[a]ll that you do about Guild Papers will be right of course [I'll] sign any you send'.[28] She had become the *de facto* Master of the Guild. That year, Ruskin expressed his desire to cede control of his home to her: 'in any thing I am trying to get done about Brantwood I am only thinking now of how to quiet you of trouble about it and leave you mistrefs of it: and its ground.'[29] While presumably thinking ahead to his own death, he also was clearly thinking of banishing himself from Brantwood. Several months later, he wrote: 'I think its very lovely having you in the Brantwood 'situation' which you were clearly meant for — and relieve me of all tubble wubble in'.[30] Similarly, he wrote again that year of his desire for her to control affairs as they related to his person: 'it seems to me a lodging of my own where Doanie could direct what was done for me if I fell ill, would be the rightest and safest thing.'[31] By voluntarily subsuming himself to her and putting her in control of his 'Mastership', his finances, his physical well-being and even his home — all of which had played important roles in shaping his identity in the 1870s and early 1880s — he shored up those markers of self. Ceding control of these to a trusted, maternal figure with whom he shared an imagined world of play enabled him to feel more at ease, less pressured and thus emotionally stronger. Their long-standing, affectionate tradition of using baby-talk ('Di Ma', 'Doanie', 'tubble wubble', etc.) enabled him to achieve this without losing face, because it allowed him to couch this actual power-shift within the imagined power-shift with which they had long experimented in their epistolary idiolects and personae.

The 1887 letter about establishing his cousin 'in the Brantwood "situation"' continues with references to Joan's stay at Brantwood. Curiously, Ruskin added: 'I've tried to ite some autographs — but it is like trying to forge my own signature my R. long leg is getting gouty — and the last iti bone is misby for want of its Doanie.'[32] This implies he was losing his sense of self without her physical presence. Yet he stayed away: as this and surrounding letters suggest, he recognized that in his current physical and mental state his physical proximity to her might destroy her. This was not a new development. As John Batchelor has pointed out, in 1876 Ruskin expressed suicidal thoughts to his cousin, suggesting to her that he was staying alive only for her happiness.[33] Commenting on sorting his 'masses of old drawings', Ruskin claimed to be 'putting them in order' 'so that peepies may know what they are, when I've got away to Rosie.'[34] He was thinking of joining Rose La Touche in death.[35] He began to reassure his cousin by saying: 'But me no want to leave oo, di ma.' The reassurance was half-hearted, tinged with both the assertion that he desired death and the implication that Joan ought to be grateful that he was staying alive for her: 'Only if it was'nt for oo, and I might go away to Rosie dectly.'[36] This passage must have put immense emotional pressure on his cousin.

Young Joan's relationship with her cousin and his mother was not one-way: they came to rely on her good-humoured companionship as much as she did on their economic support. According to W. G. Collingwood, Joan could persuade Margaret Ruskin, who was old enough to be her grandmother, to agree to things which no one else could: 'and when sometimes her son would wish to take a party in to town to see the last new piece [of theatre], her permission had to be asked, and was not readily granted, unless to Miss Agnew, who was the ambassadress in such affairs of diplomacy.'[37] Joan mediated between Ruskin and his mother, just as she later mediated between Ruskin and Rose La Touche and, later still, between Ruskin and the world.[38]

An important part of Joan's appeal was her sense of humour. When Arthur Severn first glimpsed her at a party, he was struck by 'a pretty good-natured-looking girl with frizzy hair and a complexion like a rose'. When he approached, he found '[s]he was most agreeable, not shy, and looked amused I thought at my boldness'.[39] Her playful good nature made her popular and she seems often to have been the centre of attention and catalyst of good fun. For example, Dearden describes a certain Mr. Graves's account of spending time with Ruskin and the Severns at Matlock in 1871: 'Mrs Severn is credited with the idea of forming a human chain [...]. The ladies who were present formed the anchor, with Mrs Severn as rearguard. She is also credited with the humorous idea of letting the men slip into the pond.'[40] Because Joan was playful, she was able to make those around her laugh and feel carefree — childlike.

Looking back in *Praeterita* to his formative childhood, Ruskin reminisced about his close childhood companionship with another Scottish cousin, Jessie Richardson, the daughter of his father's sister (also Jessie). His memories of her include the fond assertion that: '[w]e agreed upon this that we would be married when we were a little older'.[41] Jessie was a model of idealized childhood, linked in his mind both with exploring the outdoors and with enjoying domestic activities such as cooking; he remembered fondly his excursions with her to glean corn, which they cooked together.[42] She died in childhood, 'very slowly, of water on the brain'.[43] Because she never grew into maturity, young Jessie remained in Ruskin's memory as an idealized playmate; his perceptions of girls and ideal companions were tied to these memories. The loss of Jessie may well have set the pattern in Ruskin's mind of searching for young female companions, and there has been some critical conjecture about Ruskin and the loss of such young women.[44]

Writing in *Praeterita* about Joan's youth, he idealizes her simple, Scottish childhood for its 'habits of childish play, or education, then common in the rural towns of South Scotland'. He elaborates that 'there was greater refinement in them, and more honourable pride, than probably, at that time, in any other district of Europe; a certain pathetic melody and power of tradition consecrating nearly every scene with some past light, either heroism or religion.'[45] Joan Agnew was a product of the familial form of upbringing, akin to Jessie's and his parents'. This passage suggests that, for Ruskin, part of Joan's charm stemmed from her upbringing, which shaped her to perceive the world through a filter of shared tradition; she had a mind attuned to memory and to seeing symbolic meaning (derived from the mythic, religious past) in present 'scenes' and events. He ascribed these attributes to her Scottish roots, which he shared — Ruskin himself, although raised in the south of England, was given an essentially Scottish childhood.[46]

Ruskin wrote of yet another female Scottish cousin whose presence in his household affected him: Mary Richardson. Following the death of Jessie and her mother, '[t]he only surviving daughter, Mary,' he writes, 'was adopted by my father and mother, and brought up with me'. He notes that she 'was a rather pretty, blue-eyed, clumsily-made girl, very amiable and affectionate in a quiet way', possessed 'good sense and good principle', was 'honestly and inoffensively pious, and equal tempered'. While Mary, who lacked 'pretty girlish ways or fancies,' did not live up to the vivacious ideal of the other female Scottish cousins, first Jessie then Joan, she nevertheless added ungendered, harmonious, 'neutral tint[s]' of morality, affection and inoffensive piety to the Ruskin home.[47] These were attributes the mature Ruskin prized. The ageing author of *Praeterita* ascribed the roots of his propensity for 'pretty girlish ways and fancies,' tempered with 'good sense and good principle,' to his youthful, ten-year-old self — the self who played with the Richardson sisters as surrogate siblings. It is also important to realize that the attributes he praised in Joan's feminized, 'rural', Scottish education, endowed her with attributes he exhibited in his own oeuvre — from *Modern Painters* to *The Stones of Venice* to *Fors Clavigera* — 'a certain pathetic melody and power of tradition consecrating nearly every scene with some past light'. Much has been written about the mnemonic, mythic, symbolic and painterly aspects of Ruskin's writing, and I won't rehearse it here, but it is worth bearing in mind.

When Joan married Arthur Severn, Ruskin gave the newlyweds the use of his childhood home at Herne Hill and supported them financially. These economic gifts can be seen as controlling on his part (controlling her with her gratitude and his potential threat of withholding support), and mercenary on hers (offering him love and the feeling of having a family and a dynasty). But as Ruskin had become her official guardian in 1865, effectively adopting her, it was appropriate that he offered a dowry and supported her as a parent would a child. His parents had similarly provided him with a home for his six-year marriage to Effie Gray.

Ruskin gave his blessing to Joan's marriage, but was not entirely pleased with her choice. While one must take Arthur Severn's account of the courtship with a grain of salt, his memoir of Ruskin contains transcripts of several letters sent by the older guardian to the younger suitor. Among these is one sent to Severn on 18 March 1867:

> if I thought there was no chance of you gaining her affection, I would have advised you at once to keep out of her way. [...] I will certainly not give you Joanna, unless — (and this will not take a short time) you prove yourself not only able to make her happy, but to make her happier than anybody else I can find.[48]

Ruskin's letters to Arthur reflect his love and concern for his ward, his uncertainty about the suitability of the aspiring artist, and his curious conceptions of ideal courtship, which were coloured by his own romantic history: early adoration of Adèle Domecq, failed marriage to Effie Gray, subsequent unsuccessful attempts to win Rose La Touche. In the letter cited here, he agreed to allow the young people to court each other, essentially to place each other 'on trial'. Part of his rationale was that Arthur ought to prove himself and his love for Joan as a courtly knight might have done in Arthurian legend. He added:

> in the meantime, both of you shall use your eyes and intellects, as best you can, to see whether you cannot find someone else fitter for you. Were I your father, I should say you were quite wrong to think of marriage yet, at all[49] — and that if you did — you might get a better wife than Joanna (not a more affectionate

> — if once you could win her — but a stronger — shrewder — more serviceable one) [... .] I think I can do better for her — and mean to do so: I think I can get her as worthy a husband, in a better worldly position — only you need not fear that I shall let her be bought by anyone who does not deserve her.[50]

This letter is not entirely positive about either Joan ('you might get a better wife') or Arthur ('I can do better for her'), and offers little hope to the suitor except that his beloved would not be sold, and that — if he persevered — he might win through. Not until 20 November 1870 did the couple announce their engagement.[51] This followed an absence on Severn's part of almost three years, during which time neither young person found a more emotionally suitable match and Ruskin did not find a wealthier one for Joan.

Whether Ruskin would have been unequivocally in favour of any husband his ward might have chosen is debatable. He reacted with cautious favour to Percy La Touche's advances, but this must have been due in part to his own longing for the young man's sister, Rose: if his ward had married her brother, there would have been a permanent connection between the families. Ruskin would also have known that the wealthy young man would be able to support Joan financially. These positive considerations would have been tempered by Percy's irresponsible behaviour. He was the black sheep of his family: expelled from school, a gambler, and violent. It was to Joan's long-term benefit that this engagement was broken.[52]

Returning to Arthur Severn, there is a marked ambivalence in Ruskin's references to him in letters to Joan, echoed in Arthur's memoir. To be fair, they were probably jealous of each other.[53] In 1868, three years before Joan wed, Ruskin had written to her with a sense of anticipatory resignation to the personal loss her marriage would entail: 'for you know I must force myself into the habit of living alone, now; (for you're sure to be married to somebody before you know where you are. —) and this bit of bitter practice in the dark days [...] is good for me'.[54] He perceived any suitor as a competitor of sorts, upsetting the balance of their relationship. This is evident in another letter from 1868: 'I must get you to fall into our old pleasant ways — and live with old Greeks & Jews — and not with Ps nor As. [...] And I believe the Proper P or A, if he is to come at all — will come when you are properly helping P.A, PA.'[55] He stressed the 'old pleasant ways' they had shared before suitors Percy La Touche and Arthur Severn had appeared to complicate his idealized relationship with Joan, when he had been 'papa'.

A similar longing for the past and ambivalence towards the present is evident in letters after her wedding, such as the following:

> I was very glad of your both affectionate letter yesterday. — only you know its quite impossible for me ever to believe that any body cares for me except you. You don't mean to say that Arfie could ever be the least bit fond of me? I'm just a fusty old critical father in law — – you know he can't, possiby; he only fancies he does in his honeymoon.[56]

Ruskin was teasing, but coupled with the other letters, there is a ring of truthful anxiety here.

As an aspiring artist, Arthur Severn was undoubtedly appreciative of the wealthier, older art-critic's financial and professional support, but one cannot help but suspect that he also resented it. In an account of his wedding, Arthur repeatedly referred to Ruskin as the 'old gentleman', yet Ruskin was only in his early fifties. This wording suggests respect tinged with a desire to accentuate the age difference between the couple and their benefactor. Ruskin as an 'old man' and 'Professor' is a key trope of the memoir. It might be accounted for by knowing that Arthur wrote this late in his own life, when Ruskin's final years — as an old man — were etched on his mind. But there was perhaps an unconscious attempt to reinforce Ruskin's unsuitability to be the younger woman's bridegroom by stressing his age in contrast to her youth.[57]

Intriguingly, Arthur notes that 'the Professor looked quite the bridegroom himself, in a new bright blue stock, very light grey trousers, and almost fashionable frock-coat with a rose in the button-hole, and quite gay in manner'.[58] Again, there is a subtly ambivalent sense of Ruskin's attitude: on the wedding day of his ward, he appeared to be 'quite the bridegroom himself', rather than her 'real vice-father'.[59] While the younger man's descriptions of Ruskin on the day offer an image of Ruskin's charged emotions, the bridegroom insisted on ascribing gaiety to Ruskin; it feels forced, but whether on Ruskin's or Severn's part is not clear. Ruskin's appearance of being 'quite gay in manner' on 20 April can be contrasted starkly with the sadness of his diary entry the following day: 'April 21st Friday. Joanna married yesterday [...] For the first time since 1866. I begin work without any golden thing at my breast'.[60] He then abandoned this particular diary until April 1873, when he picked it up with: '1873. Brantwood. continues from p 140. in my father's diary book. 9th April. Wednesday.' Having begun again to use this book as his diary, he continued to do so throughout that spring — significantly, after he had established Brantwood as his *domus*. But the sense of loss in his wording of 21 April 1871, combined with abandoning this particular, physical notebook for two years, imply disapproval and abandonment.

Ruskin may in fact have considered his cousin as a possible partner in the legal, spousal sense, rather than merely viewing her as a ward, playmate and house-manager. He might have considered her his insurance option as a companion in later life should his advances to Rose La Touche ultimately fail. Although Joan Agnew was Ruskin's cousin, the connection (her 'father was the son of John James Ruskin's maternal uncle')[61] was not so close as to make a union illegal, and in fact his own parents were cousins.

If familial patterns were idealized by Ruskin, then his parents' marriage might have been the ideal model. Such symbolic, mnemonic resonance surrounded Ruskin's wife, Effie Gray. Their families were connected: they had played together when she was a child and he a young man; her home had, historically, been the Ruskin home. On one level, she represented a familial link and an echo of his childhood, which took on mythic proportions. In similar ways, Joan Agnew might, at least in the mid-1860s, have seemed a particularly suitable match for him. Ruskin's mother, Margaret Cock (later Cox) was the niece of his paternal grandmother, Catherine Ruskin. His grandmother chose his mother as 'somebody to talk to, who would not be a servant but would help to run the house';[62] as Ruskin writes in *Praeterita*, 'my mother, formed into a consummate housewife, was sent for to Scotland to take care of my paternal grandfather's house'.[63] This mirrors Joan's entry into Ruskin's household. By changing a few elements such as 'Edinburgh' for 'London' and 'thirteen years' for 'seven years', Tim Hilton's description of Margaret Cox's time in her aunt's household might apply to Joan:

> She administered the Edinburgh household with firmness and efficiency, and was to do so for thirteen years. All her youth and young womanhood was given to this home. In these years she developed an unswerving love for her cousin, John James. In time he came to love her too.[64]

Eventually, John James Ruskin and Margaret Cox established a home together and 'married in 1818, after nine years of painful waiting'.[65] A generation later, when John Ruskin and Joan Agnew were entangled in romantic associations with the La Touche family (she with Percy, he with Rose), Ruskin wrote to Edward Burne-Jones about their fall-back plan: if all else failed for them, the cousins would procure a country cottage where they might live peacefully and simply together, gardening and doing charitable works.[66] This escapist fantasy might have entailed living not just as cousins or guardian and ward, but as husband and wife. If they had done so, they would have echoed his parents.

Ruskin's marriage to Effie Grey had been annulled on grounds of non-consummation and it would have been difficult legally for him to remarry. The La Touche family was aware of this, for they consulted a solicitor, in 1871, who warned that Ruskin could not remarry.[67] This was one reason why the senior La Touches refused to allow Ruskin to pursue their daughter. It may also have provided a reason for Ruskin to hope for an informal, life-long relationship with Joan, which might have entailed all aspects of marriage (companionship, household management, etc.) except the sexual. And to a large degree — and despite her marriage to Arthur Severn — this is precisely the life-long companionship that Ruskin did enjoy with his cousin.

It is pertinent here to raise thoughts and suggestions put forward briefly in Hilton's discussion of Ruskin's 'loathsome' serpent dreams:

> the earliest dreams of this sort [...] include Joan Agnew, a young woman who was becoming closer to Ruskin, who slept under the same roof, was his ward, and whose future husband Ruskin did not greatly like. This is a time to mention — briefly and without speculation — a thought that may have occurred to Margaret Ruskin: that, if he were to marry again, John might find his best possible bride already looking after the Denmark Hill household. At all events, Ruskin's first serpent dreams occurred when he came to know of Arthur Severn's intentions toward Joan.[68]

Hilton, too, has entertained the idea that Ruskin might have considered Joan as a potential bride. Ruskin's dreams and the subtext of some personal writings hint at this. But he allowed her courtship with Arthur Severn to progress, albeit with quite frank expressions of reservation.

Ruskin's letter to Joan on 21 April 1871 hints at possible problems. It is brief, apologetic, and wishes the newlyweds '[W]hatever peace my thoughts — or words — or acts, can bring'.[69] Similarly, the last letters he sent to her before her marriage reflect sadness at no longer addressing letters to her with the name 'Agnew'.[70] His letters to Joan in the first days and months of married life repeatedly express sadness.

They must have made his cousin feel unfaithful, and — even if couched in humour and baby-talk — they exhibit jealousy toward Arthur.[71] Within a week of the wedding Ruskin wrote: 'Me mifs oo so mut. me not no fot to do. — me very sulky and seepy. — me had long walk — found fritillary fowers. and boobells — but its all no oos. now poos moos is not here. — ove to M^r & Mrs Kingsley — ittie bit to Arfie.'[72] However teasingly, he petulantly offered less love to the bridegroom than to the honeymooning couple's current hosts.

Even more cutting are the letters suggesting his cousin's absence (and, importantly, lack of letters) made him ill. This reliance on her quickly intensified. In 1866, he playfully implied that missing her — and having her letters delayed in the post — made him 'cross', affecting 'body and mind'.[73] A letter written within days of Joan's wedding is one of many to connect his not receiving her letters with being ill. Quoting it almost in its entirety, it reads: 'Me so misby, me no no fot to do. — me want my poos moos — – me feel as if I was away at Abbeville. — very ill. no etties yester day — no etties to day — bow — wow . ow — ow . ow. — Ever oos pooest poo wee Donie'.[74] The following day, he used baby-talk to admonish her for not writing and to reiterate that not having her near, or at least having her surrogate presence in the form of a letter, was affecting his state of mind:

> I am much lower than I at all thought I should or could be below my usual poor level, — for want of my ownown Poosmoos — and don't know fot to do. Me was fitened dedful for no ettie — no ettie — no ettie — no ettie — Sat-day — Sun-day — Mun –day — Two's day — me <u>so</u> fitened — at last me got wee ettie at D^r Ac.'s — To-day — here — no ettie again — me <u>so</u> misby-thisby-misby — poo — poo — poo, oos own Donie S^{t}C.[75]

He added a few extra notes on the following page, including a slightly apologetic one, 'Thats a very poking first page for my poosmoos — only it must be nice to be missed', but the initial page does not read like a joke. It is worth noting that the signature is 'S^{t}C'. This typically indicates that he was thinking about Rose. Here, perhaps, his awareness of his cousin's marital happiness made his own romantic uncertainty all the more difficult. Whether or not Ruskin consciously considered marriage to Joan, he clearly was less than delighted when she married someone else, and a certain ambiguity regarding his feelings for her continued. This is evident in a letter to her written almost a year after her wedding: 'Well, Pussie has her Arfie and I've my Pussie — and oos my Pussie and Im oos cuzzie — and at Brantwood we'll all be gay when Johnny comes marching home Ever my darling. Your own Di Pa. J Ruskin'[76] The easy flow of loves in Ruskin's mind — Joan ('Pussie') loves ('has her') Arthur ('Arfie'); John loves ('I've my') Joan ('Pussie'); Joan loves ('oos my Pussie and love') John ('oos Cuzzie') — suggests a complex set of relationships and attachments. The playful allusion to the soldier 'Johnny' returning home paints an image of Ruskin, the source of economic stability, who would return to the refuge of his Brantwood home for a period of rest and recuperation after the battles of his Professorship.

It is significant that one of Ruskin's early but protracted psychological illnesses occurred in 1871, during his first term as Slade Professor, when his mother was dying and shortly after his cousin had married. When the newlyweds went to join

Ruskin at Matlock during their honeymoon, he suffered a breakdown. Although he had sent his honeymooning cousin many letters plaintively expressing his loneliness, he also claimed he did not want to 'spoil my pussies love-time'.[77] But there is an air of protesting too much, implying that he resented both the loss of Joanna Agnew and her protracted honeymoon as Joan Severn. Earlier, in 1868, he similarly had protested too much of his independence from her, before ordering her back to his side, saying: 'you must come back, for a little while. [...] for if I *did* break down — you none of you would be pleased with me for not sending for you.'[78] Her absence could, implicitly, result in his 'break down'.

The honeymoon had already been interrupted when the bride had become ill.[79] Ruskin's illness again interrupted the honeymoon and redirected the bride's attention and affection back to him.[80] While not a major breakdown, such as he would suffer in later years, the episode of 1871 nevertheless reflects a pattern in Ruskin's life: his health, both mental and physical, tended to disintegrate when faced with the loss of an emotionally and symbolically important woman, particularly when such a loss was coupled with intense intellectual work.[81] Ruskin's 'first experience of breaking down after a prolonged spell of work' had occurred in 1840, during his second year at Oxford. While deeply engaged in academic writing, he heard that the first focus of his passionate (if unrequited) love, Adèle Domecq, had married.[82] He quickly declined physically and mentally. Another notable episode was what Hilton refers to as 'Ruskin's first breakdown [at Brantwood] in 1878', linked in part to fresh memories of his beloved Rose, despite her being three years dead.[83] What Hilton describes as his 'second breakdown', in 1880–81, appears to have had as its catalyst the loss of 'Carlyle, whom Ruskin had latterly addressed as "Papa", and who had indeed been the father of so much of the younger man's attitudes', coupled with the coinciding 'death of a well-remembered figure from childhood, George Richmond's wife Julia', as well as, again, memories of Rose.[84] That Ruskin should have had a breakdown in 1871 when faced with his cousin's marriage and his mother's terminal ill-health fits a life-long pattern. This, in turn, helps to establish how important Joan had become to him.

One of the key roles Joan enacted for him was, as the pet-name 'Di Ma' suggests, to mother him. Arthur Severn's memoir recounts an amusing yet telling anecdote from the period of illness at Matlock, describing how the invalid Ruskin was spotted dropping a half sovereign out his window to a young, female singer:

> My wife gave a sudden start, saying, 'Good gracious, that must be the Coz!' 'Impossible, Joan', I said, but she was off like a swallow to his room. I followed with more dignity, when in the room found Joan standing over the bed saying 'Is it possible? Have you dared to get up!'; head a little more under the clothes, 'Cozzie darling have you really been up?'; head quite under the clothes, 'My pettest of lambs how could you do such a wicked thing?'; head half way down the bed.[85]

Important role reversals had occurred in Ruskin's life. At the point when his ailing mother ceased to be a maternal figure because she had become an invalid, the newly married Joan Severn ceased to be his ward and took on a more powerful, maternal function in relation to him. He had long called her "amie'[86] (lamb); now he had become her 'pettest of lambs'. She had become dominant. As she expressed it in a letter to Margaret Ruskin from Matlock in 1871, he had become like his invalid mother and needed to be cared for:

> Its quite refreshing to see your son so well again! — he sits up in his bed just like you! — & looks so very like you! — & has a little white shawl (which I got for him) just like your's on! — and he asks for his books & things to be handed to him, & put back in their places! just like you — dearest Aunt[.][87]

Joan reinforced the parallels between mother and son by underlining the similes. The shawls are of particular interest. The new Mrs. Severn states that it was she who had acquired Ruskin's, which was modelled on Margaret Ruskin's. In a later letter, Joan wrote to her Aunt about the shawls again, this time responding to a letter from one of the servants: 'Kate tells me you have adopted the white shawl to wear now instead of the red! — she fancies the white less becoming than the scarlet — I don't — but not to use flattery I think you would look well in anything! —'.[88] Margaret Ruskin had ceased to wear her customary red shawl and taken to wearing a white one like her son's. The mother was emulating the son as much as he her, reinforcing kinship and symbolic parallels. As for Joan, she teasingly flattered both parties about the aesthetic appeal of their respective shawls. In so doing, she imposed her aesthetic and nurturing influence onto both her benefactors.

The security Joan offered Ruskin, and her willingness to mother him in his illness, nurtured and shaped the self-infantilized Ruskin who so enjoyed being coddled and protected. It is possible that, in this instance, Ruskin feigned illness (largely related to vomiting and lack of appetite, punctuated by moments of apparently remarkable good health) to reclaim his cousin's attention from her husband. This is an argument I am loath to make, for I don't believe Ruskin consciously did so; but the possibility is there and it is an infantilized form of behaviour. In any event, Joan was an active accomplice — a playmate — in the infantilized and feminized role-playing which came to characterize the cousins' correspondence and helped to shape the later Ruskin. That he found security in this enacted infantilism reinforces the wistful stress he placed on his child-self in *Praeterita*.

Joan not only took on maternal functions in relation to her cousin; like all relationships, their interaction was much more complex. Ruskin initially viewed the teenage Joan as a youthful companion and ward, but that soon began to change: he came to perceive her, not so much as a younger cousin to care for, but as an adopted sister, playmate and companion with whom to relax. One semi-formal role she took on was that of his most trusted and constant assistant. When Joan joined the Ruskin household, she was allocated 'three rooms in this house beautifully furnished for her amusement. The furnishing was done by Howell, Ruskin's secretary'.[89] Ruskin was aided over the years by several such manservants and personal secretaries. In an edition of correspondence between Ruskin and two of his secretaries, Charles Augustus Howell and Richard St John Tyrwhitt, Jay Claiborne writes of Howell that:

> his duties were as varied as buying a canary, answering mail, cheering up Burne-Jones, and helping Ruskin carry out individual charities such as the Cruikshank Memorial Fund. The secretaryship developed into a close friendship for a time,

and Ruskin confided in Howell to such an extent that he told Howell some of the details of his love for Rose La Touche. Howell may even have acted as an envoy for Ruskin in the affair.[90]

Ruskin befriended and trusted Howell, and he affectionately christened this secretary/friend with an epistolary pet-name: 'Owl'.[91] In Claiborne's edition of the Ruskin–Howell correspondence, Ruskin's salutations initially read 'dear Howell' until the winter of 1867–68, when 'Owl' appears.[92] The derivation of this name, a simple, childish slurring of Howell's surname, is clear enough: dropping or changing the first sound of a word is in keeping with what became established patterns of Ruskin's baby-talk idiolect. This is the same period when baby-talk began to appear regularly in letters to Joan. He used 'Owl' not only in writing to Howell, but also to refer to Howell in his correspondence with his cousin.[93] From 1868, Ruskin's salutations to Howell consistently appear as variations on 'My dearest wee Owl' until the last letter of that correspondence. This final letter, dated 4 September 1870, reverts to the more formal 'My dear Howell' to dismiss him for breach of confidence.[94] The pet-name had been a mark of trust and affection.[95]

Before betraying his employer, Howell was, '[f]rom 1866', 'in full charge of all Ruskin's affairs'.[96] For example, Ruskin wrote to him on 16 October 1868 with: 'now that you are paying Denmark Hill bills, will you please let me know how we stand'.[97] He expressed appreciation and trust with such overt statements as 'I am sincerely grateful to you, for all you are always doing for me'.[98] In wording if not quite in tone, this echoes many letters to Joan. Howell's betrayal seems to have been particularly painful because a playful friendship had developed between them; yet, according to biographers such as Batchelor, Collingwood and Hilton, Howell was never really Ruskin's friend. Rather, as Hilton expresses it, he was 'a heartless as well as a dishonest man' who used Ruskin for his own ends.[99] Ruskin's biographers imply that he saw the 'personable and plausible young man' as he wanted to see him;[100] that he constructed a perception of Howell designed to meet a need in his life. An important aspect of this construction was bestowing an epistolary pet-name onto him.

Arriving in the Ruskin household a year before Howell, Joan's initial tasks related primarily to assisting Ruskin's mother,[101] yet she gradually assumed many of the functions of personal assistant to the son. One of her earliest tasks was to help catalogue and arrange Ruskin's books. On a Sunday in January 1872, he noted: 'arranged books in various bookcases with Joan in afternoon and after tea — the best day, and most restful for a long time'.[102] The following day he added: 'Bookcases a wonder to see. Must begin Fors, February Joanna away at ½ past eight'.[103] While Ruskin greatly appreciated her help, his cousin was not irreplaceable in the discrete, individual tasks she performed. A few days later, Ruskin wrote: 'got fine Dante. Put bookcases in order with Burgess'.[104] In his cousin's absence, he had used another friend and assistant, Arthur Burgess.[105] Over the years, there were many such assistants at Ruskin's side, including: 'Sara Anderson, calm, efficient and discreet, and the secretary-disciples [William Gershom] Collingwood and [Laurence] Hilliard' as well as Jamie Anderson and Alexander Wedderburn, all of whom were with Ruskin during the cousins' difficult estrangement of 1881.[106] But it was the multi-functional Joan who spanned the second half of his life and occupied a uniquely familial position.

Although Howell is credited with furnishing Joan's rooms when she joined the Ruskin household, she later played an important role in shaping the aesthetic of Ruskin's homes, advising on furnishing and décor. This naturally evolved into her managing many of his domestic affairs, particularly as the busy — and by no means practical — Ruskin ran more than one household; in effect, she became the mistress of his homes, fulfilling the same function as a wife — or spinster sister of a bachelor brother — might do. She even seems to have looked after his grooming, for example, cutting his hair.[107]

Ruskin's letters to Joan are sprinkled with requests that she make purchases on his behalf. She acquired props and objects of inspiration for his lectures, such as the stuffed robin he wanted in spring 1873.[108] She bought household objects,[109] and ordered gifts, such as dresses for his female favourites.[110] Like Howell, Joan not only looked after such small financial aspects; she also managed Ruskin's finances by paying bills and, eventually, over-seeing household finances. This provided him with much-needed help, relieving him of some of his most onerous and stressful tasks. Ruskin's frustration with personal finances is reflected in a diary entry written after an unsuccessful attempt to list and balance just one day's expenditures: 'I really don't believe it is possible to keep count of money, if one has other things in one's head'.[111] By the 1880s, letters to his cousin repeatedly expressed deep anxiety about finances and his inability to keep track of them or effectively to curb his own spending. The fact that Joan moved from merely assisting with Ruskin's finances to taking control of them must be placed within this context. Although it was in her best interest to do so, and marked a further shift in their power dynamic, it did afford Ruskin a degree of freedom from financial pressures, which weighed heavily on him. He trusted Joan and — in contrast to Howell, whom he also had entrusted with his finances — she loved him and effectively dedicated her life to him. As well as directing his personal finances, she also helped him to keep track of the Guild of St. George funds. As early as 1873, he asked her to: 'Look at page 200 of it [big Ledger] and copy me out the state of the funds of St George'.[112] By 1887, she controlled Guild funds.[113]

She also served as amanuensis and mediator through whom Ruskin communicated with others. For example, his diary entry of 22 December 1871 includes the note 'Y. dictated beginnings of Science and Art Lectures to Joanna'. He later added a note in the margin: 'Eagles Nest', specifying the title under which they were eventually published.[114] She wrote notes for him to read in his lectures,[115] wrote catalogues for his use,[116] and transcribed notes from others' letters to him.[117] A good example of these roles appears in letters about *Praeterita*, when Ruskin sent chapters to her, requesting her approval, asking that she rework them as necessary then forward them to the printer; in October 1887 he wrote: 'It is a great comfy to me, that you like those last sentences of Praeterita', then mentioned 'retouches that you will like', which he had made to the text.[118] When contrasted with the following excerpt from a letter to Howell, this reinforces the sense that one of her roles was as secretary:

> My dearest Owl
>
> Tear off this leaf — and you will find there remain in this packet, three half sheets of new copy, which I want added at once to the end of the little pamphlet, which I return corrected. Please get the corrections made — and

> what I have left of the title printed smaller: it is not to have a title at present — nor to be by me. It is only a series of propositions offered to the Committee's acceptance.[119]

Despite the overlap between tasks his cousin performed for Ruskin and what others did for him, the degree to which he came to rely on her thoughts and memories is unmatched by relationships with assistants such as Howell and Tyrwhitt. In addition to cataloguing and arranging books, Joan joined her cousin in cataloguing his mineral specimens. For example, in June 1865, he wrote: 'I'm very glad you're coming back — I've got all our tickets under the wrong minerals. and — theres not a book in its place'.[120] She was a willing assistant who volunteered to help him.[121] One simple task was to test the quality of paper for him,[122] but there were many others. For example, 'Tyrwhitt's job seems to have been that of a research assistant, hunting odd bits of information for the lectures and later for *Fors Clavigera*. He corrected copy for Ruskin and helped him with Greek and Latin'.[123] Joan helped in similar ways, although probably not with classical languages. For example, he commented that he could not 'find lavender nor rosemary in Sowerby' but that 'if Collie Wollie showed you the place in Loudon — you could copy out for oos di Pa Loudons list of the Labiatae — which would be a great help.'[124] He thus gently asked her to record and send information to him in aid of his research. Unlike the relationship between Ruskin and Tyrwhitt, which 'seems to have been that of master and disciple',[125] the tone of Ruskin's letters to his cousin in this context is more avuncular or fraternal than masterly.

Just as she came to edit some of his public writing, Joan also handled aspects of Ruskin's private correspondence. Some letters he asked her to keep for him, in other cases the letters were to be kept for posterity. Often, he asked her to answer letters for him. Sometimes this was because he was pressed for time;[126] but at other times because he had no desire to write the letter.[127] Along with her husband, Joan also used to intercede when Ruskin had legal problems.[128]

The correspondence suggests a shared responsibility between the cousins, linked by a desire on his part to be 'useful' together; he asked her 'to resolve that every day shall bring you some true gain of knowledge or power' and to 'be made useful also by some true hand-service'. He argued that her 'safest, if not the highest happinefs lies' in such activities as 'mathematical drawing', 'illumination', 'flower painting', 'writing from [his] dictation', 'unpacking and dusting of minerals & books' and 'the study of history'. He brought this argument to a climax by saying that 'we will ^both hope henceforward to make our ^present days less dependent either on other persons, or on future hopes', finally stating that by this she 'may have [her] own little Castle in the air, beside [her] daily garden on the ground.'[129] The activities he believed gave her 'happinefs' are all ones in which he had involved her and in which they shared. Through them, he argued, she would find 'your own little Castle in the air', but this 'Castle' flowed from the assertion that 'we will ^both hope henceforward to make our ^present days less dependant [...] on other persons'. Ruskin came to rely so heavily on his cousin rather than 'other persons' that many letters express his appreciation for her care, with statements such as: 'And suppose I had'nt a Joanie to manage everything for me — what would become of me!'[130]

II · THE EVOLUTION OF BABY-TALK

'If ve'ed nevy learnt baby tawk'

The key relationship of Ruskin's later life was his intimate domestic friendship with his cousin Joan Severn. Through it, he explored his identity within a familial construct. One crucial aspect of this experiment was the way he infantilized himself, allowing himself to play out the role he saw as the ideal state of existence: a feminized and, although mischievous, essentially innocent child. A century after his death, this self is evident in the letters he wrote to his cousin.

There was no specific moment when baby-talk emerged; it evolved through interaction with his cousin and others. Sometimes it clearly placed him in the diminished position of a child with an under-developed grasp of language. Other times, it is evocative of the phrases and tones parents typically use in addressing young children, positing him as the adult using baby-talk to communicate with the inferior child.[131] Using this persona, Ruskin brought back into his private, domestic relationship with Joan the many other social relationships he had to sustain, all organized into a comfortable, personal space of a family and an owned domestic interior.[132] This provided him with a sense of both personal/psychological and cultural wholeness, offering a place wherein to harmonize the different selves represented in his different roles: cultural, prophetic, arrogant; domestic, childlike, insecure. This harmonization took place in a domestic space within his culture. Paradoxically, it empowered him in the public sphere by disempowering him in the private. These were his terms of empowerment and self-negotiation. Traces of this exist across Ruskin's writing, but they are most evident in correspondence with Joan. While a number of critics have referred to these letters in writing about Ruskin, none previously has used them as the focus of an extended project.

The public personae of Ruskin, not just as he cultivated them but also as portrayed by his literary executors, do not necessarily match the Ruskin who emerges here; but that is not to say that the Ruskin who inhabits the correspondence to Joan, and thus this book, is more 'real'. If anything, it is a less realistic version, for it grapples with Ruskin as he imagined himself to be. The Joan who appears in this book is not the woman who actually was, but the 'Doanie' whom Ruskin wanted. Just as, when looking back to his childhood in *Praeterita*, he painted his parents and his youthful self in ways that are patently distorted, so the Joan of these letters is not true. For example, Helen Viljoen's *Ruskin's Scottish Heritage* portrays Joan in an unflattering light: not very intelligent, parochial, mercantile, and a bane to Ruskin scholars for the ways she shaped and determined 'the image of John Ruskin that would eventually emerge'.[133] Viljoen's portrayal of Joan is more factual than that which emerges in this book; but what interests me here is the way Ruskin made use of his perceptions of his 'Doanie' to undergird his perceptions of himself.

On her thirty-seventh birthday, Ruskin wrote to Joan, saying: 'Oh di ma, if I only could build oo a palace with diamond windows and golden doors. and put on

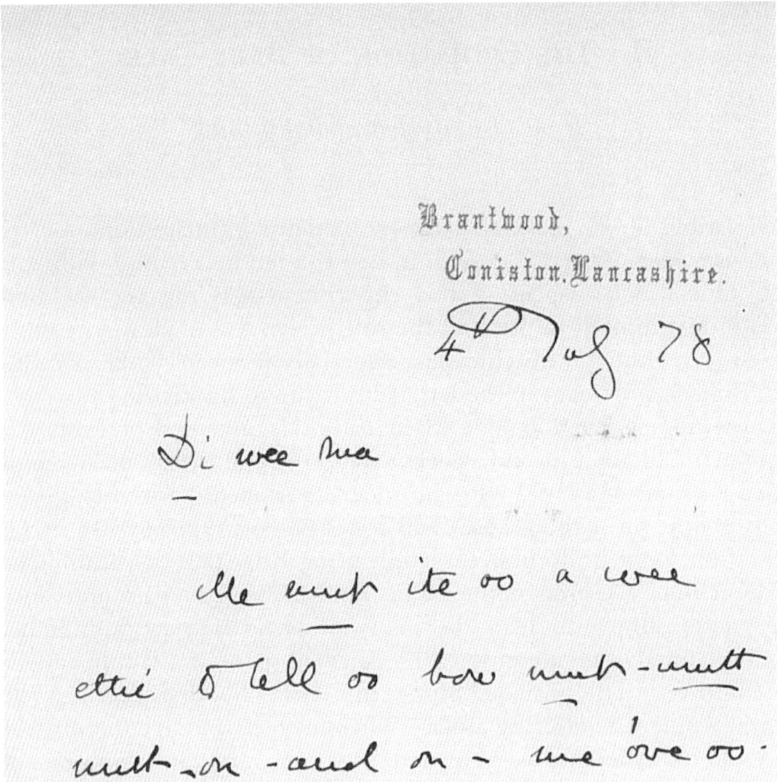

Brantwood,
Coniston, Lancashire.

4th July 78

Di wee ma

Me must ite oo a wee ettie o tell oo how muth-muth muth-oo - and oo - me ove oo - and me tant sith any longer without itin oo a wee ettie - and wei oo own poo itie

Donie

FIG. 2. Facsimile of JR letter to JS, 4 July 1878 [165]
RF L42, Ruskin Foundation (Ruskin Library, Lancaster University)

a story every birth day, as the shells do in the sea, and fill it all with music like the seashells. and have my di ma to sing to me up at the top.'[134] This excerpt begins with a term of endearment, 'di ma'. This pet-name, along with the use of 'oo' for 'you', exemplifies the ease with which Ruskin habitually integrated their shared baby-talk idiolect into his letters to her. Here, the sentiments he put forward combine with the words he chose to express a key, unifying aspect of Ruskin's identity: he was a man forever in search of such a fantasy 'home'. He longed for an idealized place — a fairytale palace — where he might consistently find comfort and peace. As this letter suggests, the power of this 'palace' would be a shared experience, mutually constructed by and for himself and Joan. He would build her the palace ('if I only could build oo a palace'), yet she would not have clear ownership of the gift. She would be in it to comfort and to entertain him ('and have my di ma sing to me up at the top').[135] It was through the shifting locus of this relationship with his 'di ma' that Ruskin most nearly built such 'a palace with diamond windows and golden doors'. He attempted to create a physical representation of this secure fairytale palace by acquiring and shaping Brantwood. But it was more effectively realized in the relational correspondence shared with his cousin. Through it, he grounded himself in domestic security rooted in memories and expressed in enacted roles. Yet this was not without complications; problematically for Ruskin as he aged, his 'Di Ma', about whom he had fantasized and whom he had tried to construct, became a real mother figure who, in reality, imposed on him constraints such as he had role-played with in his epistolary fantasies. Unlike his fantasy constructs, the reality of these constraints was not fully in his control and was not always to his liking.

Ruskin scholars have long been struck by his 'baby-talk', one of the terms he coined to describe his infantile idiolect. How his critics and editors have responded to and dealt with this language has differed markedly. When preparing a selection of Ruskin's personal correspondence for publication in the 'Library Edition', Cook and Wedderburn included a number of letters from Ruskin to his cousin; their second volume of his letters even begins with a letter to Joan Severn. Visually, the illustrations which open that volume are, first, a photograph of Ruskin at Brantwood (before the frontispiece) and, secondly, a portrait of his cousin (facing the secondary title page, after the contents and introduction). This primary positioning of a letter to and image of Joan within the volume of letters dedicated to Ruskin's later life suggests the primary importance Cook and Wedderburn ascribed to her relationship with Ruskin. But her letters do not dominate this volume, which purports to be representative of Ruskin's later correspondence; on the basis of letters reproduced, Joan Severn is on a par with the Rev. J. P. Faunthorpe (57 each). Letters to Kate Greenaway (94), Charles Eliot Norton (133) and Susan Beever (164) far outweigh those to his cousin. Based on this empirical evidence, one might expect Beever's portrait to appear where Severn's is; or that Ruskin's literary executor, Norton, would occupy this position, as the recipient of the largest number of 'business' letters. One reason why Joan appears foremost is because, while not reflected in the number of letters Cook and Wedderburn chose to include, she received a vast number of letters from Ruskin during the decades of her involvement with him: at least 2,990 are known to be extant. She was undeniably the most influential (living) person in his later life, and his contemporary editors and biographers — including Cook and Wedderburn — depended on her goodwill when producing Ruskin-related works.

Not only did Cook and Wedderburn reproduce an unrepresentatively small proportion of Ruskin's letters to Joan but when transcribing they consistently standardized the language, removing many of the more infantile tones and making the remaining traces appear to be the result of an informal and hurried pen, rather than the adoption of a specifically child-like voice. For example, in publishing the letter of 9 March 1883, Ruskin's editors removed the baby-talk salutation and signature;[136] yet they included the formal variants on these in the surrounding letters addressed to George Richmond and Charles Eliot Norton. They also standardized the spelling and removed the chatty, domestic parts of the narrative. In their editing, Cook and Wedderburn attempted to preserve their idealized image of Ruskin as an intellectual 'Master'. But their version was at odds with Ruskin's idealized image of himself as a feminized infant. In many cases, as here, his editors simply removed those sections of letters written in baby-talk, thus obscuring much of Ruskin's personality.

Ruskin wrote many 'business' letters to his cousin, a term he used to differentiate letters on serious topics, such as his public writing, his lectures, his efforts for the Guild of St. George, and financial issues, from more playfully social, experimental and phatic letters. He applied the term not only to his own correspondence on such topics, but also to those written by others. For example, in May 1882 he wrote to his cousin in response to one of her letters: 'I like the businefs letter immensely for its busywifinefs, and wisenefs'.[137] This implies that she had written to him about household finances, and the term 'busywifinefs', which combines 'business' with 'wife', means efficiently housewifely. Ruskin's letters to his cousin were rarely purely concerned with 'business'. Rather, formal talk of 'business' was generally interspersed with more plaintive and playful expressions of emotion, which were characteristically phrased in baby-talk.

While Cook and Wedderburn masked Ruskin's infantile personae, more recent commentators have tended to address this aspect, at least in passing. Tim Hilton, in a current standard biography of Ruskin, makes fuller use of Ruskin's correspondence with Joan. When citing letters that include baby-talk, he does not standardize the English, but offers readers a glimpse of Ruskin's intimate communication. He does, however, provide readers with some editorial comment on and biographical analysis of the baby-talk letters:

> These letters, which Ruskin sometimes called 'nonsense letters' became more frequent [... and] introduced all sorts of nicknames, private jokes and references. They were not, however, nonsense. They reflect Ruskin's weariness with his writing, his political pessimism and longing for his childhood.[138]

This is a succinct and generally neutral explanation of Ruskin's infantile voice in this correspondence. Lines, such as 'It's so dreadfully dismal, being a Pfessy. I can't even write baby misbinefs about it',[139] suggest that Ruskin's perceptions of society's expectations of him and his writing weighed heavily on him. He had to find ways to cope with these pressures, and this playful, petulant child-voice was one such strategy.

Arguably, although Ruskin had early used terms of endearment in writing to his cousin, baby-talk really began to flower in 1867 when he wrote his 'Pigwiggian Chaunts'.[140] It is worth noting, however, that Ruskin called his cousin 'a nice little "baby Agnew"' in May 1865.[141] The next month, he (for the first extant time in correspondence with his cousin) expressed childish puzzlement and inadequacy at a particular aspect of grammar: 'I shall be all the better of $^{\text{or for.}}$ + you', followed by the note 'It's a difficult bit of grammar that, — it always puzzles me.'[142] Within three years, such asides would be expressed in baby-talk. The first letter to use a playful, derivative name is that of 28 September 1866, which is both addressed to and signed from 'Cuzzie', implying the twinship of the cousins. This letter also includes the first extensive piece of word-play, where Ruskin began with '[t]alk of being cross as two sticks!' then used it to craft a playful image describing and elaborating on the turn-of-phrase: 'I'm as crofs as a whole crows nest of sticks. — If all the sticks creaked and croaked, as well as crofsed.'[143] Thus, the groundwork for baby-talk was apparent before 'piggies' burst into the correspondence in June and July 1867.

Because of the level of trust between them — a trust which I believe emerged from a companionship solidified through the language of childhood that they shared, as playmates, in a transportable, epistolary nursery — he could speak honestly to her. This language performed an equalizing function, enabling them to bypass differences in age and gender, which cultural expectations otherwise imposed. The baby-talk letters are infused with Ruskin's delight in their complicity; when sharing in this private, linguistic adventure 'Donie' and 'Doanie' were being naughty but essentially harmless children together. Hilton notes:

> These 'pig-wiggian chaunts', as he called them, date from his summer in Keswick in 1867. Mindful that his father had chosen a boar's head when he devised the family crest, Ruskin wrote of himself as 'Little Pig', 'or', he was to explain in *Praeterita*, 'royally plural, "Little Pigs"', especially when these letters (that is, to Joan) took the tone of confessions [...].[144] These pig-wiggian rhymes seem to have dramatised overspending, wanting things he should not have, overeating, or other minor misdeeds of the nursery.[145]

As Hilton points out, this was a confessional as well as playful mode of communication.[146] Significantly, it stemmed from an association in Ruskin's mind with his father. Baby-talk is rooted in Ruskin's construction of his adult self in light of his parents: he was 'Little Pig' to his father's implied 'Big' or mature 'Pig'. Ruskin did not really feel himself to be an independent, mature male until after his father died. Then, at 46, he effectively left the nursery, finally taking control of his own finances and experiencing a mother who deferred to him. As Dinah Birch points out, 'Ruskin's career up to 1864 had been to a large extent a vicarious fulfilment of the blocked ambitions of his father. Now he was on his own, the new male head of the Ruskin family. It was a role that perturbed him'.[147] At this moment of transition and loss, when he was pushed from the nursery and forced to bear new responsibilities, his cousin arrived to help carry the load. She also helped to maintain Ruskin's literal nursery. When she later took over the Herne Hill house as her marital home, Ruskin's old nursery became his study; and he habitually referred to it still as his 'nursery'.[148]

While Hilton's text takes a fairly neutral approach to the infantilized Ruskin, there is an implied subtext, positing the relationship with Joan as destructive. I think this is partly due to issues of space and emphasis within Hilton's biography. The baby-talk evident in the letters to his cousin is jarring, even distasteful, when removed from its natural place, embedded within the dynamic, ever-evolving correspondence. This is one reason why many critics have expressed a sinister opinion on Ruskin's baby-talk.

Although Hilton writes that 'Ruskin's first editors were not able to print any letters written in this manner and would not have mentioned the poetry from which the baby-talk derived if Ruskin had not quoted snatches of it in his autobiography',[149] he must mean that they chose not to print them, because the extant letters bear traces of their access to them. A number of letters from Ruskin to Severn have been inscribed in pencil with 'A.W.' (Alexander Wedderburn) at the top. Generally, such letters feature one or more pairs of pencilled brackets demarcating sections of the letter. In many cases, these sections correspond with letters from Ruskin to Severn reproduced or alluded to in the 'Library Edition'. Typically, the brackets mark segments written in standard English, distinguishing them from the baby-talk devices which often frame them. Generally, the brackets exclude explicit statements by Ruskin about his state of mind or finances. A good example of this is a letter Ruskin wrote to his cousin about his loneliness, the exhaustion (mental and physical) which he felt could ensue from work, and of a visit with Holman-Hunt. Wedderburn could have printed 'letters written in this [baby-talk] manner', but chose not to. Rather than transcribing in full both his version and the original letter here, I direct the reader to compare the version in the 'Library Edition' with my transcription.[150] Cook and Wedderburn omit the following: Ruskin's baby-talk salutation; discussions of his petulance the previous autumn and domestic arrangements with his cousin; comments on interactions with girls. The latter includes 'It is quite true however that I *am* very naughty about Tinys & Rosalinds — and I've less and less hope of mending'.[151] Ruskin's editors excised this potentially damning section about interactions with girls. They also edited those sections they reproduced. For example, the second set of brackets includes 'I was really very near being quite reformed yesterday all at once — by the perfectest little cherub of a five-years-old I ever saw yet in my life — Holman Hunt's little Gladys', but this does not appear in the published version. Again, this section of the letter articulates Ruskin's interest in girls, and his editors chose not to offer — and explain — it to his readers.

Hilton raises another important aspect of the correspondence: early in the relationship, 'Ruskin began to write to Joan in close domestic ways', 'demanding that she learn to cook' and using pet-names. As the cousins adopted and evolved their pet-names together, they simultaneously shared in domestic experiments. Ruskin might have demanded that his cousin learn to cook,[152] but when he took up residence at Brantwood, he too learned to cook.[153] This domestic game entailed a levelling function. It was not really any more appropriate for a young woman of her status to cook than it was for Ruskin to learn to do so: they playfully transgressed this cultural norm together.

In terms of Ruskin's self-infantilization, their shared culinary interest connects Joan with his long-dead cousin Jessie, with whom he had cooked in childhood. *Praeterita* highlights the idealized scene: his child-self and Jessie gleaning corn, which they ground and cooked into cakes as a form of practical play.[154] He also imagined himself engaging in such practical domestic play with Joan, which evolved into the reality of them literally keeping house together. Early on, they envisaged a little country cottage where they might escape from the pressures of society and live an idealized, platonic, pastoral life. Ruskin referred to this imagined, idealized life in a letter to his cousin of 26 August 1868: 'Now, if I were living in my proper simple life I should be able to walk, myself or send pussie, into the kitchen — and take the gridiron — and toast my bone thereupon ^ like Achilles till it was as dainty again as at first.'[155] This is a fantasy playhouse, which was explored in the alternative reality of their letters and in their lives together at Brantwood.

Hilton's passage alludes to another important aspect of these letters: the 'piggie-verses' associated with baby-talk confess 'overeating, or other minor misdeeds *of the nursery*'.[156] As baby-talk became established, the letters began to function as a place where Ruskin playfully could confess a different nursery-related 'misdeed': his aesthetic appreciation of girls. He was aware that this interest could be a distraction and might not gain universal approval. Although he occasionally claimed to be unable to 'jest' and use baby-talk when upset, he did use it as a means of expression during some periods of loss. Batchelor specifically links this language to Ruskin's reaction to Rose's death:

> His state of mind during this period is exemplified in his letters to Joan. He writes to Joan in a baby-language designed to show that he is simultaneously her parent and her child, and designed also, perhaps, to gain 'permission' for his experiments with the supernatural.[157]

Batchelor, like Hilton, recognizes that baby-talk could be a confessional conduit through which humbly to approach his cousin and gain her approval.

Baby-talk was not static; the idiolect of 'our wee English' evolved.[158] Sometimes, as is in the short-lived 'Mexican' of 1876 or the recurring voice of 'M. Pencil', baby-talk was not English at all.[159] Often, the derivations of words within their idiolect are traceable across several letters. Sometimes, Ruskin wrote the standardized spelling of a word, then crossed it out and replaced it with baby-talk.[160] At other times, he stated what new baby-talk term would be substituted for a standard word.[161] Often, a term was used in several letters within a short period of time, only to disappear, sometimes permanently, but sometimes to resurface after a period of months or years. 'Pig-wiggian' is a good example of this. After a period of popularity in the late 1860s, it largely disappeared, returning only in 1886, when he wrote of teaching 'Pigwiggina' to play the piano.[162] At this time, Ruskin was rereading old letters and diaries, looking for material to use in *Praeterita*. This conscious retracing of memories may have initiated pig-wiggian's re-emergence, and might explain why he christened his current playmate, the local shepherd-girl Jane Anne Wilkinson, with the name 'Pigwiggina'.[163] There were also streams which formed sub-idiolects. The most common of these was Tottish. A. N. Wilson describes the 'extraordinary baby-talk' Ruskin used with Joan, adding:

— e.g. of Scotland, he wrote to her (he aged forty-eight, she newly married to Arthur), 'There was once a bonnie wee country marnie dear — ey called it Totland — I pose because it was so nice for wee tots to play at pushing in wee bookies ... When I was the weest of tots — it oosed to be so pitty, mamie.' And so on.[164]

It should be noted that Ruskin would have classified the 'household words' cited by Wilson as a 'Tottish' (Scottish) rather than 'baby-talk' (infantilized) variant on 'nonsense', although the two are closely connected. Robson also conflates the two, referring to 'regressive baby-talk, in all its mock-Scottish tweeness',[165] but there are letters where Ruskin used standard baby-talk intertwined with distinctly Scottish pronunciations. In fact, read in its entirety, the letter cited by Wilson differentiates between 'our baby letters' and the broader range of 'the nonsense letters' before offering an extensive paragraph in the 'Tottish' idiolect. One of Ruskin's most overtly 'Scottish' letters is from October 1872, written to his cousin during one of her many visits home to Scotland: 'my mas in Totland — neebody at home — & the lassies awa [...] and there are nae lins to loup ower — and if ^{gin} there were, I'm owre auld & stiff to loup — an I dinna ken whats to be dune'.[166] If this is read aloud, followed by the following baby-talk excerpt, the difference between the idiolects is clear: '— Me dedful tired and worrited. — me's had to go and -ceive pince eopold — and sow him sings, and. mes got to go gen mowy monin. (If poo di auntie had been alive!!!) — and peepies want me to go ^{to} dinnywin and me won't.'[167] Ruskin used the Scottish variant when he wanted specifically to highlight either Joan's Scottishness or his or her physical presence in Scotland at the time of composition. Otherwise, he used a more Ruskin-standard infantilized idiolect, which tended to drop consonants rather than to extend vowels.[168]

Van Akin Burd's introduction to the 'Christmas Story' letters Ruskin wrote Joan from Venice in 1876–77 offers his perspective on baby-talk and the relationship between Ruskin and his cousin:

> Mrs. Severn (1846–1924) indeed had become to Ruskin both a daughter and a mother with whom he could now speak more freely than he had with either of his parents. Thoroughly familiar with his habits of expression and modes of thought, particularly about the lost Rose La Touche, she could understand allusions that must be explained here in footnotes. He had developed with Mrs. Severn a "little language" that he sometimes uses, particularly in the opening and closing passages of his letters, reminiscent of Swift's private language in his letters to Stella. [...] The infantilism of some of the expressions in Ruskin's letters is at first distracting, but must be understood as his language of endearment with his beloved "Joanie." [169]

The final sentence of this quotation is particularly insightful and establishes Burd's perspective as unusual among Ruskin's critics. He contextualizes it in reference to another author. And, importantly, while he acknowledges that the baby-talk 'is at first distracting', Burd recognizes that, with repeated exposure, it can make the correspondence particularly accessible. 'Baby-talk' invites the reader into this diminutive, shared world; by watching the evolution of words, and enjoying the word-play and the genuine expressions of affection that emerge, the reader is encouraged actively to participate in the relationship by deciphering the puzzle of allusions. Paralleling the transgressive acts of writing in baby-talk, the reader of these letters engages in an equally transgressive act of eavesdropping.

Ruskin did not intend these letters for public consumption. He was ashamed that others might read them. What is probably the first extant letter entirely in baby-talk was written on 7 July 1869.[170] Less than a week later, on 13 July, Ruskin suggested that others might be 'scandilized' 'at <u>our</u> baby letters'.[171] Similarly, in 1872 he asked: 'Is'nt all oos peepies [her Scottish relatives] dedfu socked 'at we tant pell any betty, oo & me — after bein Pessy and Pussy evie so long? — Me so fitened. — fot do ey all say?'[172] More than a decade later, he expressed a similar concern: 'I never write my letters for any peepies [people in general] to understand but you — – and though I leave my letters lying about — do not suppose you leave yours.'[173] He considered his letters to Joan to be private. This last letter also suggests that the baby-talk relationship was perhaps not as egalitarian as Ruskin, on the level of fantasy, seemed to want it to be. Within the intimacy of their idiolect, she was a playmate and equal. But this letter articulates a sense that his reputation could be undermined if others saw such letters by him. He exhibited no such concern that her reputation would be affected by his tendency to leave hers 'lying about'.

Although Ruskin did not want his intimate letters to his cousin to be seen by prying eyes, he was not opposed to some of his private letters being published. He gave the Beever sisters his blessing to publish *Hortus Inclusus* and he wrote to his cousin in May 1886 about the possibility of publishing a collection of his correspondence with young women: 'I really get some nice letters written just now! They'll be a lovely sequel to the auto. if theyre ever collected! and I'm getting some nice ones back! I've been obliged to clear out a compartment of a study bookcase drawer for 'under twenty' letters.'[174] His phrasing does not suggest that Ruskin considered there to have been any impropriety in these letters by young women aged 'under twenty', he found them charming and wanted to offer them to a wider readership.

Ruskin shared the intimacy of baby-talk with trusted friends besides his cousin. For example, he intended to forward to Francesca Alexander the letter where his cousin wrote, in baby-talk, 'Its' joyous to hear oo say oos a bit bitty bettie. of course oo will be all the betty-er for being dood for nufin —'.[175] Francesca lived in Florence, and the letter in question is now housed with Joan's correspondence to Ruskin. It is in an unposted envelope addressed to Francesca Alexander. The top left corner of the letter is inscribed in Ruskin's hand: 'You may like to see second page of this', directing his friend to his cousin's account of a family party charmingly dominated by the Severn's young son. At the end of the letter, he added a note to his Italian-American friend. It is written in baby-talk:

> <u>Fot</u> a tuk up Doanie she'll be if her Venetian photo is put in the Præterita! — [...] Barrand has just made an excellent copy from one of the ovey photos I had — & when I get them, I'll send them on to oo — would you prefer them, (not that I shall ever be pointed if oo don't want anything for such & too — honoured purpose for me) to the portrait Arfie did, if any illustration of the little Scotch cousin <u>is</u> wanted!'[176]

This note suggests that he had meant to send the letter on to his friend in Italy. It is not clear why he did not: perhaps because he was so taken by its description of the Severn's young son's persona as the chivalrous 'Col^l Herbert'; perhaps because he had written something at the end of the letter which he then thought better of, for the final section has been torn away, evidently excised after composition because the script on the remaining side bleeds across to nothing. In any event, this unsent letter records a shared web of baby-talk communication, encompassing Ruskin, his cousin and his sisterly friend. Not only was Ruskin sharing with Francesca Alexander the intimate communication, which he had evolved with the help of his cousin, he initiated her into the family by sending her photos and portraits 'of the little Scotch cousin'. He also discussed aspects of the publication of *Praeterita* with her, delightedly anticipating how '[s]tuck up' or vain and pleased 'Doanie' would be by the inclusion of a particularly favoured photo of her. These were the kinds of details he discussed with Joan, his 'Di Ma'; his nickname for his Italian-American friend was 'Sorella', meaning sister.

Joan knew Francesca Alexander was a trusted friend of Ruskin's. He told her that 'my thoughts are nothing now — and from day to day new lights — or shades flicker round me, — [through] which there remains now only fixed the hope not wilfully to give my Joanie or Francesca ignoble sorrow for me'.[177] This implies that their importance for him was similar, and that he considered Francesca (Sorella) to be his caretaker in a similar way to Joan (Di Ma). Joan also knew that Ruskin wrote to Francesca in baby-talk. Ruskin explicitly told her this, saying: 'I don't know if oo ikes itin to oos Donie, but my chief pleasure in life is itin to my Di Ma. I've been sending some mewys letters to Francesca too, lately which she says she likes very much — and gets up in the middle of her breakfast to answer.'[178] His account of Francesca's response to his letters suggests that Joan was not sufficiently appreciative of those she received. It also explicitly reflects Ruskin's pleasure in knowing that his intimate letters were appreciated by his 'Sorella', if not necessarily his 'di ma' at this stage. He liked hearing that his friend would interrupt her breakfast just to answer them.

'Mewy letters' was an alternate term for baby-talk. It was probably derived from Joan's earliest pet-name, 'Pussy', but it was also a concrete device used overtly by Ruskin when he recognized that he was being particularly playfully petulant. For example, in the autumn of 1872 he wrote that he would like to cry like a 'wee schoolgirl' or a 'wee kittie' then added: "Mew-. ew- ew-ew. Ever oos poo-poo-poO Donie Thats a great sob."[179] Here, 'Mew-ew-ew-ew' expressed his plaintive, whining sadness. The evolution of the baby-talk and the associated personae of 'di ma' and 'little Donie' allowed the cousins and trusted friends to communicate intimately. It freed Ruskin from mature, social constraints and roles, which he found increasingly overwhelming.

This experience of momentary freedom from the weight of work and social commitments, derived from writing intimately in baby-talk, is evident in the letter just cited. It was composed during his first term as Slade Professor at Oxford and begins: 'It's so dreadfully dismal, being a Pfessy. I can't even write baby misbinefs about it'. While this letter expresses his tiredness, loneliness and stress in the face of his Professorship, it also expresses his belief that 'My power for good to others however increases continually.' He supported this claim by telling his cousin to 'Read the notices in the papers which I send today'. Two newspaper clippings are still with the letter. One is a column-wide review of 'The Works of John Ruskin. Vol. I. "Sesame and Lilies." Sold by George Allen, Heathfield Cottage, Keston, Kent.' Although anonymous, 'John Morgan' is written in pen on the bottom. The other, unascribed, piece on 'John Leech's Drawings' extensively cites Ruskin on the topic. A further letter was evidently enclosed. In reference to this, Ruskin, sounding somewhat petulant despite his pleasure, wrote: 'Its the first time anybody ever gave me credit for knowing that things have two sides or for knowing anything besides drawing in six lessons.'[180] This expresses conflicting fear, frustration and pleasure at being appreciated, and he framed it with baby-talk, which, by linguistically diminishing him, also diminished the perceived weight of the problems. Paradoxically, it empowered him.

When Ruskin stated that 'I can't even write baby misbinefs', the letter suggests just how overwhelmed he was feeling. There are many similar letters, including another from October 1872, which reads: 'Me doin' away [from Brantwood to Oxford]. me so dismal me don't no fot to do. — Me want to give up bein Pefsor — (— me tant say at, di ma, nor ite it) — and top heer and have Joanie Ponie' and other female friends provide comfort and company.[181] This letter includes the title 'Pefsor', an uncommon variant on 'Professor'; his aside specifically links this new permutation on the term to his inability either to speak or write the word, implicitly stemming both from his real, physical problem with pronouncing 'r' and from his utter boredom and frustration with his post.

The fact that Ruskin could still use baby-talk in this letter and devise new terms means that he was not entirely overwhelmed. This mechanism still helped him relax and be playful, but as he expressed early in the relationship, 'because I write play-letters; you must not think that I am or can be, what I used to be.'[182] He did not use baby-talk when particularly agitated and recognized he could not 'jest in writing' when sad.[183] When especially upset, he used pointedly standardized English and made demands, as in the very clipped tones of 17 August 1886: 'But I am not jesting now, by any means, in assuring you that things are <u>not</u> to be on their old footing here [at Brantwood] — ever again.'[184] However, in the letter about being a 'Pfessy', written fourteen years before, he was able to use the release of baby-talk.

While aspects of the letters and the selves revealed in them necessarily stem from a subconscious level, Ruskin was aware that he used a variety of languages to evoke different personae. In one case, from November 1873, he playfully expressed his awareness of the languages he employed in different contexts — contexts he described as 'household words'.[185] On one level, this phrasing evokes Dickens's periodical and the dissemination of that other influential Victorian writer's ideologies within its pages. In the context of this letter, 'household words' implies not only the influence of cultural figures such as Dickens on Ruskin, but also the influence of his domestic setting — and those who shared it — on Ruskin the man of letters.

In this letter, Ruskin used standard, mature language to ask his cousin to help him in his role as Master of the Guild, by copying 'the state of the funds of St George', and to express the formal means of communication expected of him as

Slade Professor of Fine Art. He referred to this language as 'My own Professorial'. While he stated that this was his 'own' language, the letter suggests how his formal words were reinforced by people close to him and by different modes of communication. He alluded to the visual 'language' exemplified by the 'Door Diagram' Arthur Severn prepared for him as an illustration to a lecture. There is also an affectionate reference to the influence of his manservant, Frederick Crawley, mentioning a 'lovely bit of Crawley wawlian' in a lecture: 'gulp' in lieu of 'Gulph'. Whether this slip stemmed from Crawley's transcription of the lecture or whether it is an error typical of Crawley's spoken patterns is not clear, nor is it crucial for this argument. What is interesting is the implied interconnectedness of identity, language and communication. Ruskin perceived himself to be shaped by the members of his household: the performance of his '*own*', 'household words' is generated collectively.[186]

This letter not only implies the influence of domestic relationships on his formal, public communication, it also refers to and uses the special, informal communication he used in the secure environment of his private life: 'baby-talk'. He mentioned 'My Pesssy-wessorial', a term fusing two self-infantilizing references: 'Fessy-wessy' was the established Ruskinian baby-talk term for 'professor', while 'Pussy' was the earliest term of endearment for his cousin. The use of 'Pesssy-wessorial', as opposed to 'Fessy-wessorial,' makes the term resonate with the times he lectured her on scholarly concepts or moaned about his role as professor. In drawing the letter to a close, Ruskin placed Joan in a position she filled throughout their relationship: he had her serve as his personal assistant by asking her to send him an account of the Guild of St George finances. The term 'Pessy-wessorial' and the task he set her both allude to the professional and authoritative languages connected to his social roles (Professor, Master of the Guild) yet, strikingly, he couched them within a framework of baby-talk. This specific letter begins with the salutation: 'Darling Doanie'. It continues with the opening: 'Your letters are such comfy-wumfy', which flows through to the ending: 'Ever oos own Di Pa'. Even when asking her to serve as secretary to his culturally authoritative self ('Master' of the Guild), he issued the command in baby-talk, 'pease' for please and 'oo' for you.[187]

In a series of baby-talk letters from 1873, Ruskin asked his cousin for a stuffed robin. Like Arthur Severn's 'Door Diagram', he planned to use it as a lecture prop. Contextually, the series of letters began from Brantwood, addressed to the Severns in London. Ruskin soon travelled to Oxford to deliver the planned lecture, from whence the robin references continued. Taken together, this sequence demonstrates the flow of ideas in his mind, as well as the way terms and concepts evolved and picked up added levels of association. The robin letters begin in standard English: 'Do you recollect the Robin you gave me? on the little log. standing up? I'm writing my first Bird lecture on him. he's such a darling. There are ever so many here. One comes now generally to look what I'm doing at my stream.'[188] Ruskin's delight in seeing the live robins, his pleasure in the stuffed 'Robin', and his forthcoming 'first Bird lecture' were all connected. A few weeks later, he specifically asked his cousin for an additional stuffed robin to keep at his rooms in Oxford so he could have one at each 'home'.[189] He first requested an ' 'obbin' in a fairly extensive piece of baby-talk, childishly misspelling it by adding a 'b', and evoking a child-like pronunciation by dropping the 'r'. He then switched to more formal, professorial speech patterns to specify that he actually required the robin to illustrate his Saturday lecture. This letter is characterized by a marked division in the language: he began in baby-talk then abandoned that 'jesting' voice to make it clear that this was not just a whim but a business requirement. He even included a physical gap on the page, demarcating the change in tone. His request shifts from 'Me don't ike to take my 'obbin away from Brantwood, — because he so pitty among shellywells. — me want an 'obbin at Oxford — poo Donie tant get on without an Obbin' to 'Please — I want this as well done as its pofsible to do it — but I must have one lent, if it cant be done in time for my Saturdays lecture. — I think my Robin brings me luck, here — and won't move him'.[190] Ruskin was childishly superstitious; feeling inspired by the robin (he was writing with delighted ease at Brantwood) he would not risk disrupting such 'luck' by removing the robin to Oxford. It had become a mascot, echoing the vital, 'beautiful living ones on the lawn', bringing their vivacity inside.

References to the robin continue: 'me like my 'obbin with his mouthie open.– I wish peepies would always let me say, 'obbin' instead of wobbin [...] Send Wobbin to C.C.C. Oxford.'[191] This letter includes another shift in word usage. He had been referring to the robin as an ''obbin'. In this instance, he explicitly evoked his speech impediment and phonetically wrote the word in order to represent the way he knew it issued from his mouth: 'wobbin'. In a similar vein, he wrote a few days later about drawing robins' feathers, adding: 'Di ma. me ove oo so mut me wish me was a obbin, — me would fly to oo. Poo Donie got no fevys, ony a long beard. Poo Donie not save for three days.'[192] There is a striking contrast here between the image of the bearded professor and the infantile idiolect. Parts of these letters are problematically petulant, as though written by a spoilt child. For the reader, this disrupts received notions of Ruskin's identity. Yet, this infantile tone can equally be infused with an infectious sense of fun — of comforting play — which is endearing. Many letters express his conscious delight in this fun. Take, for example, the following extract: 'Me's had mutton top and gass of serry. How funny words are when tt one takes pains to spell 'em quite itely, Di Ma'.[193]

The correspondence with Joan and her family provided Ruskin with a portable family and a location to which he could map his identity. At the beginning of 1873, he wrote to the Severns, saying: 'So many thanks, for your letter and Arfies. So many good wishes and so much love to you both I've been looking at your photographs, for some comfy.'[194] His awareness of the Severns' love provided him with comfort, even when they were not physically present. That comfort could be, and often was, stimulated and reinforced by looking at their photographs, gifts they had given him, and their letters — and by envisaging their presence while composing letters to them. This affection and reliance on epistolary contact was reciprocal, as can be seen in the letters surrounding the death of Joan's sister Kate in the autumn of 1869.[195]

Twenty years later, in a particularly plaintive and touching letter of 1888, Ruskin expressed his perception of the unconditional love he received from the Severns. Although this letter looks back over a decade of 'pain' ('— 1878 — 1881, 82, —

85–86 — and through all this 87 from May to December') and includes mature turns of phrase such as 'no power of doing more [than] the cat does all day', it also expresses the present thoughts of a fragile person. It fluctuates in and out of the infantile idiolect in asking: '<u>does</u> oo love me too — through all the hundred fold worse than absence of the pain I've been to oo.?' And it positions Ruskin as a child in need of comfort, insecurely asking, 'Oh di ma [...] Is oo twite soo me isn't a mere bovy to oo now.' Through the baby-talk, Ruskin expressed his need for reassurance and his perception of his own precarious mental and emotional state. 'Is oo twite soo' (Are you quite sure) was a request for definite reaffirmation of his cousin's love and reassurance that 'me isn't a mere bovy' (I am not a mere bother). The act of asking — albeit rhetorically, for the bond of baby-talk actively constructed her so that she must reassure him — provided its own form of comfort, as did the imaginative leap of envisaging a response, and in reading whatever actual affirmative response he must have received. Intriguingly, a conscious awareness of constructed selves and the perceptions individuals have of each other is built into this letter. Ruskin commented of Kate Greenaway: 'How that creature <u>does</u> love me, or the idea she has of me, through any quantity of unkindness or absence.' He was aware that Greenaway's love for him was at least partially based on her — implicitly inaccurate — 'idea of' him.[196]

At the close of a letter from October 1884, Ruskin overtly expressed the value of the shared idiolect: 'Oh my di ma, fot sood ve hav done to understand each ovy if vee'd nevy learnt baby tawk? Fot <u>sood </u>ve hav done? Me's oos <u>little</u> Donie'.[197] Although few of her extant letters make extensive use of baby-talk, there are some examples of it, such as: 'Its' joyous to hear oo say oos a bit bitty bettie. of course oo will be all the betty-er for being dood for nufin –'.[198] The use of baby-talk in this letter refers directly to comments he had made about his health; she might well have been quoting his letter back to him, embellishing his baby-talk with a bit of her own in response. It is also worth bearing in mind that she had long been encouraging him to do less — even 'nufin' — in the way of intellectual work or social interaction, which she feared would unbalance his precarious mental and physical health. Her use of baby-talk here playfully encouraged him to continue the trend of relaxing. It thus functioned as a means by which 'to understand each ovy' and through which she affectionately could shape and control his actions. Baby-talk provided them both with a means by which to build kinship, placing themselves in fluctuating positions of authority, and offering them a means of shaping each other's actions and emotional state.

III · RUSKIN AND GIRLS

'Like a itie wee schoolgirl'

In June 1864, three months after the death of his father, John Ruskin wrote a letter to Mary Frances Bradford, a teacher at Winnington Hall residential school for girls, arranging to meet Bradford and several of her pupils for an evening at the theatre. He added:

> — I shall bring my cousin with me to introduce to you — a good cheerful girl whom my mother has taken a fancy to for her nurse, for the present. There's not much in her, but I think you will like what there is — Joanna Agnew is her name. She will not crowd us — the box is large — but you [the young women] will be a large bouquet for your poor thin stalk of a papa — so please dress as plainly as you possibly can to be comfortable.[199]

This light-hearted note is one of the earliest extant letters describing Ruskin's cousin. Written two months after she joined his household, he had come to enjoy her company, finding her 'a good cheerful girl'. He looked forward to an evening spent with her and other young women.

Ruskin's aesthetic eye enjoyed the company of young, preferably thin, women. For example, while staying at the Giessbach Hotel in July 1869, Ruskin wrote Joan several letters about 'Marie of the Giessbach', a friend who was ill.[200] When comments on Marie written over three days are considered together, they reflect a consciously preferred feminine type:

> She is very pretty still — in some respects prettier than she was [for me] — because more delicate — her thinned, fragile waist & neck are, sadly, graceful — and her hair cut a little short and falling behind as if she were 14 or 15 — — [...] Still she is enjoying her bit firtie mightily. — She comes peeping [... in] the morning after breakfast and stays till I send her away — and asks when she may come again, — and is happy — [...] I can't help — in spite of the sadness — being immensely amused with Marie — she is so very clever — and subtle and fun. fond of play — even in her illnefs. [...] She says such wise little things every now & then — and then nods her little head — and says — "Yes It's true."[201]

These letters also reveal that Marie debated with him on topics such as slavery, wore pretty dresses specifically to please him, and stubbornly refused always to keep him company on his terms. While Marie was very thin and looked young, this apparent youth and fragility was belied by her 'clever', 'subtle', and 'wise' personality, her distinctive mannerisms, and her strong will. She combined all of this with playfulness and the ability to make Ruskin feel she genuinely enjoyed his friendship.

Girl-women such as Marie Schmidlin were Ruskin's favoured type. Although she resonated on rather different levels, Rose La Touche, the young, thin Irish girl with whom he ultimately fell in love, was of a similar type. She too eventually wasted away. Such women, and artistic representations of such forms, appealed to him at a deeply moving, aesthetic level. When she joined his household, Joan

Agnew was slim, with what she later claimed was a 'less than 22½ inch waist',[202] but she was never a frail girl and photographs of her in middle-age suggest that she was never naturally thin.[203] Even a portrait of her from as early as 1873 suggests that she was in no danger of wasting away.[204] But her comparatively plump physique appealed to Ruskin's aesthetic on a different level: she was substantial, strong and — by early middle-age — matronly. Ruskin valued these qualities. In 1883, he wrote a birthday message, which included: 'And you're not to get thin, oo know! You and me together make a nice wee Di Ma and Donie'.[205] Her size in relation to him made her seem more maternal, nearer to the fantasy ideal he had constructed of her in relation to him: she was his 'Di Ma' or mother, and he was her 'Donie' or little child John. While her physique differed from Ruskin's preferred type, her personality — at least before she reached middle-age — fit the ideal. By all accounts, she possessed what Ruskin referred to in *Praeterita* as an 'inventive wit' and 'sense of clownish humour.'[206] He claimed to value her letters because they 'make me laugh'.[207] He could be at ease with her 'clever', 'subtle', 'wise', strong-willed, yet playful and loving personality.

As Ruskin's account of his conversations with Marie Schmidlin and his baby-talk notes to Francesca Alexander suggest, Joan was not the only woman complicit in helping Ruskin to fashion and maintain his epistolary and realized fantasy life. The use of the term 'complicit' here is intentional, despite the fact that it can have negative connotations. Within Ruskin's world, female friends were complicit. They feminized and infantilized him in ways which went against societal norms. Yet within the framework of Ruskin's web of relationships, they were complicit in the sense of Rahab, offering a domestic haven, rather than as criminals complicit in a crime.[208] Foremost of these women was his mother, who laid the initial groundwork of constructing her child as an idealized, feminized 'momma's boy'. His nurse, Anne Strachan, also treated him as a child well into adulthood. Although he addressed the girls and women at Winnington Hall as 'pets' and 'children', often referring to himself as their 'papa', they treated him as a fellow schoolgirl, rolling on the lawn and playing games together.[209] Yet the relational effect was more complex than just becoming 'like a itie wee schoolgirl'.[210] Ruskin engaged in what could thereby become a (at least to him) innocent flirtation with these girls — and their peer, the teenaged Joan Agnew — without fear of embarrassment or real danger of becoming involved in an overtly sexual way.[211]

Hilton offers two brief discussions of Ruskin as paedophile.[212] While the first, in *The Early Years*, states that Ruskin 'is typical of the condition […of] paedophilia', the later volume is more guarded in its claims and implies that this attraction primarily functioned on an aesthetic and symbolic level, positioning the idealized figures of controlled, liminal femininity as though in a painting.[213] He gives no examples of Ruskin engaging in sexual acts with girls. Similarly, Batchelor claims that Ruskin was attracted to girls and young women and he refers to Ruskin's 'sexual obsession' (with Rose). However, he also refers to Ruskin's 'unremitting state of sexual frustration'.[214] This, again, implies desire which was never fully acted on

Ruskin's Rose: A Venetian Love Story (2000) is a non-academic text dealing simplistically but at length with the Ruskin–Rose relationship, turning it into a fairytale. The authors state that Ruskin 'tried to prolong her childhood with fairy tales and pet names. He called her Posie Rosie Posie.' They add that 'Ruskin, who liked to imagine he was a child himself, took the nickname Crumpet, later Saint Crumpet, because of his kindness to beggars'.[215] This account portrays the pet-names and occasional childish dialogue as reflections of Ruskin's refreshingly child-like nature and his pure love for Rose. It suggests theirs was one of the world's great, tragic love stories. It ignores the fact that Rose was not the only person with whom Ruskin corresponded in this way.

In a marginally more recent and decidedly more academic example, A. N. Wilson's *The Victorians* (2002) lists fifteen entries on Ruskin in its index. These include his connections with notable figures ('and Alice Liddell', 'and Wordsworth'), key events from his life ('divorce of', 'visit to Venice'), and references to his writing ('on Great Exhibition', 'political contradictions of').[216] There are no references to Joan Severn or any other relative, but there is one pertinent entry: 'baby language of'. Wilson's text restates common perceptions of Ruskin, his relationships with women and girls, and his baby-talk. Like Robson, Wilson frames this exploration within a discussion of Dodgson. He contrasts the two writers' interactions with Alice Liddell and states that 'Ruskin could most cheerfully relate to females when he regarded them as presexual infants'. This is a fair and insightful comment, but part of the dynamic is missing. The key to the way Ruskin regarded such females rests in how he regarded himself when in their company and, as importantly, when imagining their company: he felt like one of them. Wilson continues with a description of Ruskin's relationship with La Touche, his 'hopeless and painful love affair — one has to use the word, though it was of course entirely Platonic, and indeed largely something taking place inside his head'.[217] This is a neat distillation of the narrative implied in Hilton's biography. Ruskin had created an idealized Rose as he wanted her to be; '[n]ot as she is, but as she fills his dream'.[218] This perception was reinforced by letters from her, particularly the one reproduced in *Praeterita*, where her voice is a strikingly fetching combination of cleverness and childishness.[219] As much as possible, he interpreted these to fit his own fantasy of her and himself in relation to her. Wilson's comment on Ruskin's imaginative construction of Rose is also pertinent, for similar relational fantasies (based on what he wanted as opposed to what was) coloured many of his relationships with women, including his cousin:

> We can all guess the truthful answer to what would have happened had Rose recovered, and had Ruskin and she attempted a 'normal' married relationship. In later life when he had gone mad, Ruskin was something of a 'liability' with the little girls at the local school, near his Coniston home. Long before this, however, in letters to his cousin Joan Agnew [...] he had employed extraordinary baby-talk.[220]

Wilson turns from the specifics of Alice Liddell, Rose La Touche and Joan Severn to suggest that Ruskin's intentions toward local schoolgirls in Coniston may not have been pure. As for baby-talk, his 'And so on' dismisses it as indicative of Ruskin's psychological state and relational inadequacies. Wilson used Hilton as a source and, by virtue of necessary brevity, his account of Ruskin's relationships with younger women seems darker.

In his account of Ruskin's fondness for young girls, John Batchelor, like Robson and Wilson, contrasts it with that exhibited by Dodgson. He states that '[a]n intense sexual attraction to little girls was a substantial component of Ruskin's sexuality'. He then notes that the women Ruskin fell in love with either tended to be 'very young, but sexually mature', such as Adèle Domecq (in his youth) and Kathleen Olander (in his old age), or women who had first entranced him when they were children and to whom he continued to be attracted as they matured into adulthood, such as Effie Grey (whom he married) and Rose La Touche (to whom he proposed marriage). While Batchelor links Ruskin's appreciation of girls to his sexuality, he argues that Ruskin was quite different from Dodgson, who was 'exclusively attracted to little girls.'[221] Ruskin's interests were broader. In a technical sense, assuming that there was a sexual interest on Ruskin's part, he would not have been a paedophile, exhibiting 'long-term sexual interest in children with the typical body shape of an under 11-year-old', but a paedohebephile, interested in 'pubescent [female] persons between 11 and 14 years'.[222] Batchelor too takes issue with applying the term 'paedophile' to Ruskin, noting that Ruskin's 'fixation' with a girl typically continued into 'the young adult life of the chosen girl' and, strictly speaking, he was not a paedophile.[223]

Catherine Robson's *Men in Wonderland* links Ruskin and Charles Dodgson (Lewis Carroll) as 'notorious girl lovers'.[224] She deals extensively with their relationships with young women; her 'Introduction' addresses standard twentieth-century perspectives on 'nineteenth-century figures who appeared to display desires other than those expected within normative conjugality'.[225] Her claim — that 'Carroll's and Ruskin's evident fascination with little girls, to be named "paedophilia" in 1906 and catalogued under "Abnormality" by Havelock Ellis in his *Study of the Psychology of Sex*,' offered 'few options' for critics, who 'could only support, deny, or ignore (and this last course was the road most taken) the portrait of the artist as pervert' — rings true.[226] I would add to Robson's statement: in looking back to Victorian minds from a twenty-first-century vantage point, we must be wary of imposing our world-views onto the past. As Weltman points out, 'even though some recent books and articles have speculatively and pejoratively labeled Ruskin a pedophile, in fact we know virtually nothing of his sex life'. She adds that '[t]he recent scholars and critics using the term *pedophile* to describe Ruskin employ it even though they agree that we have no hint of molestation'.[227] Ruskin's reputation has suffered in the wake of popular Freudian and psychoanalytic interpretations.

The type that seems to have appealed most to Ruskin was a barely pubescent girl who looked childlike, yet seemed mature — womanly — in her emotional and conversational patterns. He was aware of this preference for younger girls, and a number of letters to his cousin express it overtly. For example, in 1882 he wrote of an evening's visit with the Burne-Joneses, adding that their daughter 'Margaret had a tea of her own — and seven of her schoolfellows for guests — about her own age, — rather old, for <u>me</u> — but endurable –'.[228] They were schoolgirls, but physically mature and past the ideal. In contrast, the Rose whom he first met had been younger, just shy of ten.[229]

In the penultimate chapter of *Praeterita* Ruskin wrote that:

> Some wise, and prettily mannered, people have told me I shouldn't say anything about Rosie at all.[230] But I am too old now to take advice, and I won't have this following letter — the first she ever wrote me — moulder away, when I can read it no more, lost to all loving hearts.[231]

The chapter closes with a transcription of the letter written many years before by the thirteen-year-old Rose while on holiday with her parents.[232] Its striking tone — which Ruskin found so fetching — stems from the juxtaposition of childish playfulness and intense seriousness. There was much in this letter to captivate Ruskin: the repetitive use of pet-names ('Dearest St. Crumpet', 'Archigosaurus'); playful descriptives ('Kingfishery'); flattering comments such as 'You the author of M-Ps c^d describe it[233] Irish roses cant', which placed her in a submissive position; and childish rhetorical requests for his opinion, such as asking why, when suddenly awakened, people (here her sister Emily) invariably claim to have been awake. Her use of imagery, such as being a transplanted Irish rose when on the Continent, is precocious flowing from the mind of a child. She ends with flattery: 'You must see how we think of you & talk of you — rosie posie'.[234] The chapter which follows immediately after this transcription is 'Joanna's Care'.[235] It ends *Praeterita*. Speaking eerily of the long-dead 'Rosie' in the present tense, it is one of Ruskin's many published passages overtly haunted by the idealized image of Rose La Touche.

Ruskin's interest in young girls who exhibited surprising maturity characterized his interaction with women for much of his life. There were variations on this preference. For example two of his earliest passions, Adèle Domecq and Effie Grey, were both relatively near his own age. Both were young, yet each was aware of her feminine charms. It was not until those affections were in his past, and Ruskin in short succession both met Rose La Touche and discovered that he enjoyed the company of the schoolgirls of Winnington, that the preference for less sexualized yet mature-seeming female companionship became a set-pattern of influence on his life and writing.

In August 1888, Ruskin repeatedly wrote to Joan about 'my little Turk,' whom he had met in Dijon. One letter is particularly relevant to the discussion at hand. It includes the following, extensive postscript:

> — I enclose photo of my little Turk ^as she used to [was]^ — two years ago — the skirts are cruelly decorous, <u>now</u>; but the face is little changed — and if you take a magnifying glass to it — you will see the curious decision — She answers with absolutely the firmness and firmness and fineness of a clever woman of 25. ! Keep it with the greatest care for me. I find it rather a disturbing element in my desk — (and I shall be sure to have another flirt on as soon as I get to Sallanches.)[236]

This letter is potentially damning. Ruskin included a treasure with it: the photograph of his current 'flirt' — 'my little Turk'. Ruskin found this image a difficult distraction; it is tempting to picture the ageing Ruskin surreptitiously pulling the photo out from 'in [his] desk', lewdly to gaze upon it. This interpretation of the scene is sustainable from the text, but I am not convinced by it. An equally sustainable view of the same scene involves the aged Ruskin pulling the photograph out, not to be sexually aroused, but to be emotionally affected.

Ruskin alluded to the girl's now-lengthened skirts (he had long enjoyed seeing glimpses of shins and ankles, which he called 'eggie-pegs'[237]), but his focus rested on her face and 'the curious decision' he read there. He specified that this ideal perception was not belied by the girl's words: 'firmness [...] and fineness of a clever woman of 25. !' Thus, she exhibited the same juxtaposition of infantile youth and matronly maturity he found compelling in Rose. It is an embodiment of what he longed to find in female companions; when he did (or imagined he did) their presence infused him with a sense of play, vitality and comfort. This comfort was derived in part by the fact that he could feel in control of the relationship (he knew he was the older, dominant, male figure) yet could allow himself to relax into the fantasy of himself being a girl. Girls who were curiously playful and childish yet spoke with 'the firmness [...] and fineness of a clever woman of 25' exhibited kinship with his own circumstances. He was, after all, mature yet longing to play.

In this case, Ruskin was clearly uncomfortable with the photograph. I suspect the discomfort came from memories the girl's image evoked in him — he was torn by mixed feelings and impressions as he looked at it. Rather than destroying the photo, he sent it away from him to the safekeeping of his conscience and co-conspirator, Joan. In doing so, he asked her to join him in admiring the girl. There is no clear sense of a sexual attraction. Rather, his response seems purely an appreciation of a thing of beauty and joy, which moved him on emotional, aesthetic and mnemonic levels. Importantly, the paragraph which follows the description of 'my little Turk' reads: 'Love to my old flames at Sedgwick', where his cousin was visiting. He added: ' — Tell Mary I think it's the awfullest shame of all thats ever been awful to me, that she did'nt come to sing to me when I was ill.' Ruskin equated 'My little Turk' to other such 'flames', flames he expected would entertain and comfort him as he hoped Mary might have done in his illness.

Several years earlier he had written to his cousin from Florence, saying that he had become 'so dedful naughty,' thinking that 'a real pitty girl without any [clotheses] but roses' would be more affective than Botticelli's artistic representation of a girl robed in roses.[238] Two days later, he expressed a similar sentiment.[239] In each case, although Ruskin articulated a desire to see — and paint — naked girls, these thoughts were linked to roses. In the first, the Venus (and the dreamt-of-real-girl) is 'without any [clotheses] but roses'.[240] In the second, having thought about painting naked girls and even suggested the Severn's governess, Lockie, would be an ideal model of whom he 'could make something very Boticellesque' like the Venus, wrapped in roses, he offered his cousin a compelling word-painting of actual roses he had seen. He noted that this real, natural, ideal composition of flowers was offset by the grey-green of the olive trees; its darkness making the red roses all the more striking. He described the roses as living embodiments of ideal Roseness at their peak of vitality: '— There were no faded ones, and there were no bunches of buds making one wish they were out —'.[241] Their colours were neither too dark nor too bright, and he made a point of stating that they matched the painterly ideal, when unrealistic artists depict a fantasy: all the roses at their fantasy-fullest, without a gardener's sense of the trouble and imperfection which invariably mars their natural state.[242]

In Ruskin's mind, roses were linked to his Rose. That the naked girls of whom he fantasized appear surrounded by references to roses strongly suggests that Ruskin's interest in such girls does not rest with the girls themselves, but in the idea of his ideal girl. The letter from Rose reproduced in the penultimate chapter of *Praeterita* implies a precocious girl at her peak, neither faded nor too young, neither too bright nor too pale, a prime example of 'Irish Roses' captured at the apex of perfection. The perfect roses on the wall, the Venus wrapped in roses, the thoughts of girls posing for him, all of these resonate with his memories of Rose, not as he knew her, but as she mythically came to be constructed in his mind.

This letter mentions Lockie and imagines her as an ideal model, posing 'with her, jacket — not on'.[243] The pause created by the dash suggests Ruskin might have been picturing her stripped of even more than her jacket. But it is worth remembering, in a discussion of Ruskin's attraction to young girls, that Lockie was not a child.[244] She was the governess to the Severn children. Another letter mentions her in a possibly lascivious sense, connecting her to the notion of 'Turk': 'Enclosed cheque for dear little Lockie — I wish I could buy her [...] I wonder what she thinks herself worth, if she were to be put up like the pretty girls in Herodotus. — please ask her — I wish I was a blessed old Egyptian or Turk or something.'[245] The following year he similarly claimed the new governess at neighbouring Monk Coniston was a 'stunner' who would make nursery teas exciting.[246] This governess was not Lockie, but his letter suggests that Ruskin, who was drawn to the mnemonic, liminal aesthetic of young girls, felt a different attraction to the physicality of young women.

Having read through Ruskin's letters to his uniquely trusted cousin and her letters to him, I don't believe that he was a paedophile in the sense that we now mean it — although he was enamoured of children. To adore an other as a reflection of one's idealized self is not necessarily to sexualize that other.[247] Ruskin experienced an intense platonic appreciation of the aesthetic and symbolic appeal of girls and of ways this idealized image resonated with and shored up his identity. When, in later life, he found his interest in such girls disturbing, it was because in giving him pleasure they also evoked sad memories of past girls and lost possibilities. In some ways, this is akin to his relationship with Brantwood: he had chosen his Lake District home because of mnemonic associations of childhood holidays.[248] Ruskin could appreciate Brantwood's aesthetic, he could play and be at ease there, and for many years these experiences and the memories which accrued around them gave great pleasure and stability; over time, however, sad memories were imposed onto these and the idealized relationship he had enjoyed with his home was lost.

A letter from Joan makes clear that Ruskin's interaction with children formed a distressing mnemonic layer as he looked back to his Lake District home from the Continent in 1888. She wrote from Brantwood:

> I wish you'd open your blessed heart & tell me just why you dread coming here so? — There is yet so much possibility of happiness for us both — [...] It is only these most cruel illnesses that have ever distorted your mind, & caused me the misery I've had! — but you have been so dear & precious to me lately that the wounds are healed — no scar even left — & I want to dispel all the unhappy associations you have with the place — [...] I'm sure there is much of real happiness & enjoyment possible without the discord that a renewal of

those "classes", ^{might} bring between us — In<u>deed</u> not from any jealousy of mine — It is better to speak out — It made me furious I grant you, those girls not understanding your great goo-dness — laughing at it! — & behaving ^{insolently} to me — I can't bear to speak of it at all for the pain it may give both of us — but almost a year has gone! — & the gossip has died out! — and we can [start] happily afresh — & you would have the dearest welcome from everyone when you come! — & the respect & devotion you deserve — & your Do-anie would make your happiness & comfort in all ways a study — you can see, & talk as much as you like to any children — in the ordinary way — as other people would — not in an <u>unusual</u> way! — you will forgive me darling if I have said a word to pain you — but I don't want you to "<u>dread</u>" coming to your own beautiful Brantwood — & I thought it might be on account of what I have said — tho' I can't bear saying a word about it all now — only I feared some of these thoughts might be the cause[.][249]

The classes Joan so dreaded had been botany lessons with the local schoolgirls of Coniston. According to Hilton, these classes began in the summer of 1886 and were terminated by Joan by May 1887. He describes them thus:

> As many as a dozen children would present themselves at Brantwood for instruction, play and tea. Ruskin liked to watch the girls dancing, sometimes to tunes he had himself composed. The dances encouraged unbecoming behaviour. [...] Innocent in themselves, such romps too often excited Ruskin's mind, especially when he was tense about other matters. At such times he could behave foolishly. It is known that he proposed to adopt at least one of the girls who came to the botany class.[250]

Joan's letter suggests her concerns about the classes had related to notions of reputation. She was offended at and infuriated by the girls' rude, 'insolent' and ungrateful behaviour to herself and to Ruskin and the fact that Ruskin had become a joke to them. Even more problematic was the spread of 'gossip' — she feared for Ruskin's (and his household's) wider reputation. What I find particularly revealing, however, are the terms in which she encouraged Ruskin to return. She promised 'the respect & devotion you deserve' from the whole household and that she, specifically, 'would make your happiness & comfort in all ways a study': she offered the love and comfort he craved. Importantly for this discussion of Ruskin's self-infantilizing and -feminizing impulses, particularly as evinced through language, she added: 'you can see, & talk as much as you like to any children — in the ordinary way — as other people would — not in an <u>unusual</u> way!' I suspect that part of what the schoolgirls found so amusing in Ruskin — and what so embarrassed Joan — was the 'unusual' language he used with them. Joan's focus here is not on Ruskin's actions but on his 'talk' to the children. I suspect that, as with Howell so many years before, Ruskin had constructed an image of the girls which entailed a deep trust on his part. This trust manifest itself in the use of his private nonsense/baby-talk idiolects with the girls. The image of the bearded old professor thus communicating with the girls is jarring; it is no wonder the girls giggled and gossiped.

The spectre of Ruskin as sexual pervert recurs not only in academic discussions and popular histories, but also in word-of-mouth conversations. Anecdotally, if someone knows just one fact about Ruskin, it relates either to his annulled marriage or to his interest in girls. These popular readings of Ruskin's life relate to his infantilization: fear of mature female pubic hair, inability to be aroused by a mature female body, preference for the company of girls — these are indicative of a child-like approach to the potentially sexualized female body.

That said, Ruskin's undeniable attraction to young girls needs to be addressed, for as these examples suggest, it was a central motif of his later letters to his cousin, and it is a recurring topic of, albeit often brief, discussion by his critics. Ruskin was aware of cultural norms regarding male friendships with girls. He recognized the social impropriety of being alone in the company of girls without chaperones or intermediaries. For example, in summer 1886, he wrote about an anticipated visit from Louisa Strode and her mother.[251] When they arrived, Ruskin's response was mixed. Of the mother, he commented that she was 'a disappointment and talks too much', adding that '[t]here ought to be colleges for the education of women past 40. — before anything else is done in educational reform.'[252] Presumably the talkative mother's mind was not quick enough, her world-view not broad enough, and her company not stimulating enough for his tastes. But he was pleased with the daughter, even if she was, '[o]lder a little Im sorry to say than I pected'. He nevertheless found her: 'extremely nice; — gentle and soft,', 'in her plainness — pleasant —', 'modest & powerful. — and rather grand in features —', 'very nice — modest — useful — sensible.'[253] This description, offered over two days, stresses the girl's modesty and plainness, yet it suggests a paradoxical combination of being both soft and powerful and, importantly, a pleasant and useful companion.[254]

Ruskin followed this praise with 'Im going to have her back for a fortnight when you come. — at least — I suppose ool be tumin — some day this month? wont oo. di ma.'[255] This reveals two important things. First, it suggests that he was aware of the inappropriateness of entertaining a solitary girl as houseguest in his cousin's absence if the (disappointing) mother was not there. Secondly, it seems a calculated attempt to urge his cousin to return to him, both by inciting jealousy and by activating her role as his conscience and moderator of socially appropriate activities. A second visit did ensue, but it and his relations with 'Lou' thereafter did not live up to Ruskin's expectations. A letter from the following March implies that he blamed the breakdown of that friendship on Joan, while she blamed it on his escalating madness.[256] Reading between the lines, it seems that at some point during Louisa Strode's subsequent visit Ruskin became very angry at dinner. His cousin apparently tried to smooth things over by speaking with Louisa, probably telling her that Ruskin suffered from periods of unpredictable behaviour. The outcome seems to have been that the girl became wary and stopped playing with Ruskin in the carefree yet intelligent way he had found engaging. Instead, she became distant. She ceased to be a playmate. As always when considering Ruskin's interactions with girls, two strains of equally sustainable interpretations co-exist: Ruskin as a manipulative, self-aware paedophile or Ruskin as an adult longing to re-experience the joyful, playful childhood he associated with his idealized image of girls.

Catherine Robson makes some observations that are pertinent here, arguing that in the wake of Foucault 'it became possible to examine the case of the Victorian girl-lover from different perspectives'.[257] In light of this, she discusses why some

Victorian male writers 'reimagine[d] the young self as feminine' and she considers cultural implications of such 'repetitions of an iconic vision of the adult male and the little girl'.[258] Robson is primarily concerned with *Ethics of the Dust* and *Praeterita*. She outlines ways Ruskin equates the beauty of young girls to the beauty of stones. She argues that this was a strategy he used to de-sexualize his aesthetic (and potentially erotic) appreciation of girls. Robson reproduces a baby-talk letter to Joan,[259] then explicitly highlights the age difference between the correspondents: 'In 1869 fifty-year-old Ruskin is writing from Italy to Joan Agnew, his twenty-two-year-old second cousin'.[260] As with many readers, the surprise Robson felt in reading the letter relates not only to the apparent incongruity between the language Ruskin used here and the language he used as a cultural sage. It also relates to a sense of social inappropriateness, that such a dialogue should not occur between a middle-aged man and his young, female ward. She suggests that:

> Such regressive baby-talk, in all its mock-Scottish tweeness, invokes a welter of responses: this is of course private correspondence, never intended for the scrutiny of eyes other than Joan's, but it is startling, to say the least, to know that the author of some of the most challenging and beautiful passages of Victorian prose also wrote these sentences (and indeed many others like it in this period). [...] Ruskin's favourite things — girls, precious stones, and frequently precious stones as art objects — are bound up into a single tantalizing form. In Ruskin's particular case, the paedophile and the petrophile are one.[261]

She argues that 'the crystalline girlish self is not just the lost self of the past, but also the only true self in the present'.[262] She defines the crystalline self as both the feminized self of *Praeterita* and the idealized jewel girls of *Ethics*, concluding that, '[i]n the final estimation, Ruskin's extension of the Victorian fantasy of the gentleman's lost girlhood into a fantasy of the essential girlishness of the true self proves not to be a source of sentimental solace, but a torment'.[263]

Robson's thoughts on these letters are, like mine, concerned with Ruskin's identity and how it was played out in relationships. Importantly, she too links this with Ruskin's attempts to reconcile two selves: his ideal feminized past and his real masculinized present. However, the letters to Joan Severn are not Robson's primary focus. Based on her readings particularly of *Ethics* and *Praeterita*, she compellingly argues that 'the essential girlishness of the true self' was 'a torment' to Ruskin. Although we followed similar paths, we reached different conclusions. Having read through Ruskin's correspondence with Joan, I believe that rather than 'torment', he found comfort, albeit of a flawed and inconsistent nature, in 'the essential girlishness of the true self'. Just as Ruskin's liminal, idealized models of femininity as embodied in child-women were paradoxical, so his perception that there were points of commonality between himself and these girl-women was also paradoxical. His attempts to bridge the gap between himself and this ideal offered 'solace' to Ruskin in important ways, although his fantasy expectations were never matched by reality for sustained periods.

A possible reason for our different conclusions is that, unlike Robson, I would not claim the feminized, infantilized self to be 'the only true self in the present', later Ruskin. Rather, it was one of several true selves which fulfilled particular functions. Undeniably, this particular sense of self was problematic for him. As the note about re-inviting Louisa Strode (sans mother) to Brantwood implied, he recognized that the natural affiliation he felt with much younger women — and the easy, playful comfort he found in their company — might be frowned upon. But Ruskin was not as concerned about this as one might expect — perhaps because context is important. In a letter cited by Robson, Ruskin expresses interest in costumes worn by statues of 'wee girlies', stating that they wear 'Dust a wee Bedgowny tied about waisty with a band of jewels — If me get oo nice band of boo beads, mammy — will oo let me see oo wear oos bedgowny ike at?'[264] This seems inappropriate. From the twenty-first century, we look back and think that, whether in jest or not, Victorian Ruskin should not have asked his ward to wear nothing but a 'bedgowny' cinched at the waist with a band of beads. But there are Ruskinian symbols tied into this, which moderate the tone. 'Boo' is 'blue',[265] Ruskin's favourite colour; as Robson points out, this passage connects 'Ruskin's favourite things — girls, precious stones, [...] precious stones as art objects'.[266] Not only does the image involve Ruskin's favourite things that are external to him, it also resonates with Ruskin's internalized perception of his ideal self. The Northcote portrait of his three-and-a-half-year-old self, verbally depicted in *Praeterita* as being 'dressed in a white frock like a girl, with a broad light-blue sash', resembles a girlish figure in a woman's free-flowing bed-gown cinched with blue.[267]

Throughout his life, Ruskin chose to wear blue, particularly as an accent colour. Remembering the middle-aged Ruskin, Sidney Colvin wrote of a 'figure clad in the invariable dark blue frock coat and bright blue necktie';[268] 'invariable' stresses that Ruskin habitually chose this colour as a fashion signature. Even more common — as captured in textual accounts and colour plates of Ruskin reproduced in Dearden's *John Ruskin: A Life in Pictures* — is the 'blue neckcloth'.[269] Virtually all coloured representations of Ruskin in his daily dress feature this blue accent at his throat. It cinched his shirt at the neck, just as the similarly blue sash had his child-self's torso. The imagined 'band of boo beads', which might circle the 'wee girlies'' (and his Joanie's) waists, fits this type. Elsewhere, he wrote with delight about girls' 'tresses tied with blue'.[270] The significance of this, and his apparent excitement at it, again stem from symbolic resonance. To put it plainly, when imagining the girls so clad and in asking his cousin to emulate them, Ruskin was not motivated by sexual impressions and desires. Rather, he equated such girls to his idealized, playful, unconstrained self: the child of the portrait who exhibited the intuitive sight of an infant genius or saint. This idealized self entailed the image of one who watches. Intriguingly, Hilton writes of Rose La Touche that 'Rose's illness had both aged her and wasted her natural growth. At the same time she clung to a conception of herself as a childlike, spiritual witness in the adult world'.[271] In a strange circle of symbolism, Rose, whom Ruskin adored, became like the self Ruskin imagined himself to have been as a child.

Returning to the passage Robson cited about the statues of girls in Verona wearing nothing but 'a wee Bedgowny', it is useful to consider the lines that precede the excerpt quoted by Robson: 'Poo Donnie so hot! — biged to seep under one wee seety , and teep both windys [...] — wide open.'[272] Ruskin had been discussing bedsheets immediately before describing the girls in bedgowns. He found Italy extremely hot in the summer of 1869,[273] and wanted to sleep under just 'one wee [sheet]'; he was also intrigued by the idea of wearing more fluid, cooling clothing. The next, undated, letter in the extant correspondence was written from Venice and picks up on the description of clothing in the passage discussed by Robson: 'There were once bonnie bit girlies in Venice, mamie dee — but poo donie ony met twa, o them, dressed anything like' when he wandered through town that day.[274] Ruskin accompanied this statement with a sketch, demonstrating that one girl had been wearing a fluid headscarf and, presumably, gown. But in this letter his attention was on the head-covering and hairstyle which presented a notably unsexualized aspect of the 'Bedgowny' style of dress. This is a style of dress he also described to Dora Lees at about this point. On 31 May, he wrote her a long letter about the society he hoped to form with his cousin and any other friends who would join them. All members of the utopian society were to wear 'Costume — up to the clearly possible point of Tyrolese and other healthy peasantries ... Incompatible with quick motion, when worn in full dress'.[275].

It is also important to note that Ruskin did not write 'the wee girlies must have looked very *fit* [...] and me wish *ice* statues would come ive again', as Robson cites, but 'the wee girlies mut have looked very *pit* [...] and me wish *wee* tatues would come ive again'.[276] I have added the emphasis to each of these. Robson's reading of 'fit' and 'ice' (whether the latter is taken to mean 'cold' or 'nice' is not clear, but since Robson stresses the frozen, petrophilic nature of the girls, I suspect she means the former) is more sexually loaded than mine of 'pit' (pretty) and 'wee' (small). What follows the excerpt is also revealing. Having asked his cousin to wear a 'bedgowny', Ruskin added: 'Me will ite to wee Tonnie Won Pon to ask her too = It so vewy pît.' The focus of Ruskin's attention was not just on the Venetian girls nor his cousin; it included another favourite female friend, Constance Hilliard. What I suspect is evoked is a desire to see the aesthetically appealing images of the natural flow of fabric over natural curves, rather than the affected, structured feminine forms seen and experienced within the constraints of Victorian dress. Later that summer, Ruskin wrote a passage which similarly describes lack of clothing, this time in a painting of the Nativity: 'two delicious little angels — boy angels, with ruby-coloured wings — ∧ (and nutin else, mamie dee — At quite popy?) and as full of fun as any mortal boys'.[277] The tone is similar, but focused on boys rather than girls. Ruskin's aside of 'and [nothing] else [on], mamie dee — [Is that quite proper?]' suggests a playful but not predatory interest in lack of clothing, which is coupled with an appreciation for natural, uninhibited, useful activity. Assembled into a pattern, these passages are not nearly so sexualized as they appear in isolation.

The comfort Ruskin found in youthful companionship is evident in narratives of other encounters with girls. In June 1886, he described meeting 'seven ^Robinesque imps' on the road to Colwith and '[setting] them arithmetical questions in pence'. He added that '[T]here was one little ragged — haggard — yet not sickly — pale one with her hair flickering down like tongues of fire — I don't think I ever saw anything quite so lovely'.[278] The term 'Robinesque' is interesting. It might be meant to evoke 'Rubenesque', but it more likely symbolizes the bird, which fascinated

Ruskin.[279] The children are small and lively, like robins, and the one who most intrigued him had hair 'like tongues of fire' — redhead like robin's redbreast. His response to the most striking child was aesthetic, the juxtaposition of her 'ragged — haggard' appearance, which belied her 'little' size and youth, and her paleness, which was contrasted with hair 'like tongues of fire'. Rose La Touche is evoked in this encounter. Physically, she had been ragged and small and pale. Relationally, she had named him 'Saint Crumpet' because of his kindness to beggars such as these. In setting these children 'arithmetical questions in pence', Ruskin showed kindness by giving them coins in exchange for solving problems. He often offered such financial support to the needy in exchange for make-work projects. In so doing, he lived up to the pet-name Rose had given him: Saint Crumpet. Following what seems to have been his third visit to Colwith in June that year, his diary notes with excitement 'Went to Colwith. *Saw the first wild rose* as I was walking up the hill.'[280] Rose's influence here is worth noting; virtually all of Ruskin's interactions with children — which may be read as paedophilic and sexualized — may equally be read as innocent attempts to recapture lost memories and possibilities and fun of his youth, based on memories of playing with Jessie and Rosie and all his other lost girl playmates.

In the letters preceding this one, Ruskin begged Joan to return and keep him company. For example he had written: 'Can't you sell evy ting off at once — and come and live with oos di pa comfy and nevy go to that wicked London no mo? [...] I am doing a good deal — but theer is really no happy time in living alone'.[281] That Ruskin resented his cousin's absence is evident in the next letter, where he remarked on the 'nice time' the Severns seemed to be enjoying 'with the new stables'. Reflecting on 'what grand big peepies Arfie & Joanie are now 'in town' ', he added, morosely, 'though I did wish they wer'nt there.'[282]

After his encounter with the 'Robinesque' children, Ruskin's tone lightened. A few days after meeting them, he explained that he did not really need Joan's company. Reiterating the joy he derived from the children, he added:

> Seriously — theer is no need for you hurrying anything in town — The quiet, though sometimes a little melancholy — does me no harm. — and you being away is a good excuse for seeing nobody
>
> I was at Colwith yesterday, and have not for years enjoyed a walk in the sun to much in the old way.
>
> There are five children to open one gate —.[283]

His new-found contentment hinged on the children and his escape from work- and memory-related pressures. His reassurance that he did not need her slid smoothly into telling her about meeting five children. Whether these were five of the preceding seven, or a different group is not clear; but since he had expressed his intention to return and learn their names, they are probably the same ones. He showed them children's books, including Dame Wiggins, one of his 'calf milk of books'.[284] The appearance of this book in this context is important: to share this text with the children was to initiate them into his own childhood experience and thus himself to relive that idealized past by reading the book anew with children in his present. He also, as he had with the earlier group, gave them some coins.

46   INTRODUCTION

Ruskin ended this letter with an intriguing postscript: 'Di wee ma me ᵛwasnt a toopid, because me is'nt a wam. Oos a wam — and me's a wick.' This was very consciously written as baby-talk, demonstrated by the amendment of 'wasnt' to 'vasnt'. Ruskin was trying to show that he was 'joking', but when translated into standardized English the message is serious: 'Dear Little Mother, I wasn't a stupid/foolish person, because I know I'm not a woman. You are a woman — and I am a man'. Ruskin was reassuring his cousinly conscience that he behaved properly ('vasnt a toopid') when interacting with the children. He also expressed wistful regret at being a 'wick'; the term had emerged over the course of several letters and stems from the notion of being 'a wicked man'. It is constructed in opposition to 'wam', suggesting all men are 'wicks' and all women are 'wams'. While 'wicked donie' was sometimes the playful persona fascinated by young girls, at other times 'wick' simply refers to weakness and exhaustion, as in: 'Mondays so dull for want of a dee wee ettie from my wam. and me feels the velly wickest of wicks.'[285] The 'wickest of wicks' entails a dim, weak candle wick as well as the original derivation from 'wicked'. The use of 'wam' in this letter suggests that, in Ruskin's mind, a 'wam' was not merely a woman, but a motherly woman such as his 'di ma', referred to here as 'my wam'. By saying 'me is'nt a wam. Oos a wam', he suggested that he would rather have been born a 'wam' like his 'Di wee ma' because she safely could interact with children without fear of disapproval.

In the surrounding letters, Ruskin was concerned to show his cousin that he was behaving properly. This notion of proper behaviour does not necessarily relate to guilt about potentially sexualized interaction with children. When mentally balanced, he was very much aware of his tenuous grasp on sanity and of the need to conform to social conventions. Several years earlier, in 1878, he had written: 'Rossetti mad — and poor me, — like to go so. — if I don't mind'.[286] In 1887, he looked regretfully back on his last bout of madness, telling Joan that, if he had been properly nursed by female friends, he 'should ^ ʰᵃᵛᵉ been well in a week instead of being crazy all summer'.[287] And in June 1888 he wrote: 'I never before was so conscious of all that's wrong in me, whether in head or heart'.[288] There are many such references to his precarious mental health. He knew — and Joan reminded him — that he could quickly spiral into decline when faced with undue stress from writing or from giving lectures; he could also unravel when over-stimulated by interpersonal, memory-based experiences.

His cousin was aware that images of and proximity to girls could unsettle Ruskin. This is evident in a letter to Kate Greenaway printed in the 'Library Edition'. Unusually, it has not been edited to gloss over questionable aspects and the letter reads like a request for a graphic, if not pornographic, striptease.[289] Although Cook and Wedderburn typically removed such comments from Ruskin's letters, this letter was already in the public domain, having been published in Spielmann and Layard's *Kate Greenaway* (1905). Cook and Wedderburn must have felt it to be counterproductive to hide the letter in order to portray their idealized image of Ruskin. They chose to include it in full, perhaps to normalize the effect of its publication elsewhere. The way the letter flows, suggesting that Greenaway remove the clothing from her painted girls in order to refine her skills as an artist by experimenting with Classical life drawing, positions it as merely another lesson in art from Ruskin to one of his pupils. The contents of the footnotes suggest a different narrative. In the penultimate line, after 'round', there is a note which reads: '[Note written in pencil: "Do nothing of the kind. J. R. S."]'. Joan objected to the plan, but it is not clear whether this is because it reflected an indecent, pornographic urge on Ruskin's part, or because such images excited him on a mnemonic, associational, aesthetic level which might unsettle his mind.

Ruskin's interpretation of his cousin's interference with Greenaway is captured in a final footnote. It reads: '"That naughty Joan got hold of it — never mind her — you see, she doesn't like the word 'round' — that's all."' Indeed, as mentioned earlier, Ruskin was intrigued by what he termed 'the difference between round and oval sections in girls' waists'.[290] But the symbolic association of this fascination with waists is not necessarily sexual. Rather, the idea of waists which were allowed to be naturally 'round' or 'oval' — without the unnatural constraints of corsets and stays — is representative of freedom. It is also typical of the free-flowing dresses worn by young girls and boys at the time when Ruskin himself was an infant and resonates with the feminized and infantilized self of his epistolary fantasies.

Many of Ruskin's letters, which may be unsettlingly suggestive when read in isolation, form part of a shared pattern when read in conjunction with letters from his cousin. This is not an easy path to trace since few of her letters are extant from before 1888; by 1889 Ruskin's letters to her dry up. Nevertheless, some points of commonality exist. For example, Ruskin often wrote letters about enjoying kisses from girls. The image of Ruskin taking pleasure from receiving kisses — 'rather hard', 'long, & soft', 'and uncountable ones of any length I liked'[291] — from young girls rings warning bells in the minds of modern readers. But Joan wrote very similar letters to him, such as the following: 'I had a nice time with Connie, Harry — & their chicks — the latter such sweet loves in bed. & gave me some cuddly kisses — '.[292] If Ruskin had written about girls who were 'such sweet loves in bed' and gave him 'some cuddly kisses', he would be perceived as expressing inappropriate thoughts about the girls. But coming from the hand of a maternal woman (a 'wam'), the letter sounds sweet and innocent. As Ruskin recognized, a 'wam' can enjoy much greater freedom to interact with children than a 'wick' can. Despite apparent concerns about the appearance of Ruskin's actual interaction with girls, Joan was complicit in constructing and sustaining the mythic, feminized child-self through which he clearly derived joy and solace.

Ruskin's earliest letters to Joan suggest fondness for her, but they do not contain baby-talk. Take, for example, two letters from April 1865 written about a year after she joined his household, by which point she had become an integral part of it. Composed at Winnington School where Ruskin was surrounded by other girls and young women, both letters refer to his cousin by her given name, not by a pet-name. Ruskin signed off with the rather formal 'your affectionate cousin J Ruskin'.[293] He took an avuncular tone: '– Mind you use the carriage when you want it', and 'tell Lucy you're to have more champagne to day', casting himself in the true-to-life role of an older, familial male.[294] This tone is in response to what had apparently been a self-effacing letter from her: he assured her 'that the letter —

otherwise — is very nice — and not stupid'.[295] There is some playful teasing, for he said he should 'scold' her 'for not telling [him] more of the flirtation between M[r] Carlyle & [her]', adding: 'I'm sure it must have been very serious, this time' and laughing at her, saying '[i]t is only Scotch girls who hate summer'.[296] The teenage Joan Agnew emerges as a young girl, just like all the other young girls in whose company Ruskin then found himself: 'I tell them you are ^[a] very good girl.'[297] He implied that this place filled with other young women would be a natural haven for her: 'I wish you were here so much — you would be very happy. & have everything good for you — only too much laughing'.[298] He referred directly to the playful charms of the other young women, who had been 'rolling over & over on the grass' with him and pulling him 'fifteen ways at once', who gave him kisses and tossed their curls at him.[299] Just as his cousin teasingly had been involved in a 'flirtation' with the much older Carlyle, Ruskin had enjoyed a parallel 'flirtation' with a host of her peers, even procuring kisses. A brief aside is pertinent here: the use of 'flirtation' in relation to Joan's interaction with Carlyle is another important point of reference for discussing Ruskin's relationships with girls. Many of his letters allude to having a good 'flirt' with a much younger woman. While modern readers might interpret this as sexually predatory, when placed within the context of allusions to his cousin's playful interaction with men such as Carlyle, it instead points to stimulating conversations between the two sexes without being weighted with inappropriate or erotic connotations.

Although, in these letters, Joan Agnew was constructed as a playful girl among girls (legally a minor, she became Ruskin's ward that spring), in 1865 she had already begun to take on other functions in relation to him. She had, as previously discussed, become a reliable assistant and was a companion in his interests. They were becoming playmates and, as the earliest letter in the collection demonstrates, Ruskin set the tone: 'You needn't worry yourself with "M[r] Ruskins" and "your sons" in your notes [...] It is nicely handier and easier to say "cousin John" — highly disrespectful and improper. of course'.[300] She was to ignore the trappings of conventional age distinctions when writing to him. He encouraged equality and, over the first few years of their correspondence, a complicit playfulness was established.

Not only do the letters from Winnington Hall construct Joan as a girl among girls, they similarly construct their author. When Ruskin wrote, 'my hand shakes from rolling over & over on the grass, and being pulled fifteen ways', he had been playing with the girls as an equal. As with his relationship with Joan, his roles and self-construction in relation to the schoolgirls shifted back and forth between being equal playmates and being hierarchically placed within a master–student (or guardian–ward) dynamic.

Mature Ruskin was keenly interested in boyish activities like building model boats (or at least drawing and commissioning them), digging, chopping wood and running for relaxation, but the letters to his cousin suggest that his greatest sense of fun and ease were derived from more girlish activities. By indulging in play characterized as feminine, Ruskin attained a self-diminishing, self-abnegating power within his preferred environment. Through it, he engaged on more equal terms with his household, his girl-friends, his cousin. By extension, he experienced prolonged moments of escapist peace; but this strengthened, relaxed, fantasy self was in perpetual tension with the reality of his desire for mastery and control.

Ruskin's use of 'papa' to describe himself in relation to the girls at Winnington also reflects a recurring desire on his part to relate himself to his favourite people by casting each in a familial role. For example: he referred to Francesca Alexander as 'Sorella' (sister), Fanny Talbot as 'Momma Talbot', and Thomas Carlyle as 'Papa'. The roots of this impetus must rest with his family. Family was extremely important for the Ruskins, parents and son. The unusual dynamic of the Ruskin household and its influences on the writer have been traced by many critics, and are dealt with again here. Ruskin had grown up as the treasured only son in an aspirational household. As a successful wine merchant, his father had made the family's name on a financial level, offering physical security to wife and son. It was the son's task to make the family's name in the more genteel realm of culture: art, poetry, social thought and ideally, from his parents' perspective, religion. The domestic environment that shaped him was presided over by his mother who trained her son to be a prophet.[301] Throughout his life, Ruskin felt conflicted drives both to meet his parents' expectations of him and rebelliously to be his own person. He never fully did either. Instead, he attempted to re-conform his life and world to allow both to coexist.

The idealized 'home', and meanings entailed in that concept, was a seminal force in the development of Ruskin's self-perception. For Ruskin 'home' was an experimental place, but also the locus of self, providing security, a sense of identity and an environment within which to be creative. The domestic tinctured much of his writing, particularly so because Ruskin was an innately autobiographical writer whose texts are infused with personal narratives and memories. In their 'Introduction' to *Ruskin and Gender*, Birch and O'Gorman write of Ruskin's 'gender unorthodoxy'. They suggest that it is 'evident in the formulation of his literary authority' and argue that 'Ruskin's performativity, his capacity to adopt new voices, included his use of female subject positions. [...] Ruskin used a culturally-determined woman's place to enable aspects of his literary persona.'[302] They note that The *Saturday Review* complained bitterly of *Unto this Last* (1860), saying that the world was not going to be 'preached to death by a mad governess'.[303] Five years later, Ruskin literally adopted a governess's role, or at least that of a teacher in a girls' school, to write *Ethics*. Ruskin feminized himself.

Ruskin had male friends and disciples, but as his career progressed much of his popularity lay with women. Culturally, his *Sesame and Lilies* became the standard school prize for girls.[304] In his personal life, the majority of his confidants and friends were women. This aspect of Ruskin has received much scholarly attention. First, in editions of letters to such women, for example: John Lewis Bradley's *The Letters of John Ruskin to Lord and Lady Mount-Temple* (1964)[305]; Van Akin Burd's *The Winnington Letters: John Ruskin's Correspondence with Margaret Alexis Bell and the Children at Winnington Hall* (1969); and Virginia Surtees's *Sublime & Instructive: Letters from John Ruskin to Louisa Marchioness of Waterford, Anna Blunden and Ellen Heaton* (1972) and *Reflections of a Friendship: John Ruskin's Letters to Pauline Trevelyan*

1848–1866 (1979). Biographies, such as Tim Hilton's recent two-volume *John Ruskin The Early Years* (1985) and *The Later Years* (2000) and John Batchelor's *John Ruskin: No Wealth but Life* (2000) have drawn on a variety of sources to offer insights into Ruskin's interaction with women.

Many critics have also been interested in Ruskin's relationship with femininity and gender. Notably, and damagingly for Ruskin's reputation, Kate Millett articulated her perception of Ruskin's archetypal Victorian misogyny in her influential feminist text, *Sexual Politics* (1970). Later, in line with contemporary theoretical trends, commentators began to take a recuperative approach to Ruskin's relationships with women and the feminine. More recently, Weltman's *Ruskin's Mythic Queen: Gender Subversion in Victorian Culture* (1998) and *Ruskin and Gender*, a collection edited by Birch and Francis O'Gorman (2002), which includes Birch's groundbreaking 'Ruskin's Womanly Mind' (1988), have presented more balanced — albeit problematized — readings of Ruskin and gender. The most directly relevant to this book is Catherine Robson's *Men in Wonderland: The Lost Girlhood of the Victorian Gentleman* (2001).

Ruskin's project of feminization did not stay within the confines of his home; it coloured much of his public writing. Recently, his tendency to feminize and redefine his world in transgressively gendered (or de-gendered) terms has received much critical attention. To offer just two examples: Sharon Aronofsky Weltman has traced ways Ruskin feminized science,[306] while J. B. Bullen has demonstrated how Ruskin feminized Venice.[307] Ruskin's cultural power had been established within the aesthetic domain long before Joan entered his life. He was the author of the influential *Modern Painters*, a seminal piece of art criticism, stressing the importance of English art. Similarly, the popular *Stones of Venice* (ostensibly about the architecture of Venice but also addressing the moral state of England) was essentially an aesthetic work. His power lay in aesthetic influence, becoming a professor of fine art, not of theology or ethics or economics; and the aesthetic was, within Victorian culture, becoming ever more linked with the feminine.[308] Ruskin was interested in the two-way process whereby the private, domestic, feminine world of the home influenced the public, secular, masculine world of politics and economics, and vice-versa. Dinah Birch has referred to 'the complex association between education, religion, and myth in Ruskin's mature work'.[309] For Ruskin, these traits were tied to issues of gender and the maternal. In his own experience, his mother was the root of education, religion and myth. Notably, Weltman's *Ruskin's Mythic Queen* specifically addresses the feminized nature of Ruskin's mythic worldview and the way it pervades his writing.[310]

Ruskin desperately wanted to preside over a comforting, feminized space (such as that which surrounded his mother), which could be parallel to and congruous with his masculinized position as a 'Master'. After the death of his father and even more so his mother, Joan helped him to craft such a feminized domestic space presided over by a maternal construct. There, Ruskin developed a liminal, hybrid world whereby he attained to power. Paradoxically, his power within the wider culture derived from an aesthetic space, which was by its very definition feminine and private.[311] The locus shared with his cousin enabled him to bridge both worlds:

the feminized world of his home offered shelter from the pressures he felt within the masculinized world of his Professorship and his culturally constructed identity as 'Master' and prophet.

Afterword

Ruskin's idealized, fantasy portrayals of himself in dialogue with his cousin took on an added dimension in the late 1880s. Over the course of the correspondence, he had constructed an epistolary nursery where role-reversals were the norm. As in the pantomimes and comedies he so enjoyed, this was an alternative reality where: the part of the 'an itie wee school girl' might be played by an old man; the authoritative professor could be revealed as a bumbling 'Fessy' with a speech impediment; the fairy godmother was not an old hag, but a young and playful 'daughty' who was also a strong and loyal 'di ma'; pets, children and adults could frolic in a carefree environment; activities like rolling on the grass, running and digging were more valued than attending dinner parties, giving lectures and going to church; comfort foods like strawberries, buns and roasts, as well as social drinks like tea, coffee and wine, could flow freely; men and women could be self-sufficient, picking their own vegetables, cooking their own fish, decorating their own environment; and where jewels and gowns were readily available, to be given as tokens of affection. This fantasy was based on reality and all of these aspects were manifest in Ruskin's life. However, his power to control the plot — like an actor-writer-manager in the Victorian theatre — was necessarily limited by reality. In the 1880s, his reality was marred by increasing mental instability and by living with a real family.

Ruskin's desire to infantilize and feminize himself in an attempt to abdicate public power came most into conflict with his desire for private mastery during his banishment to Folkestone and Sandgate in 1887. There, he wrote repeatedly to Joan Severn about the girls he had seen while excitedly, even frantically, reliving his own childhood. During this period — when he strayed on both edges of sanity — he was engaged in a variety of child-like activities, including watching boats, commissioning models of boats, licking ice cream, demanding his favourite foods (the whims for which changed regularly), watching 'shrimping' girls known as 'spades and buckets', and actively disengaging himself from all public responsibility. The correspondence preceding the intensification of infantilization at Folkestone and Sandgate warrants particular attention: it is unintentionally revealing about his state of mind and his relationship with Joan. It also presents Ruskin consciously using the posture of a needy child in order to negotiate with his cousin, from whom he was estranged.

From about February 1887, his letters to Joan became ever more concerned with his doing nothing intellectual. As she had long been concerned that over-excitement might cause a breakdown, this was as much to reassure her as to reflect his true lethargy.[312] Many letters express enjoyment of activities like chopping wood, playing chess, and cleaning. He was becoming reclusive and deriving ever more joy from losing himself in physical, non-cerebral activity. The letters also became even more disjointed than usual, including flashes of anger directed at Joan and others. The cousins' relationship broke down. Unable to live in his unpredictable, unstable company, she had left Brantwood. On 8 June 1887 he offered a short, meek olive branch to her, suggesting that their private disputes and his perception of the intrusive public world (a 'false and cunning' paragraph in the newspapers) 'renders it vain for me to express any feelings of ^{the} old days at Brantwood more.'[313] This is in contrast to a letter he had written fifteen years earlier, when he had lost his mother and Rose, and was establishing Brantwood as his home: 'the home I had once — and the hopes — — all <u>broken</u> away so ill Broken isnt the [word]. Vanished. Melted — Buried — everything — and that was. Doanie the only link left to me.'[314] He had then moved into Brantwood, shaping it into an idealized 'home' with his cousin as the central source of comfort, becoming his 'sole remaining home-happineſs. Quite as much — in the real depth and support of it, absent, as present.'[315] Fifteen years later, in June 1887, she was utterly absent to him and the 'home' he had crafted in Brantwood was effectively destroyed; their relationship and his mind were disintegrating; and even memories of those past 'feelings' could not be expressed.

This is important: the childish comfort and peace he had crafted in his constructed, Lake District home were shattered by his distance (emotional and physical) from his 'poor Joan'. This, despite all the other mnemonic links (to vacations with his parents and, then, the life he had lived there) and aesthetic associations (the views and the décor). It is not clear whether the dispute with his cousin caused his madness or whether his mental instability was exacerbated by the relational breakdown. Because they were living together when the dispute began, there are no letters between the cousins suggesting the flow of events; one assumes the relational and mental breakdowns fuelled each other.

Ruskin wrote two letters dated 8 June 1887. One is clearly furious at a suspected betrayal, although it concludes with what may be an attempt at reconciliation: 'Your once. Di Pa.'[316] This places his kinship with her in the past but implies its continued possibility. The other letter is less angry but more distressed: 'I could have wept tears of blood for you, in seeing the beauty of the place — yesterday evening and to day — all lost — to Doanie and me.'[317] Again, Ruskin linked the loss of his cousin, her family, and the joy she had experienced at Brantwood to his own distress and discomfort in the home: the beauty was lost to him despite the fact that he could see it. He continued: 'Your room shall stay as you have left it. [Thomas] Richmond portrait — is put back. [...] Perhaps later in the year you might like to come down with baby & Violet'.[318] The letters of this period suggest that, in an earlier rage, he had threatened to throw her and her things out of their shared home; this letter implies they had disagreed specifically about the Richmond portrait. This must have been one of the seven portraits of Ruskin done by the Richmond brothers, probably the one of Ruskin as a young man.[319] Presumably Ruskin had taken it back during the dispute after having given it to her. As it would have been given as a mark of affection and kinship, his attempt to revoke the gift would have been a pointed intervention, communicating his belief that she had betrayed him in some way. In this letter, his anger abated, he told her he had returned it to her room and asked her to return too — not immediately, but 'later in the year'.

Attempting to reconcile with her, he had turned her room into a shrine through which to invoke her return.[320] A few letters later he sighed: 'I think you have arranged all the things in your room very beautifully. — But the sadness of entering it now.'[321] This suggests he had been entering her room, sadly to gaze at the private décor of her intimate space in an attempt to re-establish a feeling of proximity and kinship. It also links to the Ruskinian conception of domestic aesthetic: the self of the presiding genius of a space could be revealed in his or her furnishing; Joan's room was 'arranged [...] very beautifully'. But the message of the aesthetic can also be subjective: as with 'the beauty of the place' (Brantwood in general) mentioned in the first letter that day, the beauty of her room was also tinted with sadness for Ruskin because it represented her.

Like the letter of 8 June, which states the impossibility of articulating past joy, another letter begged his cousin to 'Speak no more of the Unpardonable past' making it 'as though it had never been'.[322] This resonates with a letter he had sent her nineteen years earlier, asking: 'Are there not some things you would fain forget — & cannot?'[323] In 1887, he was trying to complete *Praeterita*, which was prefaced with the assertion that, in writing it, he was 'speaking, of what gives me joy to remember [...] and passing in total silence things which I have no pleasure in reviewing'.[324] This articulates a belief that what is not spoken would not be remembered; this letter hints that this strategy of silencing offers a possibility of reconciliation. In this letter he made the dispirited request that she: 'Write to me, if you care to write, of yourself or of your children'.[325] He was asking her to write of her present, while at the same time both expressing his longing for family and presenting an image of himself as a caring member of the family, who was no longer entirely focused on having his own way.

This loving image contrasts with the tone of many of the letters which precede it. One from the previous year offers a particularly striking example:

> I am not jesting now, by any means, in assuring you that things are not to be on their old footing here — ever again. If you come here, you must come to do whatever is in your power to please me — and not only yourselves I mean to be master henceforward in this house, while I live in it — and to have the things done that I wish to be done — whether of play or lessons. — by every one whom I ask to stay in it — By you — your husband — and your children — most certainly & chiefly —
>
> And if you do not choose to please me, — you had better all of you stay in London—[326]

This letter was written as the second of a pair.[327] In the first, he had set out plans which he felt would yield 'a pleasant Autumn — for every body'. These plans included such declarations as 'no lessons!' Rather, 'the children are to go scrambling about with [Joan] and Susan to look after them, all day'.[328] The letter continued, setting out a home where Ruskin's whims would be met by all and everything done to give him comfort. He was demanding to be Master of home and family; he felt the Mastership was benign because it involved play and freedom for himself. His cousin did not agree and returned to rein him in, rather than to indulge his plan.

By the following summer he had relinquished his desire for control, writing instead in a penitent tone. The power dynamic had shifted — he was no longer the Master, he was addressing the soon-to-be Mistress. To preserve and restructure the required relationship, Ruskin was now willing to reverse their roles, placing himself in a state of complete dependence on her. By the following year, he would write such dispirited thoughts as the following, from Abbeville:

> if I come back to Brantwood it would only be to try to comfort you — [...] at Brantwood I recollect too well how I used to wander — from one room to another — one field to another — able to rest nowhere — and in mere sense of weaknefs — whether in eyes or [strained] in brain. I am far worse now than I was then. — and entirely helpless to advise — or beseech you — I will come to Brantwood if you wish it earnestly [...] when I have thought most earnestly — it always seems as if Brantwood weer the only <u>possibility</u>. — but I am so tired of seeing the leaves fall there — and I do still cling to the chances of seeing a little cheerful life. I do like seeing the French people when I am the least able to forget myself.[329]

The fall of leaves and the helpless wandering had stripped the home of its joy, but the letters of June 1887 ascribe this loss of joy to the gap left by the loss of Joan. Ruskin's once joyful and life-enhancing memories had become sad and depressing because of their association with the absent 'Doanie'. Many of the letters express this:

> The comfort your letter is to me this morning you cannot measure. You never have really known how I have loved you. — and the desolation of all sweetness to me in garden or wood, for want of you. has been the saddest thing I have ever known in all this life [. ...] The sweetnefs to me of having you to care again a little about — my room and me — and the desolatenefs of me, without you — there are no words for. [...] Oh my Doanie — how is it all to end? How much we have done and borne for each other — — in vain [...] but the distress of knowing that — that walk in the anemone wood was to be the last — has now become what there are no words for.[330]

The happiness of memories he had associated with Brantwood was tarnished by their contrast with his present state.

There were moments, too, in these letters when he spoke frankly of his madness. On one occasion he wrote that two friends 'would have come to day — but I could not let them[.] Alas, my mind <u>has</u> come back — as the waves of the Red Sea. and this state of things cannot last much longer; do with me what you think best.'[331] Recognizing his madness, he knew it might return, and he realized the need to cede control to his cousin. The next letter is — to my mind — the saddest of the entire correspondence:

> But no one can help me. now. I have lost — what might have been yet twenty years of happy life with you. Oh my Doanie — that the rest should have been dream — and <u>this</u> the wakening. and that when you were spared in that pain, when I was watching at the gate in the dawn — you were [ghos]ted back — for <u>me</u> to inflict this — [332]

This letter mourns the loss of a possible twenty years spent at Brantwood with his 'Doanie' (Ruskin was not yet seventy and his mother had lived to ninety) and speaks the horrible thought 'that the rest should have been dream — and <u>this</u> the wakening'. These thoughts, coupled with the image of his tragic last glance, make for disconcerting reading, even for the uninvolved, modern reader. The letter suggests that the sadness of these images, his sense of guilt, and the way his mind circled round them, were destroying what was left of Ruskin's sanity. He decided chivalrously to leave Brantwood so that his cousin could return to it and he potentially might free himself from guilt and destructive memories: 'in any thing I am trying to get done about Brantwood I am only thinking now of how to [quiet] you of trouble about it and leave you mistrefs of it: and its ground'.[333] Considering the connection between home and self which Ruskin articulated in works such as *Stones of Venice* and when writing Joan about establishing Brantwood in 1871–73, by eventually making his cousin 'mistress of it and its ground', he symbolically was making her mistress of himself.

Out the other side of that summer of banishment, before being fully reconciled with and returning to live out his remaining years with his cousin, Ruskin recognized that he had not always been in control of his faculties, suggesting, perhaps unfairly, that had he been nursed properly, he 'should ^ have been well in a week instead of being crazy all summer'.[334] He tempered such potentially accusatory comments by expressing gratitude to her for her 'attentive care' and noted that he had realized 'my interest was now — all of it that is left — in Francesca's stories of real people — and in peepies themselves — my Di ma chiefly'.[335] With such acknowledgements came the restructuring of the impossible dream.

He also recognized that the markers of affection had failed them. In November 1888, he wrote 'what are my good wishes worth to' his young friend Detmar Blow, 'any more than my love has been to you, my poor Doanie', adding, 'My Doanie — I have nothing to say but what I have said of my selfie — I am your poor Donie'.[336] The final dated letter in the extant correspondence, of 27 November 1888, even more clearly expresses the breakdown of communication:

> If you could see into my mind now — or for weeks back — ! — and yet — I do not know how far you have — I have not signed Di Pa lately — It is only this looking back over all times that I see what the words should have meant — Oh Doanie I am your poor — poor — Di Pa.[337]

Notably, this letter equates his letters ('I do not know how far you have') to a window on his mind ('If you could see into my mind now — or for weeks back'). It also points out that he had not been signing himself with the baby-talk term of affection and kinship ('Di Pa'). Except for the occasional use of names such as 'Doanie', baby-talk does not appear in this final series of letters. A few years earlier, he had exclaimed 'Oh my di ma, fot sood ve hav done to understand each ovy if vee'd nevy learnt baby tawk? Fot <u>sood</u> ve hav done? Me's oos <u>little</u> Donie'.[338] That particular, playful, close means of communication had failed the cousins, but the long-rehearsed posture of the penitent child dominates even without the trappings of the self-diminishing idiolect.

The fantasy world Ruskin constructed in his letters was malleable and controllable. Lacking the physical presence of his cousin before him in the moment of composition, he could construct her response simultaneously with his own offerings. By envisaging and incorporating her expected reaction, Ruskin could propose what he wanted to do, when and how (or give an account of what he had done), without the embarrassment of dealing with her real, immediate response — which might, after all, not match his expectations; through writing these letters he could feel he had her approval as his epistolary self negotiated with his imagined image of her. He could also convince himself that he was moderating his views to accommodate hers. This emerges strongly in the letters. Yet, reading between the lines, he clearly persisted in trying to advance and justify his own desires. In other words, by interacting through letters — which necessarily remove the audience from immediate reaction yet position that audience's response — Ruskin could experience imaginary control over himself and his correspondent in those moments of composition: first, because he was authoring the fantasy themes; second, because he had freely authorized her power within them and had given her authority over him. He did so by welcoming — and later longing for — the tangible and predictable response of her letters, which though not controlled by him he could take as he chose when he read them. Later, he bestowed power on her by using the medium of the letters and the enabling persona of a diminished, constructed child-self within to ask for her advice, memories and care. Through correspondence with this trusted other, whom he had also constructed as a double, he could imagine he had the freedom to decide for himself what he wanted to do and when, without feeling the pressures of real social expectations and commitments on him.

Ruskin used these strategies of self-infantilization, established early in the epistolary relationship, to comfort himself and to feel nurtured and petted. Through them, he could once again feel like a beloved only child, the centre of a stable domestic universe, where disturbing aspects of the outside world — including his own unpredictable mental and physical health — could not affect him. But they did. Although he had tried to maintain his position of authority while simultaneously positing himself as an imagined child, his erratic, real behaviour necessitated an actual power shift. His cousin, as his closest, most trusted relation, began to orchestrate his home, his healthcare, his finances, and his interaction with the public in much the same way that he had attempted to orchestrate his interactions with her over the years. He came to recognize what he called 'your maternal care for me'.[339] In this change within continuity, the stress on her identity had moved from the girl persona to the mother.

Despite losing its initial role, of allowing him to feel free from care while maintaining his position as a cultural figure of authority, Ruskin's epistolary infantilized self continued to perform an important function: it allowed him to give up control while saving face. Because he had rehearsed the infantilized self so often and become comfortable with the diminishing, disempowering child personae, he could use them as a means through which to communicate a desire to abdicate power.

John Batchelor, writing of the difficult period surrounding the death of Rose La Touche, has commented that Ruskin 'resorted to baby-talk to pledge his loyalty to Joan'.[340] This scene was played out on a number of occasions. One of the last was in June 1887, just before the time described above, when he banished himself from Brantwood. In this instance, the relative absence of baby-talk in expressing the continuing postures of the needy infant persona is striking. He tried to impress on his cousin the reality of his promises for a future relationship, suggesting that it had been fostered by baby-talk and could be sustained through a restructuring, whereby the diminished, ostensibly controllable, infantilized self would become not a mask but the reality. However, as he had recognized in 1869, this would not necessarily bring about an ideal either: 'Oh dear — I wish I were a wee Donie — and had nothing to look after nor think about — And then I should wish to be a big Donie I suppose. "Its all the same".'[341]

While being a child is not the same as being mad, there are parallels: children can get away with having temper tantrums; they are essentially self-centred, only gradually learning that they are not the centre of the universe; they need to be given lessons in social interaction, morality, safety and economics; they rely on others to direct their healthcare and their living conditions; for their own safety, they need to be contained and watched. By positioning himself as a child interested in childish things, Ruskin presented himself to his cousin as a reformed (and reformable), passive and essentially obedient figure in lieu of the erratic, truculent, dominating figure he had been. It must be reiterated that the self Ruskin portrayed in these letters to his cousin does not reflect his reality. His entourage continued to report to the Severns about his difficult behaviour; but that is what I find fascinating about the Ruskin–Severn correspondence: not any 'real' Ruskin, but Ruskin as he strenuously fantasized himself to be, in his strategic and desperate use of these constructs to retrieve the *domus* both at Brantwood and in his mind.

The parallels between young children and madmen highlight another possibility: that, in constructing himself as a child, Ruskin in some sense believed himself to be a child. This would posit the self-infantilization as a symptom of madness; this may have been the case at particular points in time. However, there is logic in many of the late letters where he adopts the infantilized posture. He clearly was thinking through problems: his relationship with this cousin, his unstable state of mind, his financial concerns. He used the infantilized personae as a language through which to organize these problems according to patterns of underlying desire.

Although he had early joked that, 'If we don't take care — wee pussie, we shan't be able to write or talk anything but pussy talk, soon! I declare I feel quite awkward trying to write English now',[342] he recognized that it could be problematic if he were to begin unintentionally to adopt the infantilized personae and associated idiolects. This is evident in letters such as the following, written during his crisis of conscience about vivisection at Oxford, where he alludes to issues of control:

> Your letters do help and fwesh and pwesh me so [...] am thinking of giving up Fessyship on account of Vote on Vivisection and nevy bovyin myself any mo with nufin. [...] It boveys me to notice that I much oftener miss letters than I used. I wrote dred for dreadful not for baby talk but real mistake and I'm a little anxy.[343]

When Ruskin began to use baby-talk and the associated personae, he had not anticipated that he would really disempower himself. He did not want the Severns to take control. What he desired was to structure a home and set of associated social relationships through which he could be a 'Di Pa', a caring yet strong paterfamilias in control of a dynasty and a *domus*. He particularly had taken on this persona after the death of his parents, when he was bereft of immediate family. Because his mother had been so central to his identity and had shaped the sheltered space where he could be secure and productive, he had to craft his own, alternative space. Although he played with gender-levelling within the domestic sphere, he needed a mother figure beyond his self in order to make good the fantasy.[344] Joan (Agnew Ruskin) Severn — his mother's surrogate in running the household and his idealized playmate — was there to fulfil the role, at first partially and in fantasy, but coming increasingly to dominate and for real.

While Ruskin wanted to recreate the controlled, secure, familial space of his boyhood and youth, he also — ironically — wanted both to be in control of it and controlled within it. The carefully crafted terms of twinship (Di Pa / Di Ma; Fessy / Pussy; Donie / Doanie) facilitated this, and the broader baby-talk idiolect, with its associated personae, offered a possible means of maintaining this illusory balance. He had actively chosen to develop them, so was 'in control', yet the dominant aspect entailed in his structuring of them was ostensibly tempered by the diminutives used within the construct. Because the fantasy superstructure was based on real relationships, those interpersonal dynamics could also take on a life of their own. Joan Severn, after all, did and did not correspond with Ruskin's imaging of her.

Notes to the Introduction

1. This image is from the John Howard Whitehouse Collection, Lancaster University [Fig. 1.1]. See also James Dearden, *John Ruskin: A Life in Pictures* (Sheffield: Sheffield Academic Press, 1999), p. 183 (Fig. 266) where it is accompanied by informal photos from that day, which Joan dominates even more clearly (Figs. 264 and 265). Joan Severn, conventionally so-named by Ruskin scholars, was born Joanna Tweddale Agnew, taking the surname 'Severn' when she married Arthur Severn in 1871. She became John Ruskin's ward in 1865 and used his name when convenient in later life. I generally refer to her simply as 'Joan'.
2. Identified as Lily Severn by Dearden, *Life*, p. 182.
3. *The Works of John Ruskin* ('Library Edition'), ed. by E. T. Cook and Alexander Wedderburn, 39 vols (London: George Allen, 1903–12).
4. Ruskin to S. C. Cockrell, 26 March 1886 in *Friends of a Lifetime: Letters to Sydney Carlyle Cockerell*, ed. by Viola Meynell (London: Jonathan Cape, 1940), p. 26.
5. These letters are infused with such baby-talk and readers are directed to the glossary. Ruskin himself did not hyphenate 'baby-talk', nor was it the word he used to denote their shared idiolect. Rather, he used a variety of terms including my preferred term of 'nonsense', which encompasses all the sub-idiolects whether infantilized or not. However Ruskin scholars conventionally refer to his playful idiolect as 'baby-talk'. See, for example, John Batchelor, *John Ruskin: No Wealth but Life* (London: Chatto & Windus, 2000), p. 265. See also Tim Hilton, *John Ruskin: The Later Years* (New Haven, CT: Yale University Press, 2000), p. 138, although on p. 438 he uses the term without a hyphen. [This volume is hereafter referred to as *Later*.]
6. 10 December 1873 [152].
7. 31 October 1872 [104].
8. For example, an undated letter from 1882 reads: 'It's a misby day. and Ive been tearing up some of my di Ma's ettie's — and it cuts me and tears me too' [1882] [182].
9. See 21 January 1887 [229].
10. 16 August 1869 [58].
11. 'Peepies', generally a diminutive for 'people', was closely allied to 'peeps', meaning children, see n.d. [May 1882] [179].

12. [49 and 53].
13. 26 May 1869 [47].
14. 26 September 1868 [35].
15. 35.537.
16. Ruskin's letters to Joan during her honeymoon express distress when too few letters appear from her. See the letters of April to June 1871.
17. In *Praeterita*, Ruskin states that Joan was 'seventeen years and some — well, for example of accuracy and conscience — forty-five days, old' on arrival in his home (35.537–38). Arthur Severn rounds the age up to eighteen (in *The Professor: Arthur Severn's Memoir of John Ruskin*, ed. by James S. Dearden (London: Allen and Unwin, 1967), p. 26).
18. 10 August 1878 [167].
19. 35.467.
20. In 1878, when he recognized 'how crazy I had been', he wrote of signing 'a pretty little page of parchment saying that if ever I'm ill — oos to have the care of me', 31 and 2 July 1878 [166 and 164].
21. See, for example, 25 May; 6 June; and 2 July 1882 [178, 181 and 183].
22. n.d. [May 1882] [177].
23. Francis O'Gorman, *John Ruskin* (Stroud: Sutton. 1999), p. 62.
24. 25 December 1884 [202a].
25. M. H. Spielmann, *John Ruskin* (London: Cassell, 1900), p. 135.
26. 27 October and 8 November 1887 [249 and 251a].
27. 9 November 1887 [252].
28. 11 November 1887 [253].
29. 26 June 1887 [240].
30. 28 October 1887 [250].
31. 18 October 1887 [246].
32. 28 October 1887 [250].
33. p.330.
34. n.d. [March 1876] [158].
35. Much has been written about Ruskin's relationship with Rose La Touche. Let it suffice here to say that she was ten years old when they met in 1858 (Tim Hilton, *John Ruskin: The Early Years 1819–1859* (New Haven, CT: Yale University Press, 1985), p. 265). [This volume is referred to hereafter as *Early*.] He became enamoured of her and proposed marriage in 1866. She initially turned him down but, with Joan as a go-between, she agreed to reconsider when she turned 21 (Hilton, *Later*, p. 99). Over the intervening years until her death on 25 May 1875, she and her parents mostly discouraged, but by times encouraged, his advances (Batchelor, p. 266). References to her permeate the letters to Joan Severn, often expressed indirectly such as referring to a letter from her as a 'crumb' or by referring to her or her parents as 'some people'. As in the letter of March 1876, she haunts Ruskin's later writings.
36. n.d. [March 1876] [158].
37. W. G. Collingwood, *The Life of John Ruskin*, 2nd edn (London: Methuen, 1900), p. 283.
38. See Joan's letter to Margaret Ruskin of 17 April 1866 [262], both for a sense of how she endeared herself to and negotiated with Margaret Ruskin, and for an example of how she indirectly relayed news about Rose La Touche to John Ruskin when Rose's parents had forbidden direct contact between them.
39. Dearden, ed., *Professor*, p. 26.
40. Dearden, ed., *Professor*, p. 42.
41. 35.63.
42. 35.69.
43. 35.70.
44. *Praeterita*'s 'The Banks of Tay' implicitly reveals Ruskin's perception of this trend. Two articles in *Ruskin and Gender*, ed. by Dinah Birch and Francis O'Gorman (Basingstoke: Palgrave, 2002) shed light on this: Catherine Robson's 'The Stones of Childhood: Ruskin's "Lost Jewels"', (pp. 29–46) and Lindsay Smith's 'The Foxglove and the Rose: Ruskin's Involute of Childhood', (pp. 47–63).

45. 35.536–37.
46. See Helen Gill Viljoen's *Ruskin's Scottish Heritage: A Prelude* (Urbana: University of Illinois Press, 1956), which offers this as an underlying argument.
47. 35.71.
48. Dearden, ed., *Professor*, p. 29.
49. Ruskin contradicted this point on 8 May 1865 when he praised early marriage [6].
50. Dearden, ed., *Professor*, p. 29.
51. Dearden, ed., *Professor*, p. 35.
52. *Later*, pp. 47, 127 and 171.
53. Ruskin admitted to being 'always a tiny bit jealous of' Arthur on 6 December 1872 [110].
54. 8 January 1868 [22].
55. 27 September 1868 [36].
56. 27 April 1871 [77].
57. That said, Ruskin referred to himself as 'an old gentleman of 54' in 1872 [116]. Ruskin seems to have cultivated this old man /Master persona.
58. Dearden, ed., *Professor*, p. 36.
59. 3 January 1868 [20], Ruskin's emphasis.
60. Bradley identifies this 'golden thing' as 'a memento of Rose acquired during that year', but he offers no proof for this. J. L. Bradley, *A Ruskin Chronology* (Basingstoke: Macmillan, 1997), p. 83. I am convinced that the 'golden thing' is a metaphor for his cousin; compare this diary entry to his letter to her of the same day [73].
61. Dearden, ed., *Professor*, p. 141, n. 1.
62. *Early*, p. 2.
63. 35.18.
64. *Early*, p. 2.
65. *Young Mrs. Ruskin in Venice: Her Picture of Society and Life with John Ruskin 1849–1852*, ed. by Mary Lutyens (New York: Vanguard Press, 1965), p. 4.
66. 14 March 1867, held at the Fitzwilliam Museum, Cambridge and cited in *Later*, pp. 120–21.
67. *Later*, p. 214.
68. *Later*, p. 159.
69. 21 April 1871 [73].
70. See 18 and 19 April 1871 [71 and 72].
71. Ruskin was also jealous of the Severn children, but was supportive of his cousin throughout her pregnancies. See 6 November 1872, 28 January and 12 February 1873 for his comments on her first pregnancy [106, 121 and 127a]. On 17 February 1873, he expressed anxiety about losing her to them [128]. She similarly expressed her fear that he would not love her 'all the same' when she became a mother [264]. Once the children emerged from infancy, he began to delight in them, teaching them lessons and, when their mother was away, writing nursery letters to her as though he was the children's nurse or governess. This direct involvement in their activities might reflect lessons in mothering learned at Margaret Ruskin's knee, since she had taken an unusually active interest in raising her son. Notably, however, when mentally agitated Ruskin's jealousy of the children would resurface. See, for example, an undated letter of October 1881: '– and let me see that even as the mother of a family, you can be interested in my present work' [174].
72. 26 April 1871 [76]. See Joan's letter of 2 May 1871 [263a], which is similar in tone.
73. 28 September 1866 [11].
74. 24 April 1871 [74].
75. 25 April 1871 [75].
76. 28 March 1872 [99].
77. n.d. [May 1871] [79].
78. 6 June 1868 [25].
79. See 2 and 7 June 1871 [84 and 85].
80. While I don't believe he intentionally fell ill, he did orchestrate their meeting to spend part of the honeymoon together, which eventually occurred at Matlock. See the letters of May and June 1871, esp. 17 May; 20 June 1871 and an undated letter from June [82, 86, 91].
81. Not only had he lost his cousin to marriage, but he was deeply concerned about Rose, who was

ill. Letters from across May and June 1871 are signed 'St C'. On 10 May 1871 he explicitly told his cousin that he had written to Rose [81].
82. *Early*, p. 53, See also pp. 35–37 and 51–55.
83. *Later*, p. 530.
84. *Later*, pp. 417 and 419. See pp. 417–26 for the broader context. Yet another breakdown occurred after the news of Laurence Hilliard's death reached Ruskin in March 1887. Hilliard died while on the Continent, reminding Ruskin of summer 1866, when Hilliard's aunt, Lady Trevelyan, died while travelling with himself, Joan Agnew and Hilliard's sister, Constance (*Later*, p. 536). This was not the first time Ruskin relived her death, see 6 October 1868 and 30 April 1869 [38 and 43]. Years later, he was still haunted by the memory of it; see 19 August 1882 [188].
85. Dearden, ed., *Professor*, p. 43.
86. The first extant example is 2 July 1867 [12].
87. Undated letter from August 1871, MS in L55 of the Ruskin Library.
88. Undated letter from August 1871, MS in L55 of the Ruskin Library.
89. Dearden, ed., *Professor*, pp. 48–49.
90. 'Two Secretaries: The Letters of John Ruskin to Charles Augustus Howell and the Rev. Richard St. John Tyrwhitt', ed. by Jay Wood Claiborne (unpublished doctoral dissertation, The University of Texas at Austin, 1969, copyright 1970). This edition comprises letters owned by the Miriam Lutcher Stark Library of the University of Texas at Austin, p. 9.
91. There is a sometimes confusing slippage of pet-names in Ruskin's letters: not only was Howell 'Owl', but Ruskin also signed himself as 'Owl'. See *The Winnington Letters: John Ruskin's Correspondence with Margaret Alexis Bell and the Children at Winnington Hall*, ed. by Van Akin Burd (London: George Allen & Unwin, 1969), pp. 667–68 (JR to Lily Armstrong, 7 March 1870, L. 493).
92. Claiborne, p. 105, n. 2 (L. 63).
93. See 26 September 1868 for the first extant use of the pet-name in a letter to his cousin. In this case, he wrote 'Howell' then amended it to 'Owl' [35].
94. Claiborne, ed., pp. 157–59 (4 September 1870, L. 97).
95. Ruskin did sometimes use negative pet-names, as in 'Lacerta' for Maria La Touche. However, he had christened her this when they were on good terms; only later did the charming attributes of snakes give way to their symbolic deception and malice. See Van Akin Burd, *John Ruskin and Rose La Touche* (Oxford: Clarendon, 1980), p. 49.
96. Batchelor, p. 193.
97. Claiborne, ed., p. 146 (L. 88).
98. Claiborne, ed., p. 149 (9 November 1868, L. 90).
99. *Later*, p. 105.
100. Batchelor, p. 193.
101. The timing of her arrival undermines Arthur Severn's claim that Howell furnished her rooms when she arrived, pp. 48–49.
102. Ruskin Library, MS 18 (14 January 1872).
103. Ruskin Library, MS 18 (15 January 1872).
104. Ruskin Library, MS 18 (18 January 1872).
105. Arthur Burgess was a copyist who worked for Ruskin. Joan did not approve of him. See 13 July 1869 [52].
106. *Later*, pp. 429 and 428.
107. n.d. [169].
108. 18 February, 8 and 14 March 1873 [129, 131 and 136].
109. 28 December 1872 [116].
110. See for example 21, 25, 28 February and 1 March 1886 [208–11].
111. MS 18, p. 29 (18 January 1872).
112. n.d. [November 1873] [149a].
113. 11 November 1887 [253].
114. MS 18 (22 December 1871).
115. n.d. [1872] [98].
116. n.d. [1864] [2].

117. He also mentioned his cousin's role as his amanuensis in a letter to Charles Eliot Norton (21 December 1868, L. 72): 'I shall simply make Joan or somebody copy them', that is, Norton's marginalia on *Modern Painters*. Bradley and Ousby also note that this is the first mention of Joan in Ruskin's letters to Norton. John Bradley and Ian Ousby, eds, *The Correspondence of John Ruskin and Charles Eliot Norton* (Cambridge: Cambridge University Press, 1987), p. 21n.
118. 22 October 1887 [247].
119. pp. 147–48 (21 October 1868, L. 89).
120. 20 June 1865 [8].
121. On 5 June 1868, he wrote, apparently in response to her offer of assistance: 'You say — can I find nothing for Pussie to do for me. Yes. I can find a great deal — after Pussie comes back — Such hard work!' [24].
122. 3 May 1871 [80].
123. Claiborne, p. 166. Claiborne underlined rather than italicized *Fors Clavigera*.
124. 6 June 1882 [181].
125. Claiborne, p. 163.
126. 23 October 1868 [42].
127. See 26 February 1883 [192].
128. For example, on 23 October 1878, Ruskin mentioned 'Arfies account of lawyer businefs' and the 'account of Mr Whistler' that Arthur Severn was 'writing out' 'for said lawyer' [170].
129. 22 September 1868 [33].
130. 18 February 1879 [171].
131. Such is the case in the first letter written largely in baby-talk, 3 September 1868 [28].
132. For a discussion of Ruskin constructing a *domus* for himself and the central role Joan played in his conception of 'home' in the second half of his life, see Chapter 3 of my unpublished doctoral thesis, 'Terms of Empowerment: John Ruskin's Correspondence with Joan Severn' (Lancaster University, 2005), pp.179–256.
133. Viljoen, *Scottish*, p. 5.
134. 4 March 1885 [206].
135. See Delia de Sousa Correa, 'Goddesses of Instruction and Desire: Ruskin and Music', in *Ruskin and the Dawn of the Modern*, ed. by Dinah Birch (Oxford: Oxford University Press, 1999), pp. 111–30. She considers the importance of music in education and the way it infused Ruskin's wider writing: music is linked to femininity and moral authority.
136. 9 March 1883 [193]; 37.440.
137. n.d. [May 1882] [177].
138. *Later*, p. 139.
139. 31 October 1872 [104].
140. For an edition of these, see *The Pigwiggian Chaunts of John Ruskin*, ed. by James S. Dearden ([n.p.]: privately printed, 1960).
141. 31 May 1865 [7].
142. 27 June 1865 [9].
143. 28 September 1865 [11].
144. Hilton's note here reads: 'XXXV, 393–94, and JR-JRS, Keswick, 2 July 1867, Bembridge MS L 33', and he quotes from the letter, see also [12].
145. Hilton's note here reads 'JR-JRS 'Abbeville — 15th 'Eptember — 'ixty-ate', Bembridge MS L 33. *Later*, p. 139, see also [31].
146. The link to over-eating raises an interesting possibility. The Ruskin family china and silver service had a boar's head in the centre. Ruskin would have been long accustomed to the irony of looking at a pig while indulging in pig-like eating in his family home.
147. 'Ruskin's "Womanly Mind"', in Birch and O'Gorman, eds, *Ruskin and Gender*, pp. 107–20, (p. 113).
148. See n.d. [1887] [230].
149. *Later*, p. 139.
150. 8 July 1882 [185] and 37.404.
151. 8 July 1882 [185].
152. See, for example, 27 September, 21 and 22 October 1868 [36, 40 and 41].

153. See, for example, 30 January and 7 February 1873 [122 and 125].
154. 35.68–69.
155. 26 August 1868 [26].
156. *Later*, p. 139; my emphasis.
157. Batchelor, p. 268.
158. 12 November 1869 [65].
159. For 'Mexican', see three undated letters, which probably date from February 1876 [155–57]. For 'M. Pencil' see, for example, 14 and 22 September 1868 and 13 August 1869 [30, 33 and 56].
160. See 13 July 1869, amended 'dear pa' to 'di pa' [52].
161. See 26 February 1879 when he informed her that she would be referred to as 'Doaneky Poneyky' and he as 'Donkey Ponky' [172].
162. 20 April 1886 [214].
163. n.d. [April 1886] [213].
164. Wilson, p. 326. The quotation here is cited to *Later*, p. 140. See 13 July 1869 for my slightly different transcription of this, with 'mamie' not 'marnie' in the first instance and 'pashing' (splashing) rather than 'pushing' [53]. Ellipses in square brackets are mine.
165. Catherine Robson, *Men in Wonderland: The Lost Girlhood of the Victorian Gentleman* (Princeton, NJ / Oxford: Princeton University Press, 2001), p. 235.
166. 30 October 1872 [103].
167. 28 November 1872 [109].
168. On occasion, he gave instructions on pronunciation, see 8 November, 1869 [64].
169. *Christmas Story: John Ruskin's Venetian Letters of 1876–1877*, ed. by Van Akin Burd (Newark: University of Delaware Press; London / Toronto: Associated University Presses, 1990), p. 29.
170. 7 July 1869 [50].
171. 13 July 1869 [53].
172. 24 November 1872 [107].
173. [May 1886] [217].
174. 17 May 1886 [216].
175. 5 March 1887 [269].
176. [269]. The date of Ruskin's additions is unknown.
177. 18 October 1887 [245].
178. 28 October 1887 [250].
179. 31 October 1872 [L 104].
180. 31 October 1872 [L 104].
181. n.d. [October 1872] [101]. See also 20 May 1869 [46].
182. 18 September 1868 [32].
183. 26 January 1872 [96].
184. 17 August 1886 [227].
185. n.d. [November 1873] [149a].
186. Another letter where Ruskin refers to being helped by others in producing his lectures is that of 18 November 1887. It also suggests the importance of acknowledging the efforts of such helpers [254].
187. n.d. [November 1873] [149a].
188. 18 February 1873 [129].
189. 8 March 1873 [131].
190. 8 March 1873 [131].
191. n.d. March 1873 [132].
192. 10 March 1873 [133]. He received a second robin and thanked his cousin for it on 14 March 1873 [136].
193. 9 November 1887 [252].
194. 1 January 1873 [117].
195. See letters of October 1869 to January 1870.
196. 22 January 1888 [256].
197. 12 October 1884 [198].
198. 5 March 1887 [269].

199. Burd, ed., *Winnington*, p. 509 (June 1864, L. 310).
200. The daughter of the hotelier at the Hotel of the Giessbach, Brienz. Ruskin's correspondence names her as 'Marie Schmidlin', see the enclosure to 10 July 1869 [51c]. She is referred to as 'Marie of the Giessbach' in biographies and in *Fors*. Hilton notes that she 'was consumptive and, at the age of eighteen, a widow' (*Later*, p. 105).
201. 20–21, 23 and 22 August 1869 [60, 62a and 61].
202. 13 May 1882 [176].
203. See Dearden, *Life*, pp. 89, 167–68,170–73, 180, 182–83, 191–92, for images of her.
204. See *Letters II* (37.facing 1) for Arthur Severn's 1873 portrait of Joan.
205. 3 March 1886 [212].
206. 35.542.
207. 26 May 1869 [47].
208. Joshua 2.1.
209. See 11 April 1865 [5].
210. 31 October 1872 [104], Ruskin's emphasis.
211. For a more a critical approach to this habit, which assumes a more active — if nevertheless repressed — sexual interest on Ruskin's part, see Mark Simpson's 'The Dream of the Dragon: Ruskin's Serpent Imagery', in *The Ruskin Polygon: Essays on the Imagination of John Ruskin*, ed. by John Dixon Hunt and Faith M. Holland (Manchester: Manchester University Press, 1982), pp. 21–43 (p. 34).
212. *Early*, pp. 253–54, *Later*, pp. 437–39.
213. *Later*, pp. 85 and 537.
214. p. 218.
215. Mimma Balia and Michelle Lovric, *Ruskin's Rose: A Venetian Love Story. 'A True Tale by Mimma Balia with Michelle Lovric'* (New York: Artisan, 2000), p. 4.
216. A. N. Wilson, *The Victorians* (London: Hutchinson, 2002), p. 716.
217. p. 325.
218. Christina Rossetti, 'In an Artist's Studio', in *New Poems by Christina Rossetti*, ed. by William Michael Rossetti (London: MacMillan, 1896), p. 114.
219. 35.529–32.
220. A. N. Wilson, p. 326.
221. Batchelor, p. 202.
222. Dennis Howitt, *Paedophiles and Sexual Offences Against Children* (Chichester: John Wiley & Sons, 1995), p. 12.
223. p. 202.
224. p. 13.
225. p. 9.
226. p. 9.
227. Sharon Aronofsky Weltman. *Performing the Victorian: John Ruskin and Identity in Theatre, Science, and Education* (Columbus: Ohio State University Press, 2007), p. 112, referring to Hilton, *Later*, p. 438 and Robson, *Men*, p. 40.
228. 2 July 1882 [183].
229. 35.525.
230. Presumably meaning Joan Severn and his other editors.
231. 35.529.
232. Batchelor, p. 203.
233. The 'it' is the view from the l'Esterelle Pass, for which this penultimate chapter of *Praeterita* was named.
234. 35.532. When Ruskin was in a disturbed state of mind about Rose, he described himself as being 'a good deal Rosie-Posiefied, and sad', n.d. [October 1872] [102].
235. Alison Milbank points out Ruskin's debt to the Bible and Dante in naming and framing this chapter, arguing that 'the choice of Joanna rather than Joan gestures to one of the women in Luke 8:3 who provided for Jesus and the disciples. The emphasis on Joan's singing and dancing in the chapter, as well as her practical care allies her to Dante's Matelda'. Milbank then suggests the redemptive, mnemonic effects of this final chapter. 'A Fine Grotesque or a Pathetic Fallacy? The Role of Objects in the Autobiographical Writing of Ruskin and Proust', in *Ruskin's Struggle*

for Coherence: Self-Representation through Art, Place and Society, ed. by Rachel Dickinson and Keith Hanley (Newcastle: Cambridge Scholars Press, 2006), pp. 90–105, esp. p. 102.
236. 28 August 1888 [258].
237. See for example 6 and 12 July 1882 [184 and 186].
238. 6 October 1882 [189].
239. 8 October 1882 [190].
240. 6 October 1882 [189].
241. 8 October 1882 [190].
242. This is not unlike Ruskin's construction of himself as a child in relation to his cousin: the ideal, infantilized self whom he constructs is quite different from the real, flawed self-infantilized Ruskin of his later years. He probably did not anticipate that disempowering himself would become real in the sense of losing the power of making decisions about his own self and home, yet this is a logical extension of his fantasy.
243. 8 October 1882 [190].
244. For an example of Lockie's epistolary voice, see the enclosure to Joan Severn's letter of 30 June 1887 [272b].
245. 15 April 1884 [196].
246. 21 June 1885 [207]. Jan Marsh notes that 'stunner' was 'the slang term for a good-looking woman', in *Pre-Raphaelite Women: Images of Femininity in Pre-Raphaelite Art* (London: Artus, 1987), p. 22.
247. Linda Austin approaches this from another perspective, arguing that Ruskin was a social élitist whose 'obvious fondness for female readers came as much from his desire to attract a leisured class as from his displaced, and much-discussed, psychological and sexual motives'. *The Practical Ruskin: Economics and Audience in the Late Work* (Baltimore, MD: Johns Hopkins University Press, 1991), p. 3.
248. According to Arthur Severn, when Ruskin announced his intention to purchase Brantwood, '[W]e said, "but do you know the position of the house?" "Yes," he said, "I know it is opposite the 'Old Man' and just the part I like, *and I have known the lake since I was a boy*."' Dearden, ed., *Professor*, p. 47; my emphasis.
249. 26 June 1888 [279].
250. Hilton, *Later*, p. 537.
251. 2 June 1886 [220].
252. 3 June 1886 [221].
253. 3 and 4 June 1886 [221 and 222].
254. For a discussion of the importance of usefulness to Ruskin's feminine ideal, see my analysis of Cinderella in 'Theatre's Heroines and Ruskinian Morality', in *Ruskin, the Theatre and Victorian Visual Culture*, ed. by Anselm Heinrich, Kate Newey and Jeffrey Richards (Basingstoke: Palgrave, forthcoming).
255. 4 June 1886 [222].
256. 14 March 1887 [232].
257. *Men*, p. 9.
258. *Men*, p. 10.
259. 27 July 1869 [54]. Robson incorrectly identifies it as 29 July 1869.
260. *Men*, p. 124.
261. *Men*, pp. 124–25.
262. *Men*, p. 98.
263. *Men*, p. 128.
264. 27 July 1869 [54].
265. It may also have suggested beautiful, derived from 'booty', as in the following which contains both words: 'my booty boo eyed wee lassie', 24 November 1872 [107].
266. *Men*, p. 125.
267. 35.21. For an extended discussion of this particular feminized child-self and the construction of genius, see my 'Terms of Empowerment', pp. 157–63.
268. Sidney Colvin, *Memoires and Notes* (London: Edwin Arnold, 1921), p. 40, as cited in Dearden, *Life*, p. 17.
269. Dearden, *Life*, p. 16.

270. n.d. [May 1882] [179].
271. *Later*, p. 136.
272. 27 July 1869 [54].
273. See 9–10 and 13 July 1869 [51a and 52].
274. 29 July 1869 [55].
275. *My Dearest Dora: Letters to Dora Livesey, Her Family and Friends 1860–1900 from John Ruskin*, ed. by Olive Wilson (Kendal: Frank Peters, [n.d.]), p. 71 (L. 31 May 1869). Wilson claims that this letter, and its companion sent to Fanny Colenso, 'are probably the earliest record of Ruskin's plans for the Guild of St George [... of which] Dora became Companion Number one and her friend Fanny Colenso Number two' (p. 73). Ruskin had, however, been describing aspects of this utopian society to his cousin and Cowper-Temple since the beginning of May. See 6 May 1869 [44]. See also his letter to Cowper-Temple in Bradley, p. 199 (4 May 1869, L. 106).
276. *Men*, p. 124 and 27 July 1869 [54].
277. 16 August 1869 [58].
278. 6 June 1886 [223].
279. See, for example, the many 'robin' letters from spring 1873.
280. Joan Evans and John Howard Whitehouse, eds, *The Diaries of John Ruskin*, 3 vols (Oxford: Clarendon Press, 1956–59), p. 1131 (June 28th, Monday). Emphasis in the original.
281. 27 May 1886 [218].
282. 28 May 1886 [219].
283. [20 June 1886] [225].
284. 35.51.
285. 7 June 1886 [224].
286. 10 January 1878 [160].
287. 25 November 1887 [255].
288. 28 June 1888 [257].
289. 37.459 (6 July 1883).
290. On 19 November 1884 [201], he described to his cousin how he 'got into a discussion — very profound, about the difference between round and oval sections in girl's waists' at a university dinner party. His own account suggests that this was greeted with good humour, but reading between the lines, it appears he was rescued from the social blunder by the wit of his friend Benjamin Jowett's who, 'after sitting smiling awhile', commented 'I cannot follow the Professor — into those <u>latitudes</u>'. Ruskin's fixation with female waists first appeared within this correspondence on 11 May 1882 [175], after he had read an article in the *Morning Post* 'that girls are never poppily in health unleſs their waists are 30 inches round.' Inspired by this, he proposed to collect the measurements of, first, the Severns' governess 'Lockie' and, then, on 13 May 1882 [176] of 'all my girl-friends' in order literally to measure their health.
291. 17 July 1882 [187].
292. 22 January 1887 [268].
293. 6 and 11 April 1865 [4 and 5]. I deal with these adjacent letters as a composite here.
294. 6 April 1865 [4].
295. 11 April 1865 [5].
296. 11 April 1865 [5].
297. 6 April 1865 [5].
298. 6 April 1865 [5].
299. 6 and 11 April 1865 [4 and 5].
300. 25 July 1864 [1].
301. In *Praeterita*, Ruskin describes his mother as a strict Evangelical who, on the model of the Biblical Eunice and Hannah, aspired for her son to be a clergyman. (35.25)
302. p.3.
303. p.3.
304. Birch, 'Womanly Mind', p. 107.
305. While Bradley's title refers to both 'Lord' and 'Lady', virtually all of the letters are addressed to the wife, often using such terms of endearment and personae as 'Philè' or '*φιλη*', 'Isolla Bella', 'Mamma' and 'Grannie', p. 9. While Bradley uses '*φιλη*', I use 'φιλη', which approximates Ruskin's script.

306. Weltman, 'Myth and Gender in Ruskin's Science', in *Ruskin and the Dawn of the Modern*, ed. by Dinah Birch (Oxford: Oxford University Press, 1999), pp. 153–73.
307. J. B. Bullen, 'Ruskin, Gautier, and the Feminization of Venice', in Birch and O'Gorman, eds, *Ruskin and Gender*, pp. 64–85.
308. See, for example, Jessica Gerrard, 'The Chatelaine: Women of the Victorian Landed Classes and the Country House', in *Keeping the Victorian House: A Collection of Essays*, ed. by Vanessa D. Dickerson (New York and London: Garland, 1995), pp. 175–206, and Beverly Gordon, 'Woman's Domestic Body: The Conceptual Conflation of Women and Interiors in the Industrial Age', *Winterthur Portfolio*, 31 (1996), 281–301.
309. Dinah Birch, *Ruskin's Myths* (Oxford: Clarendon Press, 1988), p. 4.
310. Sharon Aronofsky Weltman, *Ruskin's Mythic Queen: Gender Subversion in Victorian Culture* (Athens, OH: Ohio University Press, 1998).
311. The assumed essential femininity of art is expressed in claims such as the following by Anthea Cullen: 'Art-work was one of the few occupations considered suitable for middle-class women in the Victorian period' because it 'appeared to be merely an extension of traditional feminine accomplishments', 'Sexual Division of Labour in the Arts and Crafts Movement', in *A View from the Interior: Feminism, Women and Design*, ed. by Judy Attfield and Pat Kirkham (London: Women's Press, 1989), pp. 151–64 (p. 153).
312. For an example of her long-standing concern, see 28 November 1882 where he wrote: 'oo need'nt fear my over-exciting [or] tormenting myself again'. He sent this letter by registered post, to be delivered at Herne Hill the day after he wrote it in Dijon: he was desperate that she should read it as quickly as possible [191a].
313. 8 June 1887 [233].
314. 31 October 1872 [104].
315. 24 December 1872 [113].
316. 8 June 1887 [233].
317. 8 June 1887 [234].
318. 8 June 1887 [234].
319. See Dearden, *Life*, pp. 30–32, 49–51, 55. This is probably the portrait of Ruskin as a dapper young man (c. 1841), see Plate 5.
320. Almost twenty years earlier, he had behaved similarly after the death of her sister Kate, when Joan spent a long period of time with her dying sister and bereaved brother-in-law. On 15 December 1869, Ruskin explicitly used 'her wee roomie' as a metaphor for himself, saying: 'Ah — Doanie — when are you coming back to it?' He really meant, 'when are you coming back to [me]' [68].
321. 19 June 1887 [238].
322. 12 June 1887 [235]. See her response of 14 June 1887 [271].
323. 26 September 1868 [35], his emphasis.
324. 35.11.
325. 12 June 1887 [235].
326. 17 August 1886 [227].
327. The first of these letters mentions that he had taken morphine, which might well have affected the plans he was drawing up.
328. 15 August 1887 [226].
329. 28 June 1888 [257], Ruskin's emphasis. See Joan's letters of 26 and 30 June for the letters which sparked and responded to this one [279 and 280].
330. A composite of: 15, 17 and 26 June 1887 [236, 237 and 240].
331. 27 June 1887 [241].
332. 29 June 1887 [242], his emphases.
333. 26 June 1887 [240].
334. 25 November 1887 [255].
335. 26 October 1887 [248].
336. 24 November 1888 [259].
337. 27 November 1888 [260]
338. 12 October 1884 [198].

339. 9 September 1887 [243].
340. Batchelor, p. 265.
341. 30 October 1869 [63].
342. 16 August 1869 [58].
343. n.d. [January 1885] [205].
344. For example, just as he was leaving for a formal dinner to be attended by Prince Leopold, Prince Louis and the Dean of Christ Church, he wrote: 'me's so fitened Di Ma. & wishes me was in little Nursery, safe, at Herne Hill', 9 December 1873 [151].

LETTERS 1864–88

❖

Notes on Editorial Practice

In transcribing the following unpublished material, my aim is simply to make my own research material available to the interested reader. Because I am interested in Ruskin's self-construction and relationship-building within this composite text, it is important to capture, as nearly as possible, what he wrote in the exact way that he wrote it, preserving the idiosyncrasies. While typed versions of hand-written letters must necessarily alter the originals' appearance, it is still possible to indicate it descriptively. I have attempted to reconstruct the original without excessive annotation. The notes are intended to give basic points of explanation.

Sources. The letters transcribed here are from the manuscript letters by John Ruskin to Joan (Agnew Ruskin) Severn in the John Howard Whitehouse Collection held at the Ruskin Library, Lancaster University. These manuscripts are stored and loosely catalogued in a series of boxes entitled 'Bem L [#] / Letters / John Ruskin / to / Joan Severn / [months (where applicable)] / [year(s)]', where the separate numbers and dates are given as represented here by square brackets. Some boxes contain several years' worth of letters, while others span only a few months within one year. These letters are not yet individually catalogued, and therefore do not have individual inventory numbers. For ease of finding undated letters, I have assigned my own working catalogue system: each letter transcribed is given a number denoting where it lay in the sequence of letters extant for a given year when I first consulted them. For example, there are 142 letters from 1869, and the first is listed as '1/142, 1869'. The only exceptions have been when the content of a letter clearly indicates a different chronological ordering; in such cases, they have been re-ordered both in the boxes and in my own transcriptions. Occasionally it is evident that letters are ordered wrongly in the boxes, even though it has not been possible to establish the right chronological sequence for them; in my own transcriptions I have placed them in the best chronological ordering, while noting their position in the boxes in a footnote. I have generally retained the system of ordering in the boxes within the footnotes, for two reasons. First, many of these letters are undated and it may help readers to locate specific manuscripts if they wish to consult the original source. Secondly, because I have transcribed less than a tenth of the extant letters from this particular correspondence, my catalogue system reveals chronological gaps in my use of the letters. The year 1888 offers an extreme example of this: this edition contains just five of 220 letters. In assigning my catalogue number, I have counted the total number of letters in a given year, including each letter or telegraph from Ruskin. I have ignored empty envelopes because these probably belong to undated letters which appear at other points in the sequence. I have listed letters not by Ruskin within the letters in which they were enclosed.

Enclosures. When an enclosure is still with its letter, it has been assigned a number as a subset of the letter. For example, the letter of 9–10 July 1869 is accompanied by enclosures; so Ruskin's letter is numbered '51a', while the enclosures are '51b' and '51c'. I have included a transcription of each epistolary enclosure. If the enclosure is a newspaper clipping or some other kind of addition, I have described it or offered an excerpt, rather than reproducing it in full. Similarly, sketches and diagrams have been described verbally and I have indicated their individual dimensions, expressed numerically as width by height in centimetres.

Addresses and dates. These appear at the head of each entry alongside the number for the selections in my Appendix. If Ruskin included this information in his letter, it is repeated there, as Ruskin (and his subsequent editors, whose pencil notations have greatly aided this process) did not always put the correct date on the letters. The date in the heading is that which I have established for my own sequencing. Where possible, I deduced the date from the postmarks on the accompanying envelope, but this method is not infallible: there is no guarantee that a given letter was originally accompanied by the envelope which now houses it; and many of the letters are not accompanied by an envelope. Place of composition is also listed in the headline. When the place of composition appears in the form of letterhead, it is italicized in the transcription; but Ruskin often carried letterheads for his various homes with him when he travelled, and did not always draw attention to his writing locations. As with dates, the place given in the headline has been established when it differs from the letterhead. Places and dates in square brackets are conjectural. If the stationery is in some way unusual, this is mentioned in the general note to the letter. Readers interested in the dating of Ruskin's stationery are directed to James S. Dearden's pamphlet 'Dating of Ruskin letters: by note-paper styles'.

Later Additions. Several readers have read through these letters. These range from the intended reader (Joan Severn), to Ruskin himself, through the editors of the 'Library Edition', the various keepers of the Whitehouse Collection, and a number of scholars over time. Some have added brief notations to the manuscripts, especially 'A. W.' or Alexander Wedderburn. Typically, these are in pencil and offer a probable date of composition and list contents which help to establish the date for an undated letter or for others which are now filed near it. Brackets are also commonly added. Generally, these correspond to information reproduced or suggested in the 'Library Edition' and are often accompanied by 'AW' at the top of the page. Evidently, such pencil notations were not part of Ruskin's design and would not have been received by Joan Severn as part of the original communication. However, because this matter has played an important role in establishing the chronological order of the letters and because it is useful for tracing editorial decisions made for the 'Library Edition', I have included such references in my notes. Unless otherwise noted, all pencil notations appear on the letter rather than the envelope.

Paragraphing. Ruskin's paragraphing was inconsistent. Sometimes a new paragraph was indented; sometimes an intervening line was left blank; sometimes the multi-functional dash was inserted; sometimes a shift in the train of thought was marked simply by beginning a new line; and sometimes he used combinations of these. I have emulated his paragraphing and line length. I have tried to position postscripts where they appear in relation to the main body, rather than placing them at the end of the letter.

Punctuation. I have preserved Ruskin's punctuation, but his use of the dash poses a particular problem. It is not always clear whether a dash, a hyphen or a comma is intended; if in doubt, I have chosen the dash as the form of punctuation most used by Ruskin in these letters. It fulfilled a variety of functions: sometimes he strung several together; often he substituted it for other forms of punctuation; and — most problematically — he varied the length of it, sometimes with apparent meaning and sometimes at random. This is where I have been necessarily limited by technology: dashes are of uniform length in this edition, though each separate dash is represented. Because Ruskin sometimes added emphasis or suggested an unsaid thought by using an extra full stop, these instances have been preserved. Often, Ruskin placed his punctuation in the middle of a large space, rather than butting it against the word preceding it; assuming this to be the result of a hurried pen, I have normalized this.

Spelling. As far as possible, I emulate Ruskin's spelling and presentation, complete with superscript, subscript, crossed-out words, ampersand and abbreviations. Because I have preserved his spelling, the same word may take several different forms, even in one letter. 'Today' is a good example of this; it appears as 'today', 'to day' and 'to-day'. (Other editors have chosen 'to-day' because that is how Ruskin would have passed it in his proofs: see Burd, *Christmas*, p. 17.) I have also kept his erratic use of contractions, which generally misplace the apostrophe as in 'does'nt' rather than 'doesn't', and his archaic use of 'ſs' as a long 's'. I have copied his use of accents when using other languages (even when incorrect) and for emphasis on vowels in his epistolary idiolects. There are sets of habitually indistinguishable marks: for example, '&', 'on', 'or'; 'Mr', 'Mrs', 'W'. Usually, the correct mark can be discerned by context, but not always. In the case of doubtful marks, I have placed them in square brackets, often adding a note suggesting alternative readings. Typically, when signing his name, Ruskin connected the 'J' for John with the 'Ruskin', creating 'JRuskin' or even 'Jruskin'. I have normalized these as 'J Ruskin' or, when appropriate, 'J R'. Underlining of words for emphasis has been standardised as a single underline, although Ruskin often drew two or more.

Obvious errors. Because of the intimate, often hurried nature of these letters, there are many obvious errors. This is compounded by the extensive use of baby-talk and other nonsense idiolects. For example, Ruskin often wrote 'weer' and 'theer', rather than 'were' and 'there'. Sometimes, this seems consciously to stem from using 'Tottish', but more often it is the result of a hurried pen. Except in very rare instances (usually when a word clearly has been omitted), obvious errors are reproduced without comment, and readers should assume them to be Ruskin's.

1864

R. (now aged 45) is living in a house on Denmark Hill, with seven acres of garden, in the rural London suburbs; in 1864, he gives the lectures which will become *Sesames and Lilies*
Death of John James Ruskin (R.'s father), 3 March
J. (at this time Joan Agnew, aged 18) joins the Ruskin household, 19 April

1. 25 July 1864, Denmark Hill

Sunday

My dear Joan,

There was a great fufs last night about "Joan's letter" – It ought to have been on the table when I went to say good night to my mother. and it was not, and I looked in the drawers for it and came upon two or three, and among others [was] a little pink one, which, taking up, I said to myself – "Now – I wonder what fashionable lady has been writing to my mother – and what's up; – some of their blessed bazaars again, I suppose" – – so I threw it back into the drawer – and the letter was'nt to be found, & we had to ring for Ann[1] – & [get] her up stairs again in a bad humour – and she said the "~~Joan's~~ letter" was in the drawer – and I said it was no such thing – and so on – – and at last the pink letter was pulled out and shaken in my face, and well it might be – for I never did see such a nice change of hand brought about in a week before. It's quite legible from beginning to end – and all the letters have nice round toes and stand upright on them, and I'm really very much obliged to you. –
Well – about Mrs Fletcher –[2] mama says you must do just as you like – which I call not a right sort of message – because you can't go to Mrs Fletcher ^{so,} without being rude to mama – as liking best to go to there –
So I say – first – if Mrs Fletcher's is a draughty house and you're likely to be kept up all night dancing – you had better not go – but if its' a place wheer you will be looked after, and yet are likely to meet nice sorts of – people – it is <u>right</u> you should go – and in that case: go – whether you like it or not – especially if Mrs Fletcher really wants you. – and mama will be glad to see you at any time; she did not expect you [till][3] Monday at any rate – so it makes not much difference. You needn't worry yourself with "Mr Ruskins" and "your sons" in your notes to my mother – – It is nicely handier and easier to say "cousin John" – highly disrespectful and improper, of course, but one don't expect kittens and

---

Autograph letters for 1864 are In 'Bem L 33 / Letters / John Ruskin / to / Joan Severn / 1864–8'.

Letter 1. 1/3, 1864. Paper: edged in thick black. Pencil notations: 'Jy 25: 64'. Envelope: black sealingwax; addressed to 'Mifs Agnew. / 3. Regency Square / <u>Brighton</u>'. Postmarked: 'London. S / B / JY 25 / 64' (front); 'Brighton / C / JY 25 / 64 / A1' (back).
1. Probably Anne Strachan, Ruskin's old nurse.
2. Mrs. Fletcher may have been the wife of Lazarus Fletcher, Keeper of the British Museum Mineral Collection from 1880 and a friend of Ruskin's. See 26.1 and 34.199.
3. Spelled 'lill'.

chickens and things [inteens][4] to
behave properly.
– I'll see about the Chromothings
  – Your affectᵉ. Cousin
    J Ruskin.
  Kindest regards to John
  & Margaret[5] from us both

2. [1864?], Denmark Hill

My dear Joanna,

Please come away a
little before four, if you can,
as Mʳ Gordon & Mʳ Harrison[1]
are coming to dine – and you'll
have to drefs a little tiny bit
for them. – Besides, if this
sort of weather goes on – the
Thames may carry its bridges
away. and <u>then</u> what am I
to do about my catalogue –
(I'm beginning to forget where
we were in it.) To be sure
there are boats – if the worst
happens – but come as soon as
you can. – I'm too busy to
get out to day. Love to
Margaret & John – Ever your
  affectionate Cousin   J Ruskin

3. [1864?], Denmark Hill

My dearest Pussie

I got a tremendous scolding
last night for sending you away!
and we've been all at sixes and sevens,
to day. – Please be out at Denmark
Hill by ½ past 12 or ¼ to one.
My kindest regards, and best wishes
to mama – love to Margaret.
  Ever your loving cuzzie
    J Ruskin.

---

4. The paper is torn but 'teens' remains.
5. John Ruskin Tweddale, uncle of Joan Agnew with whom she was staying before she joined the Ruskin household.

Letter 2. 2/3, 1864. Paper: edged in thick black. Pencil notations: '? 64'. Envelope: edged in black; addressed to 'Mifs Joanna Agnew / 1. Cambridge Sᵗ.'
  1. W. H. Harrison, Editor of *Friendships Offering*, and Osborne Gordon, a clergymen. They are identified by Hilton as two friends who visited Denmark Hill in this period. See *Later*, p. 105.

Letter 3. 3/3, 1864. Pencil notations: '?64' and 'a Madame – / Madame J. [Lamos] / Hôtel Royal / Chamonix / Savoie / <u>Affranchi.</u> France'. Envelope: addressed to 'Mifs Agnew. / 1. Cambridge Sᵗ.'; Pencil notations: 'Half-sovereign / Mʳˢ S's address = / Write to Clem / with tatting patterns & / [with grey dress] / write to Mʳˢ [Sim]' (front); 'not that Im / aware of –' (back). Enclosures: two loose sheets of paper, one with four pencil sketches of a female head, each with a different hairstyle, the other has two sketches of lizards or perhaps griffins, stylized as though from stone carvings.

  Note: This letter is addressed to 'Pussie'. Because this pet-name does not appear embedded in letters until 8 May 1865 and does not appear as a salutation until 23 July 1867, this letter is incorrectly filed. Also, it is not edged in black. It has presumably been placed here because Joan Agnew stayed at Cambridge Street in 1864. I can not offer a definitive date of composition for these, so have left them where they are stored.

1865

Publication of *Sesame and Lilies*
Publication of *Ethics of the Dust* (although dated 1866)
R. continues to visit Winnington Hall, a girls' finishing school in Cheshire, to teach
R. had first met Rose La Touche in 1858, and over 1860–62 she had become the dominant
figure in his life; he sees her again (now aged 17), 10 December; she visits, 21 December

4. 6 April 1865, Winnington Hall

April.
5th ~~Mar~~ – 65.

My dear Joanna,

There are great enquiries here after you, and I tell them you are ^a very good girl. and never get into mischief. I am endeavouring to impress this upon Lily's[1] mind – . but she has no mind to impresss it upon – I think. She shakes her curls and looks out for any new chance of getting into mischief herself – next moment. I wish you were here so much – you would be very happy. & have everything good for you – only too much laughing.

Love to Katie.

Ever your affect.t Cousin
J Ruskin.

.I've told Mama to give you some money to buy velvet for me –
– Mind you use the carriage when you want it.

And tell Lucy[2] you're to have some more champagne to day.
– And don't cut the velvet too mincingly, one of the last bits does not quite cover the drawer.

5. 11 April 1865, Winnington Hall

My dear Joan,
There's only this scrap of paper about in my room[1] – and my hand shakes with rolling over & over on the grass, and being pulled fifteen ways at once, but I must just thank you for your nice little letter, and scold you for not telling me more of the flirtation between Mr Carlyle[2] & you – I'm sure it must have been very serious, this time. And to say that the letter – otherwise – is very nice – and not stupid, except about the heat – It is only Scotch girls who hate summer – The heat is divine – beatific. reviving to souls and bodies. I've not seen such a day. nor felt such a breeze – this two years – since. I was in Italy.

Autograph letters for 1865 are In 'Bem L 33 / Letters / John Ruskin / to / Joan Severn / 1864–8'.

Letter 4. 2/10, 1865. Paper: edged in thin black. Pencil notations: 'Winnington'. Envelope: black sealingwax; addressed to 'Mifs Joanna Agnew. / (Mrs Ruskin's) / Denmark Hill. / Camberwell / S. London.'. Postmarked: 'NORTHWICH / B / AP 6 / 65' (front); 'LONDON-S / 7 C / AP [?] / 6[5]' (back).
1. Lily Armstrong, (1852–1931), a friend from Winnington and daughter of Sergeant Armstrong, MP for Sligo. See Bradley and Ousby, p. 110n. Ruskin referred to her as 'Bear' or 'Little Bear', a name which also occasionally applied both to himself and to Rose La Touche.
2. Lucy Tovey, the Ruskin's parlour-maid from 1829 to 1875. See Burd, *Winnington*, p. 326n.

Letter 5. 3/10, 1865. Paper: ½ a sheet of very lightweight stationary. Envelope: black sealingwax; addressed to 'Mifs Joanna Agnew. / Mrs Ruskin's. / Denmark Hill / Camberwell / S. / London'. Postmarked: 'NORTHWICH / B / AP 11 / 65' (front); 'LONDON-S / 7 C / AP 12 / 65' (back). Pencil notations: 'Winnington', 'Ap 11: 65' (front) and '11 Apr 65' (back).
1. The letter is on the particularly thin paper Ruskin tended to use when on the Continent.
2. Thomas Carlyle, author whom Ruskin referred to as 'papa'.

– I can't make out if Crawley[3] ~~is~~ should is to
[meet
you or not – It will be late in the
evening – & I see you say you can get
on well enough without him. so perhaps
it would only bother you. Or I may hear
more to morrow

Yes 'Ill write sometimes to tell
you what we are about and how
the garden gets on – and we shall
both mifs you very much, I'm sure.
 – and I'm ever your affect[e] cousin
            J Ruskin
L. gave me five kisses yesterday!
and said I should have some more in the
[afternoon [4]
– but I lost my chance by some horrid
company coming.[5]

6. 8 May 1865, Denmark Hill

            8th May
My dear Joanna

I have been really wanting
to write to you, for some time
but have nearly been falling ill (from
having been kept indoors and at work)
and could not write letters at all – no
    nor even notes. . . But I must thank
you for your line ~~of~~ received this morning,
[which
both my mother and I were glad,
and sorry, to receive. My mother
misses you much more than I thought
she would, and says "she does not
know how she could replace you at all;
– indeed, she knows she could not" –
but she would have been glad neverthelefs
that Margarets' story had been true.

It was rather a pretty story, and
though I miss you very much myself
– too, I am more sorry than my
mother it is not true, for I attach
more importance to marriage, especially
early marriage, than she does, and as
    you know I am very remorseful
about keeping you mewed up here –
– But fancy – I've been unpacking
another Lostwithiel box this
morning, and I found you had
been wonderfully quick and lighthanded
in unrolling the papers, – it took
me twice the time – at least –
that does not allow quite for
the loss of time, when you are there,
in mischief, and insisting on having
things your own way. (as Kate[1]
knows,) – but in merely unrolling
I lost a great deal of time [in]
comparison.
We are both very sorry about the
birds nest too = and very
sympatic with you.
– and we shall both be glad
– not a little, to have you back
again – & that's all I can say
to day – no – I forgot – mama says
that you will have sometimes
recurrences of that toothache
attack – but that every attack
will be slighter – none will
ever again be so bad as that
first – Poor little pussy – it
makes me laugh still – pathetically
to think of your ~~poor~~ sad little beseeching
face – when nobody would pity you
– and even I laughed as I pitied,
pitying not the lefs – but it was

---

3. Frederick Crawley, Ruskin's valet.
4. These words have been inserted vertically into the right margin.
5. Burd identifies this 'company' as Frederic Shields and Mrs. Alexander Scott. See *Winnington*, p. 545n.

Letter 6. 6/10, 1865. Pencil notations: 'D. Hill', '1865'. Envelope: black sealingwax; addressed to 'Mifs Joanna Agnew, / M[rs] Agnew / <u>Wigtown</u>. / N. B.' Postmarked: 'LONDON / 9 / MY10 / 65' (front); 'NEWTON–STE[WART] / B / MY 11 / 1865', 'WIGTOWN / MY 11 / 18[6]5' (back). Part of this letter is reproduced in 36.482.
   1. Probably Joan's sister Kate Agnew, who married Arbuthnot Simson in 1867. She died in childbirth two years later, see 13 November, 1869 [66].

such a droll little face – not
disfigured – but [teased]² into another –
– W'ell;³ – make the most of
your liberty while you have it
– if you will come back to prison.
– Ever with love to Kate
    Your affectionate Cousin
        J Ruskin

7. 31 May 1865, Denmark Hill

Denmark Hill, s.
31ˢᵗ May

My dear Joanna.

  I had your nice little
note yesterday. – we are always
very glad to get one. the flower
is very sweet still; but hawthorns
dislike travelling. and look very
weary after it. what a comfort
it must be to you in Scotland that
some of these hardy flowers really
will [bloom] there. Your garden
looks by this time very like a bit of
the kitchen garden – The sticks, I
am sorry to see, have disappeared,
and in their stead are little rows
of things like mustard and crefs, which
I have given directions to the servants
not to mistake for salad – as I suppose
you intended them for something else;
                there are
some things coming up everywhere
which at first I was in hopes
were thistles; but the gardener
says they are only poppies; as they
have come there to please you, I
suppose – I leave them till you
send orders about them.
So you want me to give you
the highest praise of saying
that you do not want to be praised!
– No – I really can't give you such
a large bit all at once. Sugar
is all very well in candy, but
a whole sugarloaf at once would
choke you – Don't be greedy, and
I'll give you nice little clear bits
to suck, whenever you are a good girl – ¹
I shall be glad to have you back
again – I've been interrupted, & very
busy, and not very well – this last
fortnight – and could not set my
schoolgirls properly to work; so
they've done nothing but romp,
and all the mineral arranging
remains for you to do when you
come back.
– I hope you will enjoy your
sea bathing – It must be very
nice where there is hardly any
water for eight miles: – how
far have you to walk out before
you can put your head under?
I really mean what I say, when
I say we want you to come
back, as soon as you can without
breaking on any pleasant plans.
    Ever your affectionate Cousin
        J Ruskin
– and a nice little "baby Agnew".² when
I see you really don't like it, you
shall not have any more

  2. This could be 'turned'.
  3. I suspect this is an early attempt to write in a Scottish idiolect.

Letter 7. 8/10, 1865. Pencil notations: '1865'. Envelope: black sealingwax; addressed to 'Mifs Joanna Agnew. / Mʳˢ Agnew, / Wigtown. / N. B.' Postmarked: 'LONDON.S / [3] / MY 31 / 65' (front); 'NEWTON–STEWART / B / JU 1 / 186[5]', 'WIGTOW[N] / JU 1 / [1]8[6]5' (back).
  1. A line appears after 'girl', crosses to the following page, sweeps below the ideas which flow from it ('and nice [...] any more') and connects to the signature.
  2. This is the first reference to his cousin as a 'baby'.

8. 20 June 1865, Denmark Hill

Denmark Hill, s.

My dear Joanna

   I'm very glad you're coming back – I've got all our tickets under the wrong minerals. and – theres not a book in its place – – Mifs Fall[1] says you say I teaze you – I'm sure you teaze me. ~~but~~ by saying you're going away for six weeks and staying six months – however, I'm glad you've not got yourself run away with altogether. –
– Send me word by what train you're coming – that I may look after you.
The letters have been beautifully written lately – the catalogues will be lovely! – love to Kate. Ever your affect[1] Cousin – J Ruskin

9. 27 June 1865, Denmark Hill

Denmark Hill, s.

My dear Joanna

   It may be convenient to you, as you have your friend with you, to have the carriage at your disposal; I felt inclined to come for a chat on the way out; but you'll be tired enough without that – so I will just send David[1] & you can do what you like with him about setting your friend [down] – only come out then straight here. Your garden wants you, & my mother & I shall be all the better of $^{\text{or for.}}$ + [2]you, too.
      Ever your affectionate Cousin
            J Ruskin
It's a difficult bit of grammar that, – it always puzzles me.

Letter 8. 9/10, 1865. Envelope: first with red sealingwax; addressed to 'Mifs Joanna Agnew. / Mrs Agnew. / Wigtown / N. B.' Postmarked: 'LONDON [?] / [B3] / JU20 / [6]5' (front); 'NEWTON–STEWAR[T] / B / [J]U21 / [1865]', 'WIGTOWN / JU21 / 18[6]5' (back). Pencil notations: 'envl. June 20: 65'.
  1. Eliza Fall, identified by Burd as 'the younger sister of Ruskin's boyhood friend at Herne Hill, Richard Whiteman fall'. See *Winnington*, p. 554n.

Letter 9. 10/10, 1865. Pencil notations: 'envl June 27.65'. Envelope: red sealingwax; addressed to 'Mifs Joanna Agnew. / Mifs Harper / Kircudbright / N. B.' Postmarked: 'LONDON-S / 5 / JU27 / 65' (front); 'KIR[KCUDBRI]GHT / [A] / JU28 / 1865' (back).
  1. David Fudge, the coachman at Denmark Hill.
  2. Ruskin inserted a cross like an addition sign, with a dot in each quadrant to draw his cousin's attention to the note at the bottom: the first extant comment on spelling and grammar. In later letters, such comments would be expressed in baby-talk.

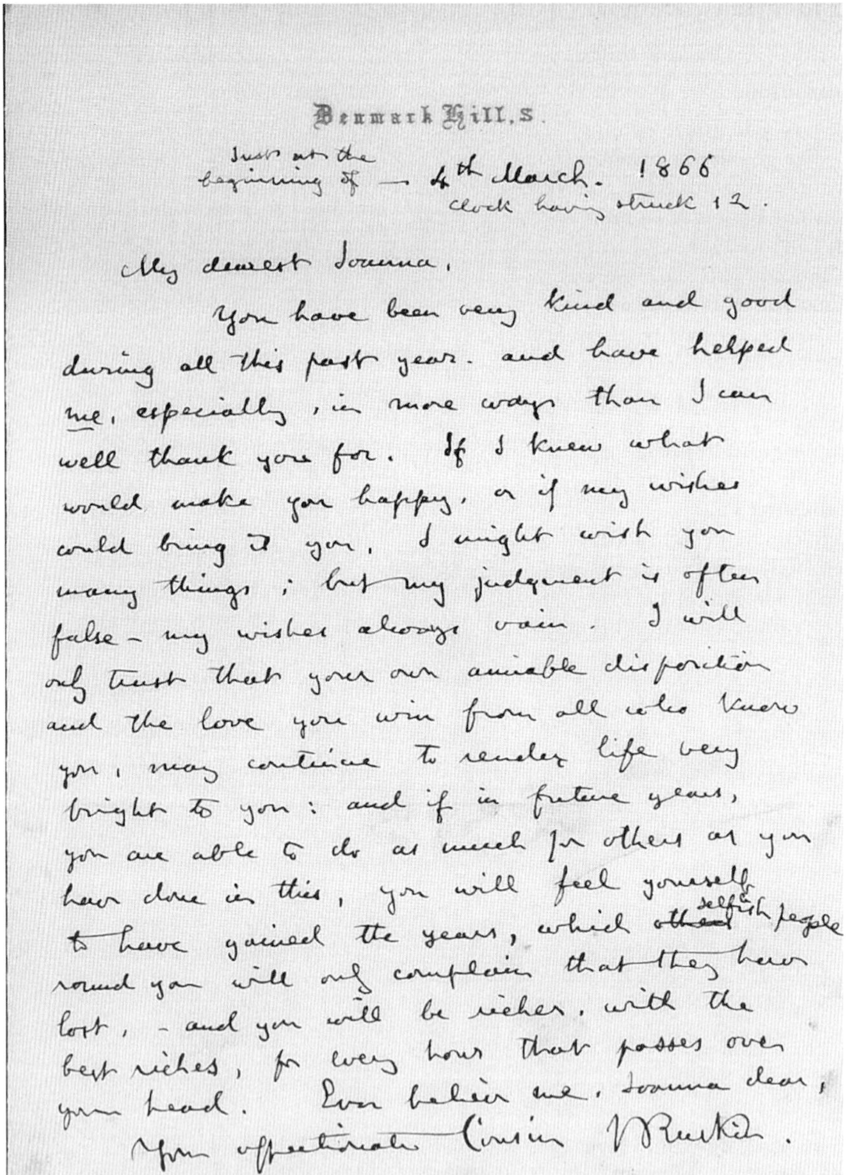

𝔇𝔢𝔫𝔪𝔞𝔯𝔨 𝔥𝔦𝔩𝔩, 𝔰.

Just at the
beginning of — 4th March. 1866
clock having struck 12.

My dearest Joanna,

You have been very kind and good during all this past year. and have helped me, especially, in more ways than I can well thank you for. If I knew what would make you happy, or if my wishes could bring it you, I might wish you many things ; but my judgement is often false — my wishes always vain. I will only trust that your own amiable disposition and the love you win from all who know you, may continue to render life very bright to you ; and if in future years, you are able to do as much for others as you have done in this, you will feel yourself to have gained the years, which other selfish people round you will only complain that they have lost, — and you will be richer, with the best riches, for every hour that passes over your head. Ever believe me, Joanna dear,

your affectionate Cousin J Ruskin.

FIG. 2. Facsimile of JR letter to JS, 4 March 1866 [10]
RF L33, Ruskin Foundation (Ruskin Library, Lancaster University)

1866

Rose's 18th birthday celebrated at Denmark Hill, 3 January
R. having proposed marriage, Rose asks him to wait three years for her, 2 February
J. travels to Ireland with the La Touches to visit them at Harristown, mid-April
R. takes Continental tour with J., his friends and patrons the Trevelyans, and their niece
Constance Hilliard, 24 April to 12 July
Lady Trevelyan dies at Neuchâtel, 13 May
While staying at Hotel Giessbach, R. meets Marie Schmidlin, 5 June

10. 4 March 1866, Denmark Hill

Denmark Hill, S.
Just at the
beginning of – 4th March. 1866
clock having struck 12.

My dearest Joanna,

You have been very kind and good during all this past year. and have helped me, especially, in more ways than I can well thank you for. If I knew what would make you happy, or if my wishes could bring it you, I might wish you many things; but my judgement is often false – my wishes always vain. I will only trust that your own amiable disposition and the love you win from all who know you, may continue to render life very bright to you: and if in future years, you are able to do as much for others as you have done in this, you will feel yourself to have gained the years, which others
[selfish people
round you will only complain that they have lost, – and you will be richer, with the best riches, for every hour that passes over your head. Ever believe me, Joanna dear,
Your affectionate Cousin   J Ruskin.

11. 28 Sept. 1866, Denmark Hill

Denmark Hill, s.
28th Sept

My dearest Cuzzie[1]
Scotland may be a fine country for everything else. but the posts in it are very odd. and it seems always about two months before I get any answer to any letter.
Anything more crofs than I am, always and altogether – I don't think you ever saw or heard of. or ever will.
Talk of being as cross as two sticks![2]
I'm as crofs as a whole crows nest of sticks.
– If all the sticks creaked and croaked, as well as crofsed, you would have a

---

Autograph letters for 1866 are in 'Bem L 33 / Letters / John Ruskin / to / Joan Severn / 1864–8'.

Letter 10. 1/2, 1866. Envelope: red sealingwax; addressed to 'Joanna, / 4th March – 1866.' This is the first extant example of Ruskin's birthday letters to his cousin. Unusually, this letter is fully reproduced in 36.502–03.

Letter 112/2, 1866. Envelope: red sealingwax; addressed to 'Mifs Joanna Agnew. / Care of, Mifs [Harper]. / Kirkcudbright / N. B.' Postmarked: 'LONDON-S / 5 / SP28 / 66' (front); 'CASTLE DOU[GLAS] / A / SP29 / 66', 'KIRKCUDBRIGHT / C / SE 29 / 1866' (back). Pencil notations: '1866'.

1. This is the first letter to address her as 'Cuzzie'. It also, reciprocally, refers to Ruskin as 'Cuzzie' in the closing.
2. See also 3 September 1868.

perfect image of my present body and mind. Downes[3] doesn't know me, – and I think Connie[4] will run away again as soon as she sees me.

I don't know – now. whether you will finally come on Tuesday or Wednesday morning. Do just as you like best –
– of course the sooner the better for me.

 Ever your loving Cuzzie
    J Ruskin.

I'll send you another last line to morrow –
– but I hope I shall have one here, first.

You may like to see the enclosed. Madame Roch's[5] translations are admirable. I think of giving her my whole 4th vol – and the papers in Reader & Geologist. – if she likes to have them.

---

3. David Downes, the head gardener at Denmark Hill.
4. Either Constance Hilliard, who had joined the Trevelyans (a maternal aunt and uncle), Ruskin, and Joan Agnew for a Continental journey earlier that year, or Constance Oldham, a pupil at Winnington who was also a neighbour at Denmark Hill and one of Ruskin's goddaughters.
5. Probably Madame Roch of Geneva. See 34.509.

1867

J. becomes engaged to Percy La Touche, but R. is barred from contact with Rose
R. makes a Tour of the North, especially the Lake District, 28 June to 25 August

12. 2 July 1867, Keswick

Keswick 2nd July
1867
(550!)
My darling wee 'amie[1]   verse for to day.
[Ps. 38th.14

You have put quite a new pleasure for me into hearing the sheep bleat on the hills – every now and then it puts me so completely in mind of the dear little pitiful ~~ones,~~ *bleats at home* ending with the comfortable
[short one!
– I had a fine long day yesterday – about fourteen to fifteen miles – over three high summits – two of them, each, 2700^{ft} – though I had only to go down 500 between them but the long sweeps of moorland which a 500 descent and re-climb mean in Cumberland, take walking. But the day was delicious, and the hill tops all in perfect peace. Downes[2] had enough of it by one o-clock – (it <u>was</u> rather hot – I must say) – so I left him and Crawley[3] to take care of each other. and got home to my own dinner at five, in much disposition for it. (Itie pigs had salmon and shoulder of a lamb.) and for tea after wards: (itie pigs had muffins).[4]
– On the ridge between the two last summits, I met two gentlemen – (In these lonely places one generally *without*
[*introduction* says something)
– The first was very handsome and I thought he would be nice too – so I capped him – and congratulated him on his choice of route. "Don't you know me"? – said he –
[laughing,
– No, I did'nt – "My name's Brayshay"[5] There could really have met me no one whom I should have been happier to see. He and his friend – an old tutor – are coming to breakfast this morning. – but they go away to day.

They've had a good breakfast. – and I a bad [one – for][6] I can't eat when I've people to look after. but itie pigs can make up some other time – They were very nice – both. I've just got your nice long yesterdays letter – I'm very glad to hear so pleasantly of [Janie] – my love to her.
It was a sadly disappointing expedition that – finding every body somewhere else.

Autograph letters for 1867 are In 'Bem L 33 / Letters / John Ruskin / to / Joan Severn / 1864–8'.

Letter 12. 4/18, 1867.
1. This is the first letter addressed 'to 'amie'. Ruskin appears to have christened Joan this as a reflection of her ability to mimic the bleating of lambs, although the name took on other connotations of being amiable and of being a friend (from the French 'amie'), as well as being a derivative of 'mamie'.
2. David Downes.
3. Frederick Crawley.
4. This is the first time he called himself an 'itie pig', a pet name which would dominate the letters of 1867 and resurface in subsequent years.
5. See 20 March 1873 for a letter fragment from a 'Brayshay' who lived in Malham; they may be the same person. This may be the W. H. Brayshay identified as the source of Record Office information on the derivation of 'Ruskin'. See 35.lx n. He is also identified as W. Hutton Brayshay of Wharfedale, Yorkshire, a letter to whom (of 18 November 1865) is reproduced in 36. 498.
6. Damaged by foxing.

– and Battersea bridge does'nt sound cheerful to me. I do wish I had you both on Saddleback.[7] But you would like Horseback better – I fancy

Send me a nice long letter tomorrow – as I can't have one the day after.

– I don't return the scraps of letters – I was glad to see them, but I suppose you don't care for them back. I'll write to Mrs Hilliard [+8] & Connie some day soon now – but I don't write to anybody but my wee piggie – generally.[9]

I hav'nt had so bad a breakfast after all! – When my friends left the
   coast clear, I set to work. and
     made the most of my time till the
_____[10]

+Apropos of Mrs Hilliards letter, which I do re-enclose, I found this story in a history

waiter came in, & I was obliged
  to stop. On which I composed the
  following moral couplets.
" When itie pigs, too sharply set,
  Have taken all that they can get,
  (And had, besides, enough. before,)
  The itie pigs – should take no more."

    Ever your loving cuzzie-piggie.
                    J Ruskin.

(Half an hour later –) Somehow – I don't feel as if I'd had any breakfast – after all.
_____

of Cumberland. "Among the latest [specimens] of the old wild race of forest men were the brothers Dodgson – who were so intent on their woodcutting that they devoted Sunday to cooking for the whole week. When they were growing old, they found the need of some domestic help & comfort – and at
                          [last, the
one relieved his mind to the other saying "[Thore] mun out, an 'tait a wife" "Aye;" said the brother –"if they[11] be a
                          [hard job,
[thou ollers] sets [yon] (one)[12] [tulk]." However he obeyed, and there was soon a wife to cook, & children helping with the faggots

13. 7 July 1867, Keswick

                Keswick. July 7th
                        1867
                –
My dearest Wee 'Amie[1]

  It is fine to day, at last; & was not bad, yesterday. and I had a walk right round Derwent-water – a good ten miles – before dinner, and another two hours scrambling walk in the evening, and slept all night long, only dreaming of being in a cathedral and hearing music and a sweet song, of which I could not make out the words, but the name of it was "Bouche douce" "Sweet mouth".[2]

---

    7. This is another name for Blencathra, a hill in the Lake District.
    8. This cross is matched, below. Ruskin inserted a line across both leaves of paper, wrote as far as 'a history' on this leaf then continued, facing, beneath the line. Mrs [J. C.] Hilliard is Mary (1827–82), the sister of Pauline Trevelyan and wife of Rev. J. C. Hilliard of Cowley Rectory. See Bradley and Ousby, 195n.
    9. As with the shared name 'Cuzzie' (28 September 1866), here Ruskin called his cousin by the pet-name he recently had applied to himself, 'piggie'. This suggests a sharing of identity. This is also the first letter in which he informed her that he wrote primarily to her, a motif which recurred throughout the correspondence.
  10. There is a line running above this postscript, which continues on the following page.
  11. He amended 'there' to 'they'.
  12. There is a small line connecting 'yon' to '(one)'.

Letter 13. 7/18, 1867.
    1. Ruskin had used the pet-name 'lamb' for his cousin before, but this is the first instance where he drew a line above the 'a' as well as placing an apostrophe before it.
    2. This is the first extant letter to Joan Agnew that records a dream.

By the way – I've had it in my
mind to tell you a hundred times,
that coloured photograph you gave
me is coloured over an original which
none of us have, and its a shame.
And though the colouring of the hair
and cheek is nice, it has spoiled the
eyes.   Try if you can get an uncoloured one[3]
10 o'clock.
And so – here comes in the letter
with the rose. and the crumb, besides
of pure manna.   –
And I'll come on Wednesday, , 'amie dear
just as you bid.
I am so very thankful for these
crumbs – for I thought she had
been put under some new forbidding
– not even to name me. and that
you were trying to keep it from me
as long as you could.
I have several notes to answer –
forgive this short one – because if
it was ever so long, it could'nt
thank you enough – or her.
Love to Mama, and Kate. & Mary.
and Arbuthnot.[4] Ever
my darling wee 'amie – your loving Cuzzie
         J Ruskin.

1 oclock
   I've been to church, and put
a sovereign which I had been saving
to buy minerals with, into the
offertory plate.

And I'm so happy. Though it's
an East Wind again.
If only it would carry me with it!
westwards.

   Write me yet a line to morrow.
With any final directions
     to Derwent-water Hotel
         Keswick
         Cumberland

14. 22 July 1867, Keswick

         Keswick
         22nd July
My dearest wee Doanie
   I hope you will be very
happy – to day – to morrow – and
ever after. – and that you will always
be happier because of your good brother
to day made yours.[1] and not lefs
happy in your tiresome querulous cuzzie
– you know – it must be nice having
somebody. to scold sometimes – and
one must'nt one's husband! – Mind that.
(and tell Kate). and love [me][2] always
    and believe me ever your loving Cousin
               John Ruskin
You were to have had a long letter
but I've been out in the rain, &
hindered. but I'm getting stronger
I've been climbing to day, as high as
your highest hill – $_{(1400)}$, in the rain & wind.

---

3. This is the first letter to Joan Agnew which is dominated by Rose La Touche. On 17 June 1867, he had written of following a carriage bearing a girl who looked like Rose. But, in this letter, he begins with the dream alluding to Rose, speaks of a photograph of the girl, rejoices in the arrival of the letter with 'the rose. and the crumb, besides of pure manna', goes to church to make an offering of thanks, and concludes with his longing to be carried 'westwards' to her.
4. These are all members of Joan Agnew's immediate family in Wigtown. She had returned to Scotland because of the marriage of her sister Kate to Arbuthnot Simson, see 22 July 1867 [14].

Letter 14. 9/18, 1867. Pencil notations: '1867'. Envelope: red sealingwax, obscuring embossed flowers; addressed to 'Mifs Joanna Agnew. / Wigtown / N. B.' Postmarked: 'B / KESWICK / JY 22 / 67' (front); 'NEWTON-STEWART / B / JU 23 / 67', '[WIG]TOWN / B / JY 23 / 1867' (back). This is the first extant letter addressed to 'Doanie' and the first signed with his formal, full name: 'John Ruskin'.
1. Joan Agnew was at home in Wigtown for the marriage of her sister, Kate. Judging by Ruskin's comment, 22 July 1867 was the day of the wedding.
2. This could be 'one'.

15. 23 July 1867, Keswick

Tuesday 23rd

My dearest Wee Pussy,

   I'm very glad Kate is'nt here! there are very bad lefsons going on in the passage – an innocent husband just called out to his wife from his dressingroom.
"Where's my lake-Guidebook?"
And the wife answered
"You ought to know!"

I've sent you <u>such</u> a packet of [nicest] letters to-day – I had torn M^{rs} H's¹ acrofs. then thought you might like to see it.
– It's very stingy and naughty of mama to write her poor boy no Sunday letter –   He won't be a good boy if he does'nt get Sunday letters. He'll go & eat too much muffin again.

So you're actually going home tomorrow! You dear nice pussy. But poor grannie! What is she to do – I shall drink to Kate's health, and good behaviour, to day.
I wonder where she's going to ????????
– Its raining here – in its prettiest way –
I believe it thinks it that it's the right thing to do.   always.

I shall write to Denmark Hill to morrow
     Ever your loving Cuzzie
             J R.

16. 25 July 1867, Keswick

Thursday Evening
25th July

My dearest wee 'Amie

   I really never Knew how well you bleated till to-day – though I always thought it delightful – but out on the moors, when I was thinking of nothing, a lamb bleated close by, and I started and turned half round – expecting to see <u>you</u>. I've had such a lovely walk – I <u>can</u> walk a little, yet, I find; and won't Rosie and I have rambles!¹ – If she had but been with me to day; – it was shower and sunshine alternately, and all the ferns glistening and gleaming and shaking in the wind; and I got from ridge to ridge of hill – and up. and down, and up higher again – till I had ^ᵍᵒⁿᵉ a round of about eight to nine miles, over two considerable hills – the last being the top of Cawsey Pike² which mama knows well – and which I came down the front of, straight to Keswick – doing the whole in four hours and ten minutes which, over soft moss and ^ʳᵒᵘᵍʰ rock, mostly against wind up ^ᵗʰᵉ hill, and including an ascent of 2500 feet, is not bad walking for an invalid. The view from Cawsey Pike pleased me more than ⁱᵗ ᵈⁱᵈ ~~twenty~~ <u>thirty</u>!
                           [years
ago – and there are the same crags and appa<u>re</u>ntly the same moss – nothing so changelefs as those strange grey mountain tops

---

Letter 15. 10/18, 1867. Envelope: lined in pink and embossed with a rose; red sealingwax; addressed to 'Mifs Joanna Agnew. / Wigtown / N. B'. Postmarked: 'B / KESWICK / JY 23 / 67' (front), 'NEWTO[N STE]WART / B / JY 24 / 67', ' WI[GT]OWN / B / JY 24 / 1867' (back). Pencil notations: 'Keswick', 'July 1867'. This is the earliest extant letter which is both addressed to 'Pussy' and is clearly dated by Ruskin. The example of 'Pussy' now filed earlier in the correspondence (in 1864) is not internally dated and I don't believe it comes from that year. This is also the first letter written in the third person and the first to refer to himself as a 'boy' and Joan Agnew as his 'mama'.
  1. Presumably he means Mary Hilliard's letter.

Letter 16. 11/18, 1867. Pencil notations: 'Keswick', '1867'. Envelope: lined in pink and embossed with a rose; red sealingwax; addressed to 'Mifs Joanna Agnew, / Denmark Hill / Camberwell / S. London'. Postmarked: 'B / KESWICK / JY 26 /67' (front), 'LONDON-S / 7 H / JY 27 / 67', '7 P / LONDON / JY 27 / 67' (back). Pencil notations on the envelope: 'Cantharadine Pomade – / Ties – Sand balls / Elastic straps' (front).
  1. See the previous day's letter to his mother for comments on his 'confidence' about Rose, which infused 'everything else' with peace (36.531). That letter also makes clear that he relied on Joan to read his mother's letters to her: 'Joan will be there to read this letter'.
  2. Here and below, Ruskin misspelled 'Causey Pike'.

– not a lichen – seemingly – more, or lefs, in thirty years.
Then I dressed, and ate a great big, pig dinner – and made these piggie-verses on it.
W[3] "If itie pigs are not at ease,
   In dining upon duck and pease,
   Replete (the Duck) with savoury seas –
   Owing , and fragrant from a squeeze
   Of Lemon, (fruit of golden trees
   In Islands of Hesperides)
– Not that, in specifying these,
   I mean to omit a slice of cheese
   Decayed in delicate degrees,
   By wise delays of g'ourmandise –
   Then itie pigs – are hard to please."

———

(Friday morning. I think, for the fourth couplet we had better read thus –
   Not that I mean, in mentioning these,
   A supercilious view of cheese, &c.

Then I sate looking out at the window at the swans on the lake – then – apropos of duck & lemons, I thought of oranges – and wrote to George – tell mama – and told him "we had'nt got no oranges".[4]
Then I had a pig-tea – and looked out of the window at an American couple who had set themselves exactly at the crossing of the garden walks.[5]

          means flower border
P Q   means Box.
          P. Q. means American couple

Then I thought I would tell you all about it. and so I've written this, and now I'm going to bed.
          [(558)!!!!!!!!!!!!!!!|||::........!⁶
(Thats notes of "admiration" (literally)) In perspective.

Friday morning. 26th July. (557)
   I have your nice letter from Denmark hill and am very happy about all.
   Ever your loving St C.[7]
Nice line from Kate, too.

17. 15 August 1867, Keswick

          15th August. Evening.

My dearest wee Fernie

Such lovely wee fernie's as I've been seeing in their little nests under the stones on Skiddaw to day!¹ (but not so prettie as my own wee Fernie, at all). – After I had sent off your letter, ² I thought I

---

3. The 'W' has been rubbed out. He appears to have started the poem with 'When' (as on in the first pig poem on 2 July 1867), then decided on 'If'.
4. See 20 August 1867 .
5. A sketch (left) with legend (right) follows. The sketch shows the crossing paths surrounded by flower borders (rows of wavy lines) and box hedges (straight lines superimposed with wavy lines), with the couple denoted in the middle by 'P' and 'Q', probably for prince and queen meaning man and woman.
6. Ruskin's emphatic punctuation here is composed of: fifteen exclamation marks; three broken horizontal lines of three marks each; two short, broken horizontal lines of two marks each; and eight dots followed by a large, dark exclamation mark.
7. This is the first letter to Joan Agnew which is definitely dated and signed 'St C', for Saint Crumpet', Rose La Touche's pet-name for him. As in the future, this signature was an indication that Ruskin was thinking about Rose. In this instance, the reference is overt: the wishful thinking about 'Rosie' La Touche's company. It may also be implicit: his interest in the American couple, represented as 'P' and 'Q', may have been perceived as a reflection of his own idealized relationship with Rose.

Letter 17. 13/18, 1867. Paper: bottom 3 cm removed from the final page; no signature. Pencil notations: '67', 'Keswick'. Envelope: lined in pink and embossed with a rose; red sealingwax; addressed to 'Mifs Joanna Agnew. / Denmark Hill / S. / London.' Postmarked: 'B / Keswick / AU [16] / 67' (front); 'London-S. / 7[H] / AU 17 / 67' (back). Most of this letter is reproduced in 36.536–37.
1. See 23 August 1869 where he comments about this summer, spent 'wandering desolately about Skidaw [... when he] could not bear to go far from that Irish sea. and have another sea between me – and – sorrow' [62a].
2. There is no other letter from 15 August in L 33, nor from the days immediately preceding it, as the previous letter in the file is of 6 August.

should like a long quiet day on Skiddaw
by myself. so I gave Crawley some work
at home, in packing stones, and took my
hammer & compass. and sauntered up
leisurely. It was threatening rain, in its
very beauty of stillness. – no sunshine – only
dead calm under grey sky – I sate down
for a while on the highest shoulder of the
hill under the summit – in perfect calm
of air – as if in a room! Then, suddenly
– in a space of not more than ten minutes
vast volumes of white cloud formed
in the west. – When I first sate down,
all the Cumberland mountains, from Scawfell
to ^the Penrith hills, lay round me like
a clear model, cut in wood – I never
saw anything so <u>ridiculously</u> clear.
– great masses 2000 feet high looking
like little green ~~knolls~~ bosses under one's hands
Then as I said – in ten minutes, the
white clouds formed, and came
foaming from the west towards
Skiddaw. – then answering white
fleeces started into being on Scawfell
and Helvellyan – and the moment
they were formed, the unnatural
clearnefs passed away, and the
mountains, where still visible,
resumed their proper distances.
I rose and went on along the
slaty ridge towards the summit, hammering
and poking about for fibrous quartz –
– when I met two people – an elderly
English gentleman and his wife – (the
right sort of thing) not vulgar – but
homely) – coming down in a great
hurry, frightened at the masses of
approaching cloud. They asked me
if they "should be lost in the fog"?
I told them, there was no fear
– the path was plain enough – & they
would soon be out of the clouds as
they went down. Well – but – are you
going to stop up here all night? asked
the lady. – "No – not quite – I answered,
laughing – but I've my compass in
my pocket. & don't care what happens"
so they went down as fast as they could

and I went on – rejoicing in having
all Skiddaw summit "hale o' mine air"
– for this couple were the only people
who had come up ~~that~~ ^to day – it
looked so threatening. It was very
beautiful, with the white cloud filling
all the western valley – and the air
still calm – and the desolate peak
and moors – motionlefs for many a league,
but for the spots of white – which were
'amies. one knew. – and were sometimes
to be seen to move.
I always – even in my naughtiest times – had
a way of praying on hill summits, when
I could get quiet on them.;.. so I knelt
on a bit of rock to pray ▬▬▬▬ [3]– and
there came suddenly into my mind the
clause of the Litany – "for all that travel
by land or water, &c. So I prayed it,
and you can't think what a strange intense
meaning it had up there – one felt
so much more the feeblenefs of the feeble:
there, where all was wild & strong.
and the[re f][4] "show thy pity on all prisoners
and captives" came so wonderfully
where I had the feeling of absolutely
boundlefs liberty – ~~no end of~~ I could
rise from kneeling – and dash away
to any quarter of heaven – east or west
or south or north – with leagues of
moorland tossed one after another
like sea waves.
Then I got up. and set to my hammering
in earnest: hiding the bits I wanted
to carry down in various nest-holes
and heaps, and putting signal stones
by them. for I'm going to take a
pony up with panniers to morrow –
to bring all down. Presently the
clouds came down to purpose – as dark
as some of our London fogs – and
it began to rain too; but the air still
so mild that I went on with my
work for about two hours; and
then sauntered down as leisurely as
I had come up; I did not get back
to the inn till seven; – (just as [you][5]
mama and you were sitting down to

3. A word has been entirely obscured by ink, 1.8 x 0.5 cm.
4. This word is blotted.
5. This word is blotted.

dinner, I had come out of the cloud on
Skiddaw shoulder – and while you weer
dining, I was sau trotting down his
flank over soft bosses of turf set with
ling.)
I've ate just the least tiny bit too much
at dinner, though – one gets frightfully
hungry from eight oclock to seven –
– and here's Crawley come to say it's
bed-time, before I've got half said that
I wanted to say.
Friday morning. I was'nt all the evening
writing this, though – I had another letter
to write.
Your ~~lovely~~ ^{dear} little note just came – It was
very teazing for you to have two letters
before the one came to put me under
right impression again.

18. 17–19 August 1867, Keswick

Keswick 17th August. 6. 7
Evening.

My darling itie Fitie

I'm so glad my letters have
made you happy. I did write them
carefully, thinking of what my itie 'amie
was feeling. (and I know, pretty well.)
But they're all true – though I chose among
true things, what I thought would
comfort itie 'amie the most.[1]
You would hardly think it, but I'm
very uncomfortable myself, with losing
count of my days. – the new 1. 2. 3
seems to go on so dedful slow. . I was
very miserable yesterday, I could'nt tell
why. but nothing gave me the least
pleasure. Today, it poured of rain all
day long. I had left some stones that
I wanted on Skiddaw top, so I

thought I might as well go and fetch
them. I got a rough pony, and a little
boy
to ride him, between two saddlebags
for the stones. and started at 12 oclock,
[^{Crawley & all 2}
– The rain got heavier every foot we
mounted. – and when we got to the
shoulder of flat moor, under the summit,
the cloud was as thick as London fog,
and I had to go by my compass.
– I struck the path for the summit without
an error of ten feet – after a mile's ^ ^{walking}
[straight
into the cloud.
The wind got fierce near the top,
and the little boy – (– in a far away way
he was like Rosie) – got rather frightened
and cold. I left him in as sheltered
a place as I could find – with Crawley
to take care of him – & went on to the
top myself – The rain was crashing
among the shingle like a water spout
but the wind, strangely enough, lulled
~~near~~ ^{just at} the summit – and I stopped a little
while then – in my usual way –
– I was wet through of course –
all about the limbs, so I could
kneel down on the stones without
caring. Then I dug up the stone I had
hidden, & came back to Crawley and
the boy – and found some more of my nests
and filled my saddlebags and braced up
the little fellow between them, and cheered
him up, ^{too} and, ^ ^{and I'm going to give him a suit of}
[^{clothes tomorrow.} set off downwards. I saw
him safe acrofs the moor into the
regular horse path – and then left him
to Crawley and came down myself by
a short cut – It rained worse at the top
than it had done at the bottom – and

Letter 18. 14/18, 1867. Paper: first of three letters embossed with a fleur-de-lis on the top left corner.
   Envelope: red sealingwax; addressed to 'Mifs Joanna Agnew, / Denmark Hill / .S. London.'
   Postmarked: 'A / KESWICK / AU 18 /67' (front); 'LONDON-S / 7 C / AU19 / 67' (back).
   Pencil notations: (all on the envelope) 'Portinscale' then (upside-down) 'Askew's Dungeon Ghill
   / Inn Upper Langdale / Cumberland –'. Part of the 18 August section of this letter is reproduced
   in 36.538–39.
  1. This is a reference to the long narrative letters of previous days. See, for example, 15 August 1867
     [17].
  2. The words 'Crawley & all' cross onto the following page. Ruskin has circled this note with two
     lines to separate it from the main body of the next page.

when I got down again – it rained at
the bottom worst of all! I got home
by ½ past four – dined at 5 and had
nearly a pint of sherry – ^ gave boy a basin of hot
[soup. rich & fine now I've had
tea too, and am very jolly. What beasts
we are! Yesterday – ^ doing nothing, & drinking
[little, in spite of all
self-examination & lecturing and proper
thinking – I was utterly wretched – to-day,
I've had a wetting and a pint of sherry,
[& I'm all right
Sunday morning. 18th Aug.
It's very odd, I always feel so much better
after these wet days than after dry ones.
I'm as fresh as a daisy – this morning.
– Not much inclined to go to church, though –
– but I shall – and see what is said to me –
For you and Auntie have, I doubt not,
been triumphing over me in a way which
you hav'nt the least businefs to do. For,
first – I suppose you read the things
which happened to me last Sunday as
if they meant that I was always to
go to church[3] – But I read them, at
present – quite differently – I read them
"If you intend to go to church, you are not
to fail in that proposed duty – because you
are anxious about your letters; but you are
quite right in questioning whether it is
good for you to go to church at all."
And this is at present a very principal
question with me.
[Alas][4] – I notice in one of your late letters some
notion that I am coming to think the
Bible the "word of God" – because I use
it – out of Rosie's book – for daily teaching,[5]

2[6]
(N.B, verse for to day, Ps. 47. 7.)
– But I never was farther from thinking
– and never can be nearer to, thinking, any
[thing
of the sort. Nothing I could ever persuade
me that God writes vulgar Greek. If an
angel all over peacock's feathers were
to appear in the bit of blue sky now
over Castle Crag – and to write on it
in star letters – "God writes vulgar Greek" –
I should say – "You are the Devil, peacock's
feathers and all. .
If there is any divine truth at all in the
mixed collection of books which we call
a Bible, that truth is, that the Word of
God comes directly to different people in
different ways; and may do so to you or
to me, to-day. and has nothing whatever
to do with printed books, and that on
the contrary, people may read that same
collection of printed books all day long
all their lives, and never, through all their
lives hear ^ or receive one syllable of "God's
word".
That crofs in the sky was the word of God
to you – as far as I can at present suppose
anything, in such matters – at all events
it may have been – And in the clouds of
19th July – and the calm sky
of last Monday morning[7] – theer
may have been the Word of God to me.
And continually, by and through the
words of any book ^ in which we reverently
expect divine teaching, in, the Word
of God may come to us: and because
I love Rosie so, I think God does

---

3. The letter referred to, from the previous Sunday (11 August), is not in L 33.
4. This might read 'Also'.
5. Rose La Touche published 'a small devotional book' entitled *Clouds and Light*. It, however, was not published until 1870 (15.417n). Nor was Ruskin referring to a manuscript copy, as the biblical verses he references to 'Rosie's book', for example Ps. 47. 7 ('For God *is* the king of all the earth: / Sing praises with understanding'), are not cited in *Clouds and Light*. Presumably the book referred to is a gift she gave him. Typically, Cook and Wedderburn excised the mention of Rose from their transcription (36.538).
6. This is Ruskin's pagination for this long letter. As he began the second and third sheets of paper, he wrote the corresponding number in the top right corner.
7. There is no extant letter from that Monday (12 August). Similarly, although he mentioned 19 July (above), the letters in L 33 jump from 9 to 22 July. Yet, this letter implies there had been correspondence on these dates which described a revelation.

teach me, every morning, by her lips, through her book. at all events, I know I get good by believing this But one mu<u>s</u>t above all things be cautious of allowing one's vanity to meddle in the matter – or of expecting a perpetual Divine help and interferences. Most peoples religion is so inwoven with their vanity that it ^ [their religion] becomes the [worst thing about them. There was a trial in the papers only the other day about a woman who had her head turned by having 500,000 pounds left her – She said she was the Holy Ghost, and whenever she went into church – said – "If only the people knew who I am!"

[8]{My wee, busy, useful pussie, cuzzies own wee pussie – please as far as you can arrange at once the following matters for me.[9]

I. I shall not be able to go with M[r] Richmond[10] to see pictures – I am resolved to see and do nothing whatever that I can help that I should <u>like</u> to ± and I should mightily have liked that –

+ I mean – of serious things. of course I shall like to take 'amies to see heathers – and the second piece of busine<u>f</u>s is

II. Please accept with heartiest gratitude the kind offer to get [us] archbishops permission to run in heather – but that George may know what he's about – & whom he's letting into consecrated ground – read him the end of this letter (no – don't – but tell him the sense of it.)[11]

III. I shall be delighted to see Willie whenever he can come, or likes to.

(Julia would get my letter yesterday morning.)}[12]

Well – I've been to church, and have made up my mind that I shall continue to go – – First; you see, the psalms for the day seemed to go straight at what I was troubling me in numbering the days. (90, 12th, and 15th.)

[and the 91st had m<u>any</u> things in it for me and the 92nd, 4th is was always an old standard verse of mine. – Well – [then] came the Obadiah & Elijah chapter – which fell in with much that I had been thinking about the fight I should have with the clergymen – – showing how priests of Baal really <u>believe</u> <u>their own</u> mission, and have to be [exposed and] ^ killed out of it – <u>can't</u> be put to [shame in their own hearts – I got a great deal too – out of all the chapter – the rainy bits – especially. Then in the second lesson, the bit about Timotheus' father being Greek, & Paul's giving way to the usele<u>f</u>s matter of form, was very useful to me. and other things – too many to speak of.[13] I got dreamy during the Litany – looking at a man who was saying it all quite straight off, and yawning, like to split himself, meanwhile. Then, they sang – (and you know the music's lovely). the 23rd Psalm – "the Lord himself, the mighty Lord", &c which was nice for me, only I had nearly

gone into a ^violent fit of – quite out –
[laughing
by unluckily thinking when they came to "cool shades, and where

---

8. This bracket (1 cm high) encompasses two lines.
9. This is the first instance of Ruskin providing his cousin with a numbered list of tasks. Later in their relationship, he would tend to herald these with 'businefs' or 'business'.
10. Probably George Richmond (1809–96), a painter and good friend of Ruskin from 1840. See Bradley and Ousby, p. 29n.
11. The bracket encompasses both lines of this afterthought on the left, but only the second line on the right.
12. This flared bracket corresponds with the one at the beginning of his business list and closes off this section of the letter.
13. Cook and Wedderburn identify these readings as 1 Kings 18 and Acts 16 (36.539).

Refreshing[14] waters flow" – of the top of Skiddaw the day before! I had to bite my lips dedful hard – and if anybody was looking they must have been shocked past all wonder.

Well – there wasn't much more till the sermon – which was upon the Bible's being a Revelation – and it ^(the sermon) was so abominably bad that it came to me as a distinct farther assertion of the Bible's being no such thing, – and the more I looked at the man, the more his ^face seemed to me like one of the ugly faces under the cathedral gutters, spouting out dirty water, – pure once, but defiled by them and the dirt of ^inside the leaden gutter they stick on – and I felt how completely here was a priest of Baal. – who wanted extinction as soon as might be, And I yet the man quite believed in himself. and in all he was saying – or trying to say. And then I came away – on the whole much helped and taught. and satisfied that from that Rosie's rose day. I was mean't to go to Church again. So I'll take you to M̅ʳ Bridges on this day[15] week – God willing. and I'm ever your own loving cuzzie
                                            J Ruskin.

It's a lovely day. and I'm going to have some dinner now. and then row about among the lovely rocks of the lake shore, till sunset.[16]

Miſs Bell[17] is sending me some money from Winnington – I told her to register the half notes to you – as I don't know if they would come safe
    in time to Langdale – where I'm going
    back on [Tuesday].
    When you get them, write to say
    you have – & the other halves will come

---

14. Ruskin amended 'refreshing' to 'Refreshing'.
15. St. Matthew's Camberwell, where Rev. S. F. Bridge preached (36.141n).
16. This message ends here, halfway down the page. It resumes at the middle of the following page.
17. Margaret Alexis Bell, head of Winnington Hall, Chester, a school for girls. Ruskin first visited the school in February 1859 and by April of that year he had lent the school £500; 'by 1867 he had paid out £1,130 15s 4d to Miss Bell' (Batchelor, pp. 200–01). Presumably Miss Bell had expressed her intention to return some of what she had borrowed.

1868

Joan's engagement to Percy La Touche is broken off
R. makes his final stay at Winnington Hall
R. visits France with his American friend Charles Eliot Norton, October

19. 1 January 1868, Denmark Hill

Denmark Hill. s.
1st January. 1868

My dearest wee Doanie

I like to write you a little
notie the first day of the year – and
I begin my care of you, which,
I hope will be both wiser &
more succefsful in 1868 than in
1867 – by peeping at a letter
which felt heavy, to see that it
was a nice one. and would'nt
spoil mine by being inside it.
– It seems (inscrutably) nice – as to
the meaning of it I'm as wise
as before I tore the envelope
I've got everything into order. and
have filled the rooms with dust
by sending Maria[1] to do her worst
in all my dens, one after
the other. I'm a half choked
– though exemplarily tidy – cuzzie
in consequence
I'm rather dismal – between the
weather – and the dust – & losing
Doanie. and might spoil
my own note – like the worst
enclosure I could put in it

– if I enclosed any more of myself.
– Love to Connie & Ettie.[2]
Ever your aff.e Cuzzie
J Ruskin

20. 3 January 1868, Denmark Hill

Denmark Hill, s.
3rd Jany. 1867[1]

My dearest Wee Doanie

We have your kind little
notes and are glad you are happy
Give my love and thanks for you
to Newton[2] and to Mifs Severn.
I forgot Walter[3] was not in town
and carried him a pretty bouquet
yesterday. but luckily asked for him
at the door – and carried it on
to Mrs Simons.[4]
The Simons dissuaded me from
Sending yesterday what I mean't
to send. It matters little. I did
as they desired.
There is a little letter for you; but
I read it, and it was so slight
and frivolous that it could not have
given you pleasure – and might
have given you pain.. I keep it for you.

Autograph letters for 1868 are in 'Bem L 33 / Letters / John Ruskin / to / Joan Severn / 1864–8'.

Letter 19. 1/78, 1868. Envelope: red sealingwax; addressed to 'Mifs Agnew / The Revd. J. Hilliard's / Cowley Rectory / Uxbridge'. Postmarked: 'LONDON-S. / X / JA [1] / 68 (front); 'UXBRIDGE / A / [J]A 2 / [6]8' (back).
1. One of the Ruskins' housemaids.
2. Constance and Ethel Hilliard, with whom Joan Agnew was spending the New Year at Cowley Rectory.

Letter 20. 3/78, 1868. Pencil notations: 'See allusions to Cowley & / Walter Severn in letter of / Jan 2' and '1868' is written above Ruskin's incorrect '1867'.
1. This was Rose La Touche's twentieth birthday. Because he thought this letter 'too dismal', Ruskin delayed posting it until at least the fifth, see 4 January 1868.
2. Charles Newton, Keeper of the Greek and Roman Antiquities at the British Museum (Burd, *Winnington*, p. 392n); married to Arthur Severn's sister Mary (*Later*, p. 130).
3. Walter Severn, an artist and brother to Arthur Seven.
4. Probably Jane Simon, wife of Dr (Sir) John Simon, good friends of Ruskin.

On no account write any more.
and remember that no one – except
in mockery, can be called a vice-
mother,[5] who wilfully hurts your real
vice-father.
After a singularly painful day
yesterday, I slept soundly. and
dreamed of going up to the ridge
of a hill whence I saw the whole
lake of Constance in bright blue
crisped waves, with mountains
beyond – fifty miles into the clear
distance
I have not had so lovely a dream
since that night when I failed
at the Royal Institution; and
I woke, as I thought, refreshed:
– but ^ in reality so utterly exhausted that I
could not paint – even in this
bright day. and fell into the
strangest depression – unconquerable.
– At last I went out and ran
for an hour round the garden
and am better. but it is very
bad for me to be without you
just now – I have no one to
tell me when I make bad faces:
and the sense of my mothers
lonelinefs weighs on me all day
long – like a quilt[6] – in my own
employments I hope to send you
a nice letter to Cowley.
– You could not expect a nice
one to day – but never mind.
– and enjoy yourself this evening.
and things will soon be righter
     Ever your loving Cuzzie
             J Ruskin

21. 4 January 1868, Denmark Hill

Denmark Hill, s.
                4th

My dearest Cuzzie
    Thank you for sweet letter
Send me a delightful account
of yesterday.
    I had a hard day of it –
till evening. but Patmore's[1]
dinner relieved me greatly. It was
simple – and every way right – with
ev nothing to give me any pang.
(– Not a wafer in the room – though
he's a Catholic.) – and only
six people altogether – A cheerful & affectionate
host – who never spoke one word
that was not interesting – & few that
were not amusing – an equally kind
hostefs – exquisitely silent, in content
that I liked to listen to her husband
better than to talk to her. Beside
me, the author of this [Talumed][2] article
an entirely gentle – soul-ful and
learned man – + opposite me – a
man of great intelligence and
good humour, making a fool
of himself ^ through vanity just to the extent
which gave me a delicious
feeling of superiority and to prevented
me from suffering from my
usual crushed sensation – but
not to the disquieting extent of
ordinary people in society –
– and a soft featured, gentle eyed
girl of sixteen, who liked what
I said better than what he
said – but only said so with
her eyes.
Now I call that rather nice?

---

5. Possibly Maria La Touche, mother of Joan Agnew's fiancé Percy.
6. This should perhaps read '[q/guilt], since Ruskin added an extra squiggle to 'quilt', making it read equally as 'guilt'.

Letter 21. 4/78, 1868. Pencil notations: '?Jan 1868'. Envelope: red sealingwax; addressed to 'Mifs Joanna Agnew. / The Rev'. J. Hilliard's / Cowley Rectory / Uxbridge'. Postmarked: 'LONDON-S. / X / JA [4] / 68' (front); 'UXBRIDGE / A / JA 5 [6]8' (back). Pencil notations on the envelope, 'John Ruskin Esq' (up the front left side) and '[maid] 2/', 'Ticket 5/', 'Geord 2/', '[keys] 7/6-', '16' '18-' (sideways, in a column down the middle back).
1. Coventry Patmore, the poet.
2. He must mean 'Talmud'.
3. Rose La Touche's birthday.

I am so very thankful you feel
so well in health – Stay as
long as you like – I miss you
sadly, but now that I've
weathered the 3rd3 I shall do.
– I wrote you a letter – to send
to Gower St. but it was too
dismal. You shall have it
tomorrow however. Auntie's love

    Ever your loving Cuzzie. J R.

Love to them all.

+He told me such a magnificent
bit of Jewish drama about
Rachel!

22. 8 January 1868, Denmark Hill

Denmark Hill, s.
    8th.

Dearest wee Doanie

    I enclose two letters, both
pretty and interesting. If you
really would like to come on
Friday, of course I shall
rejoice to g have you; but Saturday
would do quite well – for you know
I <u>must</u> force myself into the habit
of living alone, now; (for you're sure
to be married to somebody before
you know where you are. –) and
this bit of bitter practice in the
dark days – I've got a dreadful
cold too – (caught it out at dinner
on the 3rd.!)[1] is good for me – but
mama and I are getting on very
nicely now – fitting <u>in</u>.
Of course I can't come down to
Cowley, and it would be absurd
to send the carriage all that way
in this snow, when the railroad
will bring you with only an hour's

cold. So send me word to morrow
when the carriage shall meet
you – & where.
    Ever your loving cuzzie
            J R.
I am quite stupid with cold
and dismalnefs.+ Your letters
are delightful. Love to Connie
& Ettie[2]
I've only one malicious consolation
– Connie can't be skating <u>to-day</u>.

23. 4 March 1868, Denmark Hill

Denmark Hill, s.
    4th March. 1868.

My dearest wee 'Amie,
    You have always one great joy
on your birthday, the privilege of thinking
truly that other people are rather to be
congratulated upon it than you. I will
take upon me to day – therefore – the duty
of congratulating Everybody – and particularly
the little Crossing sweepers. And all I will
say of those little protege's of yours. is that I
think they set a very good example to the
public, in sweeping – not crofsings only,
but wherever they can carry a Broom.
– though I <u>might</u> say – (if I were a sulky
Cuzzie) – that since <u>you</u> have gone up
and down the hill, I find the Sweepers
more in the way than the Mud used to be.

I make you a poor little present, (though
indeed – the poorest present to my wee 'amie
would be any foolish trinket that thought
it could make her look prettier!) This is only a
foolish trinket that will try to amuse her.
– Respecting which however she may
sometimes. not improfitably reflect
1. That the great virtue of Kinghood is to
   be unmoved on attack

Letter 22. 7/78, 1868. Pencil notations: 'Jan.', '1868'. Envelope: red sealingwax; addressed to 'Mifs
    Agnew. / The Revd J. Hilliard's / Cowley Rectory / Uxbridge'. Postmarked: 'LONDON-S /
    X / JA 8 / 68' (front); 'UXBRIDGE / A / [J]A 9 / 68' (back).
    1. The dinner on 3 January was with the poet Coventry Patmore, see 4 January 1968 [21].
    2. Constance and Ethel Hilliard.

Letter 23. 10/78, 1868. Paper: lightweight. Envelope: lightweight; red sealingwax; addressed to 'My
    Wee ''Amie' in the middle with '4th March. 1868.' centred at the bottom.; part of this letter is
    reproduced in 36.548.

2. That the worthiest person on the field is a woman.
3. That Knights are active creatures who never let anything stand in their way,
4. That Bishops are people who never look – or move – straight. before them.
5. That Castles may not unwisely be built in the air, if they are carried by an Elephant – who is the type of prudence. And that a Castle which has been uselefs on one side – may usefully pass to the other.
6. That Pawns and Patience can do anything,
7th – and generally, That when things are seem-[1] -ingly at the worst, they may often mend – that we should always look well about us; – and that every body is wrong who is'nt helping every body else within his reach.
Finally my wee amie – let me hope for you that in all things as in chefs, you may bear an equal mind in loss or conquest – and remain your gentle self in both. Ever your loving Cuzzie
J Ruskin.

24. 5 June 1868, Denmark Hill

5th June

My dearest wee Pussie
Here is George's letter – all worth careful reading.
You say – can I find nothing for Pussie to do for me.
Yes. I can find a great deal – after Pussie comes back – Such hard work!

as never a Pussie had before – I don't think any Pussie but my own Pussie could do it at all! But nothing under yonder obelisk[1] – or in the Will-o-the Wisp places.
Send me a letter – however short, every day. I can't do without one at breakfast. – so I find.
Ever my dearest wee Doanie
Your loving
J Ruskin.

25. 6 June 1868, Denmark Hill

Denmark Hill, s.
6th June. 1868

My darling wee Doanie,
I have your long, sweet, letter, which is a great comfort to me already.. – but you must be of more. I have let you be as happy as I could, as long as I could; but there is something very dark happening ———,[1] and I want you here; and that speedily. You shall return to mama and Kate as soon as pofsible; but I need you just now more than they do.[2] Yet do not be afraid and miserable about me as you come: – you see how steady my hand is: I have none of the feverish retlefsnefs of the old distrefs now: but have set my mind simply to do the best I can, whatever happens: only the loneliefs, and necessity of being more or lefs cheerful to my mother, is ᵃʳᵉ too heavy upon me; and

---

1. Ruskin appears to have added 'seem-ingly' and squeezed it into the margins at both edges of the paper.

Letter 24. 15/78, 1868. Paper: half a sheet. Pencil notations: '1868'. Envelope: embossed with 'F. GRIFFITHS. POST OFFICE, CAMBERWELL GREEN.' and spray of three flowers; addressed to 'Mifs Agnew / Mrs G. Agnew / Wigtown / N. B.' Postmarked: 'LONDON-S. [E.] / 2 / JU 5 / 68' (front); 'NEWTON-STEWART / B / JU 6 / 68', 'WIGTOWN / [O] / JU [6] /1868' (back).
1. See 3 June 1868 (14/78, 1868 – not transcribed) for the first mention of this obelisk in Wigtown where the cousins seem to have shared an important conversation in 1867.

Letter 25. 16/78, 1868.
1. Here, the word is entirely obscured by a layer of ink measuring 2.3 x 0.3 cm. I assume this material has been obscured by a later reader; Ruskin typically would strike a word through, leaving it legible, or draw attention to his excision if he obscured it entirely.
2. Ruskin was encouraging Joan to return to him from her mother and sister at Wigtown. He seems to have been successful, as the next clearly dated letter is that of 25 August 1868 (not transcribed).

you must come back, for a little while.
Leave by the earliest <u>convenient</u> train
after you get this – and send me
word by telegram what train you
will come by, that I may meet
you at the station.
    Love to Mama & Kate; – I wish
I had any means of making up to
them for this cruel theft of you.
– but it <u>must</u> be, for a little while.
for if I <u>did</u> break down – you none
    of you would be pleased with me
for not sending for you.
I was at my "Paradise Row", yesterday
with Mifs Hill!³ The smell of
the stale filth is in my nostrils
yet – What an awful place!.
    Ever my darling
        Your loving cuzzie
            J Ruskin

26. 26 August 1868, Abbeville

        Abbeville. Wednesday
          26th (?) Aug. 1868.

Dearest wee Pussie
    Thank you for charming envelope &
charming letter. If anything could
startle or sadden me in that old way,
I never should have a quiet hour.
The first fishing boat I saw in Boulogne
harbour was. "Rose Mysterieuse"!
(– Did you ever hear of such a name for
a boat before?) – And here, my first
sketch is at the "Pont d'Amour"
I take it all now – with the rest of life
as a jest, or a dream, – in which one
has to make the best of the passing
moment.

At the passing moment, there is a bone
of muttonchop left from breakfast – very ill
got at by blunt knife – remaining a ruin
of mangled brown leather and torn fat
with a bloom of cold fat all over it.
Now, if I were living in my proper simple life
I should be able to walk, myself
or send pussie, into the kitchen – and
take the gridiron – and toast my
bone thereupon ∧ like Achilles till it was as
dainty again as at first. But
as it is, I send it disconsolately
away, and unlefs it gets put
into somebody else's soup – only
the dogs are likely to benefit by it.

I have a sad little letter from
Lily. – but getting one from
her at all, and one from you,
brightens the already bright morning
The weather is heavenly.
    Ever – with love to Mama
        Your loving Cuzzie
           J Ruskin

If you have not yet written to
Lily, don't write till you hear
from here – or write as knowing
her to be in great fear for her father.¹

I ∧ will enclose a	
new Franc. , tomorrow²	– it would have
Look, with your	disappointed
most powerful lens	you to-day
at the work on the	with thick letter
drapery – covered with	
<u>bees</u>, the old bearing	
of the French.	
I never saw such	
minute work in	
any coin	

---

  3. Batchelor identifies this as 'Paradise Place, off Marylebone High Street, a semi-derelict slum property which Octavia restored [...and] managed on his behalf' (p. 283). Octavia Hill was an aspiring artist when Ruskin met her in the mid-1850s. She was, by 1868 an active social reformer and later became a founder of the National Trust.

Letter 26. 22/78, 1868. Paper: this and all the letters from Abbeville of 1868 are on lightweight paper.
  1. The letter resumes in the bottom half of the next page. The Lily is assumed to be Lily Armstrong.
  2. See 3 September 1868 for an account of his attempt to send the coin [28].

27. 27 August 1868, Abbeville

Abbeville. Thursday
27th Aug. 1868

My dearest wee Doanie
I wonder what – at your fine Scotch breakfast, you would have said, could you have seen mine this morning as first served.
There was an oval tea-tray, just about the size of the bottom of one of our largest dish-covers. – painted vermilion and the paint worn through in ragged holes, the whole disguised with veil of long dirt and discolouring. On this was set – an old teapot of grey metal – a bowl of milk – slop bowl size – one table spoon – one knife, a French roll, ,butter, and some beet-root sugar. in square cakes, After all – it does not read so ill – the bread and milk alone were an excellent breakfast. but on its dirty tray. with no teacup, no plate and only one huge spoon, it had not a brilliant effect.
I have your pretty little note from the Gladstones.[1] So many thanks. How I did wish^ for you in the market place yesterday. to see a travelling dentist – dressed en Turque[2] – a splendid fellow – – with a little Turk boy and a "Turcowoman," on the top of his omnibus-built carriage – fifing and drumming the liveliest tunes while people were being cured of the Toothache below. – and enchanted with brilliant talk of affairs in Algeria – and the teeth of the Turks.[3]

I am getting on pretty well. The quiet is certainly doing me good.
Ever my dearest Pussie
Your affectionate J Ruskin

28. 3 September 1868, Abbeville

Vain hope! like all the rest!.
They would'nt register coins at the post office. I keep it for home

Abbeville
3rd Sept. 1868.

My dearest wee Doanie
Here is, I hope,[1] your franc at last: – but I am so fitened, betause so many – many wee bees might eat wee pussie moos up all, and more – pease ite soon and tell poo tuzzie
oo it all tafe.
And what oo tink? – Me found pussie moos own tick, behind laundry door – own own white tick! and me bought it to beat nasty Fench with – and it so pitty, me no like. and Fench so naughty – make poo tuzzie all so coss, as coss as <u>two</u> ticks[2]
So poo tuzzie went & bought other tick – and now he teep wee pussie's tick all tafe. till she come back. When is she coming?

It is such heavenly weather, almost too <u>hot</u>, to let one draw well, but I get a nice little time twice every day, only the subjects here have a terrible quantity of work in them – and here's Market-day come round again! and I can't write a word more

Letter 27. 23/78, 1868. Paper: lightweight.
1. The family of Rt. Hon. William Ewart Gladstone. Ruskin occasionally visited them and became a good friend to his daughter Mary; although Ruskin was also sometimes very critical of her father.
2. Here Ruskin uses the French 'en Turque' rather than the English 'Turk' as below.
3. There are a number of letters referring to Joan Agnew's toothaches, the first is on 8 May 1865 [6].

Letter 28. 27/78, 1868. Paper: lightweight. This is the first letter to be at least half in baby-talk.
1. There is a line here, connecting to the postscript above, which begins 'Vain hope!'
2. See 28 September 1866 for the last time he engaged in word-play around the phrase 'as cross as two sticks' [11].

Ever my dearest Puss,
 Your loving Cuzzie
  J Ruskin

There was a grand – open faced, red-complexioned, market^-garden woman sitting in the square yesterday – a woman came with a little child, – who while his mother was making her bargain played with the heaps of onions, rolling them all about. The market woman took no notice for ever so long – at last with a face all radiant with good humour she turned on the child – "Veux tu bien me laisser les oignons – <u>brigand</u>.!"

29. 9 September 1868, Abbeville

Abbeville 9th Sept. 1868.

Dearest wee Pussie
 I'm so glad the smallest wee Pussie has been brought back. I wish somebody would bring <u>my</u> wee pussie back to me. Do you think, if I were to send the bellman round Scotland, she would be brought back?
I had such a curious dream last night of some one whom I have not seen these thirty years, coming back –
I suppose it was only eating more mushrooms than was proper for itie pigs.
 When itie pigs eat too much mush –
 Room, itie pigs have cause to blush.
 And, like those mushrooms upside down,
 Show pink beneath their paley-brown!¹

Ever my dear Pussie
 Your affec. itie Pig.
  J Ruskin

30. 14 September 1868, Abbeville

Abbeville
Sept 14th. 1868

My dearest wee Pufsie
 Monsieur Pencil – , qui est artiste – ayant commencè un dessin d'un bel effet de sechèresse,¹ le petit zephir s'amuse a ł lui jeter de la poussiere a la figure – et a lui blanchir ainsi, les favoris.²

And that's pretty nearly all the news I can give you to-day. for I'm changing my Inn, and from the Hotel de France – like a true Briton I am going to the Bull's Head.³ For the Bull's head, as I discovered the other day from the tower of the cathedral, has a beautiful antique courtyard – and is a four turreted chateau – no less – so that I expect a corner room as at Belgarde.
But I've busy morning. and the letters don't <u>come</u> till late – so I enclose an old Froude,⁴ which please take care of for me – and you'll have something to do in making out my French and his writing. – till to morrow – and
 I am my dearest Pussie
 Ever your loving Cuzzie
  J Ruskin

Letter 29. 30/78, 1868. Paper: lightweight.
 1. See 15 September 1868 [31] for his mention of her response to this poem.

Letter 30. 35/78, 1868. Paper: lightweight.
 1. Ruskin has placed the accent on the wrong 'e'. He often does so, but in this instance it forms a pun, turning the central section into '-chère-' meaning 'dear'.
 2. [Mr Pencil, who is an artist, having begun to dry a drawing, the little zephyr is amusing itself by throwing dust onto the illustration, and thus whitened his favourites.]
 3. When Ruskin discovered an inn he liked, he tended to return to it. In fact, when Arthur Severn accompanied Ruskin to Abbeville in 1888 – Ruskin's last Continental journey – he wrote to Joan from the 'Tête de Boeuf. Abbeville' where he was staying with Ruskin (?20 June 1888, Ruskin Library MS – L64). The two undated letters written by Arthur from here in 1888 are distressing to read, with lines such as 'but between ourselves I am dreadfully bored sometimes, as I did not want to come away [to France] so early' and 'In this Hotel the Coz [Ruskin] has his old room now, and had a nice fire last night – it was so cold – I am keeping abroad as long as I can stand it – to be of service to you'.
 4. James Anthony Froude, editor of *Fraser's Magazine* and, eventually, biographer of Carlyle (Batchelor, p. 246).

31. 15 September 1868, Abbeville

        Hotel of Beef-Head. Abbeville –
          – 15th 'Eptember.
           – s 'ixty-ate.

Dearest wee pussie.
    Me so glad ~~you~~ oo ike wee piggie-wig 'oetry: me tink him bery pity too. – 'ony me too coss to ite so mut as me oosed – but me mut, for pussy moos. 'ometimes.

I've changed my inn – and am living really just as I thought – in a litt<u>le</u> castellated suite of rooms, ending in a turret stair! and with a quiet court to look into, with exquisite convolvulus', running up the whole two stories of it on strings, and running at last along the leaden gutter of the roof – looking over its edge with their purple bells, and mixed all the way up, with scarlet runners – so <u>very</u> beautiful.

The weather is lovely again – it has been almost too good, for it has made Mr Pencil, qui est artiste, draw a little too much, day after day. . and itie pigs 'ont det fat – as sey sood, if sey was ood.

Itie pig 'ought it [–][1] must go back to Hotel of France, – at first – for the Soup was <u>so</u> greasy – but all the rest of dinner very 'ice. So itie pig 'ote this 'oetry about 'oup.

" When itie pigs have had their peace
  Of mind disturbed, by soup, with grease,
  (White globes afloat in pottage thin,
  With bread, all holes, besopped therein,
  As if – to aid the Cook-maid's toil
  Each hole had held its ~~globe~~ ^{orb} of oil.)
  And can't – because their state of ang-
  -Ger, checks their fluent foreign twang,–
  Arrive at any form of slang,
  Except a simple English "Dang
  This too much Grace and too much Pang." –
  Then, itie Pigs – – should check their wish.
  To sup of that obnoxious dish,
  And pass, at once, from Fat, to Fish.

        ———

Since all admit that it is well,
That itie pigs should wisely spell.
I hope my pussie pig will see
That Anger's spelt with Double G,
Because the double g was Nes-
-cessary, like this[2] gratis S,
To give the rhyme its proper stress.

Wee. pussie has not said a word about her fall – I hope all is going on quite rightly.
    Ever my dearest puss,
        Your affectionate Cuzzie
          J Ruskin

32. 18 September 1868, Abbeville

    Abbeville, 18th Sept.
      1868.

Dearest wee Pussie
    Yes. I should like to go and stay with Froude;[1] but, Pussie ^{dear,} because I write play-letters; you must not think that I am or can be, what I used to be. When you come back, I am going to arrange all things very differently, and to be sure that we both do some thorough work, advancing and profitable, every day; and <u>mine</u> must be interrupted no more for anything. I feel the waste of the last years very fatally. and consider the question as to claims of society upon me to be now ended. – I shall live my own life, to my own mind – and it cannot be in visiting any body – not even Froude.

Letter 31. 36/78, 1868. Paper: lightweight.
    1. This mark has been blotted, but was probably an 's' for 'should'.
    2. There is a broken line connecting 'this' to the 'S' at the end of the previous line.

Letter 32. 38/78, 1868. Paper: lightweight.
    1. James Anthony Froude (1818–94), a historian and biographer whose correspondence with Ruskin began in 1862, Viljoen, *The Froude-Ruskin Friendship: As Represented through Letters* (New York: Pageant, 1966).

I hope we shall both be very
happy in the steady employment
– We always were, when we got
well into it – and I am sure grandmama
will be happier – and we must think
of her now – if we ever are to – very
tenderly.

    Ever my dearest Pussie

        Your affectionate Cuzzie
            J Ruskin

33. 22 September 1868, Abbeville

        Abbeville
    Tuesday. 22nd September
           1868

Dearest wee Pussie
    I had a nice little square
or squarish – note from you last night
so prettily directed! – I am very grateful
to you for your good – as well as frequent
writing – You say, my last letter
gave you so much to think of. I don't
know if it was that one talking of
the new way I want to set about things
when you come home – Look here – as
somebody used to say. You enjoy yourself
and give much more than enjoyment
to others, in society at present – but
that will not last, nor, from what I
see of people – is it much worth one's
while to secure! – their insecure – fancies
and esteems – or to assist their passing
pleasures. So far as you can do this
in accordance with others and really
useful work – well – But no farther.
and I want you henceforward to resolve
that every day shall bring you some
true gain of knowledge or power
which can never more be taken from
you; and ^ that each day shall be made useful also
by some true hand-service.
I think the happinefs you have felt
at different times, in your mathematical
drawing – your illumination – your
flower painting – and your more
tedious writing from my dictation –
– or more playful unpacking and
dusting of minerals & books. – and
perhaps most of all, in the new
ideas given you by the study
of history, may show you, now,
sufficiently in what directions the
safest, if not the highest happinefs
lies; and we will ^ both hope henceforward
to make our ^ present1 days less dependent
either on other persons, or on future hopes.
(– Not that any farther "future" would
be likely to disturb me.) and you
may have your own little Castle in
the air, beside your daily garden on the ground.

    Mr Pencil, qui est artiste – ayant trouvè
    des embarras dans son troisieme dessin,
    – se trouve aujourdhui un peu fatiguè –
    et ~~disp~~ s'amuse a faire la morale aux petites
                               [chattes.[2]

    Ever my dearest Pussie
        Your affectionate Cuzzie
            J Ruskin.

34. 23 September 1868, Abbeville

        Abbeville. 23rd Sept^r
            1868.

Dearest wee Pussie
    I am very much interested
in. those dreams of yours. and
as there is really no doubt of the

Letter 33. 41/78, 1868. Paper: lightweight.
    1. The word 'present' has been added, then blotted out.
    2. [Mr Pencil, who is an artist, having found embarrassing/frustrating aspects in is third drawing, finds himself a bit tired today and is amusing himself by writing ethical lessons for little female cats.]

Letter 34. 42/78, 1868. Paper: lightweight. Envelope: was loose in the box, but probably belongs with this or the next letter; addressed to 'Mifs Joanna Agnew / Mrs G. Agnew / Wigtown / N. B. / Angleterre'. Postmarked: 'ABBEVILLE / 23 / [C3] (76)' (front); 'PARIS A CALAIS [?] / 23 / [?] / (76)', 'NEWTON.STEWART / B / SP25 /68', 'WIGTOWN / C / SE 25 1868' (back).
    1. The '3' looks like an '8', but '23' makes more sense with 'rd' and matches the envelope which now houses the letter.

existence of certain forms of Second-sight, I should like you, among the first pieces of serious work you set in hand, to record in a separate locked book, most accurately, every instance you can hear of, with every circumstance ascertainable by investigation. I am going to set myself. very earnestly to accumulate evidence respecting such phenomena.

I think you will like to hear that I have written to Howell[2] to see to the walls. and ceilings of that HerneHill[3] House – for myself. I am going to fit up that room the [policeman] was sleeping in for a thorough mineral workroom. and the drawing room for a quiet study for myself. Bedrooms and library above – Dining and breakfast room below. This is that I may have my <u>art</u> all at Denmark Hill,[4] and my acids and dust out of the way. I shall still keep my choice agates – gold – &c. at Denmark Hill, but the coppers and flints – up the way.

Won't this be nice? We'll choose papers and carpets when you come home. & <u>rough furniture</u>

    Ever your loving Cuzzie
            J R.

No my dear, I am not <u>suffering</u>; But I am changed, <u>because</u> I <u>am not</u>; I never allow my mind to turn that way for an instant. – but this wholly incapacitates me from taking any pleasure in society – especially anything about marriage – and the sight of young girls, becomes painful to me. (I wrote a wickedly flirting letter to Dora[5] however – yesterday.)

Mr Pencil, qui est artiste, ayant bien avancè son troisieme dessin – remarque [– qu'il en est encore Content.[6]

35. 26 September 1868, Abbeville

        Abbeville
        Saturday. 26th Sept
            1868

Dearest wee ittie Fittie

I quite forgot you were a itie Fittie till I saw such a lovely one purple in the morning sunshine before breakfast to day. What do you think – itie Fitie – I've resolved – but mind – you must'nt say a word of it to Grandmama[1] – – to fit up that old house at ~~Denmark~~ ^{Herne} Hill for myself and my stones, so that I can hammer and drop acids and do no harm by dust or vapour ~~for~~ ^{to} my Turners – all my best stones however I shall keep at D. Hill – – I do believe I've told you before![2] – but I only heard to day from ^{Owl} ~~Howell~~[3] that the house was still free. And I've written back that

---

2. Charles Augustus Howell, Ruskin's secretary.
3. This was Ruskin's childhood home, here written as one word.
4. This was the home he then shared with his mother and their household.
5. Dorothy Livesey, later Lees, a student at Winnington. She was also given the pet name 'Doadie' by the cousins.
6. [Mister Pencil, who is an artist, having moved his third drawing on a pace notes that he is happy with it again.]

Letter 35. 44/78, 1868. Paper: lightweight.
1. Margaret Ruskin.
2. He had done so three days earlier, on 23 September 1868.
3. 'Howell' has been struck through by a horizontal line and two lines slanted diagonally from left to right. 'Owl' has been placed in the margin. Charles Augustus Howell was one of Ruskin's secretaries.

when you come home, itie Fitie.[4] and
Kate[5] and Owl[6] are to furnish all the
house for me! Only not a word
to Grandmama or she would set
her whole existence on having it
done by Mr Snell[7] like Buckingham
palace

I'm taking my tea, & catching the
post – so you must put up with
scrawl. –
I have your sweet letter about doings
and capacities, & dependings[8] on people
My dear – it was not tiring of work,
but wanting to play – that used to be
your misfortune – nor need you mind
having a treacherous memory – It will
always remember what truly interests it.
Are there not some things you would
fain forget – & cannot?
But it requires no memory to dust books,
to weed gardens – to plan furnishings –
to paint flowers – to illuminate – to cook –
to sew – or to write from Cuzzies dictation.
All that we ought to do – we always can.
 What we can't – we ought'nt – Ever your
  loving Cuzzie Piggie, . J R.

Of course you
may depend on
tried people –
But not for all your
happinefs – Divide it.
– Love as many as
you can – Trust
only – your mother,
& sisters – & me. –
and grandmama

in her own way.
& uncle John – in his –
& M^r [Harpfer][9] in his –
& perhaps – Georgie
a little bit – and
a little bit more – φίλη.[10]

36. 27 September 1868, Abbeville

  Abbeville
   27th September.
    1868
Dearest wee itie Fitie

 I have now been a month and
two days living this quiet life; and
I have done what will certainly be
useful, and give people pleasure; and
recovered some tone of health; and I
am resolved that I will not any more
enter into any kind of life under the
idea of courtesy or philanthropy, which
is destructive of my own power & peace.
– I had a quiet walk on the hills three
days ago; – in a lovely afternoon – and in
many of the conditions of the view it
resembled the view from the hills behind
Belgarde – and put me much in mind of
the lonely walks I used to take there
to look over to H.town.[1]
And to my utter amazement – & (I doubt
not) to yours – still more – I found I was
actually happier now, than then! I could
compare the two feelings exactly, as I
was breaking a piece of flint, for I
       [remembered
breaking a piece of conglomerate just in

---

4. Joan Agnew.
5. Probably Kate Smith, who became the 'Indoor Stewardess at Brantwood' (*Fors* (28. 520, 531) L. 62, February 1876).|
6. Charles Augustus Howell, Ruskin's secretary.
7. Snell & Son's (William and Edwin Snell), London cabinet makers favoured by John James Ruskin.
8. There is a line here extending to the next page and the postscript, which I've placed in a single column at the bottom of the letter.
9. This could be 'Harker'.
10. φίλη: 'filē', Ruskin's pet name for Georgiana Mount-Temple. At this time her surname was Cowper. She later became Cowper-Temple then Mount-Temple. Ruskin also referred to her as 'grannie' (see [156]). Note that I use the Greek letters which match Ruskin's choice of letters, rather than Φιλη, as it is generally transcribed by Ruskin scholars.

Letter 36. 45/78, 1868. Paper: lightweight.
 1. Harristown, Co. Kildare, Ireland, where Rose La Touche lived.

the same sort of place above Belgarde,
to take home as a "bit of Ireland", and
I remembered the weary desolate feeling
I had, and yet – you know, I had
the loveliest letter at that moment in
my breast pocket that could be – the
one about the flowers at the lecture.[2]
And now I have nothing; – but every
day I get a good piece of tolerably
useful work done – I have no torments –
(– except noisy streets or children in them)
– I am not plagued by talk – or see
people – and the worst I have to suffer
is an hour or two of thoughtlefs rest –
which I always wish were over – &
dinner time come.
Now – itie fitie, I wrote to you all
that about employment, because I won't
be taken out of this quiet life anymore
as long as it does me good: and I
won't see people – and I won't let
you go out often to tire yourself – but
I must get you to fall into our old
pleasant ways – and live with
old Greeks & Jews – and not with
Ps nor As.[3] nor any disturbing letters.
And I believe the Proper P or A, if he is to come at all –
will come when you are properly helping P.A, PA.

Mind – I'm not saying this in blame of you – I did all
I could to manage things nicely for you as I thought.
– it has not turned out well; now, I shall do what
I know to be good, in a smaller way; and that must
turn out well – in its own small way.
And – apropos of this, just now, will you please lose
no opportunity of doing and seeing cookery. I am more
and more daily impressed with the need of young ladies in
the humbler occupations of life, to make them all beautiful
and orderly again. – and I want you to be a subtle cook –
– Make a point of this – – not to plague yourself – but
learn all you can from mama – & whenever you come
acrofs a nice dish. enquire about it. and get a
recipe book – & write it all down.
It is the fête of the first Bishop of Amiens, St Firmin, today,
and I've sent Downes, with Crawley & Mr Ward,[4] to
Amiens, as I fancy there will be something in the
cathedral which will considerably astonish Mr Downes.
I took him such a lovely drive yesterday, under chalk hills

2. This letter was from Rose La Touche.
3. Percy La Touche and Arthur Severn, Joan Agnew's two suitors.
4. William Ward, one of his assistants on the journey.

for five miles, with woody dingles running up them, and
little cottages under tiny banks of dry turf, and winding walks
through broken thickets and over mushroomy downs, and
Itie Downes, "was out of the body".
Grand mama will be so jealous if she hears of my writing to
you every day that I'm only going to write every other day
after this – but longer letters.
When do you come back?. I have work heer for all this
month, I'm afraid.
Have you heard anything about the chances of that
   Glasgow election? I don't know even who are my
   opponents; or when it is decided.
     Love to Mama, Kate – & Buth. Ever your loving Cuzzie
                J Ruskin

Downes sits in the courtyard of the Inn, when
not otherwise employed – studying a French dictionary
He says it is so provoking not to be able to
speak – "The very dogs won't wag their tails for him".[5]

I enclose nice line
  from Mr Burgefs[6] about Downes

37. 4 October 1868, Abbeville

           Abbeville. 4th Oct

Dearest wee Itie Fitie,
  I have your nice <u>long</u> letter – and
nice little short one – asking about Typhaine
or [Typhugne] – late French for "Epiphany" –
– I've had a lovely day to day, sweet ~~sunsh~~[1]
sunshine and Norton[2] to drive with me over the
                             [hills
to a lovely old. French church – (French <u>specially</u>
I mean in the <u>intense</u> sense – of style
and feeling in architecture) – and
back to lunch on Partridges and
Newchatel cheese –
  Only the bills are rather long! but
they make me think all the more
of my Itie Fitie. For,

When itie pig, the other day
Had more than I proposed, to pay,
For breakfast, and what P, and A,
with T after them, call "Tay"
("Calls" would have been, if we reflect
Grammatically, more correct,
But inharmonious in effect,)
– When, as I said, – this itie pig,
Found that his bill was rather big,
He quite believed. – (before, <u>not</u> quite),
That Scottish accents must be right,
Since double P, and double A,
Pronounced in that mellifluous way,
By his wee, seepy, Seepy-mae,
Will make Pa-Pa; but not Pay – Pay.

    Ever your loving Pa-Pa.
        J Ruskin

---

  5. This postscript appears at the top of the final page, while the next appears at the bottom.
  6. Arthur Burgess, one of Ruskin's assistants.

Letter 37. 50/78, 1868. Paper: lightweight. Pencil notations: '1868'. Envelope: addressed to 'Mifs Agnew / Mrs G. Agnew / Wigtown / N. B. / Angleterre'. Postmarked: 'ABBEVILLE / 4 / OCT. / [68] / (76)' (front); '[PARIS] A CALAIS [203] / [?]', 'WIGTOWN / C / OC 6 1868' (back).
  1. Ruskin seems accidentally to have written off the edge of the page. He crossed-out this attempt and inserted the word into the left margin.
  2. Charles Eliot Norton (1827–1908), an American friend and one of Ruskin's executors. See Bradley and Ousby.

38. 6 October 1868, Paris

Hotel Meurice. Paris
6th October. 1868

Dearest wee 'Amie
I've run up here to spend two days with Norton, at Louvre and elsewhere – I have <u>so</u> many curious associations with Paris, now. First, all the Adèle[1] stay $^{story!}$[2] – with the first introduction – and the after years of avoiding Paris – – Old Studies in the Louvre – the beginnings of all future work – The coming here with the Jones's[3] – and receiving in this house, the letter <u>refusing</u> me the house at H.town – – and my going to the theatre that night with the Jones's. – Then the happy journey with Lady Trevelyan – [4] – the little flask of sherry on the way – – the buying strawberries in the market –

How execrably I write, still "look here" stay, quite clearly written instead of story.

———

A certain week in the Louvre
———

The Chartres journey – The sketching Con on the road – (one sketch still on the leaf of my Horace –) – The Champagne – Radishes – Bonbons – The Journey to Sens – to Dijon – May, V[5] Nightingales at Dijon – The leaving for – Neuchatel –
———

All is so mingled, in the light and shadow of then autumnal glades of the Tuileries.

I hope to be back at Abbeville on Thursday. There has been a gale in the channel – delaying letters – else I should have had one of yours here by this time

---

Letter 38. 51/78, 1868. One of two letters from Paris, 1868.
1. Adèle Domecq, daughter of John James Ruskin's partner in the sherry business and Ruskin's first intense infatuation.
2. Here, Ruskin has drawn a line to the left margin, where he added a note on his handwriting.
3. The artist Edward Burne-Jones and his wife Georgiana, with whom Ruskin travelled to the Continent in 1862.
4. This journey was taken in 1866, along with Joan Agnew, Constance Hilliard and Sir Walter Trevelyan. It wasn't entirely happy, since Pauline Trevelyan died *en route* at Neuchâtel.
5. This is meant to be a dash, but it is shaped like a 'V', evoking a bird in flight.

Ever your loving Cuzzie
                              J Ruskin

Last night – walking in the Boulevarde
Norton bought – for his little daughter
a little doll – six inches high – in
a green gown – only strapped over shoulders,
                                        [which
are white – with flaxen hair – and the face
almost – only the eyes a little [darker],[6]
– the very image – [7] To day
reading in his French guide
I find that at Arras, before
the revolution, there was
a society called of the "Rosati"
whose mission was to
sing of Roses, and
Robespierre was one of
them.
    I've just had such a long nice talk with
                              [Longfellow.[8]
    He dines with us to morrow[9] – and goes
                              [north
with us on Thursday.

39. 11 October 1868, Abbeville

                Abbeville. [10][11]th. Oct. 1868[1]
Dearest wee Pussie
         I have not forgotten the
date but the pen wrote unawares.
I could not manage to be quite myself
to day – allth although these two
lovely letters, from Norton & Connie,
have been a great help to me. Take
care of both. The Connies _{of the} sunset is
delicious.
I forgot to relieve your wee mindie
about the duck-hunt   It is not cruel
at all –   Ducks are used to get out
of the way of people, and flutter &
splash with much quacking, but
with no serious fear.   A fox, or _{stag or hare}
seeing the dogs gain on it is in
a real agony – as far as. a beast can
be.   But the duck does'nt care –
and, if it is to be caught you may
on occasion have your hunt – though
it is not a very highly refined
entertainment.
    I found such a pretty old castle in
        the middle of an orchard, the
other day with Norton: the fruit was
all lying on the castle floors – and I got
for three sous each, the three most exquisite
looking pears I have ever seen in France.
One was as exquisite when eaten – but
poo little piggie kept the other two
too long – and they got brown inside.
I was in quest of a Norman little c̶h̶a̶p̶ church
at the time – and near the railroad
station "Ètaples" – which – of course little
pigs pronounce in their own English way
    Where upon – they wrote these tender couplets

When little pigs, as evening dapples,
With russet clouds her fading sky,
Set out in search of Norman Chapels,
And find, instead, just past Ètaples
A castle-full of Pears and Apples.
On Dungeon floors disposed, to dry.
Then, little pigs should pay their penny,
And, if they think that there are any
Quite ripe, – those little pigs should try
Since Fate inopportunely grapples
With Jargonels too long put by.

————

Mind take great care of
Norton and Connie
    Love to you all
        Ever your loving Cuzzie
            J Ruskin
Please copy the bit about Longfellow
large, for Auntie, and send it her.

6. This could be 'starker'.
7. Ruskin left a large space here, presumably to imply Rose La Touche.
8. Henry Wadsworth Longfellow, the American poet.
9. Part of the letter from 8 October, recounting the dinner with Longfellow, is reproduced in 36.556, as is his mention on 7 November of Longfellow later writing him about the evening, 36.560.

Letter 39. 55/78, 1868. Paper: lightweight.
  1. Ruskin had written '10th' then rubbed out the number, replacing it with '11'. Although he generally would have written the 'th' in superscript, here he did not.

40. 21 October 1868, Abbeville

Abbeville Tuesday   22nd October, 1868.

  Dearest wee Pussie
I have your delightful –
letter about the two puddings.
which I am particularly pleased at
– I was not in the least in jest
about the cookery – I am quite
seriously pleased at your succefs.
– I am really well to night, for the
first time since this illnefs caught
me[1] – but still weak – not able to
bear ~~cold~~.^{chills} It is a very wholesome
warning to me – for I had no idea
how much I could be pulled back
by an attack of this kind. I have
had no cough – no cold in chest or
head – nothing but a sudden feverishnefs
turning all the wall pattern ~~to~~ into
eyes and noses – and after a night
of hot tossing to and f‸ot[2] – leaving
me ^ ^{with} just a month's progress – undone.
and nothing for it but nursing –
– The first day I went out, I was
hot in the sun & cold in the shade –
as if I had been a piece of clay –
– not alive. – and ~~it~~ $^{the\ feeling}$ has withdrawn
very slowly. I was sadly disgusted
to day taking a farewell look at
all the things I mean't to have done.
– but if I do good at this Committee[3]
it will put me into good humour
again.
My dear I am very thankful to
hear you say you are so happy. It is
very strange – in both of us: – but,
I am happier now than I was last
summer, (before October) by a great
deal. – but changed. (Don't think
this is fancy – you will see that I shall
be quite different in my way of life
and talk – but not to my pussie)
and very desolate when I am ill and
can't work – and not able to join
any more in some kinds of pleasure – for
                            [instance
– I can't have the least good from Norton's
                            [wife or children
– and had things been otherwise, I should
                            [have been
very fond of her.
But I have such plans for our Economical and
useful Future, 'amie dear!
Love to Mama – Kate & Buth.
  It is nice to hear of Kate's being up. and
looking so pretty – I was sure she would be
ever so much prettier when she was married.
    Ever your loving Cuzzie.
           J Ruskin.

41. 22 October 1868, Denmark Hill

Denmark Hill, s.
       22nd Oct. 1868
Dearest wee pussie
  I ran straight home from
Abbeville yesterday – leaving at eleven,
– staying two hours in Folkestone,
and ringing the gate bell at ½ past 7.
– to auntie's great satisfaction. All are
well – and everything looking pleasant
and I look forward to some very happy
time.+ – I am a little tired to day,
at ½ past one, with the various excitement

Letter 40. 61/78, 1868. Paper: lightweight. Pencil notations: '? 21 see envl of next letter', which is postmarked from London.
  1. He seems to have become ill immediately after his visit to Paris. While there he had met with Norton and Longfellow, and remembered past visits to the city and its mnemonic associations with various women.
  2. He wrote 'fot' then changed it to 'fro'.
  3. He is referring to a committee meeting of 'Society for the Employment of the Poor', for which he had been summoned home (see 19 October 1868).

Letter 41. 62/78, 1868. Paper: lightweight. Envelope: embossed with rose backed in red ink; addressed to 'Mifs Agnew / Mrs G. Agnew / Wigtown / N. B'. Postmarked: 'LONDON-S.E / X / OC22 / 68' (front); 'NEWTON-STEWART / B / OC23 / 68', 'WIGTOWN / C / OC 23 / 1868' (back). Pencil notations: 'D. Hill Oc 22: 1868' (on what would have been the outer leaf when folded).

and change of thought; chiefly with unpacking my parcel of Turners[1] – which are at once most delightful and most grievous to me – having been fearfully treated – fortunately the one I most wanted the great tree study, has hardly been at all injured. – and still more fortunately, the one I cared least for, – the so called lake of Brientz – , which I did not think <u>was</u> lake of Brientz – turns out to be indeed – and in the every best way. lake of +See over page   Brientz – it is the hill with the castle on it near Interlachen, under which Con and you and I had our pic nic. – and in the distance, the vale of Interlachen and the Niesen. .[2]

The two tree-studies are however the great prizes – they are worth any thing to me – being of the rarest & most powerful kind

+. I am looking for happinefs – not so much to drawing – or furnishing or the like – as in setting at once our two little minds to accomplish the problem of getting a mealy potatoe at dinner every day. Everything, when you come home, is to be subordinated to that first object. so get all the <u>accurate</u> knowledge you can in Scotland – about potatoes and how to dress them.

Now – my dear wee cuzzie – as to the time you stay in Scotland, do, unconcernedly what you think you ought, & ^{or} what you can yourself find pleasure in doing. Whenever you can come, I shall rejoice to have you – but I am well now into tranquil work, and am in no direct need of you. Tomorrow, I shall write you a quite <u>proper</u> letter, beginning "my dear Joanna,"[3] – with <u>Auntie's</u> various messages, after we have talked the matter over. but to day, I for myself tell you, for your friends sakes and your own, to do exactly what is pleasant & free. I cannot, till Saturday, tell you my own plans – I am set upon going back to Abbeville for a fortnight if possible, if the weather gets milder, – I was interrupted ~~to~~ in so much that was needful – so that till 1st December, I don't count myself <u>fixed</u>. I <u>may be</u> [however] by the committee businefs to morrow. at once.
Ever my dearest Cuzzie. Your affectionate
[Cousin
J R.

---

1. See 16 October 1868 for an earlier reference to these.
2. There are two full stops, indicating Ruskin's mind trailing off into memory. For Ruskin's description of Mont Niesen as a type of a 'conical form' hill, see 7.165.
3. If he wrote this letter, it is not in 'Bem L 33'.

42. 23 October 1868, Denmark Hill

Denmark Hill, S. E.

Dearest wee Pussie

Con and I were having the primmest little breakfast in the study when your letter came – this morning. – and Con & George and I drank your health in champagne at dinner yesterday. – but Connie is in a shy – silent – eyebrow fit – & not good for much – though very nice in temper. – But she's got a dreadful white bonnet – and its the Bonnet and Con, walking – not Con herself.

I am very much interested in your letter – It is very nice for me that you can understand me better –

I do hope you are quite well again? – Julia[1] is very nice, Please write and explain to her that I am in a grim fit of work – and can't talk or think, about anything else, yet a while.

    Enclosed Lily.
      Ever your loving Cuzzie
        J Ruskin

The great tree study of Turner's just got, is in prefect state – and quite pricelefs. The little new Geneva looks well in its frame – and Monsieur Pencil qui est Artiste, apres avoir encadré trois de ses dessins, remarque, "qu'il en est encore content". Le petit zephir – au contraire, trouve que les dessins encadrés sont tres peu amusants.[2]

Letter 42. 63/78, 1868. Pencil notations: 'Oc. 23? 68'. Ruskin had gone home from the Continent to attend 'a most important meeting of the society for the employment of the poor', see 19 October, 1868.
1. Possibly Julia Richmond, the wife of George Richmond.
2. [Mister Pencil, who is an artist, having framed three of his drawings notes 'that he is still pleased with them'. The little zephyr, on the other hand, finds that the framed drawings aren't very fun.] See 14 September 1868 [30] for his personification of the wind which was obstructing 'M. Pencil'.

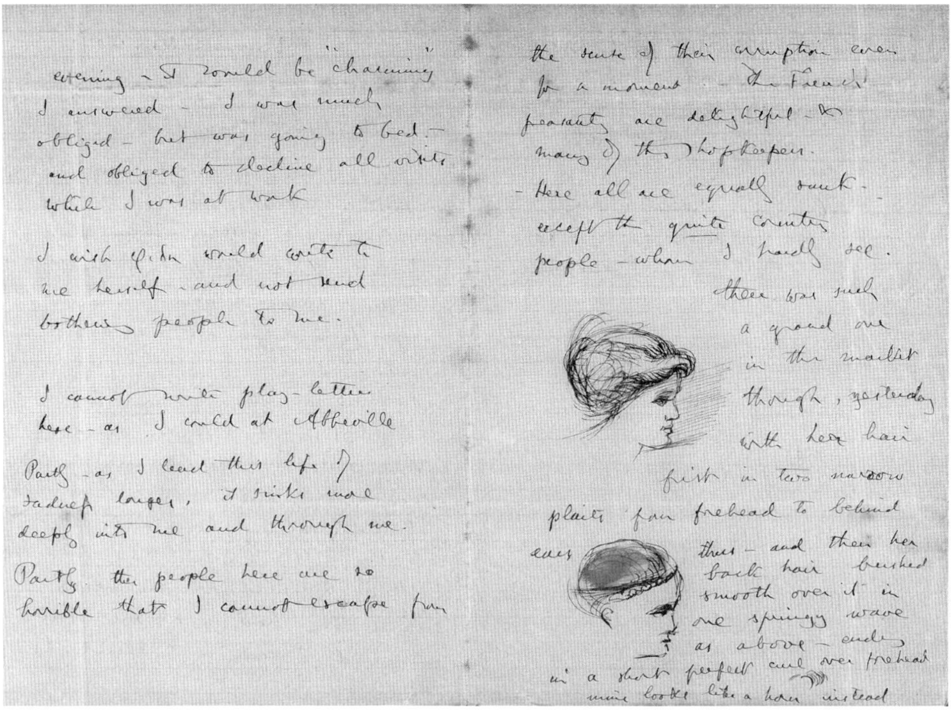

FIG. 4. Facsimile of JR to JS, 20 May 1869 [46]
RF L34, Ruskin Foundation (Ruskin Library, Lancaster University)

1869

Publication of *Queen of the Air*
R. takes Continental tour, 27 April to 31 August
R. elected first Slade Professor of Fine Art at Oxford, August

43. 30 April 1869, Neuchâtel

Neuchâtel. 30th April
1869

My dearest wee Doanie

I am in the same rooms – [1]
– but miss my wee Doanie & Connie quite miserably. and I don't care the least about anything. but hope to be better when I get to work. We have both of us had our "hard times" – since last I saw the water – (N.B – it is'nt so blue as it was, at all.). – and may hope for better ones, I should think. Here is a leaf I gathered on Lady Trevelyan's grave for you.

Love to Lizzie,[2] & thanks to all for kindnefs to you.
write   Poste Restante
         Baverno.
           Lago Maggiore
Ever your loving Cuzzie
          J Ruskin
The weather has been superb – but hazy, for
                          [Alps

44. 6 May 1869, Baveno

Baveno. Lago Maggiore
6th May. 1869

Dearest wee Pufsie

After a lovely day on the Simplon I have felt more than usually oppressed by the dismalnefs of a perfectly wet one here, in a curiously disagreeable Inn. and if I had not a wee Pufsie to write to, I don't know what I should do.

I don't think I told you that I did not see φίλη before I left. I called too early – at 4 ½ when she did not expect me till 5.. but it mattered little, for I was too ill to talk. And I have sent her a long letter from Brieg, telling her some plans I had made in driving up the Valais, seeing it entirely devastated by its rivers. I know perfectly how all this might be prevented: and I believe the best thing I could do in the rest of my life would be to begin the redeeming of this great valley
           of the Rhone; and show, with such help as I could get from good people, how the cretinism and misery of these great Alpine valleys might be ended.[1]
This would give me digging! to purpose. And you would have to come, you know Pussie – and teach people to cook. I am more and more impressed with the need of cooking, every day. There's nothing now a days between bad meat and the Lord Mayors feast. a simple well dressed delicate dinner is every day more impofsible. except at Wigtown and Denmark Hill
Write – Poste Restante Verona.

Autograph letters for 1869 are in 'Bem L 34 / Letters / John Ruskin / to / Joan Severn / 1869'. Note that all of the paper is lightweight until 29 August when it reverts to normal letterhead.

Letter 43. 4/142, 1869. This was an extended Continental journey. He did not write from Neuchâtel again until 29 August, the last extant letter of this trip.
  1. Meaning the rooms he stayed in on the 1866 Continental trip when he was accompanied by Joan Severn, Constance Hilliard and the Trevelyans.
  2. Probably Lizzie White, as she is referred to in these letters. Burd identifies her as Sarah Elizabeth White, a pupil at Winnington who lived in Liverpool. He adds that, anecdotally, she 'never married because she "gave her heart to Ruskin"' (*Winnington*, p. 461n.).

Letter 44. 8/142, 1869. This is the first of many letters with no signature.
  1. On 12 May he spoke again of his 'engineering' plans for the Rhone valley. That letter is reproduced in part in 36.566–57.

45. 14 May 1869, Verona

Verona. May 14th
1869

Dearest wee Pufsie
  What do you think I saw to night – in a garden overshadowed by tall cyprefses – looking over the city to the Alps and the far west – A <u>green</u> Rose! A bush bearing green Roses, instead of red! A whole bed of bushes like it! Real, perfectly formed single roses: with fresh green leaves. The gardener. has promised me ~~one~~ ^ a plant – as a gift – when I go away –[1]
What <u>will</u> Downes say? And what on earth – or in heaven – would somebody have said?
What else do you think I saw? The loveliest itie fitie I ever saw in my life   Ever so many itie fities all purple and blue. and like convolvuluses in glow of colour! I wonder what I shall see next.

46. 20 May 1869, Verona

Verona. May 20th.

My dearest Wee Pufsie

  I seem to be always writing letters. and you to be always – <u>not</u> getting them. I really think, by to days post I must hear of your having got ½ a dozen all at once.

I think a letter of mine to Norton's must have mis carried too – and – I hope not – one to φίλη such a long one!
Yesterday evening two ladies sent to say Mrs Cowper had told them I should be at Verona – and they had met me there – <u>would</u> I come and spend the evening – it would be "charming" I answered – I was much obliged – but was going to bed. – and obliged to decline all visits while I was at work

I wish φίλη would write to me herself, and not send bothering people to see me.

I cannot write play-letters here – as I could at Abbeville[1]

Partly – as I lead this life of sadnefs longer, it sinks more deeply into me and through me.

Partly. the people here are so horrible that I cannot escape from the sense of their corruption even for a moment. The French peasantry are delightful – & many of the shopkeepers. – Here all are equally sunk – except the <u>quite</u> country people – whom I hardly see.[2]
                    there was such
                    a grand one
                    in the market
                    though, yesterday
                    with her hair
            first in two narrow
plaits from the forehead to behind ears   [3]thus – and then her
                    back hair brushed
                    smooth over it in
                    one spriggy wave
                    as above – ending
in a short perfect curl over forehead
                    (( ))))[4]
mine looks like a horn instead
She was an entirely good honest peasant's young wife – and a pleasure to see – but still little more than an animal.
      Ever my dearest Pufsie
          Your loving Cuzzie
              J Ruskin

Letter 45. 11/142, 1869.
  1. See 14 August 1869 [57a], where he writes of carrying the plant him on his journey home.

Letter 46. 14/142, 1869. Pencil notations: '1869'.
  1. Referring to Abbeville in 1868, from whence he had written many nonsense letters.
  2. Ruskin has drawn a woman in profile with her hair up.
  3. Ruskin has drawn another profile, highlighting the plait ringing the face.
  4. This is a small set of curves like round brackets.

47. 26 May 1869, Verona

Verona
26th May 1869

Dearest wee Pussie

I've so much to write to day. and have been drawing so long. that I must just say, I love my wee Pufsie and no more – but it does me good to say that.

I do not write only to please Pufsie.
I write to please myself – it is the only refreshing moment I have in the day. except when pussy's letter comes –

Not but that my mother's letters are now very precious to me – but they make me so sad.
– and pussie's make me laugh –
– That was a very pretty one about your sister-mother the other day.   Ever your loving Cuzzie
J Ruskin.

48. 3 June 1869, Verona

3rd June

Dearest wee Pussie

The beauty beads are <u>solid old</u> Venetian glass –   But I've got some blue and white eggshells for you as well, but I don't count them anything.
I will attend to all you ask me with great delight – it is no nice to have a wee pussy to please I'm going to write pussy a long letter soon on the care of birds to be exercised by our Society. Pussy's ought to be especially entrusted with the care of birds.
Ever your loving Cuzzie

49. [2 July] 1869, Verona

.1.

Here's another Bank note for wee Pussie – Cavour. Manin – Christophe Colombus – and Dante – all for ninepence Dearest wee Pufsie   half penny[1]

Troubles to me – never come "numerable". many things have been teazing me in my letters lately. and to complete them in teazingnefs, here is my poor wee puss four days, without letters – and I'm sure its not my fault – Look here. this letter is marked 1. Im not sure about the date. but I'll find out for next letter, ^{tomorrow} and be very particular always to number my letters 1. 2. 3. &c. that you may be sure you have lost none – for ~~therers~~ there's generally some little bit of nonesense I don't want you to lose.
But I can't write even any nonsense to day – so this must be a quite worthlefs No.° <u>one</u>.[2] I hope that they'll improve in the series.
Ever my dearest wee Puss, your loving Cuzzie
JR.

Letter 47. 17/142, 1869.

Letter 48. 20/142, 1869. Paper: the bottom of the page, which would have contained Ruskin's autograph, has been cut out. Pencil notations: '1869'.

Letter 49. 37/142, 1869. Ruskin was writing to his cousin daily, sometimes more than once. If numbered letter '3' is from 4 July and '2' is from 3 July, then this must be from 1 or 2 July.
  1. The one-lira banknote is enclosed. As his letter suggests, the back of the note features a named portrait in each corner ('CAVOUR', 'COLUMBUS', 'DANTE', 'MANIN'), surrounding the larger portrait of a female labelled 'UNA'. The front of the note states its value as 'UNA LIRA', issued by the 'BANCA NAZZIONALE'.
  2. Ruskin appears to have decided to infuse the letter with 'worth' by enclosing another banknote. See the postscript at the top.

50. 7 July 1869, Verona

7th July 1869
5 .Wednesday.

Dearest wee Pussie.

No 5 is'nt worth numbering –
– only poo wee Donnie so dedful
coss that he must send it dust to
teep his wee temper.

Nobody ite. Donie any etties –
Donie to dull: –

Donnie daw till he dop pencil
out of hand – him so seepy: Den
Donnie det nooffin to wake him up.

If Donnie no get ice ettie from his
wee 'amie mammie to day – Donnie
dump as high as gass hoppies with
passion. and paps tome down again
again – nobody know where –

 Evy – dee mamie
  oos poo wee Donnie
   JR.

51a. 9–10 July 1869, Verona

7. Verona. 10th July
Saturday.

Dearest wee Doanie

It is'nt the 10th yet. but the 9th,
evening – and a very hot evening too; but
I write this overnight. because I shall
have several letters to answer to morrow
This, enclosed, the first – (which will give
you both pleasure and pain) – but not
before I've written to poor little Marie herself.
telling her I'll come and see her, and that
you and Connie will write to her directly.
I meant to have gone home by the Nortons –
but – dearly as I love Norton – I am in
no mind for the general family (especially
children } at Vevay) – and now I have
no further doubt – I shall go to Venice
on Thursday next – see Mr Brown and
draw φιλη her vignette – (a little smaller
perhaps than I intended – for her naughtinefs
in leaving me alone like this,) then
I shall go to Milan to see Count Borromeo
and then straight over the Grimsel
down on Meyringen and Giesbach.[1]

———

Don't write to Norton – (if you <u>are</u> writing)
– any word of this. – but with nice
wee line to poor Marie. and write
to Connie and tell her – Or perhaps
– I expect a letter from her now
every day – it will be best that I
tell her myself in answering.

Then I've a most touching letter
from Downes to answer – Poor fellow –
I'm really very sorry for him –
He says,
 "I <u>cannot</u> hear at all when
Miss Agnew is likely to come home –
she seems to be staying a long time".

He never says <u>I</u> seem to be to be staying
a long time! but hopes
I'm enjoying myself.

Its so hot I can't write any more

 Ever dee wee Pufsie
  Your loving cuzzie
   J Ruskin

Letter 50. 42/142, 1869. Envelope (loose in the box, but it almost certainly matches this letter) addressed to: 'Mifs Agnew / W. Milroy. Esq. / High S^t / Kirkcudbright / N. B / Inghilterra'. Postmarked: '[VERO]NA / 7 / LUG / [69]' (front); 'KIRKCUDBR[IGHT] / A / JY [?] / 18 [69]' (back). Pencil notations: 'Verona'.

Letter 51a. 44a/142, 1869. Envelope: addressed to 'Mifs Agnew / Care of W. Milroy Esq / High St / Kirkcudbright / Inghilterra / N. B.' Postmarked: 'VERONA / 10 / LUG / 69 / 4 S' (front); 'KIRKCUDBRIGHT / A / JY 14 / 1869' (back). Enclosures: calling card from Longfellow (44b/142, 1869); letter about Marie of the Geissbach from F. Locker (44c/142, 1869). See 20 August 1869 [60] for his account of the visit to Marie.

1. The Grimsel Pass, the Meyringen Valley and Geissbach (Lake of Brienz).
2. Frederick Locker-Lampson who had written Ruskin the enclosed letter from the Giessbach, which he visited with Tennyson in June 1869. See Hallam Tennyson, *Alfred Lord Tennyson: A Memoir by His Son*, 2 vols (New York: Greenwood, 1969), II, 66.

10th Really,

    I've written a pretty note to Marie – but have not Mr Lockers[2] addrefs – please
      send it me – and
        write yourself to him,
          telling him ~~to~~ all about it
How dedfuly itten – but
    wee poos moos make it out!
poo Donnie tant ite – he so ot.

51b. H. W. Longfellow's calling card

For Mr Ruskin.
    Mr. Henry W. Longfellow.
A thousand thanks. and
      good bye from all.

51c. Letter from Frederick Locker-Lampson

          Hotel Geissbach
          30 June 1869.
My dear Mr Ruskin
    I hope this will find you safe & sound at home again and that you have accomplished all for which you went so far.
    I left England about a fort night ago for a three weeks tour in Switzerland with Alfred Tennyson, this is not our first tour together, we were anxious to get some fresh air, & I think he is all the better for the change, our weather has not been [pripiteous], we spent five days at [Mürren] and past one night on the Wengern Alp.
    This letter is somewhat inspired by a book that I have been reading,
              on the
On the title page are written the words "Mlle Marie Schmidlin, from the Author, with his sincere regards, 1866.". Now do you know the writer of this book? You will be sorry to hear that Mlle Schmidlin is not at all well, the weather is cold, & she is quite confined to her room. I have had some talk with her old father, a very intelligent and gentlemanlike man. It is pleasant to see him & his wife in the intervals of the arrival & departure of guests, wander away into the pretty hotel gardens, in a most sentimental manner. We leave tomorrow for Lucerne, Rheims, Paris & London.
    I hope to be in England in about ten days time, & to go & see you, & to thank you for sending me the Drawing of that Titian Fresco at Padua. Will you send me a line about a fortnight hence to tell me <u>when</u> I may go & see you. I would take my chance, but I am rather afraid of being denied by [your] two legged Cerberus, who, faithful to you, has really been always very civil to me.
    Eleanor & I called one day to enquire about you. & heard of your safe arrival in Italy, & we were glad to have a good account of Mrs Ruskin, to whom pray present me.
    [Ever] truly
        F. Lo<u>ck</u>er

52. 13 July 1869, Verona

    9.   Tuesday
        Verona. 13th July
            1869
Dearest wee 'amie
        Still so tebby hot I can hardly hold my pen – but I get on with my drawings neverthelefs only I've begun so many – that I can't wind up ~~and~~ ^{to} get away. and don't know how long auntie and pussie can do without me! How long do you think pussie can sist – without her d~~ea~~i[1] pa. – Me want to know at. first of all. Then me must tink how

---

Letter 51b. 44b/142, 1869. On a cream calling card (7.9 x 4.1 cm). Longfellow's name is inscribed on the card, the message has been added in pencil.

Letter 52. 46/142, 1869.
    1. The 'ea' has been blotted out and 'i' inscribed on top of it.

long di pa can sist without his di pussie
– And then – you know – we must do
the drawings in the shortest possibly
sistence of the two.

I've always been afraid of vexing
you if I talked of Mr Burgefs. but
I think now I can tell you pretty
nearly what he is I soon found out
the faults you disliked so much
in manner – mode of thought &c –
– but though a deep <u>stain</u> in the surface
they are superficial – It will
be impofsible to get the stain <u>out</u> –
but it is only stain – it is not
corruption He has very fine qualities
– and all that is best in him is
least seen – much being up side
down. He has been working very
splendidly lately. and he sees <u>into</u>
things into a moment, in his slangy
way – or rather – expresses his insight
by a slangy ~~in~~ part of what he sees.
Thus, in the best early sculpture here,
of the Temptation – the serpent, instead
of coiling himself comfortably round the
tree – as usual – stretches himself
– head – neck – and half his body
far over and across to wards Eve
with an expression of passionate earnestnefs
I never saw equalled in a beast.
– That's the best temptation I ever saw
says WB. "Left <u>himself only one
turn of his tail to hold on by</u>. ! Now – that
showed that he saw the whole gist
of the thing in a moment – – though
it was only a laughable point of it
that he chose to express.

We have got on well. and I hope
I have done him good.

Seriously – I think my home coming
will be about as – on 4th page –
– I mean to try to keep to it
pretty closely. Write now to
<u>Verona</u>. again.
  Ever with love to William & Mary
    Your loving Cuzzie
        J R.

15th July. to Venice
19th July. Monday. back to Verona
26th –   Monday. Brescia
27th –   Tuesday Milan
28th   –   Como
29th   Lugano
30th.   Luino – Lago Maggiore
31st.   Faido.   St. Gothard
1st August   St Gothard
2nd August   Lungren   – (I wonder if
                                 pitty wee waiter
3rd – –   Giesbach   at Lungren yet?)
4th–5th   – – –
and so try to get to Paris by Sunday
the 8th – and home on the 10th
  – it cant be done sooner.

53. 13 July 1869, Verona

                      Verona
       13th   July

Dearest wee pussie.

    Are not Mary and William
terribly scandalized at my horrible
writing – and at <u>our</u> baby letters.
I am very much ashamed of
my writing. – But I have so
much drawing in the course of the
day that my hand is wearied of
taking care – and when it does
let go – it lets itself go all on
its back at once – and all to pieces

– And for the nonsense letters
they are the only relief I have
for a moment in the day, from
the infinite pain of seeing – and
thinking – in Italy – oos poo wee
                  Donnie
<u>so</u> – ired – and so – tick – and so eerie –
and so fightened – an so – only –
– dat if he had'nt his wee mamie to
tummy him – he don't know what
he sud do.
For Italy is one ruined cemetery – with
idle wretches lounging about it.
That is all it is –   And Europe is
coming to be little better –   There was
once a bonnie wee country, mamie

Letter 53. 47/142, 1869. This letter is not numbered, but its date fits '10' and there is no extant '10' in Ruskin's numbered letters from summer 1869.

dear – ey called it Totland – I pose
because it was so nice for wee tots
to pay at pashing in wee bookies –
– onie, en – it ought to have been
called Tot-water – or Tot-bookie –
– and not Tot-<u>land</u>. When I was the
weest of Tots – it oosed to be so
pitty, mama – it had fine geen paces
they ca'd Inches,[1] and wee bonnie
bairnies ca'd Jeans and Joanies and
the like o' that, ye ken – mamie; – wha
went paidlin aboot wi their bonnie gowden
hair and feet ~~in~~ o' snow, in the bookies, like
I dinna ken what for ~~just~~ jeust the
~~glo~~ light and the beauty o them; – and.
noo – mamie, they hae biggit big nasty
paces and gaols – and fawcktories, and sic like – a owre their bonnie
inches – and they hae filled their bookies a fu o black & boo
and green nastinefs – and there are nae mair wee trooties in
them – and the wee Jeans and Joanies are all gote
grand eddies gaein aboot to pairties an' firtin, if ye ken
  what <u>at</u> is, mamie dee – (Me always ask mamie – what <u>at</u>)[2]
and the poo wee tot of a Donnie is far awa among ugy
peepies in a land they sud ca Pot land. – for it's just a
seethin pot o' pottage o'[3] wild gourds, all fu o death,
– and nae bonnie barley meal to cast intil't, for luve –
nor for money either – or what they ca money here – whilk
is rags o paper like what Connie makes her curlies wi
– (onie no sae clean) and noo he must get his wee
breakfast – and he wishes it was porridge – and that his
 mamie was giving it till him – but its a back thing
 they ca' "cofee" and a white bit o' bread – jeust all
 – shining & round like an auld gentlemans bald pate –
 and Donnie don't ike it – and Donnie very sad – and
  Donnie his wee mammies dee wee 'bairni
    J Ruskin

---

1. See 35.68–69.
2. In the midst of this mock-Scottish idiolect, he inserted a bracketed aside composed entirely of the baby-talk idiolect. This demonstrates that these idiolects were not entirely interchangeable.
3. This is badly smudged.

54. 27 July 1869, Verona

18. Verona Tuesday
27th July

Dee-est Pufsie

I had yesterday your nice
wee letter about moonlight – which
was a great comfy and set up
for me. Mind you don't get
cold looking at the moon.
Poo Donnie so hot! – biged to
seep under one wee seety, and
teep both windys – (at it? mammy di?)
– It dos'nt ook ite. – because ey
not windy at all.) – wide open.

Mammy di – the wee girlies mut
have looked very pit, in Verona
in tummer time – : – me see by.
itty tat – –   – tatues – and me wish
wee tatues would come ive again –
– They have'nt got any thing on, [twa] speak of –
mammy di – – Dust a wee Bedgowny
tied about waisty with a band
of jewels –
If me get oo nice band of
boo beads, mammy – will oo let
me see oo wear oos bedgowny ike at?
– Me will ite to wee Tonnie Won Pon
to ask her too = It so vewy pît.

Poo wee Donnie tired – tant ite
any mo – but will have sometin
to sow his mammy. – when
he come marchin home,

Ever di mammy
ÿ Oos dood itie Donnie
J R

55. 29 July 1869, Venice

Venice 2 – poo donnie
don't no –

Di wi mamie.

This is so a wee ettie – sae
I dinna coont it naethin'[1] – – jes donnie
been ruinnin aboot the toon, and its up's an
doons o brigs,[2] till he's just oot o breath
an patience: – There were once bonnie
bit girlies in Venice, mamie dee – but
poo donie ony met twa, o them, dressed
anything like – and one was sae fat
and [soucie], she looked just like an egg
wi' a straw hat on the top o't. and
the ither was ae black – and no that bonnie
– but she had made wee curly wirlies
of hair all round her facie –
     – like at – mamie – wi a long
     black lace veil – gaein doon
     – I have botted it un
     potted it – – spoted it, I
     mean –mamie – till its
     a ugy – I canna do't in
     a hurry like at – but
she looked as if she was gaein to
sell black spectacles an had put them
a stickin round her ear. – (a fine
spectacle she had made o hersell!)
– but wee donie ike bein in
Venice again mamie – he ite
ong ettie to mowy.

Evy di mamie
oos poo wee donie
JR.

Letter 54. 55/142, 1869. Envelope: addressed to 'Mifs Agnew. / Mrs G. Agnew / Wigtown / N. B. / Inghilterra'. Postmarked: 'VERONA / 27 / LUG / 68 / [?]' (front); 'DUMFRIES / A / JY 31 / 1869', 'WIGTOWN / B / JY 31 / 1869' (back).

Letter 55. 56/142, 1869. Pencil notations: 'July 29 ? 1869'. Envelope: addressed to 'Mifs Agnew / Mrs G. Agnew / Wigtown / N. B. / Inghilterra.' Postmarked: 'VENEZIA / 29 / LUG / 69 / 6 S', 'LONDON / D / PAID / A / 2 [?] [AU] 69' (front); 'TORINO / [30] / [LUG] / 69 / [L/H] / SUC[CU]RSALENA', 'DUMFRIES / D / AU 2 / 1869', 'WIGTOWN / B / AU 3 / 1869' (back). Note that this envelope was loose and, although the letter is clearly from Venice, it is not dated. They may not belong together.
  1. He decided not to number the letter because of its intended brevity.
  2. Presumably this means the arched bridges over the canals.

56. 13 August 1869, Como

Como – 13th August

Dearest wee pussiky
   Me seen so many fine
funny things to tell pussiky but
cant to day
Me been dawing till me dop pency –
Mr Pencil – qui est artiste
apporte son dessin a l auberge –
et remarque – "qu'il en est content –
– Les habitants de Como aussie"[1]

The general criticism of the
public on my work is always
    "e preciso!"   "It is precise"
in a tone ^ of great admiration meaning – "There's
[nothing
more to be done – " – but sometimes
with occult drawback of feeling
that it is too true to be clever!
Off to-day for Lugano.
   Ever ~~your~~ oos poo wee 'uvin' Donnie

57a. 14 August 1869, Faido

Faido. St Gothard
14th Aug. 69

Dee-est Wee Poos Moos
   I'm on my way home at last
you see – sleeping to night just two miles below
Turner's pass – tomorrow morning
about 9. I shall be coming up
– I hope, by the brown stones &
blue torrent – Blue Devil of a
torrent – it should be called – of
all the devastation I ever saw in
the Alps, nothing has been like
what I saw tonight – the ruin
~~of~~ done by last year's floods

I direct this to Mr Richmond,
– it has over and over been very
positively in my mind to write to him.
– but pen & pensy dop from poo Donnies
fingys, now – but give him my dear love
   and thanks for all his good & beautiful
   letters to my mother
One of the reasons I don't write to
any one whom I care for as much
as I do for ☦ Mr Richmond, is
the impofsibility of making myself
understood, by any one in the intense anger and
[sorrow
in which I habitually live – and the
dislike I have of writing superficially
and from the mere outside of me,
to real-friends – But I will send
him some account of what I have
been doing – I hope while you are
with him.
   Ever, poos moosie dee, oos poo wee Donie
      J Ruskin
I've got three things to take care of – over
the St Gothard – myself.
1. The flower of "Madonna Verde" – Pussie
[know what
   at is? – It has come very happily with me
   in its little pot, from Verona – hitherto –
2. Wee white owange fowies in bonnie geen
[eevies,
   for my poos-moos – from Mr Bown.
3 A pillar of Con Signorios tomb – over my
[shoulder like
   a stick. I have to
   (I ~~d~~ needn't have packed.
   [icing] so [code] – !)
take mighty care of this – for if it
went ^ sideways against anything it would
break by its own weight – short acrofs –

Letter 56. 65/142, 1869. Paper: half a sheet. Pencil notations: 'Como Aug 13:69'. Envelope: addressed to 'Mifs Agnew / Mrs G Agnew / Wigtown / N B / Inghilterra'. Postmarked: 'COMO / 13 / AGO / 69 / 2 S' (front); '[?] / 1[5] / AGO / 69 [?]', 'DUMFRIES / D / AU 16 / 1869', 'WIGTOWN / B / AU 17 / 1869' (back).
  1. [Mister Pencil, who is an artist, has brought his drawing to the inn and notes that he is pleased with it, as are the inhabitants of Como].

Letter 57a. 66a/142, 1869. Paper: Unusually, the letter is written in reverse, beginning on what should be the final page. Pencil notations: 'Faido Aug 14: 69'. Envelope: addressed to 'Mifs Agnew / Care of Tho's Richmond. Esq / Park Range / Windermere / Inghilterra'. Postmarked: 'FAI[DO] / 15 / AOUT 69 [?]' (front); 'BASEL / 16 VIII 69 [III] / BR. EX', 'WINDERMERE / A / AU 19 / 69' (back). Enclosures: letter from Norton (66b/142, 1869).

– and it has base and capital, all cut out of one piece – and is <u>pecious</u>

Here's a letter from Norton Ive kept for you ever so long –

Poor dear Norton – smoothing down everything! If he had had "Verona boys" riding on his ^{pet} griffin – spitting over it – and throwing stones, sometimes at it – and sometimes at him – during his most difficult work – ~~fre~~ for days together – he would know more about the world than he does – by a great deal.

57b. Letter from C. E. Norton

Vevey, August 4, 1869.

My dearest Ruskin

I want to have news of you. It is long since your last letter came. I spent an hour or more this morning, just before dawn, in dreaming about you. I fancied you looking well, – & you were happy in your success in some great scheme for human happiness the details of which you were just beginning to give me when the house dog barked, & broke my light sleep. I wish I had heard what you had to say.

———

I had a very pleasant note from Longfellow the other day in which he spoke with strong feeling of you, & of the pleasure that your meeting in Verona had given him. Tom Appleton,. too, wrote most cordially of it, & gave me a pretty description of you perched up on your ladder, by the old tomb. "It seemed as if his ladder were borrowed from some of the old escutcheons it looked so suitable to the place! Behind him he had an admiring following of two silent English, & sundry boys of Verona whom he pronounced the worst boys in the world, & capable of any impiety, even to interrupting him"!

The Veronese boys <u>are</u> very bad, – but what provocation did not "quel malto Inglese" up there in the monument give to them! Why, he was as good as a peep-show, & nothing to pay. And very likely he had given cinquanta centesimi a quel diavolo Giovannino simply for sitting still one day for un mezz'ora, – &c eh! Signore, non c'è basta? I wish I had been a Verona boy in June.

———

We are all well & very quiet here. I am not up to much work, – but do what I can. We are happy when we are good. – but as little Sally said to me the other day when I told her to try to be good, – "Oh! but, papa, it is <u>so</u> hard." Why should not we all have been made good & happy? Is self-discipline essential? Then why cherubim & seraphim? Theology is a tangle, – & the next world more perplexing than this. So I read Omar Khayyam, – & try to make the best of Today. Goodnight. I wish you may take up the broken thread of talk again to-night.

Ever your most loving
C. E. N.[1]

Letter 57b. 66b/142, 1869.
1. There is a small, square, coloured sticker with an image of a raspberry on it, reading: 'CADBURY BROS. / RASPBERRY'.

58. 16 August 1869, Lucerne

– Love to M[r] Richmond & Constance.
Ever, dee mamie, oos poo wee Donie.
[J Ruskin

I shall be at
Giesbach. D.V.
at six. tomorrow   Lake Lucerne. 16th Aug[t].
evening.   1869

    Deeest of dee wee Pussies.
      Poo Donie down on this side of
quite big Alps. – nearer his mamie –
–but it rain – rain – rain – and poo Donie
so dull – He like bein, near his wee
mamie – but he no like leavin wee Venice
and gettin in damp – and dark – – and he
want to be twite <u>twite</u> near his dee
mamie – ^{that se may} to told him, and tumfy him.
Poo Donie must go to p- – p —-pro – fess, tings
at Oxford – Pease, mamie dee – tell wee
Donie, what peepies mean by – pro-fess – ?
Donie ike <u>doin</u> tings – : he don't know
how to pro-fess tings. Mamie
dee – do oo memby, one day – dose
dood peepies, – so very – very dood –
that came an peached till poo Donie
fell – seep –   an said evybody else was
so bad – ex – sept emselves – said
some peepies thay ca'd Cat-licks –[1]
(– Mamie dee – if at same as Puss-licks
me sood ike ose peepies) was always
so wicked, cos ey went – confessin – and
    English peopies so dood – cos ey
nevy con-fessed – nothing. Mamie
dee – pose ey nevy pro-fessed – nothin,
neither! – nor – what ey call – pro-tessed –
– nothin – neither – would'nt ey be nicer
peepies still?
—

If we don't take care – wee pussie, we
shan't be able to write or talk
anything but pussy talk, soon!
I declare I feel quite awkward
trying to write English now – but
I must write a word or two
to night – Seriously – it is very
dull and sad here. – utterly
bad weather – and I have so many
weary associations with this
dark lake – Even the Pussie &
Connie time was a little d̶ sad.
for I was frightened for Pussie –
and when I took her out for
her first little walk in the
evening – to see red sunset she was so weak
                                             [and weary
– poo Donie tebby fightened. –
I feel out of my element here, too,
<u>now</u> – and bitterly sad because
I am so. – I can't climb as I used
to do – and the cold high air puts me
all wrong in my whole system – it
has the most curious effect on me –
– just like eating unwholesome things –
– The warm Italian air seems life to me.
and I work on the buildings happily
in my increased knowledge of history
– but in on the hill side – it is always
"would I were a boy again".
I've been trying to write to M[r] Richmond
– but in vain – I could say so much –
– but – all sad. – I have done some
drawings which will interest him when
he comes to Denmark Hill again.
I saw – at Count Borromeos. the loveliest
nativity I ever yet saw – in all my
life – a little Luini[2]. The difference
between it and every other was
in its extreme simplicity – with
extreme <u>joyfulnefs</u> – everything pretty
                           and tender, and gay.
It is easy to be tenderly grave – But to be
                                        [tenderly gay!!
    I have seen many exquisitely decorated
and graceful designs of nativities – but
never one so naïve – yet so infinitely

Letter 58. 67/142, 1869. Pencil notations: 'Lake Lucerne Aug 16: 69' and 'Aug 16: 69'. Envelope: addressed to ' <u>Via France</u> / Mifs Agnew / Care of Thos Richmond, Esq / Park Range / Windermere / Angleterre'. Postmarked: 'BECKENRIED / 17 / 69' (front); 'WINDERMERE / A / AU 19 / 67' (back). Part of this letter is reproduced in 36.581
   1. Ruskin wrote 'Catl' then blotted out the 'l', replacing it with a hyphen and the separate word 'licks'.
   2. See <i>Verona and its Rivers</i> (19.444).

~~tender~~ ^sacred^ and pure. The virgin is just
going to lay the child into the little
crib of the oxen – and it is half
full of hay. and two delicious little
angels – boy angels, with ruby-coloured
wings – ^ (and nutin else, mamie dée – At quite popy?
[and as full of fun as any
mortal boys – are <u>shaking up</u> the hay
with the ~~br~~ lightest – prettiest – half
haymaker's, half chambermaidish
touch and toss of it – to make it
all nice and smooth for the baby.
– the Virgin looking into the child's
face as she lays it down with
the most passionate mother's look of
love – not adoration at all – but
just all her face suffused with a
sort of satisfied <u>thirst</u> of perfect love –
– and in the distance – a dainty little
blue angel – like a bit of cloud – coming
at the heads of the shepherds like a swallow –
– in <u>such</u> a hurry! – None of your regular
preachers of angels – that put their fingers
up – and say –. Now ^ if you please, – attend –
[^ particularly and do this: – or
Be sure you don't forget to do that – but an
eager little angel saying – "Oh – ^ my dear
[shepherds –
<u>do</u> go & see!

59. 17–18 August 1869, Samen

Samen.
11. morning   17th August. 1869.

Dee-est of wee (piggie)-pussies –

Poo Donie miss his wee piggie sadly
to day. He sitting in same roomie –
– where he fed his poo starved wee piggies –
(got nice wee girlie to firt with, this time
too – not same – but bettie – for the old one
would have been 3 years older – !) – Going
to feed wee piggie selfie with tout. but miss
his own piggies all the mo. But if oo
~~could tod~~ tood only have seen – piggie dearie –
– two wee piggies – (four-legged ones) – at
Bekenried[1] this morning. – My nevy – nevy –
nevy did see such <u>dicious</u> wee piggies for
squealin – an fightin – and going the wrong way
and stainin with their bit hoofs slip- slip- slipping
on the wet decks – with all the crew of the
steamer hanging on to their tails – pulling and
slipping the other way – Me made itie
pig ime about em, – over page –
No – here come wee girlie & tout –
—

My dee wee piggie –   poo Donie had
sut nice firtie – done poor Donies hearts
twite good. – Real nice wee girlie – not
dot up – – ony itie ed ibbon at itie neck
to fasten itie ~~grey~~ ^gey^ ~~frock~~ – gown – and se
twite popy and pitty – ony se ike to talk
to wee Donie – because poo Donie so old
and past fifty and grey haired: so se like
talk – and se <u>un</u> away ^quick^ when bell ring
downstairs and <u>un</u> back again ^ quicker – and
we talk – talk – till no more tout. left.
Now for wee piggie-imie.[2]

Dear itie pigs – on Bek'ried pier,
Whose minds, in this respect are clear –
That – pulled in front – or ~~poked~~ ^pushed^ in
[rear –
Or [twitched] or tweaked by tail or ear, –
You <u>won't</u> go there, and <u>will</u> come here, –
Provided once you plainly see
That here we want you not to be, –

dee wee piggie – oo must wait a bit
for the moral – for me had another itie
firtie – and made wee girlie tell me her name
and its' "Rosine" and now me going on
over Brunig[3] and to see poo wee Marie
and tan't ite moral till to morrow

Letter 59. 68/142, 1869. Envelope: addressed to 'Via France / Mifs Agnew. / Denmark Hill / S. / London / Angleterre'. Postmarked: 'GIESSBACH / 21 VIII', 'SUISSE / [?] / [?] 23 /AOUT / 69 / PONTARLIER' (front); 'BERN / 21 / V11169X- / [CRIEFEXP]', 'LONDON-S.E. / A S / AU24 / 69' (back).
1. Beckenried River.
2. Ruskin quotes this poem in a letter to Charles Eliot Norton of 18 August. It is reproduced in 37.582–85.
3. Brunig Pass.

Giesbach. Wednesday morning
18th August

– Dearest wee Doanie,

It rained sadly yesterday, and
the road from Samen to Brientz[4] was like
the road to Epsom in race time – No horse
for help to be had at Brunnig foot – It cleared
however – and I walked up the winding
pass among the pines – waterfalls streaming
down everywhere – moss all green – wet –
and glittering – all lovely – but the road – –
and by that – I didn't get here till nine
and poor wee Marie had been sent to bed –[5]
– and I'm up early and writing in the little
room you and Connie used to play on
piano in – and its wet, still, and
I should be very very dull if I had'nt my
wee Doanies nice pink letters – four of
them – and two from Lily. – so I can
manage to sist a little while;
– Me got boo beadies and M[r] Bowns fowies[6]
all safe – for pussie, thus far and we'll
have a repacking here – for I must
bring Pussie and Connie something from
"the shop" and I want my Poos moos
to make me a wee present. – so I'll buy
one, and se sal pay for it and bring

it down in the mornin at Denmark
hill, when I bring down hers, and we'll
open all together & see whats inside. and
   heres wee piggie moral overleaf

Dear little pigs – if only we
Could learn a little of your he-
Roism, and with defiant squeaks
Take Fortunes twitches and her tweaks,
As "ancient Greeks" met ancient Greeks;
Or clansmen, bred on Scottish peaks
To more of bravery than [breeks],
Will quarrel for their tartan streaks;
Or Welshmen in the praise of leeks;
Or virtuosi for antiques;
Or ladies for their castes and cliques;
Or churches for their days and weeks;
Or pirates for convenient creeks;
Or everything with claws and beaks
For the poor [ravin] that it seeks, –
Dear little pigs! If Lord and Knight
Would do but half the honest fight
In dragging people to do right,
You've done to-day, to drag them wrong,
They'd have the Crooked, Straight, ere long.

   Ever my darling wee piggie-pussie
      oos poo, wee, itie, piggie, Donie
         J Ruskin.

(Write here
for two days.)

60. 20–21 August 1869, Geissbach

Dearest Joanie,   Giesbach. 20th August
                              1869
   My dearest Kate

   I am afraid the pang of
parting with Joanna will make you
look with more indignation than
pleasure on a letter from any of us
who rob you of her. – but I must
write one word, to say how thankful
I am

[1]I began this to Kate ^ but was a little afraid
to go on, for fear the child should be
still ill –; when he is quite well again,
I will write – meantime[2]– will you say
to M[r] Drew that I am very deeply
pleased ~~at~~ by his kind message. that
I share sincerely in the joy which must
be felt at the recovery of his little niece.
– and that I would still beg from time
to time to be permitted to hear of her.
   I wish I could give you as good
tidings of poor little Marie. She is
very ill – I ~~think~~, [am sure] hopelefsly. It was
all brought on by precisely the same
thing happening to her which happened
to my poor wee amie – just at the same

---

4. Lake of Brienz.
5. See the following day for a brief note on Marie's health.
6. See 3 July [48] for the blue beads and 14 August [57a] for the flowers from Rawdon Brown.

Letter 60. 70/142, 1869.
   1. There is a line in ink which runs between '1869', and 'Dearest Joanie' and 'My dearest Kate'
      (above) then along the left side of the message to Kate (Joan's sister) until this 'I'.
   2. From here to the end of the paragraph ('hear of her') has been surrounded by pencil lines.

time – just in the same way – only poor wee
Marie had no sister Kate nor cuzzie Donie
to help her – nothing but the dark pines
and lonely lake – and they did not help her –
and so now – she must go where there is
– at least – no more pain.
She is very pretty still – in some respects
prettier than she was ^(for me) – because more
[delicate
– her thinned, fragile waist & neck are
, sadly, graceful – and her hair cut a little short
and falling behind as if she were 14 or 15 –
– but I know now the Pale Shadow, too well.
Still she is enjoying her bit firtie mightily.
– She comes peeping is ^(in), the morning after
[breakfast
and stays till I send her away – and asks
when she may come again, – and is happy –
– but I am afraid, she won't like my going
away.

21st August – I had, last night – my
wee Doanies note from Windermere – a quite
marvellously short post – and to day, at 12, I have
your last from Wigtown! – that, in due
course
I am so glad baby is better.
Little Louie Wood <u>must</u> be delightful –
I wish <u>I</u> was "Hugh".

There's a little more to day in mama's
letter.　　　　Ever my dearest Joan
　　　　　　Your loving cuzzie
　　　　　　　J Ruskin

61. 22 August 1869, Geissbach

Dearest wee Pufsie
　I have your pretty Windermere
letter, about the pic nic – &c. and
your being pleased with Count B.ˢ
madonna – &c. all which was
highly pleasing to me. . You must
write now – Hotel Meurice – you
know where that is?
Norton is coming to see <u>me</u> – He
is to sleep at Thun to morrow.
and I shall go down the lake and

be ready to receive him at the Belle Vue
and come back here with him on
Tuesday. Showing him the grotto
cascade on the way, where we
were all so happy.
It seems such a little time!
I think Marie will like seeing him –
She says such wise little things every
now & then – and then nods her little
head – and says – "Yes It's <u>true</u>." I told
　her of Connie's high hair.
M. "Connie is <u>such</u> a little coquette – "
R. No!?
M. Yes. It's true.
R. No – It's because shes such a
　good little actress.
M. Yes. She always acts. But she
　is very good:
R. I am sure she is – but I never
　can understand her.
M. No – because you are man, and
　she is girl. – and she is not in
　　the least like you. I can
　　understand her, for I am girl –
　　– and I see so many. I know her.
　R. I'm so afraid, now that she's
　　getting so much admired, of
　　her marrying the wrong person.
M. Yes. She will always judge
　from the outside.
R. No!?
M. Yes. Its true. Joanna is deeper.
　Connie judge with the head –
　Joanna with the heart.
R. Yes. Joanna always judges with
　the heart.　　(to <u>himself</u> – "not
　always quite rightly though.)
M. She is <u>so</u> good!
R. No!?
M. Yes It's true.

　– She has wee Doanies photograph
　in her page of "beauties" –
　– What <u>does</u> my wee Doanie
　think of all that?
　　Ever your loving Cuzzie
　　　J Ruskin

Letter 61. 71/142, 1869. Pencil notations: 'Giesbach Aug 22? 69'. Envelope: addressed to 'Mifs Agnew / Denmark Hill / S. London / Angleterre'. Postmarked: 'GIES[BACH] / 22 VIII' (front); 'BER[NE] 22VIII [?] / [?]', BASEL / 23VIII69 / BR. EX.', 'LONDON-S.E. / A P / AU25 /69' (back).

62a. 23 August 1869, Geissbach

Dearest Joan,

    I can't help – in spite of the sadness – being immensely amused with Marie – she is so very clever – and subtle and ~~fun~~. fond of play – even in her illnefs. How <u>intensely</u> happy we <u>could</u> have made her – alas – if we had come here again in that unhappy. 67. when I was wandering desolately about Skiddaw. I can't think, now, why I went there – instead of to Switzerland – It was partly for my health – partly ^ I think that I could not bear to go far from that Irish sea. and have another sea between me – and – sorrow.

Poor little Marie came in yesterday in her prettiest drefs – with a little Turkish embroidered shawl – I noticed it directly – Yes – she said – I have that "embarras de vanitè." for you, because you said you liked to see people nicely drest."

R. That was so good of you – I do so like to see pretty things – and I don't see them often – girls dress so badly now – – Look at those three, out of the window – how ill drest – But they have fine hair! (It came like lion's manes all down their backs)

M. Yes. – They are very pretty – They are Jewess –

R. How do you know they are Jewesses?

M. It is true. They all have fine hair. But I like to see girls – not horses.

R. You naughty Marie – Who would have thought our sweet, gentle little Marie could say such things –

M. I am not sweet – not gentle – I am sour –and ungentle. When people play a false note on the piano – that is like me.

R. How is it that if you are ungentle you don't like me to say that I want to make slaves of people?
              (we had talked much of America)

M. You don't want to make slaves. If you want a faithful slave – you must send for me – Here is your[1] dinner– now I will go – You are always [eating, when I come

R. – Now – Marie!

M. Yes. It is true. Goodbye. (Exit)

    The first day you are in town – see if French exhibition is closed – I wonder ~~whe~~ if you could ask where my Meissonier is, if it is [closed –[2] – and say I want it sent home – –
    If you showed this letter Mr Wallis would give it you – Or better enclosed
        Ever your loving cuzzie
            J Ruskin

62b. Ruskin to Mef^srs Wallis & Co.

        14th August – 1869

Mef^srs Wallis & Co.
Please deliver to bearer – if it is now done with – my "Napoleon" by Meifsonier. and oblige
    Yours very truly
        J Ruskin.

Letter 62a. 72a/142, 1869. Pencil notations: 'envl Aug 23: 69'. Envelope: addressed to 'via France / Mifs Agnew. / Mrs Ruskin's / Denmark Hill / S. London / Angleterre'. Postmarked: 'GIESSBACH / 23VIII', 'SUISSE.ST LOU [?] / [?] / [?] / [?] / 69' (front); 'BASEL [? III–]', BERN [?]', 'LONDON [SE] / L [?] / AU 25 /69' (back). Enclosures: request to Mef^srs Wallis & Co. for the return of Meissonnier's Napoleon (72b/142, 1869); Ruskin's autograph from a letter to his cousin (72c/142, 1869).
  1. Ruskin has drawn a line connecting the end of this line with the beginning of the next.
  2. Louis Ernest Meissonier's 'Napoleon in 1814'. Ruskin purchased it for £1,000, he would sell it in 1882 for 5,900 guineas (*Later*, p. 150).

Letter 62b. 72b/142, 1869.

62c. Ruskin autograph

[...]ing Cuzzie
J Ruskin.

63. 30 October 1869, Denmark Hill

Denmark Hill, S. E.

[Saturday.]
Dearest of wee Pufsies –
– Connie[1] has gone – and I've
nothing to console me but writing to
my own wee pussie – & thinking
she'll like to have my letter.
So she was pleased with Tukup's?[2]
Well – its all very fine peepies
saying they ove peepies – and
I pose ey do – but ey sud'nt give
peepies so mut pain –
– me dot sut big – dedful big – dump
in mornin – – see ugy ettie with
nasty ting at top – poo Donie.

———

Please put Emma's[3] mind at
rest about ingratitude. I am very
glad she has been wise enough – &
fortunate enough – to get another
situation.
Yes, dearie – I know you must
be wanted sadly at home just
now – and I will do as well
as I can and be a dood wee Donie –

Oh dear – I wish I were a wee
Donie – and had nothing to
look after nor think about –

And then I should wish to
be a big Donie I suppose.
"Its <u>all</u> the same"
— Mamie di,
Ever oos own poo wee oving Donie
J Ruskin.

The Pigeon has come back
all safe –

Connie was in an awful state
of vexation at not going <u>home</u>
for Sunday – she's gone to
her aunt's – Somebody must
be at Cowley she wants to
see – do get it out of her –
She wouldn't tell <u>me</u>, the monkey.

64. 8 November 1869, Denmark Hill

Denmark Hill, S. E.

Darling wee Pufsie-Moosie –
  (Pronounce with a nice long S –
    Puss-ss-ss.-sy – moos-ss-ss – sy –
    very delicate – you know –
    – and like a kettle singing.
    – not like a serpent –)[1]
– I'm so thankful for the little better
news to day.
And I'm immensely pleased with
three sketches I've ħ just had
given to me – of John Leech's[2] (given me)
by his Father =
1 "A windy day at the sea side'
2 "Cleaning the pictures in the
   Royal Academy"

Letter 62c. 72c/142, 1869.

Letter 63. 92/142, 1869. Envelope: addressed to: 'Mifs Agnew / Care of Arbuthnot Simson Esq / Wigtown / N. B.' Postmarked: 'LONDON. S.E. / X / OC 30 / 69' (front); '[DUM]FRIES / A / OC 31 / 1869', 'WI[GTO]WN / B / NO 1 / 1869' (back). Pencil notations: 'Oc 30: 69'; '[Tw] iglets / Louis –' (back of envelope).
  1. Joan Agnew was in Wigtown with her pregnant sister Kate, having arrived there by 14 October (see 77/142, 1869, not transcribed). In her absence, Constance Hilliard had joined Ruskin at Denmark Hill to keep him company (see 86/142, 1869, not transcribed).
  2. Tukup was a pet-name for Rose La Touche (see 83/142, 1869, Monday 25 October, not transcribed).
  3. Emma was one of the Ruskin's servants (see 96/142, 4 November 1869, not transcribed).

Letter 64. 97/142, 1869. Envelope: addressed to 'Mifs Agnew / Care of Arbuthnot Simson Esq / Wigtown / N. B.' Postmarked: 'LONDON-SE. / X / NO 8 / 69' (front); '[DUMF]RIE[S] / A / N[O 9] 18[69]', 'WIGTO[WN] / B / NO 9 / 18[69]' (back). Pencil notations: 'Nov 8: 69'.
  1. This is the first extant letter with instructions on how to pronounce aspects of baby-talk.
  2. He wrote 'Leeche's' then blotted out the 'e'. John Leech (1817–64) was an illustrator for *Punch*.

3. "The foreign gentleman performs an air on the piano."
– I never in any one of my days yet ever saw anything so wonderful – in their way. They are equal to Turner in precision of touch.

I shall probably give them to Oxford – but Pufsy must see them first.

 Ever your loving Cuzzie
  J Ruskin

65. 12 Nov. 1869, Denmark Hill

Denmark Hill, S. E.
12th Nov.

Di-est wee Mamie

[1]Poo Donie so comfy and peased that his mamie no angy. He was so vewy sowy an- pented so- incerely of bein aughty, that he –[th]ought – perhaps – he might – soon – do[2] and do it aden – for the bushes were so vewy nice![3]

The Leycesters[4] have just been here and enquired for you. very kindly They stayed till they [lost] their [brains] and won't be down at Broadlands[5] for ever so long. and what will poor φίλη do meanwhile.

But they seemed very much pleased and very happy.

(Now me must do and pactise for M West.[6] Mama di, – me thinks – inks, I mean – our wee Engłish mut pittier tan othie peepies Eng-ish – Ɨ Ever oos ovin wee Donie
  J Ruskin

66. 13 Nov. 1869, Denmark Hill

Denmark Hill, S. E.
  13th November
   1869

My dearest Joan,

 We are very sorry for you – – I – more than I could be for any other death out of this house – except one. (You – my dear – are of this house – as I hope you will feel in sorrow – more even than in joy) ––I do not know what to say to you. except that I will try to give you more and more of brother's & father's to replace sisters love – if indeed that love is taken from you. , where she is.

 Ever my darling
  Your loving cousin
   John Ruskin

Letter 65. 100/142, 1869. Envelope: addressed to 'Mifs Agnew / Care of Arbuthnot Simson Esq / Wigtown. / N. B.' Postmarked: 'LONDON-S.E. / X / NO 12 / 69' (front); 'DUM[FRIES] / A / NO 13 / 1869', 'WIGTOWN / B / NO 13 / 1869' (back). Pencil notations: '1869'.

1. This first paragraph is written in a small script, the physical size of the letters echoes the symbolic self-abasement and diminishing entailed in the baby-talk.
2. There is a shadow around the 'o', presumably to differentiate the intended 'go' from the intended 'do' after 'and'.
3. See 10 November 1869 (98/142, 1869, not transcribed) for his first account of using her brushes. Notably, that was the first letter from the period of Kate's postpartum illness to contain a high proportion of baby-talk. The baby-talk disappeared again after Kate's death, when the letter of 13 November begins with 'My dearest Joan'.
4. Mr and Mrs Ralph Leycester (37.362).
5. The Hampshire home of William and Georgiana (φίλη) Cowper.
6. Mr West was Joan's music teacher. Ruskin was making use of her class time in her absence (see 75/142, 1869, 14 October, not transcribed).

Letter 66. 101/142, 1869. Envelope: addressed to 'Mifs Agnew. / Care of Arbuthnot Simson. Esq / Wigtown / N. B.' Postmarked: 'LONDON-S.E. / X / NO 13 / 69' (front); 'DUMFRIES / A / NO 14 / 18[69]', 'WIGTOWN / B / NO 15 / 186[9]' (back).

67. 24 Nov. 1869, Denmark Hill

Denmark Hill,
S. E.

Dearest wee Doanie
 I am <u>so</u> thankful for your
t rather cheerful letter
– It is dark fog. and I am
foggy. and hard at work
besides – I'm making Lizzie[1]
copy a letter to Mifs Tollemache
about the "Order" Lizzie says
"<u>she</u> will never be one of us"
– I answer – "I hope not".
– What a mischievous thing
she's turned into!
– Great good at heart of her –
but much spoiled lately.
– Oh me – what can I tell
you to answer you a little
I've been making Downes
buy Cacti – and all
the Green House is one
mass of Prickles and
looks like an Itie Fitie
made vast, and with
a ~~bou~~ walk through it.

– Dear itie fitie pease turn
all into Down – for poor
Downes sake and mine
and be bown back to oos
pooest of poo wee Donies
                J Ruskin

68. 15 Dec. 1869, Denmark Hill

Denmark Hill,
S. E.
            15th Dec.
Darling wee Pufsie

 I got on well, last night.[1]
(– Except – that I fell quite
dedfully in 'ove!)
(– <u>Poo</u> Donie. "eally must'nt
fall about – ike at – any mo.)
– But – Me was between two sut
pitty – pitty – wee girlies – One –
just <u>goin</u> <u>to</u> <u>be</u> seventeen!
Oh – Di ma – me do so wis I was
at Woolwich – !
But me pectin wee Tonie – so
me mut make up with Tonies
and Etties.[2]
        – Me so happy, di ma,
because di ma ike her wee roomie
still. –

Ah – Doanie – <u>when</u> are you
coming back to it?

I've got to give 12 lectures
at Oxford this Spring.

Now – dear – I think I shall
have to be six weeks therefore
at Oxford.
– Could you run up, and come
here on the 3rd of January?
and stay for four weeks – and
be a little cheered? Then – Im
going to give my first lecture
at Oxford on the 2nd February.

Letter 67. 113/142, 1869. Envelope: addressed to 'Mifs Agnew / Care of Arbuthnot Simson Esq / Wigtown / N. B.' Postmarked: 'LONDON-S.E. / X / NO 24 / 69' (front); 'DUMFRIES / A / NO 25 / 1869', 'WIGTOWN / B / NO [25] / 1869' (back). Pencil notations: 'Nov 24: 69'.
  1. Lizzie White who was visiting Ruskin in Joan's absence. She arrived on 10 November (see 99/142, 1869, 11 November, not transcribed).

Letter 68. 121/142, 1869. Envelope: addressed to 'Mifs Agnew. / Arbuthnot Simson Esq / Wigtown / N. B.' Postmarked: 'London-S.E. / X / DE 15 / 69' (front); '[DU]M[FRIE]S / A / DE 16 / [186]9', 'WIG[TOW]N / [B] / [DE 16] / [1869]' (back). Pencil notations: '1869'.
  1. He gave a lecture at Woolwich on the evening of 14 December (see 120/142, 1869, 14 December, not transcribed). He had shared an earlier draft of this letter with Joan in a letter of 27 November., which is reproduced in part in 39.599–600.
  2. Tonie and Ettie were pet-names for Constance and Ethel Hilliard.

– You could go to Tyrwhitts[3]
– play with children and be
happy – Hear my first &
second lecture – Then go
back to Buth for 6 weeks.
—

Then come and be with me

in the spring time a little?
Then go back to Buth in
the Summer.?
Pussie di – Pease come to poo Donie

  Ever oos sad – <u>only</u> wee ^{di Donie}

    J Ruskin

---

3. The Reverend R. St. John Tyrwhitt was an Oxford secretary to Ruskin.

1870

R. gives inaugural Slade Lecture at Oxford, 8 February
R. and J. make Continental tour with Mary and Constance Hilliard, 27 April to 29 July
The Franco-Prussian War 'of 1870' breaks out, 19 July

1871

R. begins *Fors Clavigera*, his monthly series of public letters to British workmen
George Allen becomes R's agent, then takes over from Smith, Elder & Co. as his publisher
Fall of Paris, 28 January; Continental travel will remain hazardous for many months
R.'s old nurse, Ann Strachan, dies on 30 March
J. marries Arthur Severn, 20 April
R. arrives in Matlock for a holiday on 26 June, suffers a breakdown in July,
and is then cared for by the Severns, his college friend Henry Acland,
and his confidante φίλη (Mrs Georgiana Cowper-Temple)
R. purchases Brantwood in the Lake District, which he first visits on 11 September
Death of R.'s mother Margaret, 5 December

69. [February 1871] Denmark Hill

Denmark Hill.
    S. E.
            Saturday

Mine own wee Pufsie

[1]I must go to town without getting your letter – which my mouth waters for – I am working well for lectures & think they will be interesting. but the head. work all day long is too much for me – and I've no enjoyment of anything else, while my pussie's away.

[2]There are no words for the monstrousnefs of this war. – but it won't make people think, after all, I believe – Nothing will ever make them think –

As the French <u>were</u> to be beaten I'm heartily glad its thoroughly. – There never was such a catastrophe in the annals of war.
– Not as a soul – in France or England – has any idea of the <u>real</u> root of all these failures.

Do you remember the play I took Connie & you to see at Paris, the first time?

<u>That</u> is the kind of thing that has destroyed the French, and is destroying the English. – and no one ever speaks of it.

– Next to that – money getting and jobbery – The French army has been ruined for want of two days' food – which its Purveyors had – Pocketed.

Then thirdly – Vanity – and giddy [patednefs][3] and "Liberty'[4]

Autograph letters for 1871 are in 'Bem L 36 / Letters / John Ruskin / to / Joan Severn / 1871'.

Letter 69. 123/133, 1871. Pencil notations: '1871'; 'May 20' is just discernible, but rubbed out. It is now filed with the undated letters at the bottom of L 36. I place it at the beginning of February, shortly after the Armistice was signed at the end of the Franco–Prussian War.
1. There is a pencil bracket here, the other bracket is after 'anything' near the end of that first paragraph.
2. There is a pencil bracket here, the other bracket is after 'Imperialism'.
3. This might be 'patedness', implying the overuse of intellect, or 'spatedness', meaning a tendency to 'spat' or fight, but either of these options assume a constructed word on Ruskin's part.
4. These speech marks, first double then single but facing the wrong directions, are Ruskin's. Whether they denote a hurried hand or express particular meaning is unclear.

– The German government
is the really despotic one – the
French is a mere mockery
of Imperialism.

Dee Pussie – me no want to
talk politics – but when
I've no pussie to play with
what can me do.
  Ever oos own poo Donie
     J Ruskin

70. 4 March 1871, Denmark Hill

   Denmark Hill.
   S. E.
    4th March 1871

 My dearest 'amie,

 The sun is very bright
on this birthday of yours – and the
spring flowers are all open – I hope
the brightest & best of them will
never close, for you, and that all
your life may still be Spring.
I did not choose for you any costly
present – thinking that it was
best for you on your birthday to
practise a little wise choosing for
yourself. So I have put these little
white notes in a little house-wifely
packet – and my lambie must think
very seriously, when she takes one out!

 But the little ring – though
it did not cost Di Pa much
money – has a value in Di Pa's
eyes. It is – I mean – it holds
in its setting – the prettiest violet
Almandine he ever saw set
without foil. And that means

that Arfie's[1] love for Joanie is
to be very deep and quiet, and
to need no foil underneath; and
Doanie is to be the little diamond
in the middle of it. and Di Pa
is to be a ring round you, to take
care of you both, & pinch you a little,
– and be a little like – or in the shape of
a crown – sometimes – if you look <u>up</u> at him
  – like good children; –.
– And so all good be to you both.
Ever – dear wee 'amie
  Your loving Di Pa.
    J Ruskin.

71. 18 April 1871, Oxford

  Oxford. 16th April
   1871

Dearest Pufsie-amie

 To think that this is
(I hope) the last letter
I shall direct to "Mifs Agn.
ew. – Agnew! – (I was
writing on white blotting shee[t]
and did'nt see I had
no room.)
I think I shall always
send two envelopes, with
an old pussie one inside.
 I'm too tired to write
anything but what
you know very well –
that I shall be always
then as I am now
  Your lovingest Di Pa.
    J Ruskin.

Dear love to Connie.

Letter 70. 24/133, 1871. Envelope: red sealingwax; addressed to 'wee 'Amie, / 4th March. 1871'.
 1. Arthur Severn, who married Joan on 20 April 1871.

Letter 71. 33/133, 1871. Paper: half a sheet, folded sideways. Envelope: embossed with 'BURDEN, ENGRAVER, DIE STAMPER, & STATIONER, RYDE. I. W.' and a flower spray; addressed to 'Mifs Agnew / Mr Ruskin's / Denmark Hill / S. E. London.' Postmarked: 'N / OXFORD / AP 18 / 71' (front); 'LONDO[N S.E.] / C 7 / AP 19 / 71' (back). Note that the postmark does not correspond to Ruskin's date.

72. 19 April 1871, Oxford

> Oxford
> 17ᵗʰ April –
> 19ᵗʰ – I mean – 1871

Dearest Pufskins

I enclose you a letter I've had by me for you, ever so long – chiefly for the pleasure of directing one more letter to Pufsie Amie Agnew.

Ever your loving Di. Pa

I got your little sweet line this morning

73. 21 April 1871, Denmark Hill

> Denmark Hill.
> S. E.
> 21ˢᵗ April, 1871

Dearest Joanna.

I begin my work – or – let me rather say, my rest, this morning – with thoughts of your husband and you. – and with this poor little word of felicitation – which innocently desires to be rich but which knows you will love it – even in its poornefs. Whatever peace my thoughts – or words – or acts, can bring, be with you both.

Ever your loving   "Di Pa"
John Ruskin.

74. 24 April 1871, Abingdon

> [Ab]ingdon.¹
> 24ᵗʰ April

Darlingest Poos. moos.

Me so misby, me no no fot to do.
– me want my poos moos –
– me feel as if I was away at Abbeville. – very ill.
no etties yester day – no etties to day – bow – wow . ow – ow . ow.
– Ever oos pooest poo wee Donie
JR.
I've done good work today though.
– but <u>so</u> tired.

75. 25 April 1871, [Denmark Hill?]

> Denmark Hill.
> S. E.
> Wednesday

Dearest Poos-moos.

I am much lower

Letter 72. 34/133, 1871. Paper: half a sheet, folded sideways. Envelope: embossed with 'WATERLOWS "SECURE" LONDON' and a bird surrounded by a buckle with the motto 'INEBRANLABLE'; addressed to 'Mifs Agnew. / Mʳˢ Ruskin's, / Denmark Hill / S. E. / London.' Postmarked: 'C / OXFORD / AP 19 / 71' (front); 'HOLYWELL / B / AP 19 / 71 / OXFORD', 'LOND[ON S.E.] / [A]C / AP19/ 71' (back).

Letter 73. 35/133, 1871. Envelope: addressed to 'Mʳˢ Arthur Severn. / Care of the Revᵈ. Wᵐ Kingsley. / S. Kilvington / Thirsk'. Postmarked: 'LONDON-S.E. / X / AP 21 / 71' (front), 'A / THIRSK / AP 22 / 71' (back).

Letter 74. 37/133, 1871. Pencil notations: '1871'.
  1. The 'Ab' of 'Abingdon' is badly smudged.

Letter 75. 38/133, 1871. Pencil notations: '? 25 Apr. 1871'. The bottom third of this folded page has been neatly torn away, but there is no hint that there had been writing on it.
  1. There is a faded 'd' after the 'n'. Evidently, Ruskin began to write 'Sunday' as one word then amended it to be divided into 'Sun–day', thus adding to the feeling of baby-talk and lengthening the sense of the days slowly passing.
  2. Henry Acland (1815–1900), a life-long friend whom Ruskin met while both were student at Oxford (*The Ruskin Family Letters: The Correspondence of John James Ruskin, his Wife, and their Son, John 1801–1843*, ed. by Van Akin Burd, 2 vols (New York: Cornell University Press, 1973), II, 478–80).
  3. Rev. William Kingsley of South Kilverton, Yorkshire. He was a Turner expert (*Later*, p. 205).

than I at all thought I
should or could be below my
usual poor level, – for want
of my ownown Poosmoos –
and don't know fot to do.
Me was fitened dedful for no
ettie – no ettie – no ettie – no ettie
– Sat-day – Sun-day[1] – Mun –day
– Two's day – me so fitened
– at last me got wee ettie
at D^r Ac.'s[2]
– To-day – here – no ettie again
– me so misby-thisby-misby –
– poo – poo – poo, oos own Donie
           S^{t}C.
–See next page

I'm very sorry for Mr Kingsley[3]
My love to him.

   I am very thankful to
see you are both so happy.

Write here.

   Thats a very poking first
page for my poosmoos – only
it must be nice to be missed.
– Oh & me miss oo – mo than
tongues can tell –

76. 26 April 1871, Abingdon

     Abingdon. 26th April

Dearest Poos moos

   Me mifs oo so mut. me
not no fot to do.
– me very sulky and seepy.
– me had long walk – found
fritillary fowers. and boobells –
but its all no oos. now poos
moos is not here.
– ove to M^r & Mrs Kingsley –
– ittie bit to Arfie.

Ever oos own poo donie
     JR.
me dot no [pens].[1]

77. 27 April 1871, Denmark Hill

          See over page
    Denmark Hill.
      S. E.
        Thursday

   Darlingest Poos – moos.
   I was very glad of your both
affectionate letter yesterday. – only
you know its quite impossible for me
ever to believe that any body cares
for me except you. You don't
mean to say that Arfie could ever
be the least bit fond of me? I'm
just a fusty old critical father in law –
– you know he can't, possiby; he
only fancies he does in his honeymoon.

There's a parcel come from
Mr Brown for you – I'm so
curious to know whats in it
– Something lovely I'm sure –
There's a note which will perhaps
say. Shall I send the box.[1]
Write when you get this – to Abingdon
   Ever oos own sad – lonely di pa.
      JR.
This day last year, Lucy
says – we left Boulogne
for Paris –
Do you recollect telling me
what Lord Sligo said
and making me so happy?
And were'nt we happy
driving in by the Rue [de] Paix
that evening
   The Change! the change!
     to so many.
———

Letter 76. 39/133, 1871. Pencil notations: '1871'.
   1. This word is probably 'pens', implying he did not like the one he was writing with. In the first half of the letter, his nib produced a broad line of ink which was prone to smudging. He appears to have exchanged this for a very fine nib. Neither seems to have been to his liking.

Letter 77. 40/133, 1871. Pencil notations: '? Apr 27; 71'.
   1. Presumably a wedding present from Rawdon Brown in Venice.

78. 29 April 1871, Denmark Hill

Denmark Hill.
S. E.

Darlingest Poos moos,

Me send oo boo bell. – to show oo, me dot fairies as well as oo.
Poo Donie's stars all bite, istyday. Pitty Ina and Alice and Edith – all three – no di pa there – no di ma – Pretty Ina so pretty – pretty Alice prettier, pretty Edith prettiest – and dressed! – Well – you know how young ladies dress for private view! – but not a bit too much; and only conspicuous by the triplicity of prettinefs – Well – I came on them quite by themselves and they made themselves as charming as they – Well – I don't know
  what they could do, but it seemed
    as if they could'nt possiby have been
        charming en ^er.
– and I had them all to myself for all the time nearly – a whole hour, at least; – and as for the other people who ventured to speak to me – during that blissful time – I've put them down for never-to-be-relaxed vengeance and reprobation.

  Papa came at last, but seemed quite pleased that I had been "taking care" of them.

Then poo Donie went home to tea with Mrs Bentwick and Jessica and Jessica's little sister Venetia, who is immensely nice. and Jessica was delightful – (and besides I met Mrs Prinsefs with May Prinsefs. who is a great beauty too, and whom I had been hunting for a while about the room without in the least knowing who she was! – (did you ever know such stars, for once?) – and then – [1]all the pictures in the Academy are one worse than another – and I'm so spiteful that its' put me in the best spirits I've been in for many and many a day – – Oh – they are[2] so bad! – so bad! so[3] badd – with a double d –

all but young Leslie's, which is immensely pretty & clever – (but only upholsterers prettiness & clevernefs[4]) and a new – namelefs man – who has painted a scene form Henry the 6th which I would have bought, if I could have afforded it.

But my stars are all wrong again this morning. no ettie from my blessed poosmoss. – what shall me do!

Ever oos poo Donie
    JR

Letter 78. 42/133, 1871. Envelope: addressed to 'Mrs Arthur Severn. / Mrs Watson. / Tennant Arms / Hawnley / Helmsley.' Postmarked: 'LONDON-S.E. / X / AP29 / 71' (front); 'A / YORK / AP 30 / 71', 'HELMSLEY / A / AP 30 / 71' (back). Pencil notations: 'Apr. 29: 71.' Part of this letter is reproduced in 37.30.

1. There is a pencil bracket here, the other bracket is at the bottom of the following paragraph after 'afforded it'.
2. There are five lines under this 'are'.
3. Each 'so' has a thicker underline than the preceding one. The first is not much thicker than usual, the second is about 0.2 cm, the third about 0.5 cm.
4. These two words form an interesting example of Ruskin's inconsistent writing. Typically, he used the old-fashioned 'fs' for double 's', but in this instance he used the modern form for 'prettiness' and the archaic form for 'clevernefs'.

79. [May] 1871, Denmark Hill

Denmark Hill.
S. E.
       Saturday

Darlingest Poos moos.
 I had both <u>your</u>
letters – but not Arfies yet –
– it is very dear and sweet of
him wanting to help me about
R.[1] – I don't think anything
can be done, now, without losing
some of my influence at Oxford,
had it not been for my Pussie
I should have gone away into
a cave last October & never
come out unlefs R had come
to fetch me – but I could'nt
spoil my pussies love-time ;
– so also now, I am tied fast
by the duty of keeping my power
at Oxford, & for my greater plans –
Rosie must "pick" pansies and
leave everything she does wrong
for God to put right – as usual –
 – for the present; meantime
you and Arfie & Mamie
& Connie must all come
to Abingdon and make me
as happy as you can.

I came up with <u>two</u> pitty
Mifs Liddells from Oxford
last time – But Edith wa'snt
there – and I fell asleep![2]
I was <u>so</u> tired, that day.

    Ever oos votedest di Pa
        JR.

80. 3 May 1871, Abingdon

        Abingdon. 3rd May. 71

Dearest Poos moos
 I had your nice letter
with my mothers, this morning
I've been hard at work, giving
the men two lessons in one
and am sadly tired – but not
quite so misby as at home.

The wood hyacinths here
are <u>stupifying</u>ly beautiful –
– as lovely as gentians, but
in another way.
– So Arfie likes bad pictures,
like me; I've just been
telling Goodwin,[1] who has a
picture in the Academy, that
[t]he pictures theer are all
one worse than ^{an}other – till one
comes to Millais' landscape –[2]
which is a disgrace to human^{i}ty

– I've been doing [more][3]
pretty drawings – but
whats the use? with
no pussy to see them
and shriek

I send you a little
sketch book which Winsor
& Newton say is
well bound – I'm curious
to know how the paper
takes colour.

    Ever your lovingest
Di Pa   JR.
    Love to Arfie

Letter 79. 44/133, 1871. Pencil notations: '? May 1871'.
  1. Rose.
  2. The two Miss Liddells were Alice, of *Wonderland* fame, and her sister Rhoda. Edith, their sister, was Ruskin's favourite of what he referred to as 'the three Graces'. They were daughters of Henry George Liddell, Dean of Christ Church, and Lorina (Ina) Liddell.

Letter 80. 46/133, 1871.
  1. The letters from this period repeatedly refer to 'Goodwin' who was producing some drawings for Ruskin. Albert Goodwin (1845–1932) was a 'widely-travelled oil and watercolour artist' commissioned by Ruskin (Bradley and Ousby, p. 261n).
  2. The artist John Everett Millais, who had married Effie, the former Mrs. John Ruskin, in 1855.
  3. This could be 'such'.

81. 10 May 1871, Denmark Hill

Denmark Hill.
S. E.
10th May

Darling Pussie
The enclosed ~~three~~ two first notes have kept me in the furnace again these four days back – the third puts me in a smaller furnace of provocation with everybody. – except my Poosmoos. – forgive my, careless notes therefore of a day or two back.

I wrote a [mew] line to R. on Saturday – telling her to get well – morning

Write here. I am here till Saturday morning

82. 17 May 1871, Denmark Hill

Denmark Hill.
S. E.
Wednesday. 17th May
71.

Darling Joanie
All is right now – about letters. Yours – the last – ^ of yesterday came here this morning just when I wanted it.
I am dedful tired – and don't know fot to do – for my amie,
– I have all the letters to Abingdon quite rightly.

Now. write steadily to Crown and Thistle Abingdon and first of all – tell me what day the 13th of May is to Mamie ^ Hilliard 1 – she says it is a miserable anniversary to her.
And stay at Rievaulx as long as you [care] to day I'm quite helpleſs to say if I can come or not. but am ever your loving. di Pa,
JR
I should like all the rough way of it
[so must]

83. 27 May 1871, Abingdon

Darlingest Poos Moos
Me so velly velly glad oos both in Totland – and "so happy."
The lambs play always
– they know no ~~bet~~[1] – worse –
– And the tiny birds in their nests at [nurse]
(– Not a roof on their heads, not a penny in purse
Though its' better – after the summer weather –
To have something more, one's nest to
[feather –
Curtains of Silk – and Chairs of Leather
Put in the Charmingest way Together –
With a leaf of Rose – and a Bell of Heather –
– And if only [C.H][2] would rhyme with [V.][3]
~~it~~ I could just get one more rhyme, you see

Letter 81. 53/133, 1871. Paper: half a sheet. Pencil notations: '1871'.

Letter 82. 55/133, 1871. Envelope: embossed with 'E. JOHN. LATE WARD, DENMARK HILL. S. E.'; addressed to 'Mrs Arthur Severn / Hollidays. / Rievaulx. / Helmsley / Yorkshire'. Postmarked: 'LONDON-S. [E.] / X / MY 17 / 7[1]' (front); 'A / YORK / MY 18 / 71' , 'HELMSLEY / A / MY 18 / 71' (back).
  1. Ruskin added 'Hilliard' to specify which, since at this point Ruskin's mother, Joan's mother, and Joan herself were all referred by variations on 'mamie'.

Letter 83. 63/133, 1871. Pencil Notations: 'Abingdon' '? 27 May 71'.
  1. Ruskin apparently began to write 'better' then decided to make a poem of his letter. At this point, he added a dash pointing down to 'worse'. Subsequent lines begin straight across then slope down to the bottom right corner with ever more cramped writing as he fit in his rhymes.
  2. This could be 'T. H', but assume it refers to Constance Hilliard.
  3. This could be any number of options, including 'B', 'R' or 'L'.

– because I'm, Pussie's for ever,
—St.C.[4]
I dont know where the envelopes be –

84. 2 June 1871, Croyden

Dearest of Pussusses

Pease – Pease – Pease get well and ite poo Cuzzie but [fay] one wordie – me so sad – me so welly sad – me dont know fott _ tt tt tt tt tt to do. – Arfie writes me nice etties but I cant do without just a pencil scratch[1] – me fitened. – Me send oo all the kisses I've got – me ove oo so much so much – Pease come back pussie.

Ever oos voted St C.[2]

85. 7 June 1871, Oxford

Oxford.
Wednesday

My dearest dearest Pufsie

I was so thankful for the pencil line to day, but so longing to get near you and comfort you a little my own own self. You must not think of exerting yourself in any way before you are able. we will bear our disappointment here as we can – but you know it is very great. And I am so tired, too that I can only send poor words to my pussie – My wee, wee amie, me so sorry for oo – and for mineself. Ever your lovingest
Poo, Poo Donie.
Tell Arfie, in answer to this to write to Denmark Hill.

86. 20 June 1871, Denmark Hill

Denmark Hill.
S. E.
20th June

Darling Poosmoos.

I am so very thankful – Yes. next week will suit me exactly for Derbyshire, and that it should be nice for you too! in $^{for\ your}$ health, & all! it's too nice. +see last page I'm going to be very happy with you. God willing. most likely I shall have some news – very newsy – new-bridge-sy – perhaps. – but if not – still I mean to be happy – as I say. God willing for my work is good – just now –

---

4. Its hard to tell whether 'St. C' or the final line was written last. The dash before 'St. C' seems to connect to 'envelopes', and almost appears to have been written simultaneously between the lines. If this is intentional, he could be looking or anticipating envelopes/letters from either Joan or, since he signs with 'St. C', from Rose.

Letter 84. 67/133, 1871. Paper: embossed top left with 'IVORY'. Envelope: embossed with 'G. NEWTON, STATIONER, CROYDON'; addressed to 'Mrs Arthur Severn / Care of Wm Milroy Esq / Kirkcudbright / N.B'. Postmarked: 'C / CROYDON / JU 2 / 71' (front); 'KIRK[CUDBRIGHT] / JU 3 / 1871' (back). Pencil notations: 'Croydon. June 2: 71'.
  1. It appears that Ruskin received his first letter from the recuperating Joan on 7 June, for his letter to her from Oxford on that day thanks her for 'the pencil line today'.
  2. Ruskin was preoccupied with Rose. The next letter in the box – unfortunately undated – speaks specifically of writing to her.

Letter 85. 69/133, 1871. Envelope: embossed with 'F. JOHN. LATE. WARD. / DENMARK HILL. S. E.' and spray of flowers; addressed to 'Mrs Arthur Severn. / Care of Wm Milroy. Esq / Kirkcudbright / N B'. Postmarked: 'ABINGDON / H / JU 7 /[71]' (front); 'D / DUMFRIES / JU 8 / 71', '[KIRKCUDBRIG]HT / [JU] 9 / 1[8]71' (back). Pencil notations: 'June 7.', '1871'.

Letter 86. 78/133, 1871. Pencil notations: '1871'.

and I'm not at all sure that new
bridge is the safest for getting ^ over at
the new fields of it. The BP of
Limerick's son is very eager
to have leave to speak to people
– who know the eddies of the
river – But I won't let anybody
speak for me now – except
William or φίλη[1]
– Do you know anything of
people called [Rous] – or some such
name. – who have the impertinence
to be other peoples "friends" – ?[2]

I've been having a great read
of old letters this morning –
and – you would wonder – but –
they've [done] me good – I came
on [some] such lovely ones of L.'s!
and I've read over all that [I've]
I used to carry in my breast pocket
in 1866 – it seems as if nothing
could ever make such words vain.[3]
   Dear love to Arfie
     Ever oos lovingest poo Donie
       J Ruskin
+
   It will be at Matlock
old Bath, first, in middle
of Derbyshire. then a day
or two at Castleton,

I'n case any simple person thinks
I should ^might^ be foolish enough to
let you go into caves, please

observe –. I'm I mightnt.

87. 22 June 1871, Denmark Hill

Denmark Hill.
S. E.
22nd June

Dearest Pufsie
   It is pouring of rain. and
I feel dismal – what a shame,
When my Poos moos is better!

   I really don't know fot to do.
except to think that this day
week – God willing – my own
amie. will be comfying me.
     Ever oos ownest Donie
      With love to Arfie
       . St C .

[1]Mr Woodhouse[2] yesterday. (as
with John Simon[3] on Sunday)
as to my general health – which
is everyway helpful and cheering
     [] & nice[4]

88. 23 June 1871, Denmark Hill

Denmark Hill.
S. E.

Darlingest Moos.
   The afternoon yesterday
Was one down pour.
I went to the Athenaeum.
Wandered from Room to Room

---

1. William and Georgiana Cowper-Temple.
2. This whole paragraph is about Rose. The 'bridge' was code for a way to bridge the gulph (here 'river') between them.
3. 'L' is probably 'Lacerta', Rose's mother, while the letter Ruskin carried in his breast pocket in 1866 was from Rose.

Letter 87. 79/133, 1871. Paper: a fragment, the top and bottom third are extant and pinned together with a fine nail, but the middle 6 cm have been cut away. Pencil notations: '1871', as well as a pencilled line down the left side of the paragraph reading 'I really don't know' to '.St C.' The excised material probably related to upsetting news about Rose.
  1. What follows appears at the top of the reverse page, yet it does not flow from the bottom of the first page. Ruskin must have written on a second, now missing, leaf.
  2. Ruskin's dentist, who was also Rose's dentist when she was in London.
  3. One of Ruskin's doctors and a good friend.
  4. Most of this line has been cut away and whatever followed from 'nice' has been excised.

Letter 88. 81/133, 1871. Pencil notations: '23 June. 71.'

No Bishop.
Sate[1] for H half an hour [wondering][2]
No Bishop.
Sate for another half hour, frightened
No Bishop.
Sate for another half hour, disgusted
No Bishop – and no Dinner,
Sate for another houlf[3] – hour desperate.
No Bishop. no Dinner – & No Tea.
Drove away Home. Got home
at Ten.
No Fire. Kate [4]desperate.
Fir[5] enough in Kitchen for
Rasher of Bacon –
Kate brings [me] rasher
of Bacon.
And two eggs, rather
overdone in the hurry.
Dicious!
I mean always to have
nothing from eight to ten.
– when I can get
reasonable excuse.
This morning – enclosed
letter from Bishop.
– – Isn't it [inestimably]
comic, how all [Tuk up][6]
affairs go wrong?

I think she must be an
angel. and the Devil
is excelling himself to.
Keep me from ever seeing
her. or hearing of her.

I go to Evening Party as invited

I'm going to give the Bishop
Some L.[7] letters to read!
My goodnefs ! what a lark!
    Ever your loving S^{t}C.
I can't write now for laughing – think
    What L. would say if she knew –
        or will – when she knows.

89. 24 June 1871, Denmark Hill

Denmark Hill.
S. E.
Darlingest Pussky Mussky
  Me Two days with
no ettie. This one, came at
last. – velly short – di ma.
Dogs black-black-black[1]
for ever. no word from
lawyer – – me can't think
what will be the kind of
new life – if R[2] comes at last.
– Me quite bewildered di mamie ,
Oh – pease keep well to
come to Mat-ock.
    Ever oos own wee Donie
        S^t C.
– Love to William & Mary.[3]
and thanks for nursing my
Doanie so nicely. Love to Arfie
for sisting she shall be taken
care of. .

Auntie has sad, sad cough –
poor Auntie – all day long
and most of the night –

---

1. I have written this as 'Sate', which Ruskin uses as the past-tense of 'to sit'. The word 'Late' would also make sense here and in the following lines.
2. This could be 'wandering'.
3. Ruskin wrote 'hour' then imposed 'lf' over the 'ur', carelessly to imply 'half'.
4. One of Ruskin's servants.
5. This should be 'Fire'.
6. Rose.
7. Judging by his agitation about the angelic 'she' from whom he is barred from contact (Rose), this is presumably 'Lacerta', his pet-name for Rose's mother.

Letter 89. 83/133, 1871. Envelope: embossed with 'F. JOHN. LATE WARD, / DENMARK HILL. S. E.' and a spray of flowers; addressed to 'Mrs Arthur Severn / Care of Wm Milroy. Esq / Kirkcudbright / N. B.' Postmarked: 'LONDON-S.E. / X / JU 24 / 71' (front); 'KIRKCUDBRIGHT / A / JU 26 / 1871' (back). Pencil notations: 'June 24:71'.
1. This means that Ruskin felt deeply depressed.
2. Rose.
3. William and Mary Milroy of Kirkcudbright, Mary was Joan's sister.

The house is so sad, without
oo. – but its cruel to say
so, to Arfie & Doanie

90. June 1871, Matlock

> Matlock. Monday

Pussie, pussie dearie – me
ever so many miles nearer
oo – pease come twit, now.
– me so happy that Arfie
and oo are – cited about
Tuck up.
Me <u>not</u>, di ma,
Me velly – fillos – sofical.
– at ite – di ma?
– but it so pitty here –
pease come – di, di pussie
& Arfie.
> Ever oos own Donie
> JR.

Write [Watts] New Bath Hotel
Matlock Bath

91. [June 1871, Denmark Hill]

Darlingest Pussky mussky.

I've been very [awainy]
and lonely these several days
– two days without letter from
Pussky – how velly dedful.
Me fitened, di ma, till oos ettie
to day. Black-black-east wind
all day long. Black & cold –
no answer from lawyer.
and I quite bewildered – with
possible change of summer thoughts
and work – and mamie di – me
<u>don't</u> know FOt to do.

You may like to see the
enclosed – to the son of the B.^{p.1}
– Di pussie. pease keep velly
well – for Matlock.
> oos own Donie
> JR.

92. 12 September 1871, Lancaster & Coniston

> *Denmark Hill.*
> *S. E.*
> Lancaster. 12th Sep.^t
> Morning

Darlingest Pufs.
I've had a wonderful
walk up ever <u>such</u> a hill – to a
bit of moorland with <u>such</u> air
blowing over it – and a view of
Lancaster – !!! – ^exquisite^ ^even^ ^though^ ^spoiled
by half an infernal pitfull of
smoke between. And I feel
as if I had two legs again – instead
of two stumps only.
> Coniston. – evening

Yesterday afternoon at Lancaster
an American whom I don't
know – left me a Dante he
has just translated – then
Mr Moore came – and this
morning, Mr Edmund Sharpe;
[a nice old architect)[1] & the
Mayor of Lancaster left his card!

I've had a lovely day.
– The view from the house
is finer than I expected –
the house itself dilapidated
and rather dismal – I want
my Doanie to come & see

Letter 90. 80/133, 1871. Pencil notations: 'June. 1871'.

Letter 91. 84/133, 1871. Pencil notation: '? June 1871'. This is a fragment; while the full first page is extant, the top ¾ of page two have been excised after 'Fot to do', 4.5 cm from the base. I have placed the letter in June 1871, before Ruskin left for Matlock, although it is now filed after his arrival at Matlock.
  1. See 20 June 1871 [86].

Letter 92. 89/133, 1871. Pencil notations: '1871'. This letter is reproduced almost in its entirety, with some normalization, in 37.34–35.
  1. This is an unusual pair of brackets. To the left, it is L-shaped, to the right it is round but struck through by a horizontal line.

it dectly with Arfie, (when
I come back from Totland)
and tell me what she thinks

Ever – oo darling poosmoos
  oos own wee Donie
    JR. .

93. 13 September 1871, Coniston

        Coniston. Thursday

Darlingest Poos Moos.
  [1]Anything so lovely as the
view from my rocks was
to day – I hav'nt seen since
I was at Lago Maggiore!
– Your sweet letters all received
Write me one to Post Office
<u>Melrose</u>. I want to try and
get another walk up Rhymer's
Glen with Mary Kerr,[2] next
Sunday. I think it would
be very nice for poo Donie
– & then. me can see the
architecture of the Abby, oo know,
~~for Professorial~~ di ma – me so
fond of Archy tectur –[3]
  Tomorrow. I post to Keswick
  and so by rail to Carlisle
& see Cathedral.
– Saturday to Melrose.
I've written to lady Henry,
to ask if she, (and Mary), are
to be there. – If not – Ill
go to the Inn.
—
  Harry Acland's a good fellow![4]
to want to ~~pro~~ ^help^ my plan –

– if he'll dig. thats all that
I want.
–<u>So</u> glad you liked the
new mown hay di Ma.
  Love to Arfie
  Ever your lovingest Di Pa
    JR

Oh me – I wish you were here
or I at Dover, di ma.
You will so Dump, when you
see my rocks. and my
saxifrages.

94. 14–15 September 1871, Coniston

        14th Sept. Evening[1]

Darlingest Pussie,
  Anything so splendid in the
way of golden and blue birds,
as the pheasant I put up at
my own wicket-gate to the moors
^out of^ ~~on~~ my own heather – was never
seen except in my own Doanies
own pheasant drawing that she's
never asked after, this age.
My wrist is stiff with rowing –
I've rowed full six miles to day
besides scrambling up the bed
of a stream holding on by the
heather & – more than I cared for,
juniper bushes; – Which is exercise
also.
  There certainly <u>is</u> a special
fate in my getting this house –
  The man from whom I buy it
Linton – wanted to found
a "republic – " – Printed a

Letter 93. 91/133, 1871. Envelope: addressed to 'Mrs Arthur Severn / Mr Ruskin's / Denmark Hill / S. E. / London'. Postmarked: 'AMBLESIDE / B / SP13 / 71' (front); 'CONISTON [the rest illegible]', 'LONDON-S.E. / F 7 / SP 14 / 71' (back). Pencil notations: 'Sep 13.71'.
  1. There is a pencil bracket here, the other bracket is after 'Lago Maggiore!'.
  2. Daughter of Lord Henry Kerr. See *Praeterita* for a memory of the first such walk in July 1867 when 'Mary Ker[r] stopped to gather a wild rose' (35.557).
  3. This unusual spelling might evoke Rose's early nickname for Ruskin: 'Archigosaurus'.
  4. Ruskin's godson, son of Henry Acland (*Early*, p. 206).

Letter 94. 94/133, 1871. Envelope: addressed to 'Mrs Arthur Severn / 21. Waterloo Cresc^t / <u>Dover</u>.' Postmarked: 'AMBLESIDE / B / SP 14 / 71' (front); 'DOVER / B / SP [1]5 / 71' (back). Pencil notations: '1871'. Unusually, a pencil '2' has been inscribed at the top left corner of the second page. The numbering continues on the next page with a '3' above the line 'behind Lollies room, that you'.

certain number of numbers of
"the Republic" – like my
Fors Clavigera! and hïs[1]
printing press is still in one
of the out houses – and
"God and the People" scratched
deep in the white wash outside.
Well – it won't be a republican
~~resort~~ "centre" now – but whether the
landed men round will like
my Toryism better than his
Republicanism, remains to be
seen.
The house is built on the rock
itself – and in a recess of the hill
side – which rises <u>too</u> steeply
behind the house – almost
as the hill did at the Geisbach[2]
behind Lollies room, that you
got to by the bridge. A bridge
twelve feet long would reach the
hillside from my roof – and
I'm sorry to say, the spring which
I am so proud of has been
allowed to soak its way down
exactly there, and under the house
as far as chinks of rock will
let it. – with what result to
<u>apricot jam</u> inside – <u>you</u> may
fancy! The first thing I've
to do is to cut a trench in the
rock to carry away this drainage
– it is just like a dripping well
at Matlock, behind the house.
For the house itself! – Well –
there <u>is</u> a house, certainly, and
it has rooms in it, but I believe
in reality, nearly as much will
have to be done as if it weer

a shell of bricks and mortar.
– Meantime – the first thing Ive
to do is to build a wall up
one side of my <u>six</u> – not five,
acres of moor.

Friday.
    I've so much to do – &
its <u>so</u> beautiful, I cant
go to Scotland!
    write here. always.

    Ever your lovingest
Di Pa.
      J R.
I've been rowing & cutting
<u>wood</u> in my own woods
& am so seepy di ma –
[3]<u>nuts</u> some. I send <u>you</u>
      my first nuts –
        in a box

95. [? 1871], Denmark Hill

Denmark Hill.
S. E.

Darlingest Pussky, (Puss of the Sky,
that means)
– only my pen wont ite it.
– Me no to have no dinnie
to mowy. – Pease tum to [lunchy punchy]
(– Me send a Punchy to nite)
– Pease tum to munchy-unchy-punchy
to mowy.
– If it rains, you know dearie
we won't go. – if it does, therefore
just stop at home, and Ill come
up for a chat. But if fine,
come to lunch here. and we'll
have plenty time for our drive.

---

1. Ruskin occasionally seems to place this accent on an 'i', implicitly drawing it out to two (even three) syllables and making himself sound petulant. In this case, I suspect that Ruskin wanted a printing press of his own. William James Linton (1812–98) was a 'wood engraver, printer and republican' (*Later*, p. 212).
2. The Hotel Geissbach which the cousins visited in 1866 and to which Ruskin returned to see the ill 'Marie of the Geissbach' in 1869.
3. There is a curved line connecting 'wood' and 'nuts'.

Letter 95. 129/133, 1871. Pencil notations: '?71'. The mention of meeting for dinner matches late autumn 1871 (see, for example, 29 November 1871, not transcribed), but the apparent introduction of the term 'Pussky' might place this letter as early as June 1871, since the first dateable 'Pussky' is 24 June 1871 [89].

~~– Please send todays telegraph if you have it.~~
I was glad to see mama looking so well and happy.

Love to her and Arfie.
Ever oos oviest Di Pa.

Fig. 5. Facsimile of JR letter to JS, 24 Nov. 1872 [107]
RF L37, Ruskin Foundation (Ruskin Library, Lancaster University)

1872

R. takes Continental tour with the Severns, Mary and Constance Hilliard,
and the artist Albert Goodwin, 1 April to 27 July
Following R.'s return, he and Rose meet for the first time in six years;
he again suggests the possibility of marriage and she becomes hysterical
R. spends September and October at the Waterhead Hotel, Coniston,
to arrange Brantwood matters
R. lectures at Oxford, November and December, and develops a friendship with
Prince Leopold, youngest son of Queen Victoria, then studying at Oxford

96. 26 January 1872, Denmark Hill

My darling, of course keep Coventry Patmore – and all that you care for of autographs. And do come back   Denmark Hill
   on Tuesday   S. E   Tuesday
      – I am here still till that day week

Darling Doanie

   I really am very much obliged to you for that sweet long letter. I never in the least – naughty di Pa that I am, give you any credit for modesty and thinking it not worth while – (I am sure I never have given you cause to think so) – but I always say. There now – shes been going out to a party – or she's been late down to breakfasts – and then I'm always to be the loser.
   Di wee Doanie, I saw such a lovely French play last night, but so infinitely sad that I can't even jest in writing to day – any more than if some new grief had happened to myself

If wee Doadie[1] had'nt come and comforted me to day I should'nt have known fot to do. – she's so nice. and Im Ever oos loving Cuzzie (a little better) – J R.

97. 7 February 1872, Corpus Christi College

Love to Mama & Arfie
   C. C. C.
      7th February. 1872

Dearest Joanie

   I write to you my first letter on my new writing table. in my – own – college. It is very pleasant to me, this room – and the feeling of all – in a quiet, sad, way. Thirty-five years since I sat down first in my own rooms in college. not two hundred yards from the spot where I write.
   Your lovely letter and an exquisite one form Connie came to cheer me this morning, and I had a walk in the evening, in quiet sunshine!
   Arthur and you must

Autograph letters for 1872 are in 'Bem L 37 / Letters / John Ruskin / to / Joan Severn / 1872'.

Letter 96. 10/124, 1872. Envelope: embossed with 'F.JOHN LATE WARD.DENMARK HILL.S.E.'; addressed to 'Mrs Arthur Severn / Care of Philip Rathbone Esq / Greenbank Cottage / Liverpool'. Postmarked: 'LONDON.S.E. / X / JA26 / 72' (front) '[unclear] / 27 JA 72 / 4' (back). Pencil notations: 'Jan 26', '72'. Note that the Philip Rathbone referred to here may be the father of 'Alice' of 'Green Bank', with whom Ruskin was fascinated in November 1878.
   1. Dorothy Livesey (Burd, *Winnington*, p. 671n.).

Letter 97. 13/124, 1872. Part of this letter is reproduced in 37.49–50.

soon come down to see me.
I've bought an embroidered
tablecloth – Green, with black
edge – all over flowers, which
I am very proud of.

I have written to the Isle
of Man, sending a little
money.

Please ask Angie[1] to
get me, from Bond St.
some patterns of breakfast
sets in [Danish] china. and
to have them for me to choose,
when I come to see her
next week.

If you and Arthur will
call on Mr H. S. Marks [2]
      7, Holden Terrace
        Buckingham Palace Yard
You will see two most
interesting pictures.

Ever my darling
Your grateful and loving Cuzzie
and Di Pa.
      JRuskin.

98. [undated] 1872, Corpus Christi College

Corpus Christi College
Oxford

Darling Doanie
  Just a wee line
to say how I think of you
and what a joy you
are to me.
– Lecture's on the whole
seem to be liked.
Tomorrow's I hope will
be nice.

I read from your
writing quite nicely
  Ever your loving
    Di Pa

99. 28 March 1872, Corpus Christi College

Corpus Christi College
Oxford
28th March. 1872

Dearest Pussie
  It was <u>very</u> sweet
seeing your bright face as
far as I could to day.
I got quite comfortably down
and my rooms are nice
and I am very well.
  More sorry for the break
to people about me – not
to speak of my poor pussie.
But from this time last
year, to the servants and
tradespeople – and my friends
– the change is great.
My mother then quite well
to all appearance – and
poor Ann.[1]
And our Pussie just
going to be married.
and every body laughing
and happy.

And now – to see the
place!. I'm glad <u>I</u> can't

Well, Pussie has her Arfie
and I've my Pussie – and
oos my Pussie and Im oos
cuzzie – and at Brantwood
we'll all be gay when
Johnny comes marching home
Ever my darling. Your own
  Di Pa.   JRuskin

---

1. Possibly Sarah Angelina Acland (b. 1849), daughter of Henry Acland, generally referred to as 'Angie' (*Later*, p. 195).
2. H. Stacy Marks, R.A, a friend of Ruskins (36.lxxi-ii).

Letter 98. 108/124, 1872. Pencil notations: '72'. The letter is undated, but I have placed it in early spring, 1872.

Letter 99. 34/124, 1872.
  1. Anne Strachan, his nurse.

100. September 1872, Brantwood

<blockquote>See ovy.
Brantwood,
Coniston</blockquote>

Beloved Pussky.
 – I never feel as
if I were a bit farther
away from you; near or
far – it is all the same
to me, the thought of you
always is such a comfy to
your poor di Pa.
Please be very happy: Di Pa
is[1] going to 'joy himself at
Coniston. and say '<u>my</u> pussie'
all over the hills and lake

<blockquote>Ever oos own di Pa.</blockquote>

Di Pa joyed Arfie and
Georgie last night. Bess
  looks very well.

Di pussie,
 Poo Donie had lost
his wee pen – Just found
it again – mut tell his
amie – whenever he finds
anything he wants.

Di ma – does it tire oo to
read wee etties now?

101. [?? 1872], Brantwood

<blockquote>Brantwood,
Coniston</blockquote>

Darlin Pufsie
 Me doin' away. me
so dismal me don't no
fot to do. – Me want
to give up bein Pefsor –
(– me tant say at, di ma,
nor ite it) – and top heer
and have Joanie Ponie,
and Ilie-willie,[1] and Clochette
– and Connie-won-pon.[2]

– Seriously. I never felt the
worry of travelling so much –
The quiet of this place – and the
[lakes has] been very quiet lately,
makes the turmoil quite painful
 to me to think of.
We really had a very happy
time, all of us – (in spite
of what was underneath in
one's heart.) – and it
spoils me.
I'm really a saint, I think
after all – to go to Oxford
and be bored.
  Send me a nice "tomfy"
  ettie di ma –
  Ever oos own St Donie.

102. [October], 1872 Corpus Christi College

<blockquote>Corpus Christi College
Oxford
Monday Evening</blockquote>

Darling wee Pussky
 Here is oos Di Pa –
much nearer oo. – Twite well,
– but a good deal Rosie-Posiefied,
and sad.
  The Sunset, lovely, made him
glad he was'nt at Coniston.

Letter 100. 51/124, 1872. Pencil notations: '? Sep', '?1872'. This undated letter is the first on Brantwood letterhead, the first dated use of the letterhead is '23rd. Evening', assumed to be from 1872.
  1. Ruskin inserted 'is' in the left margin.

Letter 101. 60/124, 1872. Paper: half a sheet. The letter is filed amid a series of undated letters, some of which are tentatively ascribed to October 1872. I have placed it with the other letters concerned with Clochette, and before Ruskin returned to Oxford in late October.
  1. Probably Lily Armstrong.
  2. After a gap, the letter continued, below, in a finer pen. Connie-won-pon is either Constance Hilliard or Oldham.

Letter 102. 64/124, 1872. Pencil notations: '? Oc 72.' I have placed this letter after Ruskin returned to Oxford, but before his stay at Euston Hotel at the end of October.

where he would have seen
only grey cloud.
– Jamie Anderson[1] came in
to tea, and is coming tomorrow
with my new Balliol pupils
to breakfast.
Me tired di Ma. Mees oos
   poo Donie.

103. 30 October 1872, Euston Hotel

Euston – Tuesday
morning

Darlingest di Ma
  Oo <u>munt-nt</u> have backs,
– nor fronts – neither – =
me don't know which is wust.
– me so misby. Me wanted
a ettie so <u>pickarly</u>-[1] tickarly.
(– what is it – di ma?)
– me perfectly etched, here
– me ~~w~~ didn't want to
tum here – my mas in Totland
– neebody at home – & the
lassies awa – ower the water
to Charlie, & sic like – I'd
Charlie them! a but puîr
wee Lily, wha has nae Charlie –
– only her ~~wee~~ bit auld birdie,
that canna sing,– the [frisson]less creature.
– But – as I was sayin, theres
nae luck aboot the hoose –
– an I winna gae near it –
– an I canna see naething
here but [lums] – an I hae
nae ettie – and I'm like
to greet my een oot –
– or ~~at leas~~ to say the least
ot, blear & blin – and there
are nae lins to loup ower –
and ~~if~~ ^{gin} there were, I'm owre
auld & stiff to loup – an
I dinna ken whats to be dune
and Im oos poo wee wee Donie.

104. 31 October 1872, Corpus Christi College

Wednesday

Darlin wee Doanie
  It's so dreadfully dismal,
being a Pfessy. I can't even
write baby misbinefs about it –
I really am very utterly down
to night. Brantwood and Doanie
and Lilie & Arfie and Lollie
were too nice. . Now me got
to go dinin in the Hall with
Pfessys and Fellows, and
lonely-lonely tea – and work, &
[wory].
And seriously, the home I
had once – and the hopes –
– all <u>broken</u> away so ill
Broken isnt the [wind][1]. Vanished.
Melted – Buried – everything
– ~~and~~ that was.
  Doanie the only link left to me.
My power for good to others
however increases continually –
Read the notices in the
papers which I send to day

---

1. James Reddie Anderson, one of Ruskin's pupils and assistants at Oxford.

Letter 103. 55/124, 1872. Pencil notations: '? Oc 30 72'. Ruskin had stayed at the Euston earlier in the year, immediately after his traumatic separation from Rose. It is not clear why he returned there at this point (see *Later*, pp. 243–45, 259).
  1. There is a loopy scrawl above the hyphen which may be 'and'.

Letter 104. 63/124, 1872. Enclosures: two newspaper clippings. One, under the heading 'LITERATURE', is a review of 'The Works of John Ruskin. Vol. I. "Sesame and Lilies." Sold by George Allen, Heathfield Cottage, Keston, Kent.' It is one column wide and runs the length of the page. Although nameless, 'John Morgan' is written in pen at the bottom. The second is an unascribed column on 'JOHN LEECH'S DRAWINGS' which extensively cites what Ruskin had written on the topic. Pencil notations: '?Oc 31', '72'. In naming the place of composition, I have surmised that he was at College because of the mention of dining in halls, despite the fact that the previous letter was sent from the Euston Hotel.
  1. This appears to be 'wind', but 'word' would make more sense.

– The enclosed letter from the author of Liverpool one is very pleasant to me.
[2] I've answered, thanking him Its the first time anybody ever gave me credit for knowing that things have two sides – or for knowing anything besides drawing in six lessons.

Your letter is a great comfy to me, di ma. but if me tink how long its to be before I see di ma any mo – Me just a great big schoolboy di ma – (– ony – me would like to ky, like a itie wee school<u>girl</u>.)
    or wee [kittie][3]
Mew-. ew- ew-ew.

Ever oos poo-poo-poO Donie
    Thats a great sob.

105. 1 November 1872, Corpus Christi College

Corpus Christi College
Oxford

Darling Pufsie-Amie
    Your letter with your brother-in-law's sayings about what the Scotch think of me was a great comfy this morning – just in the very moment I needed it – For Oxford seems to me in more hopeless wreck every time I enter it. I have been as sad, about myself, as I am now, before;
– but never so hopelefs about other people.

When I was sorrowfullest in 1868, my bitterest feeling was that my influence would be destroyed again by the Irish quarrel

Now, as far as my own power is concerned, I have enough – but I think other people are past mending.

Also – I'm past mending myself – in many ways, Me so velly, bad boy di ma – – me don't know <u>fot</u> to do.
    Love to Arfie & Wm & Mary. Ever your
        lovingest Di Pa.

106. 6 November 1872, London

Wednesday

Darlin Pussky-mussky –
    I saw Newton[1] at mussy isterday.
He says – first thing – (– no – not quite) – how is Mrs Arthur?
– She's all right says I.
Is the event near – says he –
– I'm afraid so – says I –
– Tell her, of all things, not to have twins – says he.

Darlin, Pussky – I wish you were twins yourself – – and could always be one <u>here</u> and one there.

---

  2. There is a pencil bracket here, the other bracket is after 'lessons' at the end of the paragraph.
  3. The first consonant is unclear. My guesses are either 'k' for 'kittie' (but Ruskin invariably chose 'pussy' for feline diminutives) or 'sittie' for sister (but this is not a word typically used by Ruskin either).

Letter 105. 65/124, 1872. Pencil notations: 'Nov 1: 72'.

Letter 106. 66/124, 1872. Envelope: embossed with 'T.W. JACKSON, 24 & 25, ALBION STREET / HYDE PARK.' and a flower and leaf arrangement; addressed to 'Mrs Arthur Severn / [M.] Milroy, Esq, P. [F.] / Kirkcudbright / N. B.' Postmarked: 'LONDON / 4 / NO 6 / 72' (front); 'KIRKCUDBRIGHT / A / NO 7 / 1872' (back). Pencil notations: 'Nov. 6: 72', 'London'.
  1. Charles Newton.

Norton[2] dined with me
yesterday. We talked
all manner of wickednefs,
– agreed that the enclosed
article of Pallmall Gazette
was first rate – &c.
Take great care of it,
I want it
– Me so misby – misby –
misby – I really sometimes
almost wish I was
a clergyman and tellin
lies all day long – it
makes people so happy.
 Ever oos loving, faithful
  – missiby Donie.

Write to Oxford
Such a bothy wothy
to get this into envelope
& when I'd done it
[I][3] directed it to <u>Mifs</u> –
 somebody – don't know
     whom[4]
had to ite new envy.

107. 24 November 1872, Corpus Christi College

    Corpus Christi College
      Oxford
Darlin Poos,
 Is'nt all oos peepies dedfu
socked 'at we tant pell any
betty, oo & me – after bein
Pessy and Pussy evie so long?
– Me so fitened. – fot do ey all
say?
Di ma, its a bright day,
and my picties are all up.
 – Raphael in middle over fireplace[1]
  E   H
at top – Bonifazio on left –
little Sir Joshua boy on right –
Turner Bonneville below.
E. Edward Frere. <u>H</u>. Hunt window.[2]

 Then Titian Doge[3]

 Fortune Door Open[4]
on the world C[5]

  Minnies in cabbies

and my father over the
door – looking at poo Donie
where he sits to ite.
 Then Ive my Tintoret Diana[6]
between windows on my left –
but my booty boo eyed wee lassie
– I don't know <u>fot</u> to do with her
ses so pitty. Ses standin
just don beside me. at present.

Di ma peas come back
 and see it all –
  ever oos ownest Donie

---

2. Charles Eliot Norton.
3. This 'I' has been torn away.
4. The letter continues, sideways, up the left margin, to which it is connected by a rough line.

Letter 107. 78/124, 1872. Envelope: embossed with a honeycomb crest; addressed to 'Mrs Arthur Severn / Care of Wm Milroy Esq. P.F / Kirkcudbright / N. B.' Postmarked: 'OXFORD / K / NO 24 / 72' (front) 'KIRKCUDBRIGHT / A / NO 25 / 1872' (back). Pencil notations: 'Nov 24. 72'.

1. There is a sketch here of the fireplace with two pictures above and two to either side, the bottom ones on each side are lettered, 'E' to the left and 'H' to the right.
2. The 'E' and 'H' correspond to the letters on his sketch, for Edouard Frère and William Holman Hunt.
3. This line is written at the top of the inside page. Beneath it is a sketch of the arrangement in the corner of a room. It includes two paintings. One is above a door (labelled 'Door open'), the larger is above a chest, which appears to have two doors on the front, each with two panels. Ruskin has written '[minnies in cabbies]' across this chest. Sitting on top of it, he has sketched what looks like a feather coming out of a bottle, beside which is written 'Fortune on the world'.
4. This clarifies what the open door beside the mineral cabinet and beneath the portrait of his father is.
5. Sitting beneath the Doge, on top of the mineral cabinet, which is labelled below.
6. Tintoretto's 'Diana and her Dogs', which the 'Library Edition' places at Brantwood (11.376.n).

108. [25 November 1872], Corpus Christi College

Corpus Christi College
Oxford

Darlin Pussky

Mes oos pessy – and oos mine pussy. – Me tooktitit pince eopold[1] all owie the gallewys today – with hie tutor – he velly nice boy and ooked at tings vetly carefully. – me sowed him pitty Louis missal – and pitty Turners – and he gave me pitty message through his tutor afterwards about [??] my not coming to dinner – so alls ite

    Evy oos own Donie

109. 28 November 1872, Corpus Christi College

Corpus Christi College
Oxford

Darlin Poos moos.
 – Me dedful tired and worrited. – me's had to go and -ceive pince eopold – and sow him sings, and. mes got to go gen mowy monin. (If <u>poo</u> di auntie had been alive!!!)[1] – and peepies want me to go ^{to} dinnywin and me won't.)

– Di poosmoos. – when would oo like to see oos di pa? Sall him come on Thursday evening the 11<u>th</u> & stay till Tuesdays the 16<u>th</u> [&][2] go down first to Brantwood from Oxford? <u>Also</u> what me wants to know – what <u>oo</u> wants with oos di Pa. – How will oo sist without oos di Pa – till' ping time? – Me don't think me can sist, any longer – without seeing my poosmoos.
    Evy oos ovin Di Pa.

Me had nice time with petty Mifs Ls.[3] They sang and played to me – alltogevy. – Me ~~don~~ goin agen, tomowy. They came to ecties – so did Pince Eopold[4] – di Pa sy, but peepies say it was well enough

110. 5 December 1872, Corpus Christi College

Corpus Christi College
Oxford

Thursday
Darlingest of Wee Doanies
 I have all your nice letters – and am so glad you mifs your Arfie. and that he misses oo. I'm always a tiny bit jealous of him and

---

Letter 108. 79/124, 1872. Pencil notations: 'Nov 25. 72'.
  1. Prince Leopold (1853–84), later Duke of Albany, youngest son of Queen Victoria (see 20.xxxv-vi for his friendship with Ruskin).

Letter 109. 80/124, 1872. Envelope: embossed with a buckled, honeycomb crest; addressed to 'Mrs Arthur Severn / Care of W^m. Milroy Esq PF. / Kirkcudbright / N. B.' Postmarked: 'OXFORD / K / NO 28 / 72' (front); 'KIRKCUDBRIGHT / A / NO 29 / 1872' (back). Pencil notations: 'Nov 28. 72'.
  1. This bracketed reference to his mother and the pride she would have felt knowing her son was meeting with Prince Leopold has been added between the lines as an afterthought.
  2. This could be 'or'.
  3. Alice, Edith and Rhoda Liddell.
  4. Prince Leopold.

Letter 110. 88/124, 1872. Pencil notations: 'Dec. 5. 72'. Envelope addressed to: 'Mrs Arthur Severn / Care of Wm Milroy Esq. P. F./ Kirkcudbright / N. B.'; postmarked 'OXFORD / K / DE 5 / 72' (front) 'KIRKCUDBRIGHT / DE 6 / 1872' (BACK).

me no quite ike it, – but me
would ike it much less, any
other way.
I went to Wykeham House[1]
last night – though I had cold.
So had the Prince – so we
talked cold in the comfortablest
way, and it made the beginning
of things easy for both.
His tutor sate at the end of
the small table – [(no carving of corn)]
He at the side farthest from
the fire and I opposite –
(– table only about five feet
wide) – (The house is a little
on this side of Mr Tyrwhittes,[2]
and is one of the same sort.)
– Hare – or other brown, soup –
– then +herrings! – The Prince
had never tasted one!! Found
them rather soft. Talked of
herrings and char for some
time – char fo to be had
at Balmoral.
– Cutlets & chicken. Talk
got on novels. Prince never
skips. – and never looks to
see the end – hopes for the
best, all through.
"Red as a Rose is she", greatly
discussed. Said to be "out in
of bad form" a – in [the foreworn] phrase
– but very dramatic – (I suppose so!!)
Scott. of course – I recommended
the Prince, of all modern languages
first to learn Scotch. Always
Scotch as Scotts, no lefs than
Scotland.
Blancmangy pudding. Politics.
– a little – – I not caring to
bring out any of my Tory no
notions for fear they would be
thought got up for the receiver –
still less radical ones.

Then peepies talked of, of peepies.
– memories – Prince can always
remember names – [so] queen – Grandmother[3]
could'nt – one.
Grapes & preserved [pine] –
– Oxford and its ways,
The Mifses Liddell. – Prince
which prettiest? "Prince goes
for Edith" – "I can do pretty
well with Alice." – I Praised
Ina for a good girl.
– Coffee – Portfolio from
print dealer – proofs fifty
guineas each – for approval.
– Professor said – "Don't buy
any" – Prince appeared
relieved in mind.
– Drawing room.
Town of Lucerne – Queen's
stay there. Prince very happy
there – I knew all his
places – Agreed that
it was being all spoiled.
– Tea –
painting of water lilies over
side table – Well done?
– yes. – not quite right – but
– very nice. Princesf Louise –

Corpus Christi College
Oxford[4]

– Flower painting –
Gustave Dore – ? No! –
(– Did him as much harm
as I could) !)
– Ten oclock – Prince sorry
he could not come to ectie
today – Cold too bad –
– shake hands – goodnight

– Norton[5] & Ned Jones[6]
came at 12 today – Pleasantest
lunch. Then to ectie.
Ectie velly dood, me tink.
– ovy peepies say so too – tea[7]

1. Prince Leopold's house in Oxford.
2. Rev. Richard St. John Tyrwhitt.
3. The second half of 'Grandmother' extends down the margin of the page.
4. A new sheet of letterhead.
5. Charles Eliot Norton.
6. Edward Burne-Jones (1833–98), artist and good friend of Ruskin.
7. These unclear letters have been blotted and are written above the dash.

Acland then – Said "I had
been very good" at the Prince's
– So its all ite di ma.
and me's oos dood donie.
   Send me a wee kissy-wiss
      Ever oos own Donie.

111. 7 December 1872, Corpus Christi College

Corpus Christi College
Oxford

Darlingest of Dauties
   I'm so glad you're at
Mr Richmonds¹ and can
love and comfort him a little
as you do me.
– How I should have discomforted
him to day. I've been going in
at M. Angelo with all
I know – and was in good trim
and the prince was there, and
a nice University audience
and the lecture went on hotly
for an hour and a quarter –
– and I'm sure M. Angelos
none the better for it – though
   I dare say M Richmond
will say, he's none the
worse. (I should say so too
– for I dont think he <u>can</u>
   be worse.) – But really
it <u>was</u> interesting, on the early
divinity and theology of
Botticelli. – and I had
good illustrations and
everybody seems pleased
I showed the Prince in
and out – and he sent
afterwards to ask if he
might come and see
some of the illustrations

more quietly – I don't know
if he means at the galleries
or here – but said he
might come, of course.
– Di wee Dautie, give my
dear love to Tom.
– If only we were at Rome
together again –
   Oh me – how we should
fight. – perhaps its' better
   we neither of us had
older heads on our shoulders
when we weer there.

All kind messages to the
family – and many to
Arfie. The Chess message
is <u>very</u> nice. I believe
on Tuesday I must
only have afternoon tea with
you, and dine at the
Grosvenor. –
Ill write to Herne Hill
   Evy oos own Di Pa.

112. 21 December 1872, Corpus Christi College

   Love to Arfie

Corpus Christi College
Oxford

   Darlingest Poos Moos.
You may perhaps like, better
than baby talk – that
I should copy the note I
am just going to seal for Osborne
(Book in question St Paul & other poems
      by F. W. Myers)

   Sir,
   I have been in London
during the last seven days
and though your Royal Highnefs's

Letter 111. 89/124, 1872. Envelope: addressed to 'Mrs Arthur Severn / Care of Thos Richmond Esq / Park Ridge / <u>Windermere</u>'. Postmarked: 'OXFORD / N / DE 7 / 72' (front); 'WINDERMERE / A / DE 9 / 72' (back). Pencil notations: 'Dec. 7. 72'.
   1. Thomas Richmond.

Letter 112. 91/124, 1872. Envelope: addressed to 'Mrs Arthur Severn. / Herne Hill / S.E/ London'. Postmarked: 'OXFORD / K / DE 21 / 72' (front); 'LONDON [S.E.] / [? 7] / DE 23 / 72' (back). Pencil notations: 'Dec. 21 1872'. The enclosed letter to Prince Leopold is reproduced in 37.54–55.

kind letter came to me there
I was afraid to send for the book
lest any mischance should
come to it, and have only been
able to look at it to-day.
But now, much more than
most books, I have looked at
it, and learned from it. I am
very heartily glad your Royal
Highnefs likes it – but it seems
strange to me – you are
very happy in being enough
sad to enter into the
feeling of these poems already.

The 'John Baptist' seems
to me entirely beautiful and
right in its dream of him
The St Paul is not according
to my thought, but I am
glad to have my thoughts
changed. I wish the verses
were left studiously
alliterative – but the verbal
art of the is wonderful

Some of the [minor]
poems are the sweetest of
their kind I ever read –

Wordsworth with a softer
chime. I wish I had
something adverse to say,
for this [note] must read to
you as if I only wanted to
say what would please you.
That is indeed true; but
I should neither hope nor
attempt to do so by
praising what I did not
like

I will venture unlefs I receive
your Royal Highnefs's command
to the contrary, to keep the book
until your return to Oxford,
when I hope you will find
some occasion of enabling me
to show how truly I am
  Your Royal Highnefs's
  very grateful and loyal Servant
    JR

113. 24 December 1872, Corpus Christi College

Say to Downes I'm very glad
 of his letter. Give him – and his son
and your own Servants
– the same from *Corpus Christi College*
me as at D. Hill,   *Oxford*
a pound each.   Christmas Eve
 Dearest Joanie
  I send you a
letter or two which may
interest you. and all thanks
I can – for being to me my
sole remaining home-happinefs.
Quite as much – in the real
depth and support of it,
absent, as present.
I am painting a bit of
brown rock with [native] gold
and hope to spend a tolerably
pleasant day tomorrow.
– were it not for the bells..

The Cook is coming in the
morning to bring me a
cookery book, and receive
directions for a <u>plain</u> pudding
– Love to Arfie. and say I hope
<u>his</u> dinner and everything
will be right.
It is your first "merry" Christmas
– for last was too clouded.
 May you both have
many.

  Ever your own
  lovingest Cuzzie
  John Ruskin

Letter 113. 92/124, 1872. Pencil notations: '? 1872'.

114. 27 December 1872, Lancaster

Lancaster. 27th Dec
72

Darling Pufsie
 I am in the old room, where I was with you and Arfie. Ramsgate sands and all. I forgot there was a piano – You did'nt play? So odd – to be here again. – I had R's letters in my breast pocket and I suppose – thought of nothing else. But I forget how it all was. I know I went out in the morning and bought maps, and I remember bringing them to you at the Ry[1] station – and wait – wait – waiting. It seems only a minute since, now.
We met Kate and Crawley saw her safe on. Ive just had Turtle soup –. young herrings – – beefsteak – and Mince pies all of the best – and more than half a pint of sherry – and am very comfortable. Volunteer band playing Roy's wife beautifully. I wish I was Roy.
I hardly ever – you know – have anybody nice to travel with All alone to day. very comfy except from Stafford to – Never mind where – But at Stafford came a girl with yellow hair and her aunt to see her off – I made certain she would'nt get in. But she did. Veil down, and double – but looking very promising, underneath..
Talked to aunt till train went away – Very anxious about luggage in next carriage. – I made sure somebody else would come! – but nobody did. . The train went on – and the footwarmer was to be [decided][2] between us.

I looked diligently out of the side windows – in hopes that the dow at least the outside veil would go up. It did, in about five minutes. Pretty enough – – but nose too thin – hatchety – and altogether, second caste, but splendid yellow hair.
"Is the window as you like it?
"– I think I should like it a little
 higher up? – "
"Quite right, the wind is – &c. &c.
– When we got to – Never mind
 where – I had got on pretty well.
– The young lady was to get out there.
– Still anxious about luggage in
 next carriage – "It was very
 lucky it was all alone" –
"I shall be very unlucky, presently
 under the same circumstances! .
– 'Oh – somebody will get in who
 will be a pleasanter companion!
– No – madam – my goodfortune in life
 never lasts beyond a single stage.
– so I got out – and handed her
 out – and was all alone – all
 the way here.

Black day, too – and yet somehow, I'm not so far down as usual. My cold quite gone – though I was gritty this morning – many things came into my head, in the train for Brantwood work.

And. here I am at Lancaster! – so far from my Joanie – and her wee dolls house on Herne Hill
 How wonderful it all is –
– Ever my wee Doanie
with best love to Arfie.
Dited to hear of pictures getting on. ooos won own Donie
  JR.
Such a nice wee ettie from [Lizzie.] W.[3]

Letter 114. 94/124, 1872.
 1. This is shorthand for 'railway'.
 2. This could be 'divided'.
 3. Lizzie White.

115. 28 December 1872, Brantwood

Brantwood,
Coniston

28th Dec
72

Darling Pussie
   I had your sweet welcome – the only cheerful thing in the pouring day, yesterday Today, slow gaining of blue sky, from the west.
   What different modes of humour there are, possible to one. I am not sad, or vexed, in the sense for instance – that I was when I stayed at Euston, and would not see anyone. And yet there and then, I was in intense courage and vivacity for work. To day, I am quite tranquil – rather pleased with things than otherwise. – But entirely dead and depressed in energy somehow; not caring to do anything. Not caring even to rest – for I am not tired – but utterly Grey and cold in mind.
And what is strangest of all is that, being in this same temper all yesterday, I had last night, (sleeping quite soundly,) the pleasantest childish dream I've had since I was a child. You know those flying dreams one used to have, floating a little way above the ground? Well – I was first, telling somebody, – a girl – not R, so
   I suppose it was Clochette[1] – but I wa'snt much interested in her and hardly looked at her (she had no hair worth noticing and darkish eyes –) – but I was showing her how to draw angels – and she objecting to my ideal of them, I showed her exactly how angels ought to be represented flying – and *did* a bit of angelic flight in the air, lecturing upon it all the while!
   Did *ever* you know such an absurd old Di Pa!
   Now to day I have your charming whats that ^{short} for? notie – with account of
["Diddie"[2]
– (you tantalizing horrid old Doanie!.)[3]
and [fancy][4] little card
and thats all I say by
Sunday post. (Im oos) own
Donie

116. 28 December 1872, Brantwood

Brantwood,
Coniston
Sunday, 28th Dec. 72

My darling Pufsie
   I have had almost the divinest walk to day I ever had in my life. It cleared steadily from the morning on; I went out at about ½ past 12. the blue then gaining steadily

---

Letter 115. 95/124, 1872. Envelope: embossed 'T. EDMONDSON, LANCASTER' and a rose and bud surrounded by two leaves; addressed to: 'Mrs Arthur Severn. / Herne Hill / S. E. / London.' Postmarked: 'AMBLESIDE / B / DE 29 / 72' (front); 'LONDON.S.E. / E 7 / DE 30 / 72' (back). Ruskin has surrounded the top and sides of the embossed rose with five exclamation marks. It is the first use of that envelope for a letter to his cousin, and Ruskin clearly found it symbolically significant.
   1. Clochette remains unidentified and, despite the fact that some letters suggest he was taken with her as he was with Rose, this letter makes it clear that Clochette was not Rose.
   2. Sara Anderson, one of Ruskin's assistants.
   3. From this point on, the message is scrawled around the margin at the bottom of the second page.
   4. This could even be 'pussy'.

Letter 116. 96/124, 1872. Part of this letter is reproduced in 37.56.

from the west. I felt quite
tired and listlefs when I
went out – but the farther
I walked, the less I was tired
which was a satisfactory sort
of feeling for an old gentleman
of 54. By the time I got
to the rock which I took
you and Lily up – I was as fresh
as could be – and the sky
cloudlefs – the rocks already
dry – the sun making all
Coniston Water one silver shield
– I went on to our tarn, wheer
Lily was so naughty. and
it got brighter & brighter –
– Then round and to the
Waterhead – and theer was
a sunset like a Roman one –
– the lake of Thrasymene
never more glorious.
– The place is more beautiful
in winter than summer –
– the loss in foliage at first
    seems terrific and
in dark days, it is fatal ^1
and the view from the window
here does lose more than I expected
– every wheer looking like
barren moor. But when
the sun comes out. – the
hills are all gold & purple
instead of gray ^as in summer one sees
their outlines everywheer

through the copses. – the
sun coming down among the
thin woods is like
enchanted light – and
the ivy and walls ^ and waters are
all as perfect as ever –
So that I never yet had
a walk among the lakes so
lovely, and few in Italy.
and I'm actually in good spirits
to night – reading Cowley.
– and arranging my teacups
Please, I want a blue
small tea cup, there's a
saucer I can't fill..
Also – please go to Mrs Wrights
shell shop.. ^{near} Brit Museum
and ask her to choose me
four beautiful large scallop
shells, that will bear fire,
for scalloped oysters.[2]
– and before you speak of this
find out how they all are –
Mrs Wright – and the daughters
married & single – (if still)
and the son.
And ask if they've anything
new in minerals.
And love to Arfie and
I'm oos own di Pa.

————

I enclose a letter to the man
whose fresco I didnt go to see
– can you find his address & send it?

---

1. A line connects '^' to the top margin where Ruskin added the two lines from 'and the' to 'expected'.
2. The 'scalloped oysters' here may have been the shellfish, but may also have referred to the vegetable salsify. Ruskin also used scallop shells in his art. His diary entry for 8 August 1870 includes: 'Painted some scallop-shell – but my eyes were dead & colour would'nt come.' (Ruskin Library MS 16, 1870.41). A week later, on Wednesday 17 August 1870, Ruskin tallied up his recent expenses and tried to balance his books. The expenses include shells and books he had bought. Typically, the accounts do not balance and Ruskin added the note: 'All right counted. They must have given me wrong change.' (R Lib MS16, 1870.45.) In later years, he was more apt to ascribe accountancy errors to himself (see, for example 27 December 1884 [203]).

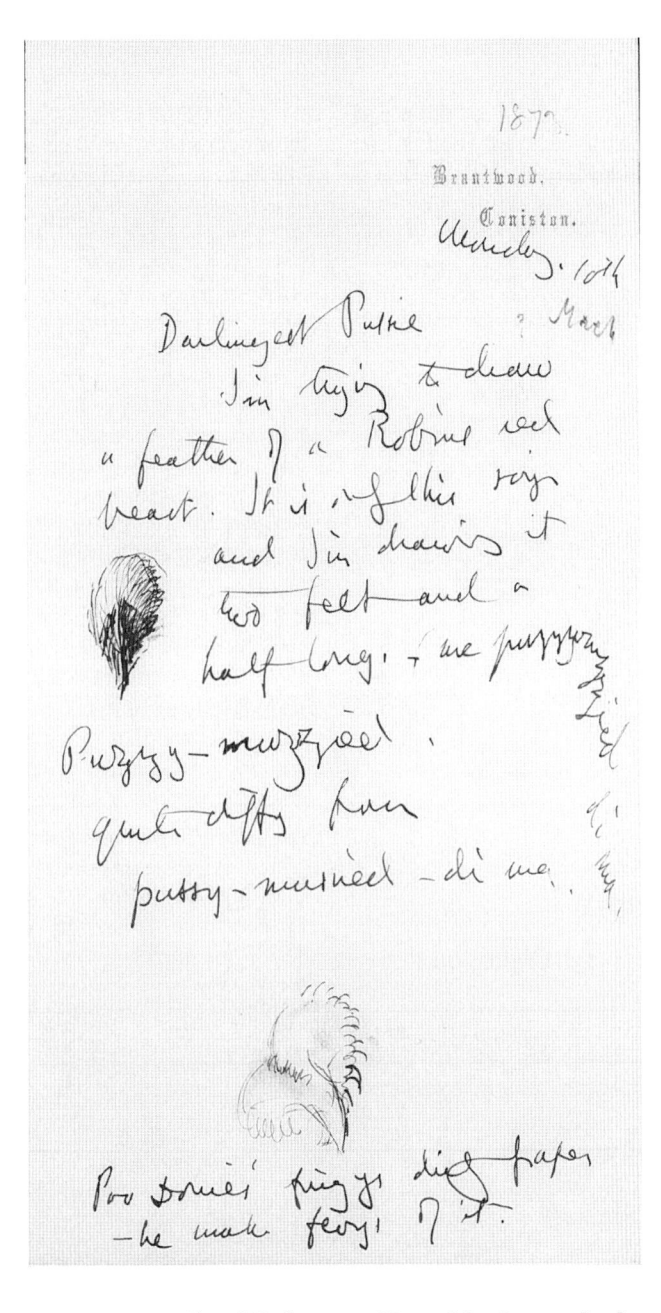

Fig. 6. Facsimile of JR letter to JS, 10 March 1873 [133]
RF L38, Ruskin Foundation (Ruskin Library, Lancaster University)

1873

Lily Severn born to J. and Arthur
R. settles at Brantwood, where he spends as much time as possible
R. begins lectures on birds in March, later published as *Love's Meinie*; Robin lecture 15 March
Severns, with young Lily, arrive at Brantwood on 2 July
R. gives the lectures later published as *Val d'Orno: Ten Lectures on Tuscan Art*,
October and November

117. 1 January 1873, Brantwood

> Brantwood
> Coniston
> 1st January. 1873

Dearest Joan
  So many thanks, for your letter and Arfies. So many good wishes and so much love to you both I've been looking at your photographs, for some comfy. and digging by my stream and ordering a railing by the spring to keep Margaret[1] from falling over.
  They come on the 6.th I'm tired and can only say, Love again & again
    your devoted Cuzzie
      J Ruskin

118. 7 January 1873, Brantwood

> Brantwood
> Coniston
> 7th Jan^y

Darling Pufsie
  I am better, but more oppressed by weather and temper than ever yet in my life – and considerable pain in arm still – This has been the most horrible day in drenching rain we have had yet – and since the Sunday before last – scarcely half an hour without it Margaret & Georgie seem happy however. Georgie says the rest is good for her My doanie must'nt go writing fourteen etties all at once! me quite fitened

It is <u>very</u> sweet of Arfie and you to feel that you are so happie in housie and that you love oos di pa

I've ordered two copies of Christina Rossettis book illustrated by Arthur Hughes to be sent to you[1] One is for <u>oo</u>. The other is for Mary.
    Now – oos to be velly dood, di
      te doanie, and for dir
    pity pitty book bout – babes and tinys –[2]
    oo must send me all ose wee Tonnie
                       [Tetches[3]
    yo oo know?
      and me's oo own own Donie

Autograph letters for 1873 are in 'Bem L 38 / Letters / John Ruskin / to / Joan Severn / 1873'.

Letter 117. 1/152, 1873.
1. Margaret Burne-Jones, daughter of artist Edward Burne-Jones. She arrived with at Brantwood with her mother Georgiana on 6 January.

Letter 118. 7/152, 1873. Pencil notations: '?73'.
1. This is Christina Rossetti's *Sing-Song: A Nursery Rhyme Book, with One Hundred and Twenty Illustrations*, illus. by Arthur Hughes (London: Routledge, 1872).
2. Ruskin appears to have quite liked Rossetti's work, although Hilton argues that he held a 'severe attitude toward her versification' (*Later*, p. 95).
3. 'Connie Sketches', presumably by or of Constance Hilliard.

119. 12–13 January 1873, Brantwood

Sunday
Brantwood
Coniston

Darlingest Poosmoos
 Me so velly glad oo
iked oos wisky-punch and
got seepy.
– I got out and had a
walk yesterday. Margaret
came with me, and I am glad
to find she can walk for an
hour and a half without being
the least tired – chattering
all the time very pleasantly,
(whether I listened or not)
Georgie seems to enjoy
herself in spite of the horrible
weather – but it is hard
 on us both.
There's an element of
hidden fire in her, now, also,
which must be a little
volcanic and awful in
constant life.
She plays old English
things to me in evening
very nicely
But me wants my Doanie
and Kisty Mins
Thank Arfie for
nice ettie about
exhibs.
<u>Cook</u> is a great find – I like
her, and all she makes.[1]
Their sheep dog comes with
her brother to see the new
works at Brantwood. and
 came (for ^{on} the walk) with
Margaret and me. He had
a plate of bones on arriving
at home. and seems likely
to attach himself here, which
I like.
I am painting ivy and
puzzywuzzled.
and can't do it. and
don't know fot to do.
I'm <u>so</u> glad you like
those Arthur Hughes[2]
– All the world is Arfie-fied –
– now. is'nt it. Oos own
Di Pa

120. [January] 1873, Brantwood

 Fabian – [Johns] Almanack
says. Me want to know
 who he was
 Monday – *Brantwood*
 Coniston

 Darlingest Pussky Mussky
 The light has come at last
– the snow is divine on the
hills – and illuminates my
study all into its corners –
I can paint – & think – and
do evything quite nicely – cept
<u>ite</u> for me's been drawin
and my hands is cold –
 Kate[1] is sure to bring [mys]
a glafs of sherry at one. it
 wants ten minutes. [2]I'm
cataloguing my books – and finishing
my coins – and really – its a

Letter 119. 9/152, 1873. Pencil notations: 'Jan. 12. 73.' Envelope: embossed with 'F.JOHN.LATE WARD.DENMARK HILL.S.E.'; addressed to 'Mrs Arthur Severn / Herne Hill / S. E / London'. Postmarked: 'AMBLESIDE / B / JA12 / 73' (front); 'LONDON-S.E. / C 7 / JA 13 / 73' (back).
  1. Possibly Hannah Stalker, identified as the Brantwood cook in Ruskin's diary entry of 11 May 1887 (Evans and Whitehouse, p. 1143); I assume that this cook is a Stalker because her dog, Maude, had been born at the Stalker's home (see [7] February 1873 [125]).
  2. See 7 January, 1873 [118].

Letter 120. 14/152, 1873. Pencil notations: 'A. W.', '(after G. left)', 'Ned's letter: Jan 1873'.
  1. Kate Smith.
  2. There is a pencil bracket here, the other bracket is at the end of the paragraph, after 'all the while.'

sort of ideal life now, so quiet
and far away – and yet with
so many pretty things about me –
and lake & mountains outside and
 my Joanie & Arfie lovin me
all the while.
(Is Oo quite <u>soo</u> Arfie likes me?)
 .One nevvy knows.
 Make him read Ned's
letter enclosed – very carefully
 – All the ovies is good
 for sometin or ovy. and
  I'm oos bofes ovin Donie

Me <u>so</u>³ peased oo iked
oos little pesent.

121. 28 January 1873, Brantwood

Brantwood
Coniston
Tuesday.

My dearest Joanie
 Your speaking of the event
as almost certain within the next
fortnight, makes me a little
serious.¹
I need not ^ ᴵ ʰᵒᵖᵉ say, my darling, that
though I am not anxious, knowing
your general good health, and the
care that you have wisely taken,
I [cld] not write any foolish
jesting letters without a very
solemn sense of the approach ^ ᵗᵒ ʸᵒᵘ of
one of those periods of life which
are intended to make us look
with closer trust to Him in whom
we live, and move, and have our
Being.
 I am afraid, in a petty way, I
 may have <u>really</u> been teazing
you about the alterations in our
pretty drawing room. (Georgie
put me in a passion by finding
fault with the carpet the
moment she came in, which
I didn't get over while she stayed.)
– Well. I have put the three
Prouts where the Hunts were,²
– (now no be angy – di ma) – and
they look <u>so</u> well in that recess
giving more height to the room.
I have put ~~six~~ ᵉⁱᵍʰᵗ pretty pieces
of china³

like that on top of cabinet
 beside the flat Japan plate.
– and I have put Constance
(Turner's.). between my two
Abbevilles; the Angelico
above. and <u>six</u> Pencil Prouts
[filling] in!⁴

– Then – the Gainsborough
wee Girly goes opposite Fair
Rosamond.⁵

---

  3. There are four lines beneath the 'so'.

Letter 121. 18/152, 1873. Pencil notations: 'Jan 28. 73'; Envelope: embossed with 'F.JOHN.LATE WARD.DENMARK HILL.S.E.'; addressed to 'Mʳˢ Arthur Severn / Herne Hill / S. E. / London'. Postmarked: 'AMBLESIDE / B / JA28 / 73' (front); 'LONDON.S.E. / D 7 / JA2[9] / 73' (back); Pencil notations: 'arrangement of / Brantwood Drawing Room' (on the envelope front, above the address).

1. This is a reference to Joan Severn's first labour and the birth of her daughter Lily. Joan Severn's sister Kate, of whom Ruskin had been fond, died from complications following childbirth in December 1869.
2. See 19 January 1873 (not transcribed) for the earlier design.
3. There is a sketch of the eight pieces of china, spread out to either side of the 'Japan plate', which is on a stand. The shelf is 8.8 cm wide, the Japan plate 2 cm high and all other items between 0.2 and 1 cm in height.
4. There is a sketch of paintings arranged in two rows of five, one above the other with the largest of each row in the centre. The paintings range in size from 0.7 x 1 cm to 2.2 x 1.4 cm.
5. There is a sketch, the central, less detailed, section represents the shelf holding the Japan plate and surrounding china, with three paintings above it in an arched alcove over the fireplace (3.5 x 3.2 cm). To the left and right are the 'Gainsborough wee Girly' and 'Fair Rosamond' (each 1 x 1.8 cm; the base-line representing the floor is 10.4 cm wide).

And – But Me must
tell oo the ovy side ovy day
— oos poo – poo fitened wee Donie[6]

122. 30 January 1873, Brantwood

Brantwood
Coniston
30th January
18673
[1]King Charles the Martyr

Darlin di Ma,
  Oos Poo Donies' in such a
passion dis mornin – he does'nt know
<u>fot</u> to do. He's a perfect Donie
the Martyr – he can't get his
soles fried to his mind; and when
he went to his cookery books to
find out how it should be done –
– though he's got three thick ones,
(– put all in order beside his geography
books – di ma, and nice wee esson
bookies –). Two of the three cooky
books say – "Do them of a fine
"brown" – di ma, – as if Donie
<u>wouldn't</u> do them of a fine brown,
if he knew how, – and the third
cooky book says. "when you think
one side is done enough, turn it."
  Di ma – how is one evy
  to learn to cook?

Hard fost, di ma. Donie
been out in his sippies to
gather snowdrops – bank so
sippy that Donie nearly
sipped down in his sippies –
– Anowy time, Donie send Kate.

Di ma – oos game of chess
all ite. Pay it again.

  [2]It's an odd game though!
  I played it first, by myself,
all through. and found it

right, before I sent it.
– Then last night, I played
it through after tea – and
stuck at the very move you
mark – Made another instead
and got on – but stuck at
last near end & put it away
in a pasin, di ma.

– Then, when me went up to
bed – me tould'nt go to seep
till me tied it again – and
it came all ite di ma –
and so it is.

Why we both went wrong
at that move, I can't
make out
I've played it again now. Its
all right – and how we <u>both</u>
stuck at that move is <u>the oddest
thing</u>!!!
You may not quite see the
  coup. Move 32. If, after
it White takes q. with R.
  Black p + R. and White
either loses his queen, for a Bishop
instead of a Rook, or is checkmated –
But I can't see myself, now why
if instead on the 33rd move, R + q
  White had played q to Kts 4th, any
      harm could have
[3]come to him. – If Black plays K.p one,
            [W.q + kts p. and is safe

  Oos sweeties sweet of a letter
come.

Yes. all the Japan vases
are just where they used to
be. I've only taken the
china for my chimneypiece
from the [floor].[4]
  Ever your lovingest
      Di Pa.

---

6. This script became progressively smaller and slanted markedly downwards. This shift in handwriting was not necessitated by space, so Ruskin has used it to denote his apologetic, hurried, playful frame of mind.

Letter 122. 19/152, 1873. Pencil notations: 'A.W.'
 1. There is a line connecting 'King' to '30th'.
 2. There is a pencil bracket here, the other bracket is after '<u>oddest thing</u>'.
 3. Ruskin had reached the bottom of the leaf and this line is written sideways up the right margin.
 4. This could be 'plan'.

123. 31 January 1873, Brantwood

Brantwood
Coniston
31st

Dearest wee Pussie
  Me so glad the
cheque came all right
& was 11/ over – Please put
  the 11 /[1] into oos little pocket.
– [2] Such a glorious walk I
had yesterday. – round the
foot of the Old Man, on the
moors. All day and sweet
grass, crisp in frost – Lancaster
sands bright in south – Fairfield
and the Yewdale crags clear
in the north. the cascades all
fringed and entangled and
netted with icicles – and
no human creature to be seen
for miles – but sound of water,
and the pleasant sense
of inhabited land below and
in the distance – and one's
own little housie glittering
on the other side of the lake.
I've half promised Connie
for this last week – we should
have <u>such</u> walks! and fancy
Connie and the new Cook!
– I do hope she'll come.
But me won't be pointed
if she does'nt . Me velly comfy.
[3]

there's no standing f[or] Tulk of
  Tuk ups! she's
out and out the stiffest – ^ I know of and
yet I've known some![4]

I forgot to enclose chess
in my letter –
When you've tried it again
send it to George – with
my question about the last
moves, please.

Di ma – I had <u>Three Robins</u>
at breakfast on the lawn this
morning.
    Mes oos wee Robin-Donie

124. 4 February 1873, Brantwood

Brantwood
Coniston
4th Feb.

  Darlingest wee Doanie
Your loving letter received
to day makes me <u>very</u> happy
and thankful. It was dear of
you to count the seven years.[1]
It[2] is curious, I am not unhappy
at all now. but have a
great feeling of intense lonelinefs.
– like Robin[3] Crusoe. It is a

Letter 123. 20/152, 1873. Pencil notations: 'Jan 31. 73'; two notations have been erased but are still visible: 'A.W.' and '[for plan / 8B]'.
1. This backslash extends over both lines.
2. There is a pencil bracket here, the other bracket is at the bottom of the paragraph, after 'the lake.'
3. There is a pencil line here, extending beside these two lines of text, which have been obscured by black ink ranging in thickness from 0.1 to 0.5 cm. Judging by the edges of letters which remain, the lines read something like: 'Me [...y] comfy with [...th's] / & ['not' or 'mut'] [out] anything [...us]'. Since 'Tuk up' was a pet name for Rose, the excised lines were probably about her.
4. There is a closing pencil bracket here, but no opening bracket for it – unless the pencil line which extends along the left side of the excised lines is the other bracket.

Letter 124. 25/152, 1873. Pencil notation: 'A.W.', '1873'; see 14 April 1873 for a letter from Constance Hilliard which may be the one mentioned here.
1. Ruskin had proposed to Rose on 2 February 1866, which must be the 'seven years' alluded to. She had asked him to wait three years.
2. There is a pencil bracket here, the other bracket is near the end of the letter, after 'talk things over'.
3. Ruskin's current fascination with birds and, particularly robins, is evident in the shortening of 'Robinson'.

different state of mind from
any I have ever been in.+

A glorious sunset last night.
Bright sunshine to day, with
cold north wind.

– I am so very glad Arfie
and you liked my letters to

⁴+chiefly made uncomfortable by a
naughty fancy for Clochette!

Mʳ Smith.⁵ I will not
be in any ru hurry – I should
not be surprised, myself,
if I got six or seven thousand
for those copyrights.
– I have several businefs
letters to answer & must
be short.
I come up on the 10ᵗʰ
but of course shall stay
in town. Not at Euston
– some Hotel in Piccadilly
to be near booksellers &
talk things over.
oo is rather a pokin wee
pussie, just now – me mut say
Evy oos own Di Pa.

125. [7] February 1873, Brantwood

No Connie to be had.¹
Papas are horrid wretches.
– all but oos own Di. Pa.

Brantwood
Coniston

My blessedest pussie
These long letters are
such dites to me – oo tant think
– All so full of pitty sayings,
and thinkings, and doings, too.
– Please – the Cornhill was
sent in your portmanteau – ever
so long ago! – says Crawley.²
Everything of the kind I find
is packed off to my pussie
instantly.
Maude³ came with me
for a hill walk yesterday. – we
called on Mʳˢ Stalker⁴ – at the
farm you know. and she was
very very glad to see us.
us, for I left Maude outside,
though I had noticed that
she trotted on before ᵐᵉ to the
Farm door with great alacrity.
– but in five minutes came
a pitiful and appealing Scratch
at the door. 'It's Maudie,
mother', said little Agnes,
– appears apparently quite
acquainted with Maudies
peculiar and private Scratch.
– So Maudie was let in
and lay under my chair all
the time of the visit. – being
as I found, a puppy from
that cottage.
⁵Mrs Stocker was baking –

4. These two lines appear at the bottom of the first page and follow from the '+' several lines above.
5. Given the context of books, this must be George Smith of Smith and Elder, publishers. See Ruskin's letter to Norton of 18 February for his dispute with the publishers over copyright (Bradley and Ousby, pp. 280–81, L. 217).

Letter 125. 26/152, 1873. Pencil notations: 'A.W.', '? Feb 73', 'after Feb. 4'. This letter must be from just before 8 February 1873 because of the reference to Lily Severn (Fisy) possibly being born on the 8th.
1. Ruskin had hoped one of the Constances would be able to visit him.
2. Frederick Crawley.
3. The Brantwood cook's dog, which Ruskin seems to have appropriated.
4. A shepherd's wife, the family lived in 'Lawson Park' above Brantwood (*Later*, p. 320). Note that Ruskin's spelling of her surname is erratic.
5. There is a pencil bracket here, the other bracket is at the end of the passage about Mrs. Stalker, after 'this nice country'. The 'Library Edition' of *Fors Clavigera* (28.256) includes a note which offers a transcription of this section. The editors made several changes. They spelled Mrs. Stalker's name correctly, they wrote '22' in letters and they excised 'Di ma' from the penultimate line.

– a great lesson for me
– A large pot, hung
over the hearth well covered
with thoroughly hot turf,
held six or eight small loaves
side by side at the bottom.
On the flat lid of the pot were
loaded two inches more of
hot turf. The bread was
baked in an hour, Mrs
Stocker said – and I never
saw any that looked nicer.
    She had baked so for
22 years.
        I shall really
know something worth
knowing at last. Di ma –
in this nice country.

– Maude lay all the
evening by the drawingroom
fire. Puss peeps round
the legs of the sofa at her –
– then goes away to the piano,
– makes a rush, and gets on
the back of my chair – then down
my arm onto the table – examines
everything – puts her nose into
the slop basin – and at last helps
herself to my bit of butter –
but immediately rolls ^{it} into the
salt – and won't have anymore
to say to it. .
    How splendid if Fisy would
come on th 8th.![6]
    Ever oos poo di Pa.
        JR

126. 11 February 1873, London

11th February. 1873
Brantwood
Coniston

My darling
    Im so very thankful.
I send you my love. I know
you must be quiet. That love
I hope never disquiets you.
        Ever your Di Pa.
        And Fisy's di Gran Pa.

127a. 12 February 1873, London

Brantwood
Coniston

My wee Doanie
    Is oo velly proud – and
velly happy?
So is oos di pa. . My wee amie –
– me's been so fitened – and so
sad – all these days. – me did'nt
know fot to do. Knowing that
my wee amie was going to have
such dedful pain –
But Arfie says you were so brave
and good. . Pease – di mammie –
oo mut ove poo – poo – Donie, all
y same?
Me would write mo. but mutnt.
– Me will ite moosin etties, if
me can – when oos bettie.
    Ever oos own ovin-ovin-ovin Donie
– Me joyed Arfie so [muts] to day. His
pics quite bu̲ful

---

6. 'Fisy' is a nickname for the Severns' unborn child. Like 'Fitie', an early pet name for Joan (Agnew) Severn, it means 'Thistle' and evokes her Scottishness. Ruskin's birthday was 8 February, so presumably his cousin had suggested that he and his surrogate grandchild might share a birth date. In the end, Lily arrived three days after his birthday.

Letter 126. 28/152, 1873. Envelope: embossed with 'F.JOHN.LATE WARD.DENMARK HILL. S.E.'; addressed to 'Mrs Arthur Severn.' Pencil notations: '? London', '?Grosvenor Hotel'.

Letter 127a. 30a/152, 1873. Envelope: a folded piece of Brantwood stationary; addressed to 'Mrs Arthur Severn. / Herne Hill / S. E.' Postmarked: 'LONDON [N] / FE 12 / 73' (front); 'LONDON-S.E. / G 7 / FE 13 / 73' (back). Enclosures: one is a fragment (30b/152, 1873); the other is a newspaper clipping headed 'THE CHESS MATCH BETWEEN ENGLAND AND FRANCE IN 1843.', which summarises that match and lists all the moves made. Pencil notations: 'envl. Feb 12: 73.'

127b. fragment

nothing distresses me more
than the undisturbed [possession]
of a crooked pic^t,

128. 17 February 1873, Brantwood

>Brantwood
>17th Feb. morning

My darling
I have just been reading
in St John's Gospel – (N. B –
which I don't read now but
to dispute – mostly –) – the bit
about – "She remembereth no more
the anguish." I am always
able to conceive pain – and was
very wretched for the last fortnight
before the 12th not in any grave anxiety – – but in
mere terror of the great pain for
my poor poor – wee – wee Doanie.
– But I can't at all fancy
the following part of the verse – the
joy that a child is born. Is oo
really so velly peased with it,
di ma? Will oo always ove
oos poo Donie just the same?
Me fitened – di ma? Is oo velly
much peased. Pease no be peased too mut
    Di ma – Evy oos <u>own</u> <u>old</u> poo Donie

129. 18 February 1873, Brantwood

Tuesday.

>Brantwood
>Coniston
>~~1st Oct.~~ ^{1}

Darlingest Poosymoos.
    Do you recollect the
Robin you gave me? on the
little log. standing up?
I'm writing my first Bird
lecture on him. he's such
a darling. There are ever
so many here. One comes
now generally to look what
I'm doing at my stream.
    Stream! we're nearly
reduced to dipping out of the
lake for tea! no rain for
three weeks.
    Please tell Arfie I have
his "Blottesque" letter – and
am glad of it. and that
I want him to find
out a good bird stuffers
and get me, not stuffed
nor set up, but merely
fine specimens – a lark
– a skylark – a swallow,
a swift – and a nightingale.
– and send them all in a
box down here.
I think it may amuse
Arfie to do this – or
would set Burgefs to it

My darling me ove oo
so mut, me don't know
<u>fot</u> to do. Oos Donie.

Letter 127b. 30b/152, 1873. This is on a scrap of paper, apparently the bottom half of a sheet of writing paper.

Letter 128. 33/152, 1873. Envelope: embossed with 'F.JOHN.LATE WARD.DENMARK HILL.S.E.' and a fern and leaf arrangement; addressed to 'Mrs Arthur Severn / Herne-Hill / S. E. / London.' Postmarked: 'AMBLESIDE / [B] / FE17 / 73' (front); 'LONDON S.E. / 7 / FE 18 / 73' (back). Pencil notations: '1873'.

Letter 129. 34/152, 1873. Pencil notations: 'Feb.^{18} 1873'. Envelope embossed with 'F.JOHN.LATE WARD.DENMARK HILL.S.E.' and a fern and leaf arrangement; addressed to 'Mrs Arthur Severn / Herne Hill / S E. / London'. Postmarked: 'AMBLESIDE / B / FE 18 / 73' (front); '[LO]NDON-S.E. / H 7 / FE19 / 73' (back).

1. Ruskin must have reused a sheet rejected some months earlier.

130. 2 March 1873, Brantwood

> Brantwood
> Coniston
> 2nd March

My darling

   I send you one
separate word of thanks and
what blessing I have power
to give, for your own birthday.
Heaven be with you always
Day, and Night.

   Ever your most loving
> Di Pa.

131. 8 March 1873, Brantwood

> Brantwood
> Coniston
> [8th March 73[1]]

My darling wee pussie

Me want oo to give oos Donie
a wee present, mamie di,
for Donies birthday. – he
had'nt any from any body –
– poo Donie.
– Mamie di – me want
anowy wee Robbin. Me
don't ike to take my 'obbin
away from Brantwood, – because
he so pitty among shellywells.
– me want an 'obbin at
Oxford – poo Donie tant
get on without an Obbin.
Di ma, will you please
give Donie anowy obbin. and
have him tuffed and set up
on a pitty banch, for Donie
to show at his ecties?
– Please – I want this as well
done as its pofsible to do it
– but I must have one lent,
if it cant be done in time
   for my Saturdays lecture.[2]
– I think my Robin brings
me luck, here – and won't
   move him, – he's standing
   beside me so daintily, now,
and two such beautiful
   living ones on the lawn

   Sweet Ettie just come
Only Crawly, Not Jackson[3]
to be in the lodge.
   Jackson was only to come
because somebody was
wanted to be near.
     Ever your loving Di Pa

132. [?] March 1873, Brantwood

> Brantwood
> Coniston

   Darling Pussie
     me like my 'obbin
   with his mouthie open.
– I wish peepies would
always let me say, 'obbin'
instead of wobbin
– What a sweetie of
a nurse that must have
been.
– Here's a sweetie ettie
from nice married lady –
send it me back. to
Oxford. Send Wobbin
to C.C.C. Oxford. and
I'm ooooooooooo<u>s</u> own Donie

Letter 130. 48/152, 1873. Envelope addressed to 'Mrs Arthur Severn / Herne Hill / S. E. / London.'; Postmarked: 'AMBLESIDE / B / MR 2 / 73' (front) 'LONDO[N S. E.] / D 7 / MR [15] / [73]' (back). Pencil notations: '73'.

Letter 131. 53/152, 1873.
1. This might read '8th March 73'.
2. His Saturday lecture was given on 15 March 1873 (Evans and Whitehouse, p. 741). The bird lectures, of which the robin was the first, were published in *Love's Meinie*.
3. Jackson was the Outdoor Steward at Brantwood (28.531).

Letter 132. 149/152, 1873. Pencil notations: '73?'; (and, on the reverse) 'Mrs C. Church –', 'Lily – ', 'Mrs Smith', Sara P. P. Carver.'

133. 10 March 1873, Brantwood

> Brantwood
> Coniston
> Monday. 10th

Darlingest Pussie
  I'm trying to draw
a feather of a Robins red
breast. It is only this size[1]
    and I'm drawing it
      two feet and a
      half long. – (me puzzywuzzied di ma)[2]
Puzzy – wuzzied.
  quite diffy from
    pussy – mussied – di ma,

[3]Poo Donie's fingys dirty paper
  – he make fevys of it.

Di ma. me ove oo so mut
me wish me was a obbin,
– me would fly to oo.

Poo Donie got no fevys, ony
a long beard. Poo Donie
not save for three days.

Such a long walk, me had
isterday, di ma. Maude
goes with me always. but
Maude is too old to approve
of <u>long</u> walks, or going up
hill. All the way <u>up</u> the
hills, she follows me step
by step, a yard from my
heel – with a – " I wish
you would'nt go any farther"
      expression

  Then – when I turn, she takes the lead,
– and, looking back occasionally to see
if I'm following, shows me the best and
shortest way home. Yesterday I came ^ in
                          [going to
a bit of steep wall, which, ~~going up~~, I was
afraid she could'nt get over. I called to her
  to be taken by nape of neck and pulled over,
but she turned aside – went two or three yards
down the hill to another place, and was over in
a minute. Coming back, she took me a hundred
yards higher up, where there was a hole
                         [underneath
the wall which we could both creep through.
– Then she lies on the drawing room rug
all the evening. Last night she came up to my
                                 [room
to see Crawley brush ~~ha~~ my hair, and begged to
  be allowed to sleep by the fire, so I let [he][4]
her – and she was perfectly quiet all night.

134. 12 March 1873, Brantwood

> Brantwood
> Coniston
> Friday

Darling Joanie
  I very wrongfully
    forgot to congratulate you both
yesterday. on the sale of
the picture. and on the delightful
[businefs] of the critique – which
is quite true and deserved.
  – Do you think you could
receive me on Monday? – I
want to see a book I've
just bought without seeing, on
Ned Jones'[1] and the keeper
of Print room at B. M.s[2] report
– so I should like to come up
on Monday, & see my book
of books. – my Keepsake, &
  Forget me not, & Book of Beauty
– my own wee Joanie –
in <u>her</u> museum, – if I
may.
And could you find
a room for Kate on Tuesday?

Letter 133. 55/152, 1873. Pencil notations: '1873', '? March'.
  1. There is a sketch of a feather below left (1.5 x 2.1 cm).
  2. The line makes a right-angled turn after 'puzzy' and continues down the right margin.
  3. This is preceded by a sketch of two feathers (2.5 x 2.5 cm), the centre of which are formed by smudged ink.
  4. This line is written sideways up the right margin.

Letter 134. 57/152, 1873. Pencil notations: '? Mar 12', '73'.
  1. Edward Burne-Jones.
  2. British Museum.

She wants to see baby so.[3]

This is to be posted from Lichfield. – write a line to morrow to C. C. C. – and tell me if I may come

– What Maude will do, for [these] ten days. – She never leaves me now for a minute, if she can help it, night or day. – and won't lie in any part of the room if but near my chair – On the rug, in the drawing room – but in the study, beside me in the corner between the book case & mineral cabinets

F.G[4]

Missed her
 she moved of course[5]

Thats the least bit better – .
 no more time

135. 13 March 1873, Lichfield

Brantwood
 Coniston
 Lichfield.

My darling
 I wrote hastily from Coniston – If you have made arrangements between Thursday & Tuesday about the Christening, don't put them out. – write to morrow if you would like me from Monday to Wednesday – and Saturday to Tuesday, or from Thursday to Tuesday unbroken. I can come to the Christening of course, my darling. theyre always in the morning – are'nt they. only, if I come on Monday till Wednesday – I must be at Oxford Thursday to Saturday.

 Pease di ma – me would like to call baby
 Buttercup.

– or Daisy – (for Con.)

or Pansy –

or Cowslip –

or Pinkie.

or Mossy – (for Moussie)

me's got evy so many names
 but the post going
– Evy oos own darlin Donie
 All the same here – as
 when we were all together

136. 14 March 1873, Corpus Christi College

 I slept well enough – after writing a savage letter to Connie. and I hope ectie will be nice.

 ~~Brantwood~~
 Oxford ~~Coniston~~
 Saturday morning
Darling Doanie
 Tuesday next will

---

3. This Kate is probably the 'Brantwood indoor Steward' (28.531).
4. This is followed by a sketch of the dog in the corner of a room, apparently on a carpet (11 x 9 cm).
5. The letter continues on the reverse with another sketch, this time a closer view of the dog (10.5 x 8.5 cm).

Letter 135. 58/152, 1873. Pencil notations: '? Mar 13. 73.'

Letter 136. 60/152, 1873. Envelope: Ruskin wrote a postscript on the front: '(Robin's Come – / Delicious!)'; addressed to 'Mrs Arthur Severn / Herne Hill / S. E. / London.'; Postmarked: 'OXFORD / N / MR 14 / 73' (front) 'LONDO[N S. E.] / D 7 / MR [15] / [73]' (back). Pencil notations: ' ? Mar 15: 73', '18.71' (on the reverse of the final sheet, which suggests this letter was not always with this envelope).

do beautifully for me. and
I'm so glad we're to be by
ourselves.
Connie & I have been doing
nothing but quarrel lately – but
I daresay we can mange to
live in the same house for
a day or two more.
As a matter of feeling, I should
– even now, – have liked Rose
better than Lily.   But I
dread the evil star.
    – Di Ma – Me sood like 'Poppy'
        best of all –
            No – see over

Oh – my di – di – di-est ma –
– pease – do <u>pease</u> let it
  be Fifle!

– The Robin is <u>so</u> lovely
The very ditefullest
Wobbin[1] me evy did see

Enclosed is nice –
I mean to catch
after noon post with
this if possible – On
Monday, I shall go to
British Museum first.
to fetch this book that Ive
bought[2] – I shall come by
the morning train – David
to be at station about one
oclock I suppose – and I
shall be out with my own
di ma about four.
I'll send accurate hours
by my tomorrow letter
for Monday morning.
   Ever your lovingest
      Di Pa
Yes. – Arfies lake of [Lenor]
    all most right

137. 19 March 1873, Corpus Christi College

Corpus Christi College
Oxford

Di Ma,
    Its velly coo-el of oo
to send oos poo Donie to school
He no like it at all.
How's itie Illie di Ma?.
Is se <u>velly</u> dood – now she's a
itie Christian?[1] Me will be
velly dood, di Ma – if oo
would'nt send me to school.[2]

Lecture went off very nicely
I think – The Prince came to
hear it again! – and Acland.
– and the three Graces,[3] tell
Connie – looking very nice –
I never saw Ina looking so
pretty – I'm going to tea
with them and the princefs
Louise to morrow – Mrs Liddell
said she left it to Alice
to ask me, because she knew
I would'nt come if she did herself –
– I'm velly – bedient to pitty
Alice, di ma – me [so] dood, me
don't f know for to do.

Me velly seepy di ma –
– Dood nite.
    Evy oos own poo Donie

  1. Here, Ruskin wrote 'robbin' then changed it to 'Wobbin'.
  2. See 12 March 1873 [134].

Letter 137. 62/152, 1873. Envelope: addressed to 'Mrs Arthur Severn / Herne Hill / ~~ELLC~~ S. E. / London.' Postmarked: 'OXFORD / N / MR 19 / 73' (front); 'LONDO[N S. E.] / D [7] / MR [20] / 73' (back). Pencil notations: 'Mar 19 73.'
  1. Lily Severn recently had been christened.
  2. There is a pencil bracket here, the other bracket is two lines later, after 'Acland'.
  3. The Liddell sisters.

138a. 20 March 1873, Corpus Christi College

Corpus Christi College
Oxford
20th March –

Darlin' Pussie
   – Me was so fitened
to day about Prin cefs – and.
– theer was no Princefs after all.
– they kept her hearin peepies
playin 'Bach' till she had no
time to come in to tea – away
by 5–8 train. Deanery[1] full
of peepies – Prince fetch in 'em
all after him. me had a
word with pitty Alice quietly
and ran away. When I got
to my rooms – (quite seriously relieved
in my mind, for I was so ashamed
of my [hands]) I found 'Bob'
in my room writing me a note –
He looked so well – and seemed
to enjoy his chat with me.
– Asked if I had been at the
music – No I had'nt – never
   could attend to any music
now. Did'nt I to Cons
asked Bob; – "Oh = yes = to
Con's – but only to look after
her [accompaniments]."

He had just bought Carlyle's
past and present. I told
him he was a good boy
and must be a good boy –
and read it ^every^ word from
beginning to end.
He orders his own dinners, now –
and I advised him not to
be afraid of baked mutton.
– I hope to be <u>home</u> at
soon after 5 tomorrow.
   Evy oos own ownest Donie
   my Di, wee, Di-wee wee-Di didima.[2]

138b. A. Liddell invitation and J. Ruskin response

Deanery
Ch. Ch.   19. March 73

Dear M[r].. Ruskin
   We are so sorry
you do not mean
to hear the beautiful
music; but will
you come in
and hear all
about it after
it is over, at
4..30 after P. M.
and meet the
"Princess Louise:
do please come
Believe me
Very sincerely yours
Alice Pleasance Liddell

Answer –
   My dear Mifs Alice
I am sure I shall like to
hear you telling me about
the music – or about anything
else you like to tell me,
much better than any
music – unlefs you would
sing it to me without the
organs and the trumpets and
[strumings] and things; but even
in that bright historical light
Im afraid I shall never
come to think of Bach as other
than sounds from Wonderland.
   But I'll come, on <u>any</u> pretence
   being ever,
     Your faithfullest Servant.
         J R.

Letter 138a. 63a/152, 1873. Envelope: addressed to 'M[rs] Arthur Severn / Herne Hill / S. E. / London.' Postmarked: 'OXFORD / [D] / MR 20 / 73' (front); 'LONDON-S.E. / [H T] / MR 20 / 73' (back). Enclosures: Alice Liddell's invitation with Ruskin's response (63b/152, 1873); a fragment of a letter from Brayshay (63c/152, 1873). Pencil notations: '? 1873'.
  1. Home of the Liddells.
  2. The end of this line curls down the right margin.

Letter 138b. 63b/152, 1873. Paper: embossed with a stylized image in red ink.

138c. Brayshay fragment

(.5.)
one, that you could commend!
  Oh how I <u>do</u> wish that I could make myself of some service to you. The only people (my father & Mother) that I seemed to feel I had duties, owing to, <u>before</u> you; are dead, & gone from me; &, I faithfully trust, at rest: – it always seems as if, after them, my next duties are to <u>yourself</u>: as some slight returns for all <u>your</u> goodness to <u>me</u>. –
  I am <u>only now</u> at the close of long wearisome duties as Executor of my poor father's will – &c: &c: – & so am not able to be properly at work, yet, at

(6.)
drawing: – In a couple of months I hope to be settled down at my little house at Mal--ham: & to get quietly to work.
  How thankful I should feel if I ever could do any work that would give you a spark of pleasure or satisfaction: or, if that is to be denied me, if I could do anything that you could in <u>any</u> way make use of – for purposes of charity, or anything, – <u>for others</u>. – (?)
  Is it at all possible that when I get to Malham I may <u>ever</u> have the great pleasure of a visit, or even a "<u>call</u>," from you? I would do everything in my power to make you not regret it! My wife desires to be kindly remembered to you. & I am always
                [affectionately yours, my dear Mr Ruskin   W^m. Hutton Brayshay. –

139. [25] March 1873, Brantwood

       Brantwood,
           Coniston. Lancashire.
My darling
  I got a terrible fright by opening Arthur's letter two hours after Lily's – (not expecting one – & <u>only</u> reading Lily's in my morning work time)

I am so far thankful that you have had something to go through showing both Arthur and me how you really bear pain. It will make us both still more tender & loving to you than we have ever been. – for sometimes even <u>we</u> used to have moments when we thought Joanie was tired perhaps a wee bit too soon. Now we shall both know.

But me so misby, till I hear again –
Oh my di-di di Joanie –
– <u>pease</u> don't ~~go~~ ^try feeding babies any more.
My sweet – it may a little amuse you to know how happy Downes is! So very Downsy Pounsy[1]
and ^ he and I together – ~~we~~ have found a new Rock – in the wood where I never, had been and its going to be prettier than anything else in Brantwood.
  Oh my pussy – my pussy – to have oo were, "<u>twite</u> well Di Pa" once more!

  Love to Arfie

  Ever your <u>doting</u>
       Donie

Letter 138c. 63c/152, 1873.

Letter 139. 66/152, 1873. Pencil notations: 'Mar 73'.
  1. The letter resumes, upside down, on the following page.

140. 2 April 1873, Brantwood

> Brantwood,
>   Coniston.

Darling Joanie
   Of course you know how unhappy I am when you are ill I dare not think of it – or should be too misby. Please give up nursing directly. and get a stout wet nurse. I know its' the only way. You can't do the child justice in your present state. It is not your fault – you have done all you could
    Ever my own darling,
      Your sorrowful Di. Pa
        JR.

141. 6 April 1873, Brantwood

> Brantwood,
>   Coniston. Lancashire.
>   Palm Sunday

Darling Joanie
   I am too uncomfortable about you to be able to write cheerful or amusing letters. But I am not tormenting myself with any anxiety and am greatly relieved by hearing baby is weaned. – Arthur sent me mamies letter – I took the liberty of reading it. & have sent it to her – asking for mine – Ever your devoted di Pa.

I am doing things here with Downes which I want to keep a great secret – till my Doanie comes. Then, I think – she will both keem and dump. She must make herself able to do both.

I am very well, myself again. to-day. .

142. 15 April 1873, Brantwood

> Brantwood,
>   Coniston. Lancashire.
>   15th April 73

Dearest Joanna
   I am so constantly in sadnefs that your beautiful letter can hardly make me more sorry – but it makes me feel more resolution to be what I can to you, always, to the best of my powers. Not that 'resolution' is ever needed to be kind to you. but sometimes – to be kind to myself, for your sake. Now that I must so far as ^{is} in me, be mother as well as father to you, I must strive to have peace in my own heart; that I may preserve it in yours.
   I will write to Mary.

   Elkanah's saying to Hannah[1] {"Am not I better to thee than ten sons?" has been murmuring in my ears up and down the woods. One mother is better than ten sons. But you are that yourself, Joanie, now

---

Letter 140. 72/152, 1873. Envelope: embossed with 'F.JOHN.LATE WARD.DENMARK HILL. S.E.' and a fern and leaf arrangement; addressed to 'Mrs Arthur Severn / Herne-Hill / S. E. / London'. Postmarked 'AMBLESIDE / B / AP 2 / 73' (front); 'LONDON-S.E. / 7 / AP 3 / 73' (back). Pencil notations: 'Apr. 2: 73.'

Letter 141. 73/152, 1873. Pencil notations: 'Apr 6: 1873'.

Letter 142. 81/152, 1873. Envelope: addressed to 'Mrs Arthur Severn, / Herne Hill / S. E. / London.' Postmarked: 'AMBLESIDE / B / AP16 / 73' (front); 'LONDON S.E. / 7 / AP17 / 73' (back). This letter is reproduced almost in its entirety in 37.65.

  1. Elkanah is the husband of Hannah, an archetypal biblical mother (of Samuel), I Samuel 1.8.

and I will be at least
– all I can, to you.
    and ever your lovingest
    – and gratefullest
            Di Pa – besides

143. 20 April 1873, Brantwood

Sunday,
Brantwood, 20th April
Coniston. Lancashire.

My dearest
   I am very glad you
wrote to me all that was
in your heart. Pray do so
always.
It would not be right for
me to tell you all that is
saddest in mine. Sometimes
the flowers make me
much more sad than the
wind and rain: and
the distant views always
make me think of my
father in his grave. And
the mystery of it all becomes
perpetually more terrific
to me. But it is because'
I am not moved enough
by it, that it is so
woful. – because I am
not trying enough to
do right. & feel low, as
base, as well as unhappy.

I know you can't understand
this. but it is so.
The only thing to be ^{by any of us} done is
to be kind & cheerful always
———

See over page

[1]I enclose
cheque (for horse –
and a little
present besides)
   My dear – I don't   – with love to Arfie
care about twenty babies
if only you and Arfie
can come, after 17th May
– The baby doesnt <u>the</u>
<u>least</u> annoy <u>me</u> by
squalling – I'm only
sorry for its loving
mamma, being
        Ever her own Donie

Dearest love to Lily
    & thanks for letter

   The harbour <u>will</u> be a beauty
   but will take me, as near
   as I can guess – of. ^{my} Robinson
   Crusoe work, till the year
   1880, before it is done.
   But Arfie will be able to get
Lake in where it's <u>shaded</u> soon
            enough, – the
            earth in A.
            is terribly thick.
[2]Beach   A

144. 4 May 1873, Corpus Christi College

Corpus Christi College
Oxford
        Sunday Evening.
My darling,
   I was up at five, as usual
this morning. Wrote letters till
8. (from 6) – chapel – wrote
lectures till one. Had M^r
Dixon of Newcastle to lunch.[1]

Letter 143. 83/152, 1873. Pencil notations: '1873', 'A. W.' This letter is partially reproduced in 37.65–66.
  1. This final aside is squeezed into the top right corner of the final page.
  2. Written at the centre of a rough sketch of the harbour (8 x 3.5 cm).

Letter 144. 92/152, 1873. Envelope: addressed to 'Mrs Arthur Severn / Herne Hill / S. E. / London.' Postmarked: 'OXFORD / N / MY 4 / 73' (front); 'LONDON-S.E. / G 7 / MY 5 / 73' (back). Pencil notions: 'May 4. 73.'
  1. Presumably the cork cutter Thomas Dixon of Sunderland, the recipient of Ruskin's 1867 letters published as *Time and Tide, By Wear and Tyne.*

Alice Liddell asked me to
come & see her – on her birthday.
– Went, & found people besides –
Had to talk – (cousin of M^rs
Barrington² at Venice)
– Went away for a walk.
– Met [Cannon Liddon]³ – Theology
for an hour. – Dinner in Hall –
– your nice Mr Anderson
to tea –
No rest, all day till this
minute – and now I'm
puzzled whether you'll
have put off the young lady's
visit – or will be disappointed
as much as I shall' be
if I don't come.
If you want me very much
send me a telegram,⁴ and as soon as you get
[this
I'll manage to come, by eight
oclock –

 Ever your lovingest
  Di Pa.

145. 2 June 1873, Brantwood

  Brantwood,
   Coniston. Lancashire.
    Monday .
My sweetest of possible pussies
 That letters should have
missed yesterday – of all days!
– when I just wanted them to
go right. – and they 'trusted'
somebody. and somebody was
too late for post.
Me so seepy – di ma. Me been
up since five ocock.
– Venice¹ is learning the clock
because I make appointments
with her, and she can't read
the timepiece. Her² mother
has made her a pasteboard model
with two hands to push about.
That's what I call education.
But I perceive that little girls
never want <u>any</u>body to teach
them – what do you call
it di ma – what you used
to do so – oo know – Firtin?

– Of course Venice & Maude
 are great friends f by this
 time. So down at the
beach yesterday, Venice was
kissing Maude all over the
head – So I said. "You know
Venice, I can't have <u>that</u>
going on, and I getting none –
If you don't stop directly, Ill
have one myself. Whereupon
Mifs Venice instantly gives
Maude another. Whereupon, I
 take one myself, as I said; and
then – for I was going t̶o̶ up to
the house, I said – Now Venice,
– mind you don't go out on the pier.
– and I won't be long –
"And I shall kiss Maude all
the while you're away," says Venice.

Di Ma – me ove oo so mut –
 me don't know fot to do.
 is that Firtin?
  Evy oos own. Donie

---

 2. Perhaps Mrs. Russell Barrington (37.715).
 3. This could be 'Carson Liddo'.
 4. There is a line here, crossing the margin to the message transcribed to right.

Letter 145. 106/152, 1873. Pencil notations: 'June 1–2 73'.
 1. Venice Hunt, the eight-year-old daughter of William Henry Hunt, and one of Ruskin's goddaughters (*Later*, p. 259).
 2. Two words have been superimposed on each other: 'the' and 'Her'.

146. June 1873, Brantwood

Brantwood
Coniston

Friday.
Darling Pussie
How the days fly – but as they bring me nearer to sight of mine own poos moos I won't complain

Venice begged leave to have her own kitten – so it was sent for. You <u>never</u> saw such a little rogue. It is every wheer in the room at once. – usually sits on somebodys shoulder – climbing up from the floor if one's quiet for a minute – <u>Will</u> be on the table – (whipping or no whipping) – & will put its paw on every word I write as the pen finishes it –
– I've been obliged to give it a bit of bread it eats my bread! with rapture!![1] to get leave to write this. When the bread's done, I shall have to put it in the cupboard

– Such lovely weather M^r & Mrs Hunt have had, and I think I'm doing them good – There now – Pussies at a Turner, scratching the glass to get inside – Now shes up on my shoulder – now she's on the table, purring like a steam engine – now she's [slapping] my. hand – now shes rubbing [the nib] of my cork pen. –[2]

– Now shes up on my shoulders again – now down the other side now walking over the paper – now licking my glass of sherry – now poking up a drawing with her head under it. . – but all with an intense affectionateneſs & confidence which is wonderful. The other cat went & sulked for an hour about it last night – sitting like an owl on the corner of the railings –
– There now she's found my watch chain, and I shall have no more peace Now she' has actually sat down <u>on</u> this sheet – at the top, and is watching every word I write – Well – my dautie – I wish everybodys letters needed no more watching.
Love to Arfie, many times over.

Ever [mine] own
your devoted Di Pa

It's so sweet of you, not minding my going ~~up~~ down by myself.

147. 27 June 1873, Brantwood

Brantwood,
Coniston. Lancashire.

Darling Joanie.
Me so dedful pointed at oos not coming till Wednesday, me don't know fot to do. But its best Crawley shall set down all about the trains.

Letter 146. 110/152, 1873. Paper: this reverts to an older style of letterhead. Envelope: embossed with 'F.JOHN.LATE WARD.DENMARK HILL.S.E.' and a fern and leaf arrangement; addressed to 'Mrs Arthur Severn / Herne Hill / S. E. / London.' Postmarked 'AMBLESIDE / B / JU 6 / 73' (front); 'LONDON.S.E[.] / 7 / JU 7 / 73' (back). Pencil notations: 'June 6 73.'
1. Ruskin used bread to blot his ink when writing.
2. This line of text is particularly unclear, presumably because the kitten was playing with the pen as he wrote.

Letter 147. 113/152, 1873. Pencil notations: '?June 27 73'.

If it is a fine day I shall
meet you at the bottom of
the lake – Geographically
I mean – not hydromically.

My dear, I'm so very grateful
for the word about Ireland.
The enclosed is from
another mad friend[1] – a
very worthy person – and
may amuse you. a little

– Poor Maudie has just
taken a fit of putting her
nose under my elbow
wanting to be patted, which
is greatly disturbing to my
letter. Oh me, I wonder
~~wha~~ how my work would
have got on, if I had ever
had R. coming in and wanting
to be petted.

It is getting on very well
just now – though very slowly.

I enclose also a line from
Ned Jones,[2] which is very
delightful to me.

Oh my pussie, my pussie –
please come back pussie –
   For the hills look blue,
   For want of you –
   And the lake and I, black, pussie.

   – Ever oos own   Di Pa.

148. 8 November 1873?, Corpus Christi College

Best thanks for the statue-table –
That little goat is the most wonderful
   piece of cutting I ever saw in my
life. But what
on earth does one
do with it? to   *Corpus Christi College*
               Oxford
keep it safe?   8th Nov. answer by return of
                             post

My darling Joanie
   For the present, leave
your money where it is: for
the following reasons.
You observe that as a preference
shareholder, you only get your
dividend by swindling the
old shareholders.
William Milroy[1] does not see
any impropriety in this; but
if he has money in rails, he
will in a year or two perceive
the [impropriety] of the Third
Order of Preference Shareholder
who will by that time be
Swindling <u>Him</u>.
And this Third Order of
   Preference Shareholder will
probably be the last. For
in a few years after that
– the British Public,
Blockhead though it be
to its inner brain, and
rogue to its marrowbone,
will perceive that a dividend
on a railway is only a tax
on its passengers – and is
exacted partly in lives and
limbs.
And the British public
will abolish dividends on
railroads – as on <u>other</u> roads.
You might ~~as~~ just as well
buy a share in an obnoxious
   Turnpike – which did <u>not</u> mend the roads,
it piked, as a share in any Railway going.
There is not a man in them – who stays
in them, but will be ruined in the next
ten years.
      Ever your lovingest Old Fessy.
      whom you had better trust than
      any present man of busineſs,
      unleſs you mean to live by
      jumping from one swindle to
      another. Which is a most
lucrative line of life: but not one for my pussy.

  1. 'Another mad friend' tied to the reference to Rose suggests that, by this point, he assumed she was mad.
  2. Edward Burne-Jones.

Letter 148. 120/152, 1873. Pencil notations: '? 1873'.
  1. Husband of Joan's sister Mary.

149a. [after 10 November 1873], Corpus Christi College

Corpus Christi College
Oxford

Darling Doanie
 Your letters are such comfy-wumfy – and I'm so glad to [learn]¹ of Arfie's new subject – one I entirely delight in myself. Im just going to share his Door Diagram !!! to day.
I've three languages ~~neu~~ now, – of my "household words" My own Professorial. My Pesssy-wessorial or [Bibsesasevingsy]² – And my Crawleywawlian. – I've just come acrofs such a lovely bit of Crawleywawlian in my ectïe last written. – Gulp of Genoa for Gulph of Genoa.

 Don't oo run away home without tellin me first – my wee Doanie & Arfie? .

– Please – theres a big Ledger next window in bookcase behind [ww].
Look at page 200 of it and copy me out the state of the funds of St George

 Ever oos own Di Pa

149b. fragment, 10 November 1873

 Whitby
 Nov. 10th
 '73¹

to have also 4 of the Cabinet portraits, the other 2 shall follow by post.
 Hoping they will

150. 6 December 1873, Corpus Christi College

Corpus Christi College
Oxford

Darlingest Pussy
 ¹ Yes. – time does fly just – for busy – and – in certainly many lights and ways, happy, people like you and Arfie and – Donie. With all my grumbling over what might have been – or what I crave for, or what I have lost, I am not unconscious of the much good I have, especially in power of giving pleasure of help.; and ~~it is~~ ¹ ᴵ ᵃᵈᵐⁱᵗ ⁱᵗ ᵗᵒ ᵇᵉ really a very comfortable thing for an old gentleman to be able to sit in a cathedral stall to hear Bach music – ᵃⁿᵈ to have Ediths to flirt with, Princes to walk with – and Pussies to love.²

I am ^ ᵃˡˢᵒ ᵗᵒⁿⁱᵍʰᵗ in a very comfortable

Letter 149a. 132a/152, 1873. Pencil notations: '? Nov.', '1873', 'copy state of Funds of St G', 'AS Door Diagram'. Enclosures: fragment of a letter.
 1. This could be 'hear'.
 2. 'Bibsy' was a pet-name for the infant Lily Severn, and 'Pessy-wessy' was a pet-name for himself as professor, so this line refers to baby-talk.

Letter 149b. 132b/152. Paper: the top 8.5 cm of a sheet of writing paper; at the top of the page, there is a sketch of a holly branch, signed 'G Sutcliff'.
 1. The place and date of composition are all that remain of the beginning of the letter. This section is not in Ruskin's hand, but the rest of the fragment, overleaf, is.

Letter 150. 125/152, 1873. Envelope: addressed to 'Mrs Arthur Severn / Brantwood / Coniston / Windermere'. Postmarked: 'OXFORD / R / DE 6 / 73' (front); 'AMBLESIDE / A / DE 7 / 73', 'WINDERMERE / A / DE 7 / 73' (back). Pencil notations: 'Dec. 6. 73', 'A.W.'
 1. There is a pencil bracket here, the other bracket is near the end of the letter, after 'a little exacting'.
 2. Edith Liddell, Prince Leopold, and Joan.

room – all my own – have
four wax candles and a nice fire –
– a college dinner about to be
brought up in state – admirably
cooked – A Titian portrait
in the corner. Turners Bolton
Abbey over the chimney piece –
– ~~my~~ 15 sketches by Mantagna[3]
under my table – any book in
London that I like to send for –
– and a balance of about a
thousand pounds ready money
at my bankers –

And I think – in claiming – or even expecting – any extraordinary shows of pity or condolence from my fellow mortals – I am perhaps a little exacting

Who should walk in this afternoon but Drewett[4]
He is well in for his physician's work and
likely, I should say, to be a very great man.
He is very happy – and thinks ~~the~~ his examination
to morrow will be 'great fun". – "such a queue with
the examiners to make a little go a long way"
Ever di Pussie
Arfie & oos loving Di Pa

151. 9 December 1873, Corpus Christi College

Corpus Christi College
Oxford
– Tuesday evening

My darling Pussie
    Is oo at home
oo di wee sweet di Ma.
    Me's just goin out to
dinsey win – me so fiten ed Di Ma
That second call of Princey was
to ask me to dine with Prince
Louis of [Hess] to night – and
the Dean of Ch Ch[1] is going with
me – I mean – me's goin with
him – and me's so fitened Di
Ma. & wishes me was in little
Nursery, safe, at Herne Hill.
—
Me's back, Di Ma. –
It was very nice, but I was a
little frightened – The Vice Chancellor
– Dr Acland – Profesfor Max Muller[2]
and Prince Louis's gentleman
in waiting – Baron – I forget
what – made up the party.
I sat on prince Leopolds left had –
– the Baron on his right – Prince
Louis opposite Prince Leopold –
The Vice Chancellor on his right
Professor Max Muller on his left.

    3. Andrea Mantegna, whom Ruskin classified as an 'Art Master' from the 'Age of Masters' (19.443).
    4. Dr. Dawtrey Drewitt was an Oxford pupil and friend of Ruskin (24.xxvi).

Letter 151. 132/152, 1873. Pencil notations: 'Dec', '? 1873', 'A.W.', 'Dines with Prince & Prince Louis', 'To lunch with / Princess of Wales'. Ruskin's diary entry of 10 December 1873 ascribes these events to the previous day, the 9th. See Evans and Whitehouse, p. 770.
    1. Henry Liddell.
    2. Frederick Max Müller (1823–1900), Professor of Comparative Philology (Evans and Whitehouse, p. 769n).

Acland & the Prince's tutor[3]
at head & foot of table.
> whom I like very
> much indeed.
In the evening, Prince Leopold
& Max Muller played
a long duet from [Musowbuler]
– It was very strange the feeling
of sitting by and having two such
players to play to me. But me
likes my Pussie betty.[4]

– I'm to meet the Prince at
the Taylor Gallery tomorrow –
I believe Prince Louis is
coming with him.
Then to morrow evening I'm
to have another nice time of
it – the three Mifs Liddells
by themselves – I'm going in
to be played to, , and to have a
real quiet little bit of enjoyment.
Then on Thursday I'm to lunch
with the Princefs of Wales. –
– Di ma, me's oos own poo wee Donie
– pease, no angy; . me will
ty to do all my lessons after
the nice parties.
  Ever oos own Donie.

152. 10 December 1873, Corpus Christi College

> *Corpus Christi College*
> *Oxford*

My darling Pussie
  And oos at home! –
– and me's comin – and oo
will pet me and make a
wee baby of me – Me so tired
di Ma. – me want to be put in
wee cradle, and sung to sleep.
– I had to receive the two
princes at the gallery this
morning. They were both
~~et~~ entirely nice – and looked
at all the Raphael drawings
and at Turner's and wee Donie's
and seemed to think their
morning pleasant. And the
Baron – [^^^^^^^^^^^^f^^^^][1]
Poo Donie ty to ite his name in
> German
– was very eager in asking
me to come and visit him
in Hesse-Darmstadt – He's
some relation to prince Louis
– but me nevy no nothink

Me's goin to have fine wee
firty with Ina and Alice
and Edith[2] – all three, to night –
– Gracious – if Connie knew!

Here's a nice little note from
Ina. – Yesterday – and
another's just come from
Wykeham house – so I shall
have to lunch to morrow with
the Princefs & dine with Prince
Leopold – Lunch will be
a dreadful thing – fifty or sixty
  people I suppose, at the
Vice Chancellors. – but M^rs
Te says the Princefs 'wants to
see me' – perhaps it's only
her form of putting it.

I write to Girlie –
  (Broad Greer Lodge
    Thornton Heath.)
to night – to say, if <u>you</u> call
who you are: – Do you
think you could manage
to call on Friday or Saturday
so that she might perhaps
come on Sunday and stay

---

3. There is a line connecting 'tutor' to the 'I' of the note below.
4. Ruskin wrote 'better' then amended it to 'betty'.

Letter 152. 126/152, 1873. Pencil notations: 'Dec', '?1873', 'Wed', 'A.W.', 'Gallery with Prince & Pr. Louis', 'Girlie', 'Juliet Tylor'. Ruskin's diary entry for 11 December 1873 places the events of this letter on 10 December (Evans and Whitehouse, p 770).
  1. Ruskin filled three lines with mock-script. The name should be Frederick, Grand-Duke of Hesse-Darmstadt (*Later*, p. 305).
  2. Lorina, the wife of Henry Liddell and two of their daughters, Alice and Edith.

Monday, – without my driving over theer – for I'm rather in confusion with all this unexpected break up of my time. – If she could stay till Tuesday – Julia Tylor[3] might come from Tuesday to Saturday.

Ever you own
Di Pa.
Dear love to Arfie
– How's [Mrs Handly]?

Ever you own
  Di Pa.
Dear love to Arfie
– How's [Mrs Handly]?

---

3. Probably Juliet Tylor, daughter of Alfred Tylor of Carshalton, Surrey (*Later*, p. 222).

1874

Arthur Severn Jr. born to J. and Arthur
R. participates in Ferry Hinksey road-digging experiment with undergraduates of Oxford
R. makes Continental tour, 30 March to 23 October:
spends much of May copying Botticelli's *Zipporah*;
receives letters from Rose, September and October
R. sees Rose on return from Continent, and then divides his time between Oxford
and London, where Rose is staying at the Queen's Hotel, Norwood
Rose returns to Ireland, 15 December
R. returns to Brantwood for the turn of the New Year

153. [early 1874?], Corpus Christi College

Corpus Christi College
Oxford

Sweetest of Pussky-musskies
I had a lovely walk
to day, feeling more myself
than I've been since that
Sunday morning at Coniston
Church door. – I had a far view
of Oxford, in sunny mist, from
a hilltop – wheer I had not been
~~sc~~ since I was 21. And "The
skylark oer the furrows sung," as
I did then
I've sent you a fairy book, for that
child. Her letter was frightfully
rosaceous. – but she <u>can't</u> run
away from us ^ yet for a week – or
ten days –, anyhow –, can she?
But this fairy book seems really
very nice. I've read the
story of the Corrigan. I think
Rosie must be a Corrigan
turned wrong side out – and
wanting ^ to kill people by hurting them –

I've found the other portrait
of you. I want to come back
and finish it – and make a
drawing of Rosie.
Notice that the fairy book
is by a Scotch man.
I've sent a book on French costume
and furniture to Rose – I hope
it will amuse her a good deal
Love to Arfie & Bibsie
Ever your aff^e run & poor Di Pa
JR

154. 10 [March 1874?], Brantwood

+^{1}Chest on table from
Mr Talling.^{2} No wee Joanie
to sit on the bench. & unruffle
Brantwood,
Coniston. Lancashire.
Tuesday 10th
My dearest wee Joanie
Your letter today is
perfect in sweetnefs and fitnefs;
exactly what I wanted. The relief
of seeing the Rose one is very great.
partly in showing me she is better;
– more in showing that she has
not yet begun to tire of my
Joanie, and that there is some,
constancy in her.

Autograph letters for 1874 are in 'Bem L 39 / Letters / John Ruskin / to / Joan Severn / 18??'.

Letter 153. 3/245, 1874. Corpus Christi College letterhead. Pencil notations: '?1874', '?Jan. Feb' and 'Fairy book for child'.

Letter 154. 16/245, 1874. Pencil notations: 'R', 'A.W.' '?1874', 'March?'.
 1. Ruskin placed a dot in each corner of this cross and its mate, below.
 2. Probably Mr. R. Talling of Lostwithiel, Cornwall 'from whom Ruskin purchased many minerals' (36.499, see also 26. 449–51).

³ Yes. – it is bad for me to be alone
– yet only alone can I do my work:
only alone, or, ^ if it could be! as it used to be,
with my own Joanie, all to myself.
Don't cry out, dear, that you're just
the same. You love me as much –
or more; – but you can't unpack
my minerals for me, + and drefs
Bibsie – and talk to Arfie, all at once
– you need'nt think it – nor need I.
– My work is going on, now,
very splendidly. but exactly
as it did when I was alone
^ 10 years ago at Boulogne & Lucerne,
– through an infinite sadness,
which, to relieve, then, I had
my weekly letter from R – and
vague hope – at all events
pofsibilities of hope. And
my Father & Mother. and Ann.

Now. – I have no hope – no
future – no Father – no mother –
– no Rose – and only the
third part of a Joan. I oughtn't
to have so much – but believe
I have that.
It is curious that my work for
my geological lectures required
me first of all – or nearly so,
to complete the map I left
unfinished – breaking off – at
Harristown – to watch Rose ^ at play on
the Lawn. She threw up
her mallet at me – calling
to me to come down. I would
not. for I said I must finish
my map. I did not go down –

But I did not finish my map.
That one will never be touched
more – but I must make another

On the other hand, I have now
enormous power and responsibility
and try to feel like Frederic
the Great. – if only the weather
would let me feel anything.
Bitter north wind & snow
today. but good light for my
work, which prospers. The
giving up lectures does not mean
any giving in. but that I
have no heart or strength for
speaking . and could not have
looked people in the face, the
sorrow so sucks the life out of
me; – but it increases the
thoughtful power, and I'm doing
really more than if I were at Oxford
But Princy-wincy will be vexed.
He really wanted to hear me
lecture again, and those good
Americans will be vexed –
But – I am really helped & comforted
to-day by the earnest, faithful,
loving work Louise has done for me.
in drawing. She is a very noble
girl.

   Yellow chairs in drawing room
Drawing room chairs in my own
turret room, look ever so nice
– Globes in study – old drawing room
[cellarets] in hall – So velly nice
   oos own Donie   Di Ma

---

   3. There is a pencil bracket here; its mate appears after 'Americans will be vexed – '.

1875

Agnew Severn born to J. and Arthur
R. remains at Brantwood into January, then makes a tour of the Dales
Death of Rose La Touche, 25 May
R. receives telegram informing him of Rose's death, 28 May
R. makes extended visits to Cowley (Hilliards) and Broadlands (Cowper-Temples),
October and December; at the latter he attends séances, and believes he feels Rose's presence

1876

R. embarks on what will prove an almost year-long Continental tour, 24 August
He stays mostly at Venice, becoming obsessed with Carpaccio's *Dream of St Ursula*
(see Burd's *Christmas Letters* for his important correspondence to J. during this period)

155. [February] 1876, Corpus Christi College

   Di wiema –
   In <u>Mexican</u> –
'I love oo.' is
ni-mits-tsika-waka-thasolta –
and a Kiss is a
   tetenamiquilitzli
   Dieu merci, says the
Frenchman who learnt Mexican
   Quand on a prononcé
le mot, on a bien merité
la chose.[1]

156. [February] 1876, Corpus Christi College

Corpus Christi College
Oxford

Darlingest Joanie
   How nice to make oo
laugh so at oos lessons
in Mexican!. We mut
both learn Mexican dectly
because it will puzzywuzzy
peepies so mut mo than
baby talk.

Di Ma, mes not tumin
home to mowy, betause
me's got to take so many
tings to London Instit, and
it will really be less
fatigue to me to go theer
straight from here, than
to pack em all at Herne Hill
and go in early. So I'm
coming on Tuesday early
to town – arrange evything
and come out to early
little fetchment dinnywin
at five o cock.
– but me'll ite again early
to morrow –
Oh my di wee pussy how
nice it is to have oo
to give ecties to. oo, and
φίλη, are all my 'audiences',
really – only poo Donie wont
have his grannie this time
But his dee wee ma will
do twite well
Evy oos – own Donie

Autograph letters for 1876 are in 'Bem L 41 / Letters / John Ruskin / to / Joan Severn / 1876–7'.

Letter 155. 25/130, 1876. Pencil notations: '?Feb 76' 'Mexican' '?1876.'
   1. [When one has said the word, one deserves the thing].

Letter 156. 26/130, 1876. Pencil notations: 'Mexican', 'Feb?', '1876' on a half-sheet of letterhead.

157. [February] 1876, Corpus Christi College

Corpus Christi College
Oxford

Di wee ma
  Here's some little tissoo,
– it sound almost like "kiss oo'
paper. – and some Hortitultural
tings – and mixed etties – nice
old Rawdon Brown and [Tony]
and me will be at Herne Hill
to mowy. at a little after
four to dress – if David will
be at the station at two –
and George with his wooden
& velvet things at London
Institution at three.[1]
  Evy di wee Ma –
    Oos own poo Donie.
Vi-mits-tsibāwakā-thosolta

158. [March] 1876, Corpus Christi College

Corpus Christi College
Oxford

Darling Pussky
  Anything more horribly
tantalizing than thinking of
how nice it would have been
to have – pised oo, last night
and been 'at home' for y̆ oo –
can't be. But oh dear, I
tood'nt – evy body has something
for me to do. and my masses of
old drawings are in such a
litter. I'm putting them in order
and retouching, & leaving – so that
peepies may know what they are,
when I've got away to Rosie.
But me no want to leave oo, di ma.
Only if it was'nt for oo, and I might
go away to Rosie dectly – me should
ike it. only perhaps, – she would'nt.
Oh my poo wee Doanie, me
so fitened at those nasty sea
lions a̶t̶ barking at oo, Whatever
is they like?
Enclosed is a Kevvy letty! sent
without any addrefs!
  Did oo see t̶h̶e̶ Zipporah,[1]
di wee ma – and did she
look nice. ? and have they
got the one from the
Arundel?
And I'm oos poo lonely Di Pa

Letter 157. 27/130, 1876. Pencil notations: 'Mexican', 'Feb?', '1876', 'George with wood & velvet to LM'.
  1. Possibly for the lecture on Heraldry, given a the London Institute on 17 February 1876, see Ruskin's diary entry for 19 February (Evans and Whitehouse, p. 885).

Letter 158. 47/130, 1876. Pencil notations: 'Zipporah', '? Spring 76'. I have placed this in early March, partly because Ruskin spent a relatively large amount of time at Oxford in March, and partly because I suspect the 'pise' might have been a birthday surprise for Joan.
  1. See Hilton for a discussion of Ruskin's fascination with Botticelli's *Zipporah* and how, in 1874, he began to conflate Zipporah and Rose (Later, pp. 275–76).

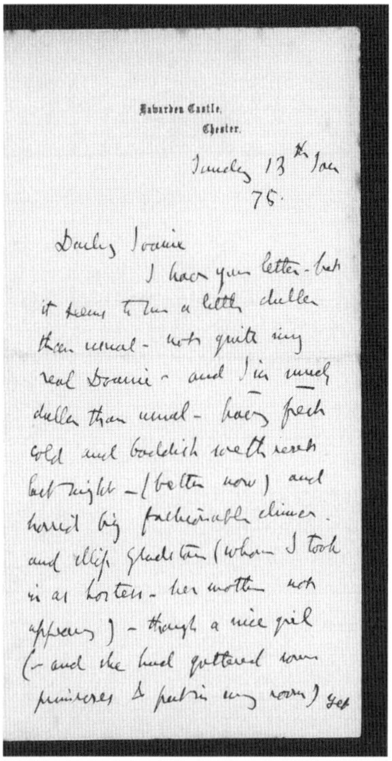

FIG. 7. Facsimile of JR to JS, 13 January 1878 [162] RF L42, Ruskin Foundation (Ruskin Library, Lancaster University)

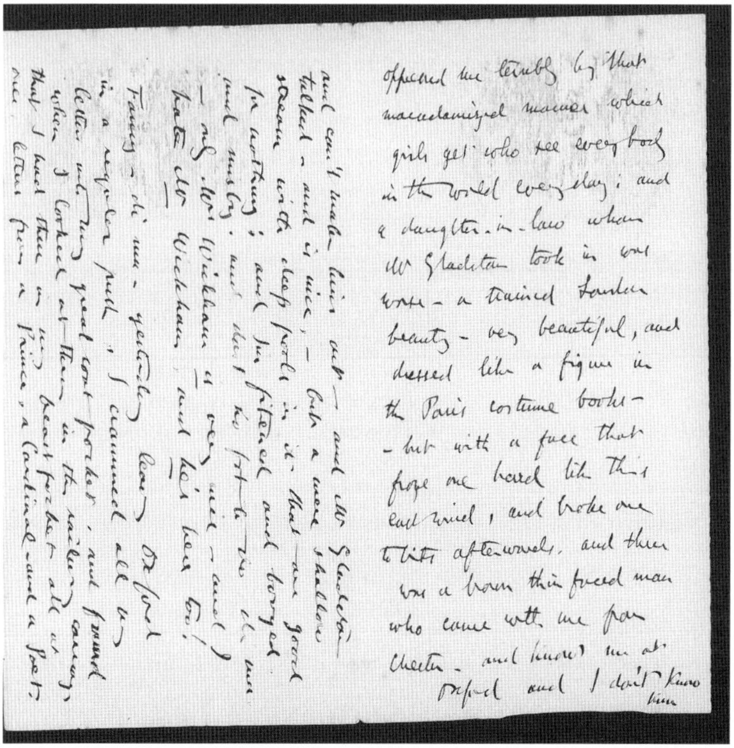

1877

R. returns from his long Continental tour, 16 June
R.'s review of a London exhibition in *Fors* 79, July, describes Whistler, at this time
a rising young artist, as a 'coxcomb... flinging a pot of paint in the public's face'

1878

R. suffers a breakdown, February to April
Whistler's suit against R. for libel is heard at the High Court, 25 November; Whistler wins
damages of one farthing, and is bankrupted by his legal costs
R. resigns the Slade Professorship at Oxford

159. 1 January 1878, Windsor Castle

Corpus Christi College
Oxford

Windsor Castle – 1st Jan. 78
Di wee Doanie
I've just twenty minutes
of the first day of the year left,
to send you one more line: – There
were only the Prince – Mr Collins –
his physician – and I, at dinner –
and it was very nice, but I had
a little too much weight of
conversational responsibility on me.
– Evening very pleasant afterwards
– the librarian being an old friend
of mine at the Brit Museum.
– and the Prince sent for the
[Luciande]¹ & Raphael drawings
and went right through them
with me. At the end, he
made me write my name in
his "birthday book" – with date
1st January 1878, & Windsor.
– Curiously, though most of
the days had before been
more or less occupied by
other people, the 8th Feb^y
was wholly clear. – so that

my name was the first on
that page.
'Wednesday morning,
Oh di ma, its so
tebby – window looks out
into [sandy] courtyard – like
Abingdon gaol – Oh di ma
how lucky oo and me
dont live in no nasty castles
– oos poopoopoomisby
Dipa.
Enclosed letter nice,²

160. 10 January 1878, Corpus Christi College

Corpus Christi College
Oxford
10th Jan 77
Darling Pussie
¹I have <u>greatly</u> enjoyed
Marks visit. but eve$_r$, since,
the interruption of my plans
by the Windsor visit, have
fallen into confusion deeper
& deeper, and at the beginning
of the year it is ruinous – <u>so</u> that
to my deefp² sorrow I am

Autograph letters for 1878 are in 'Bem L 42 / Letters / John Ruskin / to / Joan Severn / 1878–80'.

Letter 159. 2/65, 1878.
  1. This could be 'Lucinda'.
  2. This footnote is on the reverse of the first leaf.

Letter 160. 5/65, 1878. Pencil notations: 'A.W.' , Ruskin's '77' has been struck through and replaced with '78'.
  1. There is a pencil bracket here, the other bracket is at the end of the paragraph.
  2. Ruskin wrote 'deef' then added a 'p' to the 'f'.

forced to give up Gladstone[3] altogether, & Brantwood for perhaps yet another fortnight – I don't know – I'm just done up with overwork and no exercise; and dare not attempt more – and in them great houses one never has an instants' rest from breakfast till 12 at night.

– Tell Downes I recollect now about the stone –
It was <u>my own</u> ordering about the packing to Baxter. All part of the confusion – two pieces worth 10/ and 8/– – gone like glass.
Ive sent Prince Leopold my fathers' copy of the Seven Lamps, and must buy an American edition for myself![4]
I went to see the Union Frescoes with ~~Ro~~ Marks – <u>Such</u> a ruin! and Woodward[5] dead, Rossetti[6] mad – and poor me, – like to go so. – if I don't mind
Ever your lovingest Di Pa
Lolly is happy and helpful to the utmost

161. 10 January 1878, Corpus Christi College

Corpus Christi College
Oxford
10th Jan[y]. 78.

Darling Pussie
I have rejoiced in Mark's visit, but ever since the Windsor interruption have fallen into a state of confusion which is now wholly oppressive and inextricable. – and I feel so exhausted that I am obliged not unwillingly to give up the Gladstone visit. It is a distress to me to feel how this will vex and disappoint my puss more than I can say. – But I am sure it is wise: my head is beginning to fail me in the way which admits of no farther strain;
one of the chief and ~~vexatrousest~~ most stinging things being – that I've lost Sir W. Scotts pen – and it not mine![1] Pray search instantly for me everywhere – that you can think of. I never showed it at Windsor – but am terrified it may have got thrown out of my box theer.
Ever your woful but loving di Pa.
JR.
Enclosed letter was first written – I send it only to show by its illegible scrawl how unfit I am to be more troubled.[2]

the Pen was wrapped in a piece of white paper[3]

3. Despite this hint that he would not go to visit the Gladstones at Hawarden, he had arrived there by 13 January [162].
4. See 35.238 for Ruskin's letter to Prince Leopold in response to the Prince's thank-you for the book.
5. Benjamin Woodward, one of the architects involved in building the Oxford Museum (*Early*, p. 218).
6. Dante Gabriel Rossetti had been involved in designing the Oxford Museum and painting the Oxford Union murals (*Early*, pp. 221–24).

Letter 161. 4/65, 1878. Pencil notations: 'A.W.', 'Scotts pen lost'.
1. Sir Walter Scott's pen been lent to him by Mrs A. G. Butler.
2. It is worth noting that even this, second, version (above) is not very legible.
3. This final postscript was placed at the top of the reverse of the first leaf.

162. 13 January 1878, Hawarden Castle

Hawarden Castle,
Chester. Sunday 13^(th) Jan
78.

Darling Joanie
I have your letter – but it seems to me a little duller than usual – not quite my real Doanie – and I'm much duller than usual – having fresh cold and baddish [wetherest] last night – (better now) and horrid big fashionable dinner. and Mifs Gladstone[1] (whom I took in as hostess – her mother not appearing) – though a nice girl (– and she had gathered some primroses & put in my room) yet oppressed me terribly by that macadamized manner which girls get who see everybody in the world everyday: and a daughter-in-law whom Mr Gladstone took in was worse – a trained London beauty – very beautiful, and dressed like a figure in the Paris costume books – – but with a face that froze one hard like this east wind, and broke one to bits afterwards, and there was a brown thin faced man who came with me from Chester – and knows me at
    Oxford and I don't know
            him

and can't make him out – and Mr Gladstone talked – and is nice, – but a mere shallow stream with deep pools in it that are good for nothing; and I'm fitened and bovyed and misby . and dont no fot to do, di ma. – only M^(rs) Wickham is very nice and – I hate Mr Wickham, and he's here too!

Fancy – di ma – yesterday leaving Oxford in a regular push, I crammed all my letters into my great coat pocket, and found when I looked at them in the railway carriage – that I had there in my breast pocket all at once, letters from a Prince, a Cardinal – and
                      [a Poet.
Prince Leopold Cardinal Manning and Mifs Ingelow.[2] – and all as nice as nice could be. you shall have them after [Susie] has seen them.
Me mut answer them all di ma, so goodbye.[3]

163. 12 February 1878, Brantwood

    Lily's Birthday
Has'nt it just brought me Good?
Brantwood,
    Coniston. Lancashire.
11 Oclock 12^(th) Feb. 1878.
My darling Pussy –
    It is entirely cloudlefs. and I think I must go out and have a little choppy-pop.
    I've written, this morning the enclosed six pages, – one is two half pages. of which perhaps you may like to keep the rough one for oos selfie. – and this must

---

Letter 162. 9/65, 1878. Paper: 'Hawarden Castle, Chester.' in red ink. Envelope: embossed with 'THOMAS & HARDING, 157, PICCADILLY, LONDON'; addressed to 'M^(rs) Arthur Severn / Herne Hill / S E / London.'. Postmarked: '[CHESTER] / [?] / JA 13 / 78' (front); '[HA]WAR[D]EN / C / [JA] 13 / 78', 'LONDON. S.[E.] / E 7 / JA 14 / 78' (back).
  1. Presumably his friend Mary Gladstone.
  2. Prince Leopold, Duke of Albany; Cardinal Henry Newman (1808–92, see Bradley and Ousby, p. 214n); Jean Ingelow, poet.
  3. There is a sketch of the view from a window in Hawarden Castle, across the formal gardens to the folly behind the castle. The sketch covers the full width of a page (11.2 cm) and is 9 cm high at the centre and 14.2 cm high at the tallest edge.

Letter 163. 20/65, 1878.

I think, end, with what
little I may add or revise –
my W. H. H[1] work just now
– which I am thankful to
have been permitted to
do in a way pleasing to my
faithful old friends – if it be so
Then . I want you really
<u>to read</u> the first two
pages of the introduction
to Tuner catalogue
– You [and][2] Arfie may like
to glance at the rest.
Then please send it all
in to Huish. who will
be expecting it.[3]

No mo di ma – me's
got such a lot of lovely
loveletters to answer
such a beauty from sweet
old Connie!

    Evy oos poo old
    wicked Di Pa.

Dear love to Lily.

A little nice bit besides
to my Baby.
And a good big bit besides
to Arfie.

And a great & good big bit
besides to Papa Arfie.

164. 2 July 1878, Brantwood

Most true regards
to your dear old friends
if you are still   2nd July 48[1]

with them.   Arthur is <u>so</u> much better!
Darling Pusswoosky.

We're off <u>this</u> <u>very</u>
morning at last<u>!</u> to be
nearer my pufs every hour –
and nearer Diddie![2] – and
me's twite well and I've
sîgned a pretty little page
of parchment saying that if
ever I'm ill – <u>oos</u> to have
the care of me – but thats
<u>means</u> <u>Diddie</u> and oo,,[3]
mind at, di ma. If you
had sent for Diddie to nurse
me, me would have been quite
dood, dectly. – mind oo do, next time
– and meantime mes oos own and Diddies
    di wee poo Donie.

165. 4 July 1878, Brantwood

Brantwood,
Coniston. Lancashire.
4th July 78

<u>Di</u> wee ma

Me <u>mut</u> ite oo a wee
ettie to tell oo how <u>mut</u> – <u>mutt</u>
mutt – on – and on – me 'ove oo –
– and me tant [sist][1] any longer
without itin oo a wee ettie –
and me's oos own poo itie
    Donie

---

1. William Holman Hunt.
2. This could be 'or'.
3. Marcus Huish, a director of the Fine Art Society. See Hilton for a discussion of Huish and the Turner Catalogue *(Later*, pp. 373–75).

Letter 164. 28/65, 1878.
1. This should read '78'.
2. Sara Anderson, Ruskin's secretary.
3. There are two commas. Usually, a doubled punctuation suggests a trailing off of thought, but in this instance I suspect it represents the twinned 'Doanie' and 'Diddie' working together.

Letter 165. 29/65, 1878.
1. This could be 'fish'.

166. 31 July 1878, London

31st July. 78

Di wee wee Ma,

How does or did di Diddie det to Wigtown to care of John Simson[1] Esquire! – me no understand – but me wishes me was John Simson Esquire with all my Doans and Diddies – Give my darling as much love as she can hold in both hands, and then shake some more all over her.
[2]I dined at Knowles's[3] last night and sat next the Card^l.[4] – and had some diteful talk – – but could'nt tell him how crazy I had been. for everybody was talking politics and so was he. The out of placest looking person I ever saw in such a company. All the others regular MPs – all votes and interests – except the Free thinker Holyoake![5] Me twite well di Ma Arfie keeps better. and enjoyed himself I think both days at the Gallery.

I had a nice little time with Mary too in the afternoon yesterday. and walked out from [Harley] S^t here in a minute or two less than an hour and three quarters – and I looked at all the photographs of pretty girls in Regents S^t – and watched one or two real ones a while, which kept me. I did the three miles and a half from Parliament S^t to your gate in an hour & five minutes – and had some tea and a toasted bun – and enjoyed my dinnywin afterwards N B. Mifs Anderson's – ! are the best Buns – after all! – I hope to send you another wee Pinie-winie to day.

—

We get off to morrow – really, I hope Malham
        by Settle,
            you know

Enclosed from Mr B is in answer to my note yesterday. I'm just going to drive in to him straight

– No mo – today – (only [some] mo love to Diddi) and I'm ever oos own poo wee
            Di Pa.

167. 10 August 1878, Malham

Malham 10th Aug^t

Sweetest Pussky

Your letter gave me a great deal of relief and pleasure to day. – relief because I feared you were doing too much. and I did not like you being 'footsore' – and pleasure,

---

Letter 166. 30/65, 1878. Pencil notations: 'A.W'.
1. The mention of 'Wigtown' implies this is part of the extended Scottish family in Wigtown, possibly John Simson the father of Arbuthnot Simson who was, in turn, the widower of Joan's sister Kate.
2. There is a pencil bracket here, the other bracket is at the end of the paragraph after 'the Free thinkers of Holy oake!'
3. James Knowles, an architect, a founder of the Metaphysical Society, and the Editor of the *Contemporary Review* and *Nineteenth Century* (*Later*, pp. 252, 396).
4. This is short-hand for 'cardinal'.
5. George Jacob Holyoake, a 'reformer' and 'agitator in popular causes' (17.415).

Letter 167. 37/65, 1878.

because the two scenes with the
dumb lady and the country girl
were very delightful to me. I can
so well fancy the joy of the poor
lady in talking to my Joanie.
– and the country girl must have
been like ƒ my Joanie herself
when she was one – oo know, oo
would have been fitened too, Doanie
if oo had found a cake with nothing
inside. And Arfie says so too
and that oo would have sent
the whole bazaar into fits!

    I'm getting on pretty well. but
only pretty well, and
longing so to be home with
oo and [Nyache][1] & the children
again

    I've sent a little letter
and present to Diddie at
Mr Simson's? is that right
No post from here tomorrow
– Oh my di wee Doanie – fot
shall me do if I tan't wite
when I want to.

    Ever your lovingest di Pa

168. 13 August 1878, Malham

    Malham
        13th August
           .78.
Darlingest di Ma

    How <u>dicious</u> oos ettie
this morning! and it
promises another from
Carlisle. and to think of
your being at the Thwaite!
– how lovely! But I'm
in the middle of step and
stair diagrams of Malham
Cove ^ and can't write I've sent one to Arfie
which will – (oh – I did'nt
think of that! – perhaps it'll
give him another fit of rheumatism)
– I don't know what – its so
tebby. Dear love to Susie &
Mary.[1] and tell Susie I've no
consolation of existence [here][2]
but Ducks, and now &
then a Wagtail – I'm always
trying to coax the ducks
ashore – but they wont
come , yet – and my
breast is contracted therefore[3]
but I'm ever oos own
        lovingest Di Pa.
Does oo recollect doin
them things, di ma?[4]
    I'm doin all
      the Cove like
        that!
    I shall drive
<u>some other peepies</u>
crazy – any how –
to keep myself from
being too odd!

1. This could be 'Wyache'.

Letter 168. 40/65, 1878.
  1. Susie and Mary: Beever sisters, neighbours at Coniston, see *Hortus Inclusus*.
  2. This could be 'now'.
  3. This metaphor alludes to a tale from the *Arabian Nights* about a woman with a bird dress. See undated letter 25/65, 1878 (not transcribed).
  4. There is a diagram of three-dimensional blocks, stacked largest at bottom, smallest on top, like a flat pyramid (4.7 x 4.2 cm).

169. [undated], Brantwood

Brantwood,
  Coniston. Lancashire.
Sweetest [Ponnie]

Me's oos poo Donie –
but oos cuttitet all my
hair off – and everybody
shrieks the minute they see
me – you've had your
hair cut.!

Me's been so Kevy this
morning. My Sausage
got cold when half through.
– and I put the cold bit
into the shovel – and rolled it-it
and rollditit about over
the fire till it fizziditt
– and got quite hot – and
blazeditit a little bit – and
then me ateitit it all up.
Lollie's[1] really better
and we all enjoyed
our tea and [Marrowing]
I hope [Tora] likes Forester?

Ever your lovingest Di Pa

170. 23 October 1878, Brantwood

Brantwood,
  Coniston. Lancashire.
    23rd Oct
Sweetest Pusswoosky
  Arfie got home in
lovely time last night: and
his accounts of you all are
quite dicious, only I'm mewing
and moping over my pussie's
headache.

You must be having a fine
time of it, though, with those
girls; and the two maids
with Mifs Bell. I wish
I was there to see it all!

Here are some more
enclosures: one letter of your
own, long kept to be returned.

Arfies account of lawyer
businefs very satisfactory.
and he's writing out an
account of Mr Whistler[1]
for said lawyer, which
will be diteful
Me so lazy, di ma, me
don't know fot to do.
– me's oos own poo-poo-poo
wee wee wee [mufbymufbymufby]

  Donie[2]

Letter 169. 53/65, 1878. The ink on this letterhead is much redder than all the others dated 1878. I think it was written in a later year, but as none of the clues ('Lollie', '[Tora]' or 'Forester') can clearly be pinned down to one year, I have placed it where it is currently filed.
  1. Laurence Hilliard, brother of Connie and one of Ruskin's secretaries.

Letter 170. 59/65, 1878. Pencil notations: 'Whistler'.
  1. James Abbott MacNeill Whistler. The account was being written for the Whistler v. Ruskin libel trial (*Later*, pp. 356–57, 396–98).
  2. Unusually, the 'i' is dotted with a circle.

1879

R.'s mental state remains precarious, but he continues work, and spends most of the year at Brantwood

171. 18 February 1879, Brantwood

Brantwood,
Coniston. Lancashire.
18th Feb. 79

Darling wee Doanie
   Ive set Elsie to work
to find receipts, if possible
[1]'Its enough to make one take
up one's astrology again,
to find out what star is
bringing this pestilence of
vulgar nuisance to bother.
me ^ all this year just when I'm set on
my flower work and ought
not to have a thought shaken.
And suppose I had'nt a
Joanie to manage everything
for me – what <u>would</u> become
  of me!' . All the same
its rather interesting this
forgery businefs and the
insanity connected with it.
For you know he might
just as easily have got
fifty as thirty eight, when
he was about it! I knew
him to be mad, a year ago.

I'm ordering such lovely plants
di ma – Irises and lilies
and things that will grow
here as those gladioli do.
and some for your greenhouse! .
funny twisty wispy ones!
   And me's oos own grateful
di Pa. – Receipts will come
  to morrow. if possible
     Ever your loving J Ruskin

172. 26 February 1879, Brantwood

Brantwood,
Coniston. Lancashire.
Wednesday

Darling wee Doanie
   Mes invented two new
names for you and me!
Oos my Doanikie-Poanikie
and mes oos Donikie-Ponikie
  – Otherwise 'Doaneyky P<u>o</u>neyky'
  and   'Donkey   Ponky'
– Snow two inches deep
again all round the house
I can't write a word
o̶f̶ I've been doing lots
of Lilywork. Nursy
came up to say Lily
gets on with her
knitting! exquisitely.

but <u>poor</u> wee – Lily
is so downhearted because
she has'nt a ettie from
her di ma.
I told Nurse how <u>tebby</u>
busy you weer for oos
donkeyponky.

   I'm very sorry for poor
David. you know that
  I'm sure.
     Ever your lovingest
       Di Pa

Autograph letters for 1879 are in 'Bem L 42 / Letters / John Ruskin / to / Joan Severn / 1878–80'.

Letter 171. 11/53, 1879. Pencil notations: 'Forgery', 'A.W.'
   1. There is a pencil bracket here, the other bracket is at the end of the second paragraph, after 'a year ago'.

Letter 172. 15/53, 1879. Pencil notations: '? Feb 26. 79'.

1880

Violet Severn born to J. and Arthur
R. spends the first half of the year at Brantwood, leaving only to give public lectures
R. visits France, 21 August to 5 November

1881

R. spends all but one week of 1881 at Brantwood
R. suffers breakdown, 20 February

173. 17 February 1881, Brantwood

Brantwood,
Coniston. Lancashire
17th *February*
1881

My darling Lily,
So many thanks for your pretty Valentine; – and I am sure <u>you</u> should thank the <u>Fairies</u> for bringing your mother to see you on your birthday, and for putting it into <u>my</u> head to give you a pretty silken dress – I will tell you some day how the Fairies teach silkworms to spin the silk : – the <u>first</u> lesson they have to teach the little things is that they must be very industrious all their lives – then, that though they're only worms, they can, if they're industrious make the loveliest dresses for little Lilies like you. – and then, they show them how they must eat , *mulberry leaves* and how they must sip dew: and then how they must make their leaf huts – and then how they must spin all day long (I don't know how long their working day is though, but I'm sure its the right length – the fairies know.) And then the fairies tell them they must rest – and that their work is to dress beautiful little and great – ladies, who when they are wise, do as the fairies bid <u>them</u> and spin, – golden threads. And thats all I have time to tell you today – but I wish I were with mama to see you in your fairies dress – for spring. Perhaps they'll give you pretty dreams, even when you put it off – and will watch by your bedside – and sweep the floor for you during the night – only you can't see <u>them</u>. –. you know – green and blue dresses cant be seen with open eyes – [on] in the night – so nobody believes in fairies – except [1] – but only dreamed of with shut ones
– I'm in a tebby hurry
and am making a mess
Ever your lovingest[2] Di Pa.

174. [October] 1881, Brantwood

I am afraid this letter is very badly written – but I had rather write prettily when   *Brantwood,*
I have nicer things.   *Coniston. Lancashire.*
to say.   *Sunday*
My dear Joanie
Your yesterdays letter was the first, since you went to London, that has said

---

Autograph letters for 1881 are in 'Bem L 43 / Letters / John Ruskin / to / Joan Severn / 1881–82'.

Letter 173. 4/52, 1881.
1. This line of text has been added below 'night', in small letters, with a squiggled line connecting the phrase to 'night'. The rest of the message, clearly aimed at Joan, is written in the margin.
2. There are three dots over the 'i'.

Letter 174. 9/52, 1881. Pencil notations: 'Legacy', '? Oct 81'.

a word about any of my
books, or anything that
people were saying of them.
If you were a little more
interested in either the
Scott paper's, or the history
of Amiens, and of –. several
other places, – which are
at present my true work,
– you would not immediately
think me out of my wits
because I tell you [some][1]
truths either about Lacerta
or yourself – which are not
subjects of my usual talk
to you. I usually treat
you ∧ ^only^ as a loving child or
loving pet. But you are
now on the point of forgetting
that I cannot always
be amused by the ballets,
or the Rogue's march or
the Christy minstrels. .
– Try to recover some
of the feeling you used
  to have when I taught
  you your drawing –
– and let me see that
even as the mother of a family, you

can be interested in my present work,
– and can trust me to choose the
instruments of it – whether [Haxton][2] –
                              [Burgefs,[3]
– or Randal.[4]
I recommend you also to recollect carefully
as far as you can – all that I said
to you in walking down to the Marshall's[5]
^harbour^. ~~pier~~ that day. And – act on it.
   – I have got a legacy of £19. – from Mifs Fall[6]
– I suppose for a mourning ring. – which
I have not the smallest intention of wearing
I will send it you when I can find
the paper. and I want five pounds
    sent to Mr Dawson out of it.
It is at least, [some][7] little comfort to me, in
                                     [this
  time of extraordinary – health – to see
  how much better <u>you</u> get on without <u>me</u>,
  than I without you.
      Ever your lovingest Di Pa.
You will probably answer, eagerly, that you
                                    [<u>do</u> care
about the Scott papers, and my books.
                                  [How is it,
then, that you never ask whether I am
                                       [getting on
with them?

1. This could be 'simple'.
2. Hilton transcribes this as 'Hackstoun', *Later*, p. 429. W. Hackstoun was an artist and copyist for Ruskin (39.253).
3. Arthur Burgess, engraver and artist employed by Ruskin (39.92).
4. Frank Randal, an artist employed by Ruskin (39.438).
5. The Marshall family were neighbours at Brantwood, living in Monk Coniston.
6. Possibly Eliza Fall.
7. This could be 'one'.

1882

Herbert Severn born to J. and Arthur
R. suffers severe breakdown in March, improving by April
R. makes Continental tour, 10 August to 2 December; he meets the American-born illustrator
Francesca Alexander in Florence, 8 October, and she will become a lifelong friend

175. 11 May 1882, London

Thursday 11 May
82

Darlingest Doanie
I had a very sweet
day for my Fathers birthday
yesterday. Drove in open
Hansom, enjoying fresh air
all the way in to T. and Mackrells[1]
– ^was^ at ^the^ entrance to Bond Court,
by 10, 55 AM! ^where^ I met
good Mr Baker![2] we went
in together, found both partners
and chatted till 12 – usefully. .
Then Mr Baker came with
me to Fishmongers Hall
wheer we met Arfie to see
exhibition of model ships
(and I drew the Norman Sea King's
   of ninth century, found ~~at~~ in
opening [tumulus], in 1880) – then
Arfie went to sketch Thames, in
lovely day, and I, with David
(whom I had left to bring
Arthur in, not wanting ~~him~~ David at
Walbrook) – drove to [Epitots] to
lunch, and then to British
Museum, where the head of

Minerals, Mr Fletcher, – showed
me a unique diamond with[3]
   a six rayed star, <u>dark</u>
   seen through every
   side. so. size of entire
             (show Collie)
a . . .◊   stone. a!

Then I recommended
purple velvet instead
of white cotton! – and mean
to send Mat[4] to [bring][5] some
to show.
Then I left my card on
Froude: and <u>walked</u>
from Onslow Gardens through
Knightsbridge to Duke's Statue
where I went into the
Park and observed – various objects – of
scientific interest. Then I walked down
to end of Grosvenor place – where I had told
   David to wait. – drove home – had tea
(with an egg, from [Lucastes][6] – my own
                                    [boiling –
– and I <u>buttered</u>[7] other 16, myself.) then
into garden wheer I walked for an hour
before dinner – Evening closed with Arfies
beating me at chess – but he had a fight for it!
I slept perfectly well and have done a nice
bit of geometry for Collie Woll[8] before

Autograph letters for 1882 are in 'Bem L 43 / Letters / John Ruskin / to / Joan Severn / 1881–82' [letters 1–90] and 'Bem L 44 / Letters / John Ruskin / to / Joan Severn / July-Dec 1882' [letters 91–216]. Ruskin began to use blue-flecked paper rather than the white (or occasionally cream) of earlier years.

Letter 175. 8/216, 1882. Pencil notations: 'H. Hill', 'Waists & chrystals', 'Diamond', 'M [Baker]'.
 1. 'Tarrant & Mackrell'.
 2. George Baker, Mayor of Birmingham who 'look[ed] after the Guild's affairs' (*Later*, pp. 357 and 437).
 3. Ruskin drew a sketch at the left side of the paper (1.5 x 1.4 cm). Beneath it he added a smaller sketch of the actual size of the diamond (0.3 x 0.3 cm).
 4. Martha Gale (*Later*, p. 434).
 5. This could be 'buy'.
 6. This could be 'Lancaster', 'Lacertas' or something else.
 7. This could be 'battered'.
 8. William Gershom Collingwood, one of Ruskin's secretaries

breakfast. As I walked through Knightsbridge.
I saw rather a pittier phot of Princefs Helen
and bought it to send oo, as enclosed:
but, please
di Ma, there's an article in
the Morning Post of today –
(sent also) which makes me
velly anxious about peepie's
healthis – particularly Lockie's,⁹
It says – Di Ma, that girls
are never poppily in health
unlefs their waists are 30 inches
round. Now Di Ma, could
oo be so velly good as to take
a little measure of satin riband
and send me the <u>exact</u> measure
round Lockie's waist, – when she
has'nt got anything on; oo know.
di Ma – so that oo can run it
quite fine: – its velly important
for me to know. before I write
anything more for young ladies.
– And me's so much obliged
for [nici chart] of the rooms Di Ma
and for nice news of Mifs Beever¹⁰
and me's velly well for my
tea, this afternoon, and it
promises to be fine, and me's oos poo
wee deserted Donie.

176. 13 May 1882, Herne Hill

Saturday
13th May

Darlingest wee Ma
What a sweet oo is, to
send me my measures so
quickly – It will be <u>such</u> a
new light in science – proportion
in crystals – and waists – all
at once – and, di ma, what
oo said about shoulders is
velly intyecting –. and, I think

I must make all my girl-friends
measure each other for me – and
me tink, di ma that it would
be a little rude to ask about the
shoulders, – so me will only
ask for the measures round the
neck. & round the waist – and
round the garter, and round the
ancle,
and then, di ma – I think
I can guess the rest pitty well
– only <u>those</u> four must be given
very fine & close –
And <u>was</u> oo really di ma
– less than 22 ½ – !! How
much lefs? – You must
tell Lockie <u>she</u> must'nt
get married on any account
of – or what a little
dumpy-dump she'd be!

I'll write to Lady [Bateo']¹
dectly and ask her to
tea with Mary Wakefield
– I rather enjoyed my
tea with the [Tylors],² only
Master Arfie cut in and
carried them off to <u>his</u> domains.
which was'nt fair. I won't
have him splitting my
Vampire Queen that way –
– he shall go to his club –
and smoke.
I had rather a nice time
at the Tennants – Don Carlos
was there and Sir C Dilke³
and everybody very pleasant
– and Dolly dicious – She
took me out by the garden
gate – and put her face
so close in saying goodbye
I had like to have kissed her
before all Whitehall! and
the Horse Guards!

---

9. The Severn's governess.
10. Susie Beever.

Letter 176. 11/216, 1882. Pencil notations: 'Herne Hill', '1882', 'The Tennants'.
1. This could be 'Baker'.
2. The family of Alfred Tylor, who had three daughters, see *Fors* 54 (June 1875), (28.353).
3. Sir Charles Dilke; see 36.332 and 37.588 for letters from Ruskin to Lady Dilke, see also 20.7n.

She's been painting
<u>such</u> pitty pics of nymphy
               wymphys
With no – nofin at all on! –
– She asked – did I mind?
– but I said I did'nt mind.

More Rook [Pie][4] from
M[r] King and I've sent
him a lovely letter of
thanks, though I say it
Arfie won another game
last night – and quite
off the bat!
     Evy oos – <u>ovin</u> and, <u>voted</u>
        Di Pa.
How lovely it must be to
see Agnew go down the
lawn! Mind he don't go
into the Sweet Briar! – or
   the <u>road</u>! though.

177. [May] 1882, Herne Hill

Friday

Sweetest Doanikey – Poanikey
  I like the businefs letter
immensely for its busywifinefs,
and wisenefs: and indeed
I have more Turners than
I want, and should much
like to buy in a little more
stock than I have, for I'm
ashamed now of the bankers
receiving this small dividend.
– The report of the Meifsonnier
is very encouraging. and
Huish wanted to buy it
straight off – But I mean to
see what it will bring –
Any how you need not be the
least anxious about your
new building expenses – for

it is sure to ~~cower~~ cover
much more than those.
and – if Christie's people
have a good water colour
sale coming on – Ill clear
off my light Turner
sketches. and some of
the drawings which I
do not need – and get
a Pot of money to potter
on with at ease.
   But I am glad to hear
what you tell me of the
cheapnefs of Brantwood
– I should'nt mind
myself taking rooms – which
they'd be glad to give me
in old Christ Church, when
I wanted to be near London – and, if I keep
well I shall be much abroad too
so that Arfie might really throw up this
house altogether ± and take the Lewis
and Brett[1] and, all the china for the
new rooms – ^ at Brant. or suppose we
make a [pairing] off sale of Turners and
blue [hawthorns]?
   <u>There's</u> a stroke of businefs for you! –
Dear love to Collie, and tell him I
   want the volume of my ~~quee~~ green
big ten volume Sowerby[2] which has
   the Labiatae in it. Ever your lovingest
                          Di Pa
[3]+Im enjoying the garden, though
   Peonies marvellous. and all sorts
     of nice things coming. snapdragons
         and lily.

178. 25 May 1882, Herne Hill

25th May

Darling Joanie
   First about the music.

---

4. This could be 'Pic'.

Letter 177. 21/216, 1882. Pencil notations: '? May 82', 'Meissonnier came', 'Perhaps sell Turners'.
  1. Ruskin owned works by both artists: John Brett, A.R.A. (39.86) and John Frederick Lewis, R.A. (39.310).
  2. James Sowerby, illustrator of *English Botany* (39.573).
  3. This footnote appears across the bottom of the page, at right angles with the main script.

Letter 178. 22/216, 1882. Pencil notations: '1882', 'H. Hill', 'Tidying', 'Meissonnier', 'A.W.'

– It merely encumbered me
here. and I could not
keep the lessons Mr West[1]
gave me, and my own – in
any order among it. If you
will choose out any of it
that is worth binding – and
return it arranged in the
order you would like, I will
at once send it to Mr Simpson
   [2]My real comfort and
happinefs I find, so far as
the last is possible to me,
depend far more upon little
things and tiny orderlifses
than on quantity of possession.
   You also, if you have
everything at Brantwood
when the new building
gives you room, tidied
as far as those big boys
will allow, – will have
twice the comfort with
servants & everybody.
   [3]Arfie is gone into town
with the Meissonnier, which
he has carte blanche to
put in any hands he
chooses: and I am much
inclined to have rather a large
sale of whatever I don't want
– my eyes now will serve me
for crystallography – but I can't see Turner's
touch as I used to. and it would be nicer
to <u>buy</u> in some stock and feel that one
had turned the corner! at 63!

Baby on Thunderstorms is delightful!
   Tell Collie Wollie to answer that lady
with a Yes. – as polite as he likes!
   and that I'm so glad he keeps his interest
in the diamonds. – I am sadly <u>cut</u> by
them myself. worse than Lockie Cut me
when she went away to Tunbridge Wells
(How she could! or you could let her!)
   I never <u>can</u> make out. Evy oos own Di Pa

179. [May] 1882, Herne Hill

Tuesday

Darling Joanie
   I am so very thankful
for your effervescent account
of moor land expedition. and
thankful in many other
directions, that thus far,
my plans have succeeded.
in this first real trial of
them under my own direction.
   How tantalizing though
for <u>me</u> to hear of those
[hyain<u>phs</u>] = Silver tresses
tied with blue!   so pitty
di wee ma.
And that nest! – just
   above the crumb-place!
but you don't expect
to be able to keep that
long! from those peeps and
eye-peeps and shy peeps
and far from shy peeps of
your's?
Tell Collingwood his
diamond diagrams are
overwhelming and I
feel as if I were going
to be carried away by
a roc, out of the Valley
of Diamonds.
I shall show them at
British Museum directly.
– but can't write about them to-day
having a revise from Jowett.[1]
– I'm getting on fairly well with
my work – but am growly wowly to
a bitter – and acid manner. which
totally ends all my musical interludes.
and on the whole makes me unpleasant
to everybody. But I'm in for the grind of
it now. & must keep on. ^{Arfie very good in}
   [coming in for chess.
   I forget how the rooms are arranged –

  1. Ruskin's music teacher.
  2. There is a pencil bracket here, the other bracket is at the end of the sentence after 'possession.'
  3. There is a pencil bracket here, the other bracket is at the end of the paragraph after '63!'.

Letter 179. 28/216, 1882. Pencil notations: 'H. Hill', '? May', '1882'.
  1. Henry Jowett, Ruskin's printer.

who sleeps in mine?
Baby on the 'Mauvais Pas' must be dicious!
                    Evy oos ovin   Di Pa

180. 4 June 1882, Herne Hill

                    Sunday, 4th June
                         82
Darlingest wee di Ma
    After a dicious little tea
with Francie, last evening, Arfie
came home in high feather from
the Meifsonn^r. sale. – and no wonder.
– you know, if wes bof poppily
piccolocomical, di ma, it will
last evy so long! – But I'm
really very happy that you won't
feel the least uncomfy now about
the new house.
The two telegrams about baby
are an immense joy to me; and
I hope to be a little less 'deplorable'
to Mr West tomorrow.
I made Francie play –. [St Kennedy]
and she said it was such a pretty
tune! I thinks <u>she'll</u> like my
wee moosie betty than Mr West.
Mr Schmidt[1] is coming in
this evening for a cup of tea
and to play chess, as Arfies
going out. and me's rather
betty today, and have got some
nice work done
    ,Nufin mo to tell oo di ma.
except that there are certainly
95 peaches on the wall –.
How many did I say. ?
before? They hide so among
the leaves.
What a feast [me'll][2] have
eatin [of em] all up.

Evy di ma
    oose little Gobble Johnnie
    (It looks like a
    new sort of [Fiswis!])[3]

181. 6 June 1882, Herne Hill

                    6th June. 82
                    – wet and dark as
                    November!
    Sweetest Doaniky
        It is very funny, you,
Herdson, and Coward[1] being
all as delighted at "breaking
into the house" as the children
would be in [unroofing a]
Doll's one; not to say an
ingenious and jolly society of
"Three jolly-burglars." It is very
nice to hear of my very dear wee
Joanie enjoying herself, and of
Baby's 'taking possession of
the Lodge.'
Arfie came home to tell me
of the Meifsonnier just after
Francie tea. so it was
a pleasant evening altogether.
I am pretty sure Christie
won't charge more
than 5 per cent which on   6090
would be – say   305
                            5785
and on the small
Geneva theres 200,
    or less 10   180
                            5965
The more immediately interesting
question being, <u>when</u> they pay.
My impression is they [normally]
take three months credit.

Letter 180. 34/216, 1882. Pencil notations: "?A.W.', 'Meissonier', 'H. Hill', 'Francie at tea', 'last (evg)'.
  1. Given the context of Mr West (Ruskin's music teacher), this might possibly J. H. H. Schmidt who developed a musical notation for prosody (31.xxxiii).
  2. This could be 'we'll'.
  3. This could be 'Feswish', either way it probably mean 'fish' in fessy-wessy/baby-talk.

Letter 181. 37/216, 1882. Pencil notations: 'A.W.' and 'Sale of Turner'.
  1. Dawson Herdson was Ruskin's gardener (27.lxxii), while Mr. Coward seems to have been employed at Brantwood (38.331).

[2] The Turners arrived quite safe last night. and look charming One, the [Faido] gorge sketch[3] I shall never part with but if Christie's are still in good activity as I think I shall send in all the others with good protection orders to Arfie, who will watch the sale. I think he brings – me luck – whether in buying or selling

Di wee ma, Im so puzzled because I cant find lavender nor rosemary in Sowerby – I think, if Collie Wollie showed you the place in Loudon – you could copy out for oos di Pa Loudons[4] list of the Labiatae – which would be a great help. Ever your lovingest – loneliest –
— longingest – poo poo wee wee
Di Di Pa

As many loves to Agnew[5] as he can possibly count. and say his Di Pa has the sincerest sympathy with these Arithmetical recreations.

182. [undated] 1882, Herne Hill

Saturday

Darling Wee Ma
  The nice long gossipy letter was a great comfy to me this dismal morning – but it's so dreadfully dark I can't do the visiting cards properly. I enclose three however, as I'm very eager to wait upon Dolly in her own house.
So glad Arfie's better. How singular that he should feel the [woooping] so! but I've great fsimpacy with him myself.
  Susie writes me a long, perfectly written piece of gossip too – and Mrs Talbot's[1] coming but me's vely dull – di ma.
  It's a misby day. and Ive been tearing up some of my di Ma's etties – and it cuts me and tears me too' – – but there's no oom for all of them in my wee drawer
  So many thanks for them Di Ma
    Evy oos poo wee Donie

183. 2 July 1882, Herne Hill

2nd July.   Sunday afternoon

Darlingest Pugwagsie
  I've had a nice time of it since this time yesterday, rather. – I sent word to Georgie[1] I would be there by six. – and it was really a sweet afternoon. and it so chanced that Margaret had a tea of her own – and seven of her schoolfellows for guests – about her own age, – rather old, for me – but endurable – fauts di mieux. So when I got there, the tea was over, and they were all playing ball in the garden – – Whereupon I asked leave to come too, and then Ned himself

---

2. There is a pencil bracket here, the other bracket is after 'buying or selling'.
3. A small sketch of the painting is to the right (4 x 3 cm).
4. Mrs. J. C. Loudon's *Flower Garden of Bulbous Plants*, plates from which are referred to in 21.229, 235 and 243.
5. Joan and Arthur's son.

Letter 182. 42/216, 1882. Pencil notations: '1882', 'visiting cards', 'A. better', 'Mrs Talbot coming'.
  1. Fanny Talbot, a widow who made a gift of land to the Guild of St. George. Ruskin referred to her as 'Mama', see *Dearest Mama Talbot: A Selection of Letters from John Ruskin to Mrs Fanny Talbot*, ed. by Margaret Spence (Manchester: Bulletin of the John Rylands Library, 1966).

Letter 183. 61/216, 1882. Pencil notations: '1882', 'A.W.', 'at opera with G B-J / again / in a fortnight'.
  1. Georgiana Burne-Jones. The rest of the family are also referred to in this letter: her daughter Margaret, husband 'Ned' (Edward) and son 'Phil' (Philip).

– and so we made a ring on the lawn – and the game was, to throw the ball always when nobody was ready to catch it – And it was rather pretty, and nice,
    Then – when I got hot, which I did in half an hour or so – I went indoors, and the girls sat on the grass and sang, – outside in the last sunshine. – making an [extremes Sonesaurian]² picture. Then it was time to go to the opera – though it didn't begin till ½-past 8. Georgie and I are quite of a mind about being early!
    So we got in & comfy at 10 minutes past eight – – and then we had the most dicious performance of Don Giovanni I ever was at. Not because
        of Patti, (who is no actress – but merely a lively [and rather vulgar young woman –) but because <u>the whole</u> cast was good, and the great choruses studied and perfect – as I've never heard them yet – It was one feast of glorious sound for three hours – lasting till nearly a quarter to 12 with <u>very</u> short intervals Patti spoiled the ['la ci darem'] by too fast time; but sang all the rest ~~al of the~~ ʰᵉʳ songs clearly and carefully. – and the men singers were superb. – Then we had a lovely moonlight drive to the
        Grange – supper on pigeon pie and
                    [champagne –
and Ned gave me his room to sleep in. full of no end of sketch books – At breakfast –
                    [Morris,³
– whom I was ~~b~~ most happy to see – and
                    [Margaret
and Phil. – then up in Neds room again,
                    [long talk
quietly, over sketches – Then a visit to
                    [Margarets
room – and nice time with her and mama – then Lunch – Chicken; & currant and cherry pie! and a strawberry or two (stolen off Margaret's plate). – I engage to come again in the same way – this day fortnight – and Ned gives me three lovely little sketches – and I drive, home – where I find Christie's cheque for £5800,,18,,0. – which I mean to take in to Tarrant and Mackrell to morrow and buy £5500. stock, and pay – [over plus] into banker's for cashy wash. I expect Allen to bring me £100 to morrow at breakfast; and I shall have quite a lovely balance, in spite of June bills coming in. (I owe Arfie 3 pounds for gravel walk will he have it at Coniston or when he comes back?) Walter⁴ writes me such a pathetic letter about the Dudley⁵ that I must
    give in, ~~be~~ [for] a Counsellor – Love to Arfie
        Evy oos ovin Di Pa⁶

The gooseberries are all very red on top of the wall!

184. 6 July 1882, Herne Hill

Darling di ma
    What a <u>precious</u> long ettie! – I am so [ovy] glad you like the opals. I'm going to send you another bit of the 30/¹ lot – won't <u>it</u> tonish
    my wi di ma, & Lockie and everybody! but can't pack

---

2. This could be 'extreme Louesaurian'.
3. William Morris.
4. Probably Walter Severn.
5. Dudley Gallery.
6. The letter continues in the right margin, divided from the main body by three sides of a rectangle.

Letter 184. 66/216, 1882. Pencil notations: 'H. Hill', '? July 6', '1882', 'Opals', 'Tiny White', 'advice about piano', 'Turner to go on 22ⁿᵈ', 'breakfast with / Gladstone', 'Diddie to dinner'.
 1. This slash extends into the next line, which Ruskin did not begin until after it.

– it to day. Im just – off to
breakfast with Gladstone – &
then Im going to read with
the Cardinal – and then I'm
going to [draw]² minerals at
Brit Mus. and then I
call on Papa and Mama
and Diddie, at Warwick ^{Gardens}
Sq. and carry off Diddie for dinner!

Di wi ma, I nevy, – no –
nevy – got such a lot of
long, soft-hard, kisses, as
Tiny White³ gave me yesterday
– before all the company too! –
–. finishing off with a little
side-roll of cheek – so nice!
I met Lady Wilde there!
and heard that Oscar⁴ was
still the faithfullest of my
disciples!
Tiny has nice large soft eyes
and flaxen hair, and,
– rather pretty eggiepegs. but
one may see prettier. – in the
Park. – still, she's a find.
All that advice about
    piano is dicious – and me
will do exactly what you tell me. and
be evy so conomical. – But I've got a
£600 balance at bank now, – with 1900
due from Mʳ Kennedy – all sure. and
eight Turners to go at Christie's on the 22ⁿᵈ
– even if I don't sell either Fluelen or Savoy.
– it will be a pretty penny farther
    Evy oos own wee [queesy]

185. 8 July 1882, Herne Hill

Saturday.
Darlingest wee Doanie
    I am sure you need not
be afraid of warning me, at
any time or about anything,
so long as there is not any
special subject on which we
chance to be at issue. I would
not take any warnings last
autumn, because we were at
issue whether the house should
go on, or not, – and I thought
you fancied me ill only because
I had changed my mind
about it. But now,¹ I only
wish I had you here to watch
me – and tell me when I am
tired – for often I am, when
I don't feel it, and am not,
when I am stomachically
languid and miserable. But
the fact is, that though I have
been going about so much, I have
been extremely cautious, all
this while, – writing absolutely
nothing, except necessary letters
– so that all book excitement
is withdrawn, and keeping
off all subjects of sad thought –
–. In spite of which I am
always so sad, when I am
alone that for the first time in
my life, I have sought company
as a distraction.
It is quite true however that
I am very naughty about
Tinys & Rosalinds² – and I've
less and less hope of mending

---

2. This could be 'show'.
3. Tiny White was a child actress. Ruskin had met her through the Webling sisters, Rosalind and Peggy who were child performers specialising in recitation (*Later*, pp. 426–28 and 438–39).
4. Oscar Wilde became friends with Ruskin, then Slade Professor of Fine Art, while he was an undergraduate at Oxford in the early 1870s; surprisingly, he took part in Ruskin's Hinksey Road building project in 1874.

Letter 185. 70/216, 1882. Paper: two sheets. Pencil notations: '? July 8', 'H. Hill. 1882', 'Visit to Hunts', 'Mascotte alone', 'A.W'. This letter is partially reproduced in 37.404.
1. There is a pencil bracket here, the other bracket is at the end of the paragraph after 'distraction'.
2. Tiny White and Rosalind Webling, child performers.

– though I'm going to put off
the peacocks feathers to morrow
because I'm going to wee
theaty to night (La Mascotte)³
and think it would be a little
too bad – Saturday & Sunday
          and all!
⁴I was really very near being quite reformed
                    [yesterday
all at once – by the perfectest little cherub of a
five-years-old I ever saw yet in my life –
                    [Holman
Hunt's⁵ little Gladys. I [had an]⁶ entirely
                    [happy
afternoon with him, and her, and her mother –
– entirely happy because first, at his studio;⁷
I had seen, approaching completion. – out
                  [and out
the grandest picture he has ever done, which
will restore him at once, when it is seen, to
his former sacred throne – It is a "flight into
Egypt," but treated with an originality, power
and artistic quality of design, hitherto
                  [unapproached
by him Of course my feeling this made – him
very happy, and as Millais⁸ says the same, we're
   pretty sure, the two of us, to be right!
Then we drove out to his house
at Fulham, which is aesthetic
if you like!! – such eastern carpets
– such metal work! – such 16th century
caskets and chests – such sweet
order in putting together – for
comfort and use – and three
Lucca della Robbias on the walls!
– with lovely green garden outside
and a small cherry tree in it
before the window looking
like twenty coral necklaces
with their strings broken, falling
into a shower.
His wife is liker φίλη than
any other woman I know – though

of course not so lovely; – but
very beautiful too – Gladys is
a round-faced child of the
purest-pale angel type with
blue eyes, fuller of love than
I ever saw child's eyes before –
She knew me by the King
   of the Golden River – and had
been much expecting me, and
when she came in and I saw
what a creature she was, I
knelt down to get her kiss; her
mother said. "Could'nt you put
your arms about his neck"? She
did so – and then burst into
tears. Her mother took her
quietly away, and she went
into the garden to get me a rose
She gathered <u>one</u>, with one pansy,
and some jessamine – but gave them
to her little brother to give to me.
   We talked over many things
and long times ago, at tea –
– pretty cups and perfect
strawberries & cream, and
Mʳˢ Hunt picked my strawberries
for me just as naturally
as <u>you</u> would have done. She was
so thankful for my praise of the
   new picture.
– I've had a visit from Mʳ Newman
the anemone painter – in far
better health & spirits and
have almost promised to meet
him at Lucca in September!
Now I'm going to have a
rest – and quiet tea – and
Mascotte all to myself!
   Evy oos own ovin poo wee
   di pa.
   Autograph of Hunt enclosed
      may be interesting to
      some people

---

  3. *The Mascot*, a comique opera by Edmond Audran.
  4. There is a pencil bracket here.
  5. William Holman Hunt, Pre-Raphaelite artist.
  6. This looks like 'hxd air', but I think the '/' in the former (forming 'x') was a failed attempt to clarify the 'a', while the apparent dot over the 'ir/n' is an error.
  7. There is a distinct accent over the 'o', but I assume it is meant to represent part of the semi-colon. If my assumption is wrong, the end of the line reads: 'at his studió,'.
  8. John Everett Millais, artist and husband of Ruskin's former wife, Effie.

186. 12 July 1882, Herne Hill

12.th

Sweetest wee Doanie
Here's Arfie all right
and nice – and here's Collie
Wollie too – (but he's had
his hair cut!). and I've
just been told about the
Rose painting! and the
Moonlight! and the Study
with me in it.[1] and its
all so velly nice!!.!
And. di wee Ma, the
Nieces[2] and I all went
to see Clara. $^{last\ night}$ – and they
were dited, but they stand
up for Connie instead! – But
Clara has blue eyes – and
Flaxen hair! – and tapering
eggie-pegs. and is such a dote.
And we had a lovely little
darky private box – and ices
and sponge cake, and I got
the carriage for them in
a minute and they went
home to supper and I to
Cup of tea and beezy bo.
And I'm going to take
M^r & Mrs West to see
'Money' on Saturday. or
perhaps, to the Opera.
And I've got Rosalind
in peacocks feathers for tomorrow
– tea – and a note from
Tiny's mama, saying Tiny is coaxing her to ask
me when they're by themselves – so – as they're
close by the Regents park – I think I shall
go and see some beasts on Sunday and
have tea – with Tiny.
– Love to oo all and me's oos own poo
wee 'voted di Pa.

187. 17 July 1882, Herne Hill

Monday.
My letters here are safe for tomorrow
I only go by the 2.30 $_{45}$ train
from Kgs +.[1]
Sweetest –diest – pittyest
Di Ma
Enclosed letter gives
you my addrefs till Saturday
when I must be back
heer to go on with some
dicious work I've got leave
to do in arranging the chalcedonies[2]
at Brit Mus.
– I had a fine time of it
yesterday! Three or four rather
hard kisses from Louise – one –
– long, & soft, from Maude – who
is a pretty bright-eyed brown
creature – (with brown eggie pegs
very pretty.) – and uncountable
ones of any length I liked from
Tiny – whose phot – with her
little sisters – I enclose – It was
a lovely afternoon – and I went
round from Thorpe House by
the Zool. gardens, and had
a cobra and a little rattlesnake
poked up for me –. and a little
play with a nice English snake

Letter 186. 74/216, 1882. Pencil notations: 'July 82.', 'A. back. & Collie', 'At Mascotte with / nieces', 'Wests to see "Money" / on Sat'.
  1. The Collingwood portrait of Ruskin in his study. See Dearden, *Life*, Plate 25 for the final copy.
  2. The previous letter, also dated 12 July 1882, identified the nieces as 'Tot[tie], Mat and Claudie'. Only two were 'nieces', Claudia was Arthur Severn's sister, and married to Frederick Gale. Their daughters were Martha ('Mattie') and Marion (*Later*, p. 363.)

Letter 187. 80/216, 1882. Pencil notations: '?July 17', 'H. Hill 1882'. This letter has been torn diagonally across the top, separating a piece measuring roughly 13 x 10 cm. The pieces are still grouped together.
  1. Ruskin was travelling from King's Cross Station to Sheffield where he would help arrange the museum.
  2. This is a type of quartz.

who wanted to get up my sleeve.
and had to be pulled out by
his tail. A little rhinoceros
is getting quite good, in the
elephant garden – and opens
his mouth for [leaves] in the
civilest way. And the
pelicans weer lovelier than
ever – also the spoonbill.
Thank Lockie for her lovely
little note – which is a great
comfy.
I'm off early to Brit Mus.
Di wee ma, me ove oo so,
I should like to go on writing
all day. Evy oos poo poo wi Pa

188. 19 August 1882, Sens

    Hotel de l.'Ecu.
        Sens. 19th Aug.
        Saturday
  Di wee ma.
    This is rather a tipsywipsy.
notie – me's been drinkie too mut
Cote-Rotie – with dicious Fowl-rotie
at lunchy punchy.
– All the same I've been vely
melancholy in that corridor. does
oo memby, di ma, – lady Trevelyans
room – – and the big saloon? –
– Seventeen years ago, di ma –
+ Seventeen years ago!
– We're off for Avallon at last –
by 4 oclock train. and I hope
to have [ubby] etties tomowy
mornin – we shan't get there till
nine.
+ Sixteen – only. I believe – But to
think of it – ! Does oo memby
the nightingales at Dijon?
– Oh di ma – if I had those years
back again! oos poo di pa.

[1]I've made rather a good
drawing of chalk cliffs, to day
and the little snapdragons
and convolvulusis – !! ! ! !

189. 6 October 1882, Florence

    Florence Friday   6th
Sweetest di wee mawa
  I had yesterday your
funniest little note about
Francie – with her's enclosed
– her letter to Annecy was
too late. but I'll soon get it
as I'm going back there as
fast as I can – this Florence
makes me wretched –
partly thinking of old times in
it – I see, di wee ma,
the hotel we were in when
Mrs Hilliard nursed Kate
was the <u>Aruo</u>, not this, but
I think <u>I</u> must have been
here in 74.
I'm going out to breakfast
with Newman. and must
leave this to be posted, before
getting my letters this morning
  I'm quite well; but the
ruin of the place, and partly
the change in myself – not for
the good – makes me melancholy
  – Di wee ma – me's got to
be so dedful naughty – me
don't know fot to do – I used
to think Botticelli's little Venus
the nicest thing to see in
the world, but when I saw
her again yesterday I only
thought that to see a real

Letter 188. 109/216, 1882. Envelope: addressed to 'Mrs Arthur Severn / Brantwood / Coniston / Ambleside / Angleterre.' Postmarked: 'Sens / [7 19] / [AOUT] / [VONNE]' (front); 'AMBLESIDE / A / 21AU / 82' (back). Pencil notations: '82', 'A.W.'
  1. There is a pencil bracket here, the other bracket is at the end after 'convolvulusis'.

Letter 189. 109/216, 1882. Envelope: embossed with 'E. GOODBAN FLORENCE'; addressed to 'Mrs Arthur Severn / Herne Hill / S E / London / Inghilterra.' Postmarked: 'FIRENZE / 6 / 10.82 / 12M / FERROVIA' (front); 'LONDON-S.E. / W 7 / [OC] 9 / 82' (back). Pencil notations: 'Oct' '82'.

pitty girl without any [clotheses][1]
but roses would have been
so much nicer!

    Me's oos poo old wick of a Di Pa
– Love to Lockie – How does she know
the advertisement was'nt from me?

190. 8 October 1882, Florence

    Florence Sunday
        8th

    Dee-est wee Ma wa
    Your's of 5th safe to
hand. rather comfying the poo
Donie in saying oo tink all's
safe for a fortnight: and also
rather sticking up poo wee Donie
in saying Arfie likes his Zip –[1]
– I've really been sauntering through
the [leppizii] this morning, thinking
if I'd really set myself to be a
painter, I could have done little
Zips! – and Tips – and little Doras
and Norahs – and little Kiss-me-Alices
in Kistial palaces – as pitty as other
peepies – I think, even now, if I'd
only the chance of doing – suppose –
Lockie with her, jacket – not on, I could
make something very Boticellesque of her
– but I've never the chance!
– Also I'm rather tuck up about my
sciptions, and Arfies being so
pickular about keeping all my
etties twite safe. I only wish

me tood give oo my sciption of
the way the hedges of roses grew
over the walls – yesterday afternoon
under the grey of the olive trees.
– There were no faded ones, and
there were no bunches of buds
making one wish they were out –
but only little blushes and gushes
all about, of the reddest rose colour
that is'nt dark – and the brightest
that isn't pale. put in just as a
painter would who had'nt any trouble
to grow them – but could touch them in
– bunches at a time – They grew
    together – here & there like grapes,
and then went glancing away up and down
                    [among the
olive leaves, like firflies.[2]
– I've been reading your account of little
                    [Arthur
drawing his large boat with many jibs and
a big crew, and hoping it might hang in the
'box [room]' to Collie, who is greatly delighted
                    [by it[3]
– as me too, di ma. and Baby's song of the Keel.
and her sending of herself to the 'Hospital'
                    [all
equally dicious
I got all my letters quite safe, and shall
get them all safe at Luccia, You may
still write there.
    Evy di di di ma wa
        oos poo little powo-wowd
            Donie

---

  1. This could be 'clothings'.

Letter 190. 156/216, 1882. Envelope: embossed with 'E. GOODBAN FLORENCE'; addressed to 'Mrs Arthur Severn / Herne Hill / S E. / London / Inghelterra.' Postmarked: 'FIRENZE / 7 / 10 [8]2 / 3S / F[ERR]OVIA' (front); 'LONDON-S.E. / LC / [OC 9] / 82' (back). Pencil notations: 'Oct 82', 'Joan roses'.
  1. Short for 'Zipporah'. Initially derived from Botticelli's 'Zipporah', the term came to be associated with Rose and with girls in general.
  2. Presumably Ruskin means 'fireflies'.
  3. Collingwood was in Italy with Ruskin, so Ruskin is not referencing Joan here, but telling her that he has shared the narrative with Collingwood.

191a. 28 November 1882, Dijon

Dijon. 28th. Morning

Darling di wee ma
  I got your lovely letter here last night – about liking me to draw flowers better than to write. But oh – my di wee ma – me ta'nt draw fowies as other peepies can. – and me can, though I say it – write things that they can't – that nobody but oos poo wee Donie can, in their wee way And there are such things as dooties – (confound them – at custom houses and everywhere else!) but oo need'nt fear my ever over-exciting [or]¹
  tormenting myself again. – And – di wee ma – think what exciting work – what killing sorrow – I had – in 1872 – 1874 – 1875 – and that all after. 1865–1866. of such bright hope! ²I'm writing in the room that poor lady Trevelyan had – and the sun's bright – and I shall see the Nightingale valley as I pass by to Paris, where she had her last happy day! Think of it all, di ma – it was <u>those</u> things that made me ill – never my work. . At the back of my bed last night there was the little door wheer it was [Amies]³ great joke of the journey to peep in, in the morning & catch me asleep.
All that has passed away now – into quiet twilight – and <u>if</u> they really want me at Oxford, I musts go. – not to talk – but to finish what I began theer and left like a house without its roof.
  It's a nasty nuisance those gossiping papers fidgetting you – – I could have put it all right for you in ten minutes – if I had been at home. but I can't write any more to-day

Ever your lovingest Di Pa

191b. Ruskin's menu of 25 Nov. 1882

GENÈVE
HOTEL DES BERGUES¹

MENU DU	25/11.82.	N° 20
POTAGE	Consommé aux perles	
POISSONS	Truites au bleu S^{ce} Câprus	
RELEVÉS	Gigots de mouton	
ENTRÉES	Palmis de Pardreaux	
LÉGUMES	Haricots verts Sautés	
ROTI	Poulets Rôtis Salades	
ENTREMETS	Poudding aux pain S^{ce} Vin Rouge Pattiseries	
DESSERTS DIVERS		

TOURNEZ S.V.P.²

Letter 191a. 204a/216, 1882. Envelope: addressed to 'Mrs Arthur Severn / Herne Hill / S E / London / Angleterre'. Postmarked: '[GARE] DE DIJON / 28 / NOV. / COTE D'OR' (front); '[HERNE HILL S.E. R.] / A / NO 29 / [82]' (black ink, so this is registered mail). Stamped in purple ink with: 'GRAND HÔTEL DE LA CLOCHE / DIJON / 28.NOV.82 / EDMOND GOISSET / Propriétaire'. Enclosures: a copy of his menu for that day (204b/216, 1882). Pencil notations: 'A.W', 'Nov. 82'. This letter is partially reproduced in 37.422.
  1. This could be '&'.
  2. There is a pencil bracket here.
  3. This looks like 'Annies', but is probably 'Amies', meaning Joan.

Letter 191b. 2.04b/216, 1882.
  1. There are curving pencil lines here, reminiscent of the carved arm of a chair.
  2. The reverse offers information about the 'SOCIÉTÉ DES MAITRES D'HOTELS DE GENÈVE'.

1883

R. resumes the Slade Professorship
R. gives the lectures which will become The Art of England
Kate Greenaway, the writer and children's-book illustrator, spends a month
at Brantwood, 10 April to 7 May

192. 26 February 1883, Brantwood

Brantwood,
Coniston. Lancashire.
26th Feb. Evening

Di wee ma
  I had no time to
write of anything this afternoon
but I enclose a letter. from, I
suppose, some lady I ought to
remember in Ireland – but
[all]¹ that time is mere chaos
to me now, and confused
with the dreams since. – would
you kindly answer her – saying
that I asked you to say so,
and have no letters of her
Fathers, but have grateful
memory of his hospitality
and kindneſs. I enclose also
a wee Doanie letter I've been
long in [getting]. and a [newsp]²
slip about a monkey which
may amuse you and chicks
I think I shall stay here
quietly till you can get
Miſs Green-away³ to come.
Then hyacinths will be
out before we know what
were about.

193. 9 March 1883, Oxford

          Brantwood,
Oxford   *Coniston. Lancashire.*
          9th March 83

Dearest wee ma
  ¹I think the lecture
went off nicely. the Vice Chancellor
(Jowett) made a very pretty
speech of welcome afterwards
The under graduates cheered
no end, and Baxter said
the people going away who
could'nt get in were like
a church coming out.
I was obliged to promise
to give the lecture again
to morrow. After lecture
I went to the schools, – saw
my old Turners; made the
young ladies class beam by
looking over their shoulders –
and praising each for what
was praisable – many <u>weer</u>
drawing very nicely, (quite
the most succesful part of
the lecture was the account
of Miſs Lilias's first lesson.)²
Then I went and had tea
with M^{r} & Mrs Macdonald
and the omnipresent Mrs Talbot!
And nice dinner heer; but
now I'm tired and must
go to bed and me's oos
    own wee <u>real</u> Fessy
      Donie Ponnie

  Autograph letters for 1883 are in 'Bem L 45 / Letters / John Ruskin / to / Joan Severn / 1883'.

Letter 192. 19/157, 1883.
  1. Ruskin wrote 'alll' then blotted out the third 'l'.
  2. This should read 'newspaper', but Ruskin has written off the page.
  3. Kate Greenaway, artist and good friend of Ruskin

Letter 193. 30/157, 1883. Pencil notations: 'A.W.' This letter is partially reproduced in 37.440.
  1. There is a pencil bracket here, the other bracket is after 'Miſs Lilias's first lesson.)'
  2. Lilias Trotter, artist and, later, missionary.

194. [March] 1883, Oxford

Wednesday Evening

Darling Di Ma.

The lecture went off very nicely, though I felt more tired than usual afterwards owing I suppose to the heat of the room. I had a lovely drive with Acland afterwards – and found among my letters an invitation from the Princefs Louise of Dessau to go and stay there (Auhalt Dessau) – with two – (perhaps younger!) – countesses – who seem to be very nice – daughters of the [?][1] Prince George of Auhalt –

Di wee ma – if I was only not such a poo sy wee boy, me'd go. but me tant – and me'll be at Brantwood with my di ma.

Evy oos ovin Donie

Letter 194. 33/157, 1883. Pencil notations: 'Oxford', 'March?', '83'.
  1. This word is illegible, but 'grand' would be appropriate.

1884

R. remains mostly at Brantwood until September with J. and her children;
he is teetering on edge of breakdown
R. stays at the Euston Hotel, London, for the first two weeks of October,
then begins erratic lectures at Oxford

195. 19 May 1884, Brantwood

Brantwood,
Coniston. Lancashire.
Monday

Sweetest Doanie
I was up at the Wilkinson's[1] yesterday, and found thats the mother had been ill exactly as you have – with fainting [&][2] nearly fainting fits – severe cough and general weakness; she's getting over it, but looks pulled down. it must be epidemic. – The Father looking strong and happy. ~~Mary~~ Jane Ann[3] has got a pet lamb, who was extremely charming in getting between everybody's legs every minute – and I only wish I could remember or spell the rich Lancashire in which the Father told me "there was no kind o' mischief that could be thought on, that that lamb would'nt be into, when it was a week or two older".!
(Telegram just come – so dicious!)

– and that there was'nt a Creature in the world so hard ~~difficult~~ to manage as a pet lamb – "wherever you went, they'd be in it." – How Arfie and I ever have managed our pet lamb, I can't think!

As I walked up the road to the house, I saw Jane Ann running full speed down, and of course, thought it was to meet me! – When she was within fifty yards she turned her back straight on me, and I saw she was after a stray hen and – chickens, (I supposed –) I called to her and told her how disappointed I was, – but she said she'd never seen me! – So we drove the hen and chickens up the hill back together. They turned aside at the opening to a little ravine opposite the farm, and ~~Mary~~ Jane seeming satisfied I asked if they would stay there. Oh yes, says she, they'll go into the Beck. Do chickens live in a
[Beck, said I
'Them's Ducks' !– explained Annie.
Di wee ma me's got two young ladies comin to tee-wee – and me's

Autograph letters for 1884 are In 'Bem L 46 / Letters / John Ruskin / to / Joan Severn / 1884'.

Letter 195. 30/123, 1884. Envelope: red sealingwax; there is a 0.3 cm strip of brown substance which could be a hard wax down the centre front, which had extended across the height of the envelope, now 5.5 of the 9 cm remain; addressed to: 'Mrs Arthur Severn / Herne Hill / S. E / London.' Postmarked: 'AMBLESIDE / C / 19MY / 84' (front); '[LOND]ON.S.E. / 7 / MY20 / 84' (back). Pencil notations: 'May 19:84'; 'get a chair & / lets be the two / children sitting under / a tree [so] – with / chairs in hand', 'Lockie', 'Deuce', 'Lucky B' (on back of envelope).

1. Shepherd family living in 'Lawson Park' in the 1880s, the home inhabited by the Stalkers when Ruskin first moved to Brantwood. Young Jane Anne Wilkinson became a special friend of Ruskin's.
2. This could be 'or'.
3. Ruskin twice wrote 'Mary' then changed it to 'Jane' in this letter. This might be an error (perhaps he was thinking of another Mary) or it might be meant to bring to mind the nursery rhyme 'Mary had a little lamb'.

been out all [day]⁴ nearly
and me tan't [say] no mo.

[I] took a fancy to one
in Susies passage, last
week. Susie and I agree
to call her 'the Sparkler'.
they live just beyond
Lolpollie. somewhere.
Mes oos own poo wee
lonely Donie.

196. 15 April 1884, Brantwood

Brantwood,
Coniston. Lancashire.
.15.ᵗʰ

Darling Joanie
 Enclosed cheque for
dear little Lockie – I wish
I could buy her with
the piano – it's a horrid
shame I can't. I wonder
what she thinks herself
worth, if she were to be
put up like the pretty girls
in Herodotus. – please ask her.
– I wish I was a blessed old
Egyptian or Turk or something.

 But di wee ma, what
does oo mean by
getting nothing for the
Venice sketches – and
yet having to pay back
the 100. – you cant have
to pay back the 100 after
theyve sold all those
small sketches – ? [However]
– I've done with the Fine
Art Society, henceforward

– and I don't think they'll
make much of their £100.
So many thanks for
copying out Ellis ettie –
&c & &. and all
the long chat.
I enclose some etties – and
have you read Punch of the 10ᵗʰ
all through – and looked it all through.
—————————————¹
Pease di Ma, Me should like to go to see
 [Excelsior – oo
 know oo oosed to sing it – so pitty.

 Evy oos own pooweewee Di pa

Ned says in a letter to day about
painted glass. – of Morris² – with
tone of sorrowful injury.
"I've urged him to steal his wifes gold
ornaments and boil them up and get
a true ruby" – (colour) "and he won't. –
 he wont !

197. [May?] 1884, Brantwood

Brantwood,
Coniston. Lancashire.

Darling wee wee Doanie
 ¹I am so thankful
and happy to day. – about
you, who are the principal
'sky' to me just now –
but fearfully sulky about
the bitter plague wind which
takes every atom of pleasure
out of May for me. except
in having comfortable light
for indoor work, and sometimes
sunshine for minerals.
I ask (to day) M. Chesneau²

---

 4. This word and the one below have been torn away by the envelope glue. The spacing and context suggest 'day' and 'say'.

Letter 196. 19/123, 1884.
 1. This line connects from the bottom of the second 'through' to the beginning of 'Pease', below.
 2. Edward Burne-Jones and William Morris.

Letter 197. 40/123, 1884. Pencil notations: 'A.W.', 'Chesneau', 'Dressler'. 'Jane Anne', '1884'.
 1. There is a pencil bracket here.
 2. Ernest Chesneau, a French writer on English art who had corresponded with Ruskin since 1867 (*Later*, p. 490). His son, Emilien, is named below.

and his son to come down
on Saturday and stay till
<u>Wednesday</u> – then <u>they</u> must
leave, as Conrad³ comes on
Tuesday, – and oo-o-oo –

Oh – <u>oo</u> <u>o</u> <u>o</u> O O⁴

on Thursday. D.V. – di ma.

– Me's twite well – but
a little bovyed with
light beginning at two
oclock – birds at three
and things in general at
four – which I have to
lie abed all the while.
⁵I engaged Jane Anne for
shepherdess yesterday and
to day, to take care of my
wheat – I was greatly surprised and pleased
to find her on the watch with a <u>real</u> Crook!
and to find that it is really useful to
catch the lambs with.
At school they are teaching her the collects! .
– of which she does not of course understand
one mortal word! However I explained to
    her to day the meaning of 'Ascension'
      and made her pronounce fairly clear to the
      end. – sitting with her under a juniper tree!
(Don't tell Kate for goodness sake!) – and
                             [I think
    she was just as well there as at Mifs
                            [Yewdales.⁶
But she has found out where the sheep got in
    and stopped the gap. – so I suppose she'll
                            [have to
           go back to school tomorrow.
  I think perhaps Arthur
might like to get a glimpse
of what Mʳ Chesneau and
his son Emilien are like –
– I believe they will be at
Mifs Leech's. 65. Kensington
Sq. on Friday

198. 12 October 1884, Canterbury

Cantᵇʸ 12ᵗʰ Oct 84

Darlingest di Ma
    There's no post from
the North here on Sunday,
so in the first place I must
send you a doleful
    MMMEEEEEEWWWW.
(– really, that <u>does</u> look very plaintive!)
and then – proceed at once to
mere businefs.
I'm very glad you sent me the
6ᵗʰ Gibbon, for I've found something
very useful in it; but it was
the 7ᵗʰ that I wanted – please
post that to Oxford. 84 Woodstock
Road; and also, I've left behind
in the most extraordinary manner
all that I had done & Diddie
had copied of my Fifth lecture
"Protestantism." – It may possibly
be in <u>her</u> drawer in the old
dinning room – or it <u>might</u> be – but
improbably, in my drawer,
topmost under the bookcase
next bow-window; on my left
as I sit, or it <u>might</u> be in
ᵒⁿᵉ ᵒᶠ the two uppermost drawers
of the old bookcase – opposite
the other window – Oh my
di wee ma what tubby wubby
mes givin oo – only <u>nevy</u>
mind if oo tan't find it
for its one I can quite
easily ite ovy again. &
I dont want it for a month
yet. Send it to Oxford if found

–Enclosed from W.B was
weelly illywistible – so me's
written to say he may
    keep a stall for me.

  3. Conrad Dressler, a sculptor (*Later*, p. 489).
  4. Below, there are two circles with rays extending from them like two suns. The central circle of each is 1.1 cm across, the varying lengths of rays extend to make each circle measure between 2 and 2.8 cm across.
  5. There is a pencil bracket here, the other bracket is at the end of the paragraph, after 'the lambs with.'
  6. She was the local school mistress at Coniston.

Letter 198. 52/123, 1884.

Then – di [weemee], does oo tink
that [Sairey] would take me in on Thursday
for dinnywin & bed? Me can
always go to British Hotel – mes goin
to Oxfy on Fiday.
   Oh my di ma, fot sood ve hav done
to understand each ovy if vee'd nevy learnt
   baby tawk? Fot <u>sood</u> ve hav done?
         Me's oos <u>little</u> Donie

199. 15 November 1884, Balliol College, Oxford

POST OFFICE TELEGRAPHS
Handed   Oxford Office 4–13   Received 4–32
in at the   here at

From   To
John Ruskin   M^{rs} A Severn.
Balliol College   28 Herne Hill
Oxford   London [S7]

Fifth Lecture given every one
pleased and I am quite
well

200. 15 November 1884, [Balliol College], Oxford

      Monday Evening
      Darling Doanie
         What a lark it is having
you tell me to keep out of
   the way of girls! just when
I'm taking command of the
High school and two colleges
of them! I had a delicious time
too this morning with the little
Brasseys! at breakfast – two
finished little fringy and frank
9 & 10 year olds.
I wish Arthur would'nt
make remarks on my looking
tired &c. I'm no more tired
than I am after any Brant
wood dinner.
Fifth lecture finished off
to day. Ever you loving
            JR

201. 19 November 1884, Balliol College Oxford

Balliol – 19th. Morning
   Sweetest Doanie Poanie
      Violet shall come and
give me lessons on the Organ.
, one of these days.
   [1]I had such a lovely
dinner <u>out</u> last night –
with the Master at a
nice quiet couple's Professor
and Mrs Marshall.[2] M^{rs} M.
and I got into a discussion
– very profound, about the
difference between round
and oval sections in girl's
waists. Jowett's after sitting
smiling a while – "I cannot
follow the Professor – into
those <u>latitudes</u>"!!
   Ever oos ownie Di Pa
            See over.

[3]Off my sleep more than anything

Letter 199. 88/123, 1884. Telegram from Ruskin. Envelope: pre-printed with '<u>TELEGRAM. / NO CHARGE FOR DELIVERY.</u>' (front); 'WATERLOW & SONS LIMITED, LONDON WALL.' (back); addressed to 'M^{rs} A Severn / 28 Herne Hill'. Postmarked on the telegram: 'HERNE-HILL / C / NO15 / 84 / N^E.RAIL.STATION.S.E.' Pencil notations: 'Nov 15', '84', 'Fifth Lecture'.

Letter 200. 89/123, 1884. Pencil notations: 'Nov 15: 84', 'Fifth Lecture'. Ruskin's handwriting was becoming ever more erratic during this period.

Letter 201. 91/123, 1884. Paper: half a sheet. Pencil notations: '? Nov 1884', 'AW', '(over)'. This letter is partially reproduced in 37.499.
   1. There is a pencil bracket here, the other bracket is at the end of the paragraph, after 'latitudes " !!'
   2. Professor Alfred Marshall.
   3. A line connects this paragraph to the 'but' of the postscript, which is at a right angle to the main text.

– they ought to have been here yesterday
– [4]I hope to have a nice time with you on Friday week, with all worries over – I'm rather worse than[5] crofs tonight because I found a lot of beautiful fragments of Magdalen in a heap under the [restoration] – I'm going with the Master to call on the President tomorrow morning, and save them if [possible.
– but its like fighting singlehanded against the sea.   Part of sulking but about delayed pictures.

202a. 25 December 1884, Brantwood

   Brantwood,
    Coniston. Lancashire.
  Christmas 84
Di wee ma
 Twenty letters to day
but none from my di ma.
but I'm sure a lovely one's
coming. – and I send my
di ma all sorts of good hopes
and felicitations – on everything
but her Di Pa – who's been so
naughty and [twarvy] he does'nt
know fot to do. he'll nevy be
so nevy no mo. he wants his
di ma to take care of his
money for him.
He's a little tiny but bettie
but velly bad.
 Evy her poo Donie

202b. Letter from I. Low

       Is'nt this a
J. G. Low *Memorandum* pretty answer
 From   to my letter saying
Low, Scott & Co.,   his pic
Silk Mercers.[1] *133 High Street,* was [so] good[2]

   Montrose, 23 Dec 1884

D.ʳ Sir
 Your kind report to hand yesterday
for which I beg you to accept my
best thanks. As you have sent no
a/c for your trouble father bids
me send you a brace of Pheasants
& which I have sent on per parcel
post today. Regarding the Verdict
it is just as we expected as we
had no history or anything to guide
us except the workman ship. I may
state that I employ all my leisure
time in painting & Sketching from
nature & I can assume you find
welcome relief from business in that
occupation I have also consulted
some of your works in the references
Library here & found satisfaction & benefit
therein Allow me again to thank
you for your kind trouble &
if ever so far North as Montrose
you can drop in if you have
the time to spare as we always
have a Vacant bed & plenty
of rich scenery both in Sea &
Country
 Wishing you a merry Christmas
  & Returns of the season

 I am yours

  Ian G. Low

  <u>23. High St</u>

---

4. There is a pencil bracket here, the other bracket appears after 'sea.'
5. The 'than' is in the margin.

Letter 202a. 117a/123, 1884. Envelope: red sealingwax (twice); addressed to 'Mʳˢ Arthur Severn / 28. Herne Hill / S E / London'. Postmarked: 'AMBLESIDE / P / DE25 / 84'. Enclosures: letter from Ian Low (117b/123, 1884).
 1. Low has struck through these three lines and inserted his name, above.
 2. This note is in Ruskin's hand, the 'so good' could be 'no good'.

203. 27 December 1884, Brantwood

> Brantwood,
> Coniston. Lancashire.
> 27th Dec. 84

Sweetest Doanie
   Most thankful I am
for both your notes of
Xmas & yesterday – relieving
me about Lily.
   ¹I feel entirely unable now
to engage in or for anything.
– I am writing out the Sir H²
lecture in a form for publication
but do not think I can come
up to town or do more than
vegetate this spring. I am so
seriously frightened at the feeling
of collapse, and the sense of
despondency is so terrible
that if I once get interested
in anything here, I will
not leave it.
   Your new greenhouse looks
quite beautiful. – finishes
the group admirably. and
I'm still good for that and
our life here. – but I am
utterly aghast on casting
up accounts to see what
I have let slip since
I went up in October merely
through holes in my pockets.
There's cheque after cheque
for cash – which went, I
absolutely don't know how, beyond cab-fares!
I never was so puzzled or vexed by expense
before in my life!³

Lollie⁴ seems happy to be here & says
his room is comfy.
   Evy your loving Di Pa
   I daresay I shall have another
   packet of mixed things for
   tomorrows post as well

204. 31 December 1884, Brantwood

> Brantwood,
> Coniston. Lancashire.
> 31st Dec. 84

D[ar]lingest Joanie¹
   ²You know well how
happy I wish all years to
be to you & your's. I trust
I may be myself spared
to see it and not spoil it
for a few years more. I am
a little tiny bit better every
day but very bad still.
Allen send's me £150 to day
"making 1650 for the year –"
if that holds, I ought to be
able to live upon it, somehow?
– but what I've been doing
with my money this year
I can't make out, no how!
Ive spent 200 pounds in
small cash and don't
recollect buying anything
but an umbrella!
Di wee ma, I really think
oo'l have to manage my
munny for me; and [Amie]³
must see theer are'nt any
holes in my pocket.

Letter 203. 120/123, 1884.
   1. There is a pencil bracket here, the other bracket is on the final page after 'in my life!'.
   2. Sir Herbert; '[t]he lecture on Sir Herbert Edwardes had been given at Coniston on December 22, 1883, and was afterwards expanded into *A Knight's Faith* (Vol. XXXI.). The proposed lectures in London [...] were not delivered.' (37.499)
   3. Two days earlier, on Christmas day, he had asked Joan (in third person baby-talk) to take over his finances. See transcription above.
   4. Laurence Hilliard.

Letter 204. 123/123, 1884. Pencil notations: 'A.W.'
   1. This page is torn, so that the 'ar' of 'Darlingest' is missing.'
   2. There is a pencil bracket here, the other bracket is after 'umbrella!'
   3. This could be 'Annie'.

I think you may be amused
by a little girl's letter from
Selby – and my answer, which
you've only to post.[4]
2. Tarrant & M. – very nice at end
3. Connie's dog, very nice
– you may as well see my
answer to him –
4. Dr Elizabeth Blackwell, delightful
5. "A little cheque" wrapped in an acc^t of Dawes
which please pay out of it and begin
keeping my pockwocky money for next year
6. A Dudly election – pease ask Arfie
what it means, I thought I was
on the 'council' centuries ago.
7. A delightful letter and leaf of
printed Gossip from Councilgeneral
of Algiers.
And so – di ma, mes oos poo Donie and
me hopes ooll be a happy wee hug
and snuggywug all day tomowy Love to Arfie &
chicks.   Poo Donie.

[4]. Here begins a list of enclosures sent with this letter, none of which are still present.

1885

R. spends most of the year at Brantwood with J.
Resigns the Slade Professorship once again, 22 March
Major breakdown in July, diary ceases on 20 July until sparse entries on 18 October
Praeterita begins ('completed' in 1889)

205. [winter or spring] 1885, Brantwood

Friday

Sweetest Doanie

Your letters do help and fwesh and pwesh me so– [1]The weathers changed yesterday and is so cold and I've a headache bilious, and shivers all day. and am thinking of giving up Fessyship on account of Vote on Vivisection and nevy bovyin myself any mo with nufin.

I think I <u>never</u> saw such tebby tearing, dredful wind.
It boveys me to notice that I much oftener miss letters than I used. I wrote dred for dreadful not for baby talk but real mistake and I'm a little anxy.
I hope Agnews heel is better.
I'm going to take a great rest, anyhow
    Evy oo di di mamie
       oos Wee wee Donie

206. 4 March 1885, Brantwood

Brantwood,
*   Coniston. Lancashire.*
4th March 84
Sweetest Doanie minie
And me did'nt have any pise for oo, after all.
– was there evy such a dull dolt of a Duncie Donie? Oh di ma, if I only could build oo a palace with diamond windows and golden doors. and put on a story every birth day, as the shells do in the sea, and fill it all with music like the seashells. and have my di ma to sing to me up at the top.
   – Pouring rain – still – and fog, – but the day's all bright and nice to me because [its][1] my di Ma's birth day.
Lollies[2] painting such a petty pic of our steps and waterfall. He says hes been itin a cheeky ettie to my di ma
   Fot <u>can</u> it be?
Love to Arfie of both sizes

Autograph letters for 1885 are in 'L 47 / letters / John Ruskin / to / Joan Severn / 1885–86'. All are on flecked blue paper with 'Brantwood, / Coniston. Lancashire' in red lettering, unless otherwise noted.

Letter 205. 45/74, 1885. Paper: cream paper he received from Susie Beever, first used on 6 January 1885, which suggests this may have been written within a day or two of that. Pencil notations: 'Giving up Professorship', 'Agnew's heel', 'A.W.', '?85' (originally '?84' then amended).
1. There is a pencil bracket here, the other bracket is after 'Vivisection'.

Letter 206. 48/74, 1885. Envelope: red sealingwax; addressed to 'Mrs Arthur Severn / 28 Herne-Hill / SE / London'. Postmarked: 'AMBLESIDE / C / MR 4 / 85' (front); 'LONDON-S.E. / C7 / MR 5 / 85'. Pencil notations: 'Loll painting waterfall'; '[1885]' (in ink, square brackets).
1. This has been torn away by the glue of the envelope.
2. Laurence Hilliard.

and all the children
& mes oos poud wee
lovin Di Pa

207. 21 June 1885, Brantwood

>Brantwood,
>   Coniston. Lancashire.

Longest day 85
 Darling di wee ma
  I'm much bettie
to day. The girlies[1] came
with me to tea at Ethels
yet[y]. to meet the Monk
Coniston[2] governefs – She is a
stunner!! – my goodnefs, what
nursery teas we shall have
with Clennie at one end of the
table and she at the other.
and oo and me di ma, [on][3]
our Ps and Qs. opposite in
the middle.
  Some day perhaps we could
have that old gentleman of
eighty to play us the violoncello.
The girlies seem very happy
Lily's[4] making a lovely drawing
of Mifs Yewdales.[5] She's [done]
four boys doing sums, with
a big slate behind – and
there to be a row of girls
from [there][6] all across the
pic.
I find her doctor brother
is at Halifax just now
so I've asked him too, till
Thursday – when I believe
they must all go. – but
we don't know if he can
come yet, only they thought
it ever so kind of me to
ask him
  Rainbow morning – clearing up
– but very windy! Girls gone
to church with Martha!
  Evy oos poo wee Donie

Letter 207. 71/74, 1885.
  1. The Severn's daughters.
  2. Monk Coniston was the home of the Marshalls, neighbours at Brantwood.
  3. This could equally be 'on', 'or' or '&'.
  4. Lilas Trotter who, according to Evans and Whitehouse, was then visiting Brantwood with her sister, Minnie (p. 1113).
  5. The Coniston schoolmistress.
  6. This could be 'them'.

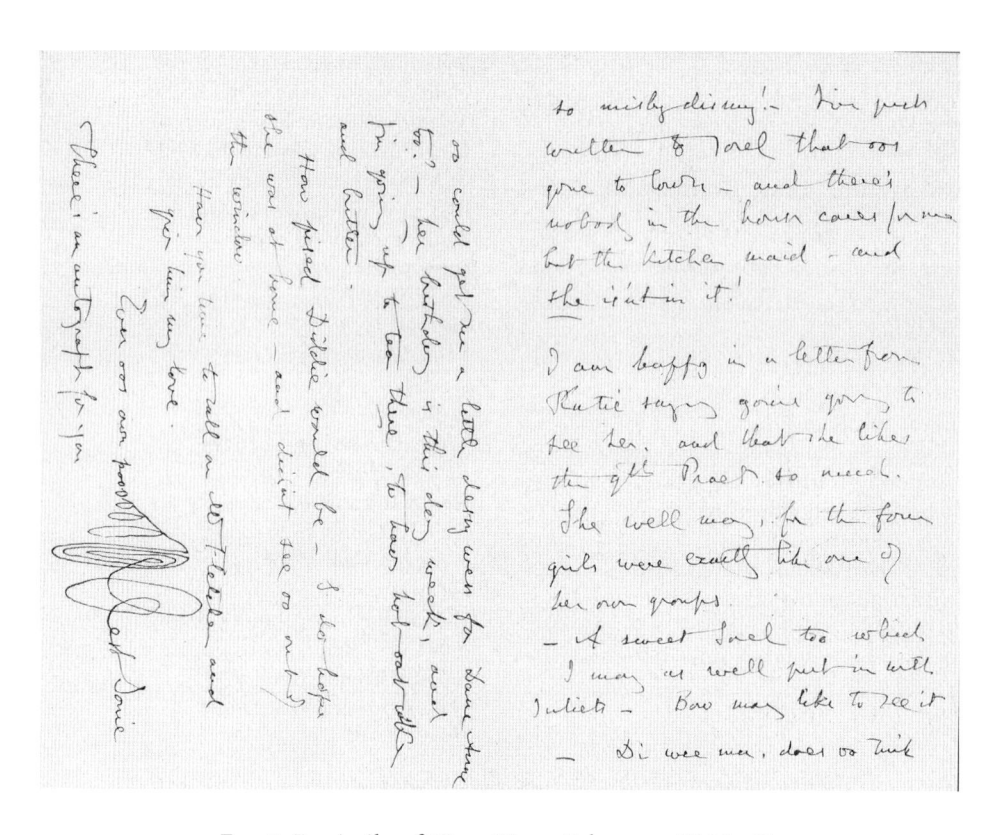

FIG. 8. Facsimile of JR to JS, 21 February 1886 [208].
RF L47, Ruskin Foundation (Ruskin Library, Lancaster University).

1886

Mostly spent at Brantwood
R. and J. have a major argument, 8 April; such severe arguments recur throughout the next year, tempered by periods of penitence

208. 21 February 1886, Brantwood

21st – Feb. 86.

My dear <u>Violet</u>
  I am most grateful
for your note – and glad in
your memory.
——
  Di Wee Ma. – Me <u>is</u> so
ecococomical. – this is a
spoiled sheet – but oo won't
mind? – I began Violet
instead of Juliet in answer
to enclosed.
– Post card just come. So glad
the poo wee wee etties wer'nt
lost. Di wee ma – me <u>is</u>
so misby dismy! – I've just
written to Sorel[1] that oos
gone to town – and there's
nobody in the house cares for me
but the Kitchen maid – and
<u>she</u> is'nt in it!

I am happy in a letter from
Katie[2] saying you're going to
see her. and that she likes
the 9th Praet so much.
She well may, for the four
girls were exactly like one of
her own groups.
– A sweet Sorel too which
  I may as well put in with
Juliets – Bow[3] may like to see it
– Di wee ma, does oo tink
  oo could get me a little dressy wess for
                              [Dane Anne[4]
too? – <u>her</u> birthday is this day week, and
I'm going up to tea <u>there</u>, to have hot oat
                              [cake
and butter.
  How pised Diddie would be – I do hope
she was at home – and did'nt see oo out of
the window.
  Have you time to call on Mr Fletcher[5] and
give him my love.

  Ever oos own pooooooOest[6] Donie.
There's an autograph for you

209. 25 February 1886, Brantwood

Brantwood,
  Coniston. Lancashire.
        25th
  What larks and games you
<u>are</u> having – you di wee ma!
– <u>such</u> a Kev oo is! – and
now the sun's come I'm rather
joyin myself here – and Clennie's[1]

Autograph letters for 1886 are in 'L 47 / letters / John Ruskin / to / Joan Severn / 1885–86'.
All are on flecked blue paper with 'Brantwood, / Coniston. Lancashire' in red lettering unless
otherwise noted.

Letter 208. 5/92, 1886.
  1. I assume this is short for 'Sorella', meaning Francesca Alexander.
  2. Ruskin wrote 'R' then turned it into a 'K'.
  3. This is an unidentified woman who may have been named 'Hannah' (see 2/92, 1886, not transcribed).
  4. Jane Anne Wilkinson.
  5. Lazarus Fletcher.
  6. These 'os' are attached, becoming progressively larger, ranging from 0.1 to 3.3 cm high. The penultimate one is circled like a snail's shell.

Letter 209. 6/92, 1886. Pencil notations: '? Feb 86'.
  1. 'Clennie' McClelland, governess to the Severn children

been quite good these two days
– Oh me – I dar'nt ask how
[Ina]² was looking.
I've answered enclosed card by
asking Sir John to bring Mifs [Lutbach]³
to see Brantwood – when their
tour time's up.
Arfie's been chopping to day
and greatly delighting Jane Anne,
– di wee ma does oo tink
the dessywesses <u>will</u> come in
time.
I'm dying to know how you
enjoyed Irving,⁴ and if oo
was fitened. – but I wish oo
could go to W. B.⁵ too? I would
spare you a day for him gladly
Nothing pickler to enclose
to day. I pects a petty ettie
from Duchefs to mowy.
   Di ma. mes oos poo little boy
– when are you going to see
my Grannie?⁶
   – oos ovin Di Pa

210. 28 February 1886, Brantwood

Brantwood,
*   Coniston. Lancashire.*
    28th Feb
Sweetest Doanie Poanie
–
   I missed the post
on Friday because I was
so worried with those
rascally servants – I was
thinking of turning them all
off in a bunch and ordering
a fresh lot from London –
– but Mary's got to be
such a postman, I should
miss her – I think I shall
send off old Gooseberry¹
anyhow – for I believe its <u>her</u>
fault mainly that Lizzies²
cut up rough –
She went home without
asking my leave – and
I can't let the Kitchen
have all its own way like
that.
I've given all your messages
to [Nyache]³ – who is gone off
piously to church. I wish
Clennie would learn some
manners there – and give
me my candle properly.
   I took Lily⁴ to tea at the
Bells.⁵ I think I never saw
a girl more rightly and sweetly
speechless with pleasure than
Libbie over that Tartan [Fall].
It is really a lovely thing –
fashion wholly out of question
and everybody was equally pleased. I had
two <u>perfect</u> eggs and a muffin.
Im going up to Jane Annes to tea to day
Hav'nt opened parcel yet!⁶
Me twite well – and got my blackbird
and five robins and three tits for company
    How tebby that <u>Faust</u> must have been
for my poo di ma!
    Arthur's been chopping wood in the
most resolute style. to Jane Annes entire

  2. This could be 'Iona'.
  3. This could be 'Lublech'.
  4. Presumably this is a reference to a performance by the important Victorian actor–manager Henry Irving (1838–1905).
  5. Wilson Barrett, another actor–manager.
  6. 'Grannie' is probably Mrs Cowper Temple.

Letter 210. 7/92, 1886. Pencil notations: '86'.
  1. This was a cook or kitchen maid in the Ruskin household.
  2. A Brantwood servant.
  3. This could be 'Wyoche'.
  4. Lily Severn.
  5. This was a family living in Coniston, probably that of John Bell, identified by Evans and Whitehouse as 'Registrar of Births and Deaths at Coniston', p. 1141.
  6. Jane Anne Wilkinson, neighbouring shepherd girl.

approval and glorification
Icicles exquisite. Lily told me the
whole story of "little women"
coming home from the Bells
– very nicely.
    Me's oos poo old Donie –

211. 1 March 1886, Brantwood

>Brantwood,
>>Coniston. Lancashire.
>>>1st March.

Darlingest Doanie
    I got up to Jane Anne's
'tea' – and it was all very nice
but I was disappointed in
the frock – and it had lace
round the cuffs which you
know I abhor.
Where are you to be on <u>your</u> birthday?
– When you are at Herne Hill –
please have Alison's Europe
packed and sent – and, if
its about any where, Stauntons
Chessplayer Handbook.[1]
Enclosed from Collie[2] nice –
– Mrs T.! Terrific!
with playful pontivenefs I've
smashed her up. – but you'd better
go over her with a rolling pin, when
                you write next.
Clennie and Arthur 'go on' no end
When I'm not there! – They
always stop the minute I open
the door. How <u>you</u> put up with it
I can't think!
Ever your loving & shocked,
           Di Pa

212. 3 March 1886, Brantwood

>Brantwood,
>>Coniston. Lancashire.

My deedy dïest-Weedy – I mean,
Flowery-weest-Doanie Poanie

So many and many happy
returns – And you're not to
get <u>thin</u>, oo know! You and me
together make a nice wee Di Ma
and Donie – mes as fat now as
me wants to be – so oo must still
make it up for me a little

Your nice long letter only came
this morning. will answer to morrow
    This is just to send you a years
back of love in the day.

    Evy oos poo wee di Pa

      See over

    "The stitches is comin loose
– some on em was only tacked
together" Jane Anne on her
gown to day.

213. [April] 1886, Brantwood

>   See inside
>Brantwood,
>>Coniston. Lancashire.
>>>Easter – Wednesday

Darling Doanie   It's Janie's
                 <u>own</u> correction
[1]I am tired of ~~ritting~~ ^{writing} though
verry well to day and
so glad: Violet[2] is better
I forgot to tell [Thait]

Letter 211. 8/92, 1886. Pencil notations: '? 86', 'Books to be sent'.
   1. Howard Staunton's *Chess-Player's Handbook* (37.232).
   2. W. G. Collingwood.

Letter 212. 10/92, 1886. Pencil notations: 'Mar 3. 86'.

Letter 213. 27/92, 1886.
   1. From 'I am' to 'Pigwiggina' is in a childish hand, with a few flourishes (such as a rather large and loopy 'V' for 'Violet'), written by Jane Anne Wilkinson.
   2. Violet Severn, daughter of Joan and Arthur.

How much I wanted her
to give the Cross. i beg
Janey sine herself your
affect.^{e} and Obed.^{t}
    Pigwiggina³

    Vainly – my – love my science tries
The mystic scene to localize.
For here the difficulty lies –
– Or rather, on the bank – arises,
What was at first a single Pise⁴
Is changing into double Pises.

214. 20 April 1886, Brantwood

    Brantwood,
      Coniston. Lancashire.
        20th April
Darling Doanie   86.
    Its all very fine about
Lockies¹ new companionship –
I think – if she'd come just now
and give me a little – it would
be more to the purpose.
– However, I'm thankful for Piggie,²
and Baxter's³ ducks, who are really
an immense Social power. One
meets them every wheer – sometimes
they're in the garden, – ~~every~~ any wheer
in the wood – and to day in the
fishpond – where their glossy
backs dipping in the sunshine
were delicious. Bramble⁴ is also
extremely busy helping Baxter
to do a new piece of work for oo

di wee ma – it will be <u>such</u>
a 'pise'. – you never did!
I've taught Pigwiggina to know
A, B, C$^\sharp$ and E on the piano
and to write our bell tunes out
in booful crotchets & quavers.
with [missims]⁵ to finish.
I knew that Sunset of Arfie's
would fetch peepies. – I hope
my purple mountains are keeping
nice and dark
I wont mifs telegraph.
    Me's oos poo itie Donie
I send two Acad. Tickwickets

215. 9 May 1886, Brantwood

    Brantwood,
      Coniston. Lancashire.
        Sunday
Darling Doanie
    Wet morning, – and
nobody to watch coming down
stairs – and poo Donie very
sad. – but thankful. <u>so</u>
thankful – that Violet's better.
and going on bettering.
    Kate¹ is writing me quite
lovely and helpful letters.
Also Sorel.²
Autobiog. going. on steadily –
but it won't be so funny.
    I can't make out about the
times I used to be alone in
the D. Hill drawing room with

    3. Jane Anne Wilkinson.
    4. See 20 April 1886 for Ruskin's mention of a 'pise' (surprise).

Letter 214. 31/92, 1886.
    1. The Severn children's former governess, who seems to have become a nurse, see [272b].
    2. Jane Anne Wilkinson.
    3. Peter Baxter, Ruskin's valet.
    4. Ruskin's dog. See 'James S. Dearden 'John Ruskin's Dogs' (Bembridge, Isle of Wight: Desktop Studio, 2003).
    5. This could be 'vimins'.

Letter 215. 29/92, 1886. Pencil notations: 'After Easter', ' 86'. Having cross-referenced this letter with diary entries for Sundays during this period, 9 May is the apparent date of this letter. Ruskin mentions 'Wet morning', but many of the Sundays mention snow rather than rain. Others include references which he would have mentioned in a letter to Joan and only on the 9 May does he mention difficulty with writing his autobiography (Evans and Whitehouse, p. 1126).
    1. Probably Kate Greenaway.
    2. Francesca Alexander.

mama in the evening. Were
you much away from us, after
you came? – What year did
you come first in. to stay?

Ever your poo wee Di Pa

216. 17 May 1886, Brantwood

> *Brantwood,*
> *Coniston. Lancashire.*
> Monday

Darling Di Ma
 I've such a lovely
letter of thanks from Mr West![1]
To think how grateful every
body is to me, except that
Clennie!.[2] Really, when Scôtch
people <u>are</u> horrible – they're
– <u>very</u> horrid.
 I think you'll be amused by
Mr West's observations on
my new musical system
as described to him to day.
 I really get some nice letters
written just now! They'll
be a lovely sequel to the auto.[3]
if theyre ever collected!
and I'm getting some nice ones
back! I've been obliged
to clear out a compartment
of a study bookcase drawer
for 'under twenty' letters.

But I'm making Susie[4]
and even Mrs Talbot,[5] rather
happy too!

(Susie is a wonder –
Just look at this enclosed!)
And I'm really much better
If you could only get that
pillow arrangement carried out –
– I should really be all right.
 Ever your lovingest Di Pa

217. [May 1886], Brantwood

Books all *Brantwood,*
right – but I *Coniston. Lancashire.*
was'nt told   Tuesday.
of them! <u>founɖ</u> them to day!
 Darling Joanie
  I never write my letters
for any peepies to understand
but you – – and though I leave
my letters lying about – do not
suppose you leave yours. You
ought to be very thankful
I can jest about anything.
Poor Burgess[1] is dead, and
will be for all the remainder
of my life, a burden, on my
conscience – and writing
Praeterita and walking up
and down the garden alone
is'nt the liveliest way of spending
this one of the few springs that
may be spared to me.
However, I have been wonderfully
well these last seven or eight
days – and I quite think it
is best that you are all of you
in London just now – if you

Letter 216. 44/92 1886. Envelope: red sealingwax; addressed to (typed) 'MRS. ARTHUR SEVERN, / 28, *HERNE HILL, / LONDON, S.E.*' Postmarked: 'AMBLESIDE / [?] / MY17 / 86' (front); 'LONDON.S.E. / C 7 / MY 18 / 86' (back). Pencil notations: 'M^r. West', 'May 17. 86'.
  1. Ruskin's music teacher.
  2. Clennie McClelland, the Severn children's Scottish governess from the Isle of Skye.
  3. *Praeterita.*
  4. Susie Beever.
  5. Fanny Talbot.

Letter 217. 49/92, 1886. Pencil notations: '? May 86', 'Burgess', 'Marks'. Note, if the 'Burgess' is the artist and copyist Arthur Burgess, then this letter must be from 1887, when Hilton states he died (*Later*, p. 521). However, lacking other definite evidence, I have left this letter where it is currently filed.
  1. Probably Arthur Burgess.

don't overtire yourself.
Enclosed from Faunthorpe[2]
is sad to me, about Ireland,
and I had a 'private' letter
from poor little Aggie Marks[3]
– which saddened me about
her Father's selling no pictures
now.
The Academicians should
long ago have had a proper
reserve fund to support each other in hard times
– I wrote back [however] that if they were all
sold up and had to live a caravan,[4] they'd
   be ever so much happier than in that house.
– It was'nt to borrow – but I think she
wanted a little present to go & see her sisters
baby with – I told her one baby was as
good as another – she might find plenty
to nurse close by. I dont think I ever wrote
such grim letters as I've been doing lately
Enclosed mixed lot of different peepies may
moos oo a little. Oos ovin Di Pa

218. 27 May 1886, Brantwood

> Brantwood,
>   Coniston. Lancashire.
>   27th May 86

Darlingest Di Wee Ma
   Mes been goin on bit-bit-bit
bit-bitin my poo wee moofsie
mo and mo, till its all in bits!
– But oh deewee est di ma
what pagues and pagues houses
is! Can't you sell evy ting
off at once – and come and live
with oos di pa comfy and nevy
go to that wicked London no
mo? Me thinks you sood – always
did think so.
– I am doing a good deal – but theer
is really no happy time in living alone
– and me's gettin so coss and woss
and sulk and wulk – there's no speakin
to me. And I don't mind oos
missin the pwimwoses – for me
thought ood get peachweechies
and applepappies[1] – but the
Oak Ferns! just in their light
of always-sun-on-it green!
and to no di ma to see dem!

I send you one of the really
nicest letters I think I ever
had from Mrs Talbot.[2]
I'm taking much more pains for
her – she really deserves it.
Also one from Susie,[3] very
charming and marvellous.
– and a pretty and graceful one
from the Irish Queen.[4]
Di wee ma, how is it I
never, so far as I recollect
– heard of – much lefs saw
which I would have so liked to, Uncle Charles?
– I have a sweet note from Eleanor to day.

Me wotedit half a dovsy etties to oo, in
my head, isterday and did'nt get one
posted . I think I made Albert Fleming[5]
very happy in an afternoon walk – and

---

   2. Rev. John Faunthorpe, Principal of Whitelands College, Chelsea.
   3. The context implies she was the daughter of artist H. Stacy Marks, R.A.
   4. An 'in' appears to be missing.

Letter 218. 53/92, 1886.
   1. Ruskin is referring to Joan missing the blossoms of these fruit trees at Brantwood by staying in London too long.
   2. Fanny Talbot.
   3. Susie Beever.
   4. See 30.344 for Ruskin's response to a letter from the Rose Queen of a high school in Cork that year.
   5. Fleming was a lawyer and Companion of the Guild of St. George. With Marion Twelves, Fleming founded the Langdale Linen Industry and revived the local traditions of spinning and weaving, and he was editor of *Hortus Inclusus*, see Jennie Brunton, 'The Late Nineteenth-century Revival of the Langdale Linen Industry', in *A History of Linen in the North West*, ed. by Elizabeth Roberts (Lancaster: Centre for North West Regional Studies, 1998), pp. 93–118. Joan did not trust him, see her letter of 26 June 1888 [279].

showing him pises.
– Wain again to day. Ah. those poo woo twolips!

   Evy di wee ma oos ownponie
       Donie
– What was it Frederick liked in the new numbers?

219. 28 May 1886, Brantwood

Theres too much to explain in Susie[1] – but you'll like to see I'm making people comfy. Mr Mason came to ask for a little sub to a testimonial to Mr Howells, which I gave him £2.   *Brantwood, Coniston. Lancashire.* 28th May

Di wee ma pease make out oos di little bill all straitywait.

Sweetest Di ma wa
 It is a little comfort to oos poo Di Pa to hear of your nice time with the new stables, and to think[2] what grand big peepies Arfie & Joanie are now 'in town' – though I did wish they wer'nt there.
If Baby and Violet could only see the Ducks on the Lawn, out of the Drawing room window. They look <u>so</u> nice, and fat, and funny. and they know they should'nt be there so well. – and scuttle away as hard as they can waddle the moment they see me at the study window. And it is immensely curious how instantly they <u>do</u> see!
 Enclosed from Mrs de P. will be satisfactory to you.

– Never any letters provoked me more! – the piece about the flatterers especially. – which in my final answer to this, I have severely referred to

The watch has come <u>booty</u> and strikes booty – but Ive put it in my ^{big} gold mineral drawer, for dear old Aunties is ever so much pleasanter to wear – and goes <u>so</u> sweetly.
Di wee ma, <u>can</u>[3] oo tell me how old Auntie[4] was on 2nd Sept – 1844. ?

 Di wee ma – <u>won't</u> it be like Mr Briggs when the masons come, to open the door? If you've an Instit Catal. – or are going there
[– look at 'You stay with Baby'.
– Also, I think I should rather like 'Caught
[Tripping'
Oh dear – to think me tant ite to my Di
[Ma Tomowy
– theer are such horrid lots of Sundays. . Oos
[poo wee Donie

220. 2 June 1886, Brantwood

   Brantwood,
    Coniston. Lancashire.
2.33   2nd June –
51. K – Ks 6th. 51.p. – Bp 6

Darling wee ma –
 Its no use sending this move to Mrs Talbot! I've 'sent in my resignation' instead – and me's oos own eccocomical Donie, andthoughtoowoodnt mind the paper being saved. My poo woo di ma, to be thundered and itinged till she toodnt wite to her poo Donie! I'm really pleased to find that I could dine and breakfast

---

Letter 219. 54/92, 1886. Pencil notations: '86'.
 1. Presumably this is a reference to an enclosed letter from Susan Beever to Ruskin (no longer with the letter).
 2. This was 'they' then amended to 'think'.
 3. This 'can' is underlined three times.
 4. Margaret Ruskin.

Letter 220. 57/92, 1886. Pencil notations: 'Louisa Strode', 'Mr Moor', '? 86'.

with Mr Moore¹ really without
fatigue! even with benefit to appetite
and I'm not fitened for Louisa²
and her mother, who come
by 6. train. Mr Moore left
by carriage at 10 for Windermere
to go across to Durham, as lovely
a line as there is in England
– and the days fairly fine.
Clouding a little now – but
after rain yesterday the hills
were blue and trees fresh – and
Ive seldom enjoyed a walk in
the wood more.
We're cleaning out fishpond
and find such a lot of fine
fish in it – toutywouts no end of
fat – and charywars no end of
pink! Must wite to poo M^r
West. – me's oos own good itie boy
                    Donie

221. 3 June 1886, Brantwood

Brantwood,
Coniston. Lancashire.
3rd June –
Morning

Sweetest Di Ma.
  I am getting nicely on
with my company – Louisa
Strode is extremely nice; – gentle
and soft, as the exact reverse
of Clennie in all particulars.
– ~~but~~ ^and^ in her plainness –
pleasant – as Mifs C in her
prettinefs is – Well, theres no
word for what she is.
The difference between Louisa

and our self-pushing friend
of the long letters, not less striking
L. modest & powerful. – and
rather grand in features – Older
a little Im sorry to say than I pected
Also the mother is a disappointment
and talks too much.
¹ There ought to be colleges for
the education of women past 40.
– before anything else is done
in educational reform.

  You will I hope be heee
to enjoy the visit proposed
in enclosed. note

How **tood** oo forget what oo
tolld oos di pa? see enclosed.

– So glad Ellie liked letter
No fear of my forgetting
doggy poggy Im rather
pleased that the engraver
seems taking his time over it
Ever your lovingest Di Pa Wa –
                    wave.

222. 4 June 1886, Brantwood

Brantwood,
Coniston. Lancashire.
4th June

Darling Di Ma
  Its rather a short allowance
of di ma this morning. M. E. W.
– And I havn't much time
myself – for [M^r] Moore & Mifs
Lou have taken up these days
Lou is very nice – modest –
useful – sensible. and Im going
to have her back for a fortnight

---

1. Probably Professor Charles H. Moor of Harvard University, Evans and Whitehouse, p. 1128n.
2. Louisa Strode was '[a]n Edinburgh friend, daughter of a naval officer' (Evans and Whitehouse, p. 1129).

Letter 221. 58/92, 1886. Envelope: red sealingwax; addressed to (typed) 'MRS. ARTHUR SEVERN, / 28, *HERNE HILL,* / *LONDON, S. E.*' Postmarked: 'AMBLESIDE / C / JU 3 / 86' (front); 'LONDON.S.E. / C7 / [JU 4] / [86]' (back). Pencil notations: 'Louisa S', '86', 'A.W.'; a different hand has added: 'letter from Willet re. / OW Holmes filed separately'.
  1. There is a pencil bracket here, the other bracket is at the end of the sentence, after 'reform'.

Letter 222. 59/92, 1886. Pencil notations: '86'; a different hand has added: 'Enclosure from [OE Owans] filed separately'.

when you come. – at least – I suppose
ool be tumin – some day this month?
wont oo. di ma.
The Azaleas are all <u>blazing</u> out
and quite astonished peepies to day!
– they thought they looked so
much better on the bank than
in pots.
Enclosed letter pleased me
mightily and Ive given him
leave to print what he likes

    Di Ma, mes oos own poo wee
        Donie

223. 6 June 1886, Brantwood

Brantwood,
    Coniston. Lancashire.

Sweetest Doanie
    <u>All</u> your loves indeed!
You don't mean that Crab Blossom
sent any?
– I'm sending – very much the
contrary ^ of love, about everywhere.
(– You'd better ^ go and look after poor
Kate a little if ever you're up the
road).
I'm glad to hear of the Robins. Mine
have all left me, of course, but
I took up with a lot of seven
Robinesque ^ imps in a bunch at the cottage
half way from Colworth[1] to Traveller's
Rest – yesterday two boys and five girls, and
set them arithmetical questions
in pence – and I'm going back
next week to learn all their names
There was one little ragged – haggard
– yet not sickly – pale one with
her hair flickering down like tongues

of fire – I don't think I ever saw
anything quite so lovely –
    Traveller's Rest landlady better
– nice white & pink – House being
'done up' – all plaster & sand
. I had to go on and tea in
the other inn. – Walked down
and round by the ^ ford and old bridge but
felt very feeble. Afterwards
went to look at the force – It
is pinned all over its rockbreast
with daffodil buds –
Ate two eggs and a lot of
bread & butter for tea – but am
bilious and out of sorts to day – and no end
                          [of cross.

224. 7 June 1886, Brantwood

Brantwood,
    Coniston. Lancashire.
7th June
Di'est wee ma
    Mondays <u>so</u> dull for
want of a dee wee ettie from
my wam. and me feels the
velly wicked of wicks.
Me is petty well. but so lazy.
I like Baxter[1] to Row me or Joe[2]
to drive me and nevy to have
no trouble myself. Its an awful
bore to talk – and if Mary would
only eat my dinner for me, Id
give her such a big extra wages[3]
Ettie was quite carried off
her feet and head by those
azaleas! They do look wonderful
on the bank. Im too lazy
to go and gather you any
but theyre all this sort of thing[4]

Letter 223. 62/92, 1886. Pencil notations: 'June', 'May ? 86', 'Colwith'. This was probably written on Sunday, 6 June 1886, coinciding with Ruskin's first diary entry about visiting Colwith Force (Evans and Whitehouse, p. 1129).
  1. This should be 'Colwith'.

Letter 224. 64/92, 1886. Pencil notations: '?86'.
  1. Peter Baxter.
  2. Joe Wilkinson, one of the Ruskin servants (Evans and Whitehouse, 1135n).
  3. These are all servants at Brantwood.
  4. A row of four flowers (plus a fifth, below) are roughly painted in shades of yellow and orange (ranging in size from 1.5 to 2 cm).

and anything else
you like – They
make poo Donie quite fitened
lest its the bank blowing up
with dynamite.[5]

Then the wody dendys
are that sort of thing
and me's oos poo no
sort of a thing – poo Donie
Heres Herdson[6] just passed the
window and Ive sent <u>him</u> to
gather some leaves for you

225. [20 June 1886], Brantwood

Brantwood,
Coniston. Lancashire.
Sunday Morning
Sweetest Di ma
I am so very thankful
for the good news of Agnew[1]
and so grateful for the long
letter
<u>Seriously</u> – theer is no need for
you hurrying anything in town
– The quiet, though sometimes
a little melancholy – does me no
harm. – and you being away
is a good excuse for seeing nobody
I was at Colwith yesterday, and
have not for years enjoyed a
walk in the sun so much in
the old way.
There are five children to open
one gate – standing against it

it[2]   – I find I havn't
a distinct idea of the general effect
of children – but theyre in
sizes

Joseph Annie Charlie Eliz.th Dinah.[3]
I took five of your new sixpences
for them – Richters childs book
– and Dame Wiggins.[4] – I showed
them Dame W. first – and then
said – here was a prettier book
for Dinah. Elizabeth immediately
possefsed herself of the Dame,
with a look indicating her perfect
satisfaction with the arrangement.
How diteful the [Aurist on]
Arfies pictures! – and I'm so
glad to hear you keep him to his
work. Oos own old idle Di Pa

Di wee ma me ^{v}wasnt a toopid, because me
is'nt a wam. <u>Oos</u> a wam – and me's a wick.

226. 15 August 1886, Brantwood

Brantwood,
Coniston. Lancashire.
Sunday
Darling Doanie
I'm keeping very well
– except that the nights seem
long – whether I sleep or wake
– the sleep is still fretted with
the idea of of the torment during
the illness. But the cold has
gone away marvellously – some

---

5. To the left, Ruskin has drawn a single rhododendron blossom painted in blues and reds (2.3 cm).
6. Dawson Herdson, gardener.

Letter 225. 63/92, 1886. Pencil notations: 'June 86', 'Agnew's cold', 'Colwith'. Ruskin's second diary entry referring to a visit to Colwith Force is made on the 20 June 1886, referring to the 19th. This letter may correspond with this, but no other references clearly coincide.
1. Agnew Severn.
2. Presumably Ruskin means the fence. He has drawn a five-slatted fence with rough figures in a row, arranged from shortest (left, 0.5 cm) to tallest (right, 1.2 cm). The whole sketch, including the fence measures 2.1 x 1.4 cm.
3. A line extends up from each of these, each line longer than the next ranging from left to right: 'Joseph' 0.5 cm, 'Annie' 0.6 cm, 'Charlie' 0.8 cm, 'Eliz.$^{th.}$' 1 cm, 'Dinah' 1.4 cm.
4. *Dame Wiggins of Lee*, one of Ruskin's 'calf milk of books' (35.51).

Letter 226. 89/92, 1886. Pencil notations: '86', 'Aug 15'.

of those morphine [& specucuantion]
lozenges checked the beg ing
cough at once.
– I am working really well
at music – and have quite
lovely plans for everything
when you come back. In
the first place, there are
to be no lessons! the children
are to go scrambling about
with you and Susan to look
after them, all day – and
Clennie is always to be ready
to play to me, – or make notes
of my compositions. – and
it will do her ever so much
good to help Jane Anne
a little in the wood. Violet
and Baby shall have lovely
gardens – full of wild raspberries
and what not, and Lily
shall have lovely rides on
Norway[1]
and when Clennie[2] has written down my
compositions – she will enjoy playing them.
– and may also help Diddie to keep my books
in order.
   – I think I see my way to a pleasant
Autumn – for every body

   Ever your lovingest
      Di Pa

227. 17 August 1886, Brantwood

Brantwood,
   Coniston. Lancashire.
My dear Joan
   I was certainly – in
some degree – jesting – in
the letter you answer to day.
   – But I am not jesting
now, by any means, in
assuring you that things are
<u>not</u> to be on their old
footing here – ever again.
If you come here, you
must come to do whatever
is in your power to please
<u>me</u> – and not only yourselves
I mean to be master henceforward
in this house, while I live
in it – and to have the
things done that I wish to
be done – whether of play
or lessons. – by every one
whom I ask to stay in it
– By you – your husband
– and your children – most
certainly & chiefly –
   And if you do not choose
to please me, – you had
better all of you stay in
London. I am not yet
so paralytic as to need more
looking after than my servants
are capable of. – Ever your – Di Pa.[1]

   1. Presumably this refers to a horse.
   2. 'Clennie' McClelland, governess to the Severn children. She was from the Isle of Skye (*Later*, p. 485).
Letter 227. 91/92, 1886. Envelope: red sealingwax; addressed (typed) to 'MRS. ARTHUR SEVERN, / 28, *HERNE HILL,* / LONDON, S. E.' Postmarked: 'AMBLESIDE / C / AU17 / 86' (front); 'LONDON.S.E. / C 7 / AU 18 / 86' (back). Pencil notations: 'For Joan' 'Aug 17. 86'.
   1. This letter seems to have brought Joan back to Brantwood. Ruskin's diary entry for 21 August reads 'weary week, chiefly past in quarrelling with Joan [...] Joan and her people came yesterday, when the Almanack says "Black cock shooting begins" – ', Evans and Whitehouse, 1132.

1887

In May, R. becomes violent towards J.;
the Severns leave Brantwood for London
R. moves to Folkestone in October, then to Sandgate

228a. 19 January 1887, Brantwood

Brantwood,
Coniston. Lancashire.
Wednesday

The 2nd is exactly the right day to come on. R[1] seems strangely prompting all arrangements, just now even to <u>Endwell</u> Road [r.] – please keep to the 2nd –
  Darling Joanie
Money sent to day[2]
  [3]I am very happy in your letters now – and to know that we are doing as you wish about the children – But they have been a great gladnefs to us. always. and babys finding the cameo was really providential. The packet of letters – the china Rosie' – inspire – not <u>excite</u> me, to the best work I only settled finally to day the name of. Chap 1 of Vol III. 'Otterburn'. It is to introduce Wallington and Connie at 9 years old.[4] The IXth Chapter is to be
  'Joanna's (charge: /care?
unlefs I think of one not liable to make you like Joan of Arc at the head of her cavalry.
  That <u>one</u> number has to describe all relations between Auntie[5] & you – I had no idea how I should
  have to comprefs in finishing
Dr Parsons[6] here to day, says I'm quite well – I think so too.
                    Your lovingest
                         Deapa.
  I should like Lacerta's[7] addrefs.
     Why does'nt she write to me.

Autograph letters for 1887 are in 'Bem L 48 / Letters / John Ruskin / to / Joan Severn / Jan-Sep 1887' and 'Bem L 49 / Letters / John Ruskin / to / Joan Severn / Oct-Dec 1887'.

Letter 228a. 7/170, 1887. Envelope: red sealingwax; addressed to 'Mrs Arthur Severn / 28, Herne Hill / London / S E'. Postmarked: 'AMBLESIDE / C / JA19 / 87' (front); 'LONDON.S.E. / C7 / JA20 /87' (back). Enclosures: invitation by Violet Severn with comments by Ruskin (7b/170, 1887). Pencil notations: 'A W', 'Jan 19 / 87'.
  1. Rose, who had died in 1875.
  2. This line was inserted at the end.
  3. There is a pencil bracket here, the other bracket is near the end, after 'I think so too.'
  4. Constance Hilliard; she was actually eleven, not nine, when Ruskin first met her at Wallington, home of her aunt, Lady Trevelyan, see Virginia Surtees, ed., *Sublime & Instructive: Letters from John Ruskin to Louisa Marchioness of Waterford, Anna Blunden and Ellen Heaton*, (London: Michael Joseph, 1972), pp. 51–52 (16 August 1863, L. W.37).
  5. Margaret Ruskin.
  6. Dr. George Parsons, whose practice was 'at Hawkshead, some five miles from Brantwood', he 'first treated Ruskin in 1873' (*Later*, p. 387).
  7. Maria La Touche.

228b. Invitation by V. Severn and J. Ruskin

> Brantwood,
> Coniston. Lancashire.

D E H E D

H i J N G

W N[1]

This is Violets invitation of Mifs Watson[2] to tea – written at my study table

229. 21 January 1887, Brantwood

> Brantwood,
> Coniston. Lancashire.

Darling Joanie
Your letter to day is quite [de]licious.[1] Here are two – which you must copy for me. How could you ever think either you or Connie would be *out* of Praeterita. You run through the entire third Vol.
Ever your lovingest Di Pa

230. [undated] 1887, Brantwood

> Brantwood,
> Coniston. Lancashire.
> Sunday

Darling Doanie
How funny and [squincy deary] that you should be at Diddies[1] when she was writing of silks! – I wish you would tell me what I don't like to ask her, how their incomes are affected by the two late deaths. Please, will you bring Rosie's phot with you. – & the one in my nursery – & send it down registered better[2] – without its frame in strong boards
I'm keeping quite well, D.G, – but am sorry never to see the children I hope I shall, to day. – Tennie is such a romp that I suppose she suits them – they never seem to – want me –
Your post card about parties immensely nice.
Your lovingest Di Pa

231. 3 March 1887, Brantwood

> Brantwood,
> Coniston. Lancashire.
> 3rd March

Darling Doanie
No, Doanie isn't 'described' yet – but I'm beginning to think how it is to be done – I believe I shall have recourse at last to an engraving from one of the Venetian phots. I

Letter 228b. 7b/170, 1887.
1. These 'letters' take up the centre ¾ of the page. The 'J' of line two and the 'N' of line three are backwards. They were written in pencil by Violet Severn and sent to her mother with an explanatory note by Ruskin beneath.
2. Marion 'Tenzo' and her sister Lizzie Watson were then visiting Ruskin (*Later*, p. 534).

Letter 229. 8/170, 1887. Pencil notations: '? Jan 21st 87'.
1. The 'de' have been obscured by a piece of the envelope which is now affixed to the letter.

Letter 230. 15/170, 1887. Pencil notations: '?Jan. 87' and '85?' changed to '87?'.
1. Sara Anderson.
2. This should perhaps be 'letter'.

Letter 231. 20/170, 1887. Envelope: red sealingwax; addressed to 'Mrs Arthur Severn / 28. Herne Hill / S. E / London'. Postmarked: 'AMBLESIDE / C / MR 4 / 87' (front); 'LONDON[.S.E.] / C[?] / MR [?] / 87' (back). Pencil notations: '87'.

shall ask Arfie at dinner to day
– I'm so glad he's happy. I've
been so heavy & moppy that
he might as well have the
dripping well at [Knaresborough]
for company – but he has always
something to moos me with
   I came on enclosed this morning
put aside for Dilecta. but perhaps
its the least bit too gushy. You may
like to keep it – I would, if I
thought I should long be able
to keep anything. Whats to
become of all my heaps of
rubbishy drawings and diaries
I can't think.
I'm a little bettie to day
however. By all means let
Mr Myers have my name
   Ever your ownie Di Pa.

232. 14 March 1887, Brantwood

> Brantwood,
>   Coniston. Lancashire.
>   14th March.

Darling Doanie
   You've quite spoilt Lou
Strode for me by what you
must have said when she
was here – when I was no
more off my head than you are
yourself – and was only angry
at dinner because I was very
much provoked at it – But she
only sends me rubbish like this (see scrap with
                                   [birds head)[1]
now, and stupid formal letters.
[2]I am greatly delighted with
my own letters to Susie of
which I have revised the first

instalment! – but see what
Albert[3] says of them! at end
of his note
       Just when I had
set up to be rigidly ecconnommicle
– and saved £50 on Milton –
comes this from Stodart – and
I could'nt but send it to the
poor man. I like his letter

Here's your nice Sunday line.
I'm glad you saw Mrs Liddell
and Mrs [Skene]. and that
Arfies drawing pics for children
I'm sending him his 'bit
of game' to himself as
you've enclosures enough.
Im very well just now.
No Night mare any mo. but
   Mes oos poo Donie for
all that

233. 8 June 1887, Brantwood

> Brantwood,
>   Coniston. Lancashire.
>   Friday

My poor Joan
 [1]I meant to have
written kindly again, to day
but a paragraph I find
has been inserted in all the
papers – false and cunning to
a point which I had not conceived
possible – renders it vain for me
to express any feelings of the old
days at Brantwood more.
Heaven's Will be done – in what
remnant of days may be
spared to us both.
   Your once. Di Pa.

Letter 232. 29/170, 1887. Pencil notations: '87', 'AW'.
   1. This bracketed section is written sideways down the right margin.
   2. There is a pencil bracket here, the other bracket is three lines down, after 'instalment!'.
   3. Albert Fleming, who was editing Ruskin's letters to Susie Beever.

Letter 233. 42/170, 1887. Envelope: red sealingwax; addressed to 'Mrs Arthur Severn / 28 Herne Hill / London / S. E'. Postmarked 'AMBLESIDE / C / JU 8 / 87' (front); 'LONDON.S.E. / [C7] / JU 9 / 87' (back). Pencil notations: 'June 8', '87', '?A.W.' See her response of 11 June [270].
   1. There is a pencil bracket here, the other bracket is after 'Brantwood more.'

234. 8 June 1887, Brantwood

> Brantwood,
> Coniston. Lancashire.

8th June 87

My poor Joanie

I could have wept tears
of blood for you, in seeing the beauty
of the place – yesterday evening and
to day – all lost – to Doanie and me.
Your room shall stay as you have
left it. Tho¹ Richmond portrait –
is put back. – the Hunts on left
of fireplace were injured by damp
I will put something else pretty
Perhaps later in the year you might
like to come down with baby & Violet
– Nearly the first letter I found to day
was the account of Violet's illness

Send me word about how you are.
as soon as you can.

> The two

drawings, Liber and Rookes, you
had marked 'private' had
simple short hand notes [on themes]
of passages to be written respecting
them both, at a time when I was
in hardest & usefullest work, this spring
– spoiled so cruelly for me.

I am glad to have the opal back
and to see how well it joined.

> Ever your much sorrowing.
> Di Pa

235. 12 June 1887, Brantwood

> Brantwood,
> Coniston. Lancashire.
> Sunday –

My poor Joan,

Write to me, if you care to
write, of yourself or of your children.
Speak no more of the Unpardonable
past. – till you wish – as much as I
that it should be – as though it
had never been.

> Your sorrowful Di Pa.

236. 15 June 1887, Brantwood

> Brantwood,
> Coniston. Lancashire.
> Wednesday
> 15th June 87

My Doanie

¹The comfort your letter is
to me this morning you cannot
measure. You never have really known
how I have loved you. – and the
desolation of all sweetness to me in
garden or wood, for want of you.
has been the saddest thing I have
ever known in all this life –

But that you are out again –
watching – the children in the daisies
and have had your dear Bishop
to see you – and could keep him
for two hours, is such a comfort; and
I have been <u>twice</u> to see Susie
and she is all <u>her</u>self again –
to my utter thankfulness.

Letter 234. 43/170, 1887.
1. This is shorthand for 'Thomas'.

Letter 235. 44/170, 1887. Envelope: addressed to 'Mrs Arthur Severn / 28 Herne Hill [S] / London. /S E'. Postmarked: 'AMBLESIDE / A / JU12 / 87' (front); 'LONDON. S.E. / 7 / JU13 /87 / R' (black ink rather than the usual red-brown, presumably because it was sent registered mail), 'LONDON.S.E. / C7 / JU13 / 87' (back). Pencil notations 'June 12 87'. The front of the envelope has swirling pen scrawlings on it, reminiscent of a monogrammed letter such as a large, stylised 'R' or 'L'. It seems to have formed part of the original underlining of 'London.' and 'SE'. See her response of 14 June [271].

Letter 236. 45/170, 1887. Envelope: red sealingwax; addressed to 'Mrs Arthur Severn / 28. Herne Hill / S. E / London.' Postmarked: 'AMBLESIDE / C / JU 15 / 87' (front); 'LONDON. S.E. / C7 / JU16 /87' (back). Pencil notations: 'A. W.'
1. There is a pencil bracket here.

I will attend to everything you
send me word about
Dr Louis Carré first
Dear love to Baby..

　　Ever your poor Di Pa.

I keep fairly well. but am totally
unable to do anything beyond
a letter or two. – and I sleep
languidly – in exhaustion of sorrow.

237. 17 June 1887, Brantwood

　　　Brantwood,
　　　　Coniston. Lancashire.
　　　　17th June 87
My Doanie,
　　^1The sweetnefs to me of
having you to care again a
little about – my room and me –
and the desolatenefs of me, without
you – there are no words for. I take
all care I can, and hope that
the languor on me – and infinite
sorrow, – however hard to bear
are better than if I were trying
to force interest in anything. The
letters from Francesca are very
beautiful about you.
　　Baby's message is honey & balm.
– and that you are better brings
back some light into my tired
eyes. Oh my Doanie – how is it
all to end? How much we have
done and borne for each other –
– in vain.
Last year at this time I was
only getting sleep by taking brandy
at night. I took no wine yesterday
at all and slept withou[t] [dre]ams

so I trust you need not [be in]
fear about me, except [that] I
die of sorrow – slowly. The [w]onder^2
is – it has not been – quickly.
　　Dear love back to Baby – and
　　Violet must have some too, this time

　　　Ever your poor Di Pa

238. 19 June 1887, Brantwood

　　　Brantwood,
　　　　Coniston. Lancashire.
　　　　19th. June 87
Oh my Doanie,
　　Francesca thinks of
you only, I believe, just now –
her only hope for me is that
you will return to me.
Violet and Baby digging are
joys to me – but I hope you
use the word 'sunstroke' of
Agnew, only of such feverishness
as cannot but follow any school
game as <u>he</u> plays it, in this heat.
^1I do scarcely any thing all
day but lie in the beds of moss,
or in the shade of rhododendron
or pink hawthorn: – I have put
some lovely bits of Francesca
together for next Folk in Apennine

Lily's letter is here – with thanks
which I did not deserve for
sending Leech' It was before
given to her. I think you
have arranged all the things
in your room very beautifully. –
But the sadness of entering it
now. – Ever your poor Di Pa

Letter 237. 46/170, 1887. Envelope: red sealingwax; addressed to 'Mrs Arthur Severn / 28 Herne Hill / London / S E'. Postmarked: 'AMBLESIDE / C / JU17 / 87' (front); 'LONDON. S.E. / C7 / JU18 / 87' (back). Pencil notations: 'A W'.
　1. There is a pencil bracket here, the other bracket is near the end of the letter, after 'not been – quickly.'
　2. This and the preceding lines have been marred by sticking to the envelope seal, but the words are mostly discernible and some still clearly legible where they are attached to the envelope.

Letter 238. 48/170, 1887. Envelope: red sealingwax; addressed to 'Mrs Arthur Severn / 28 Herne Hill / London. / S E'. Postmarked 'AMBLESIDE / A / JU19 / 87' (front); 'LONDON. S.E. / C7 / JU20 / 87' (back). Pencil notations: 'A W'.
　1. There is a pencil bracket here, the other bracket is at the end of this paragraph, after 'Apennine'.

239. 23 June 1887, Brantwood

Brantwood,
Coniston. Lancashire.
23rd June 87

Darling Doanie
So many and many thanks for the letters, as in old days. and for keeping affairs in order for me still. I will do everything I can to save you from farther trouble. My days are very desolate now.
    For I am ever your loving
        Di Pa.

What lovely brooches those are you have sent the maids!

240. 26 June 1887, Brantwood

Brantwood,
Coniston. Lancashire.
Sunday

My Doanie
    The love you send me at the end of your letter is worth more than worlds to me – and believe me, in any thing I am trying to get done about Brantwood I am only thinking now of how to [quiet][1] you of trouble about it and leave you mistrefs of it: and its ground.
I have still more strength than I could have thought possible. but the distress of knowing that – that walk in the anemone wood was to
        be the last –
has now become what there are no words for.
I am thankful that Mattie is coming down to Ethel.
Mary and Baxter and all of them are ever so good to me[2] – What is to become of them when I am gone?
. . Many and many a letter comes that ought to make me a little glad for what has been.
    But I am in all things now
        your poor-poor Donie

241. 27 June 1887, Brantwood

Brantwood,
Coniston. Lancashire.
Monday 27th

My Doanie
    Mattie came to see me yesterday, looking so bright and good.
Ethel & she would have come to day – but I could not let them Alas, my mind has come back – as the waves of the Red Sea. and this state of things cannot last much longer; do with me what you think best.   Your poor Donie

242. 29 June 1887, Brantwood

Brantwood,
Coniston. Lancashire.
29th June 87

My poor Doanie
    I have sent to Dr Parsons[1]

Letter 239. 51/170, 1887. Envelope: red sealingwax; addressed to 'Mrs Arthur Severn / 28. Herne Hill / London. / S. E'. Postmarked: 'AMBLESIDE / C / JU23 / 87' (front).

Letter 240. 53/170, 1887. Pencil notations: 'June 26', '87'.
  1. This could be 'quit'.
  2. Servants and friends at Brantwood.

Letter 241. 54/170, 1887. Pencil notations: 'A W', 'June 87'. Envelope: red sealingwax; addressed to 'Mrs Arthur Severn. / 28 Herne Hill / London / S. E,'. Postmarked: 'AMBLESIDE / C / JU27 / 87' (front).

Letter 242. 55/170, 1887. Paper: half a sheet of Brantwood letterhead. Envelope: red sealingwax; addressed to 'Mrs Arthur Severn / 28. Herne Hill / London. / S E'. Postmarked: 'AMBLESIDE / C / JU29 / 87' (front); 'LONDON. S.E. / C7 / JU 30 / 87' (back). See her response of 30 June [272a].
  1. Ruskin's local doctor at Brantwood.

enclosing your note, which he
ought to have. But no one can
help me. now. I have lost
– what might have been yet
twenty years of happy life with you.
Oh my Doanie – that the rest should
have been dream – and this the wakening.
and that when you were spared in that
pain, when I was watching at the gate
in the dawn – you were [ghos]ted back
– for me to inflict this –
      Your poor Donie
overleaf[2]

243. 9 September 1887, Folkestone

(Written before my last – as far
as over page.
     Brantwood,
      Coniston. Lancashire.
     (Folkestone.) –
Darling Di Ma.
 I can't think what Arfie
is doing at the Bishop's. Does he
sing in the chapel in a surplice – ?
He can't find anything to paint
in those poor little sandstone ditches
– nor any glades of trees as at Sedgwick
nor any sailing as at Brantwood. Does
he tell stories all day, and you, dance
finger-ballet?
Apropos of sailing I find the boats (toy)
are made here without any rudders just the
same as at Coniston but I hope at least
to get good models of the rigging of
a cutter and a lugger – the one pushed
mainly by her main sail – & the other by
her fore sail. And your maternal care
for me will be satisfied by my
arranging to stop all Sunday at Hythe
and recover some position in the
Clerical world.
I am delighted by all you tell
me of Rose – and of Lily's
going down into the dungeons and
up to the battlements – not did [I]
ever doubt your having happy
times there – What I complained
of was that you thought it happy
for me to have no companion
but – Mr Baxter,[1] and no
lectures on Ravenna to hear, but
only Mr Baxter's observations under
the inspiration of American drink
("What I wishes to tell you Sir, is
that your legs is swollen". . &)[2]

I had a perfectly glorious scarlet
dawn over the Calais sea, today
Friday – after a night of the serene

---

 2. The letter had continued, but the second page has been torn away.

Letter 243. 76/170, 1887. Addressed to 'Mrs Arthur Severn / Rose Castle / Carlisle'; postmarked 'FOLKESTONE / D / SE 9 / 87' (front); 'CARLISLE / B / SP10 / 87', '[TONTIES BO] / D / SE9 / 87 / FOLKESTONE' (back). Pencil notations: 'Sep. 9: 87' and (sideways on the right side of the front of the envelope) 'Dr Ewart / 33 Curzon St / Mayfair'. Ruskin arrived in Folkestone on 21 August and was then staying at the Hotel de Paris.
 1. Ruskin's valet, Peter Baxter.
 2. There is a jagged symbol just inside the bracket. I have represented it as '&', implying etcetera. It may equally be a visual representation of exasperation, or a failed first attempt at forming the bracket.

waning moon, and another [Rochester] boat as come
with its family – a red scarfed Mother – like Mother [Bucca]
and a grand red faced hard working Father – stout son
and dear little 7 year old daughter – and I had a talk
with an excursionist old lady about her Pomeranian
dog, on the pier at Sunset, – and any quantity of fullsail
ships in distance – and – as nearly as possible – Connie Gilchrist
at sixteen, – edging nearer me, . evidently with purpose of letting
me find something to tell her about the Sky. And in fine
Ive resolved to stay here till Christmas – and then come
up to my old nursery, and take everybody to the Drury Lane[3]
Pantomimes.
  Me evy so seepy with getin up to look
at the Moon. me's oos poo wee Donie

244. 9 October 1887, Folkestone

  Folkestone
  Sunday
   9th Oct. 87

Darling wee pussie

 I've sent the 12th Praet
to Jowett[1] telling him where to
put in the two pages I sent you.
I hope it will not have tired
you too much to copy them.
 I sent also the 4th Folk
with a pretty bit added to replace
the uggie one taken out.
And the 5th Folk, which is
very beautiful, in a state which
Jowett can work with your
self into printable form.
  That, with a preface, if I
can write one, shall end the
Christ's Folk – and I shall leave
Francesca's letters for you, with
her permission, to [print – listing]
each one according to date

I am dreadfully ashamed
of myself for having presumed
on my strength, and plagued
you as I did – But you
know – and Diddie knows
how all my anxiety was to

---

3. It appears as though Ruskin indistinctly scrawled 'theatre', with the '-atre' trailing off, then superimposed 'Drury Lane' over the line representing '-atre', transforming the first three letters of 'theatre' into the word 'the'.

Letter 244. 98/170, 1887. Addressed to 'Mrs Arthur Severn / Brantwood / Coniston / Ambleside.'; postmarked 'FOLKESTONE / F / OC 9 / 87' (front); 'CARNFORTH / C / OC10 / 87'.

get you back safe to your
husband & children. – and
it seemed to me that I had
a new piece of work to do, alone.

It was finding the Turner skies
unchanged that threw me
quite off the idea of going to
France. Nor do I wish I had
gone. but finding all my
walks & sails now cut short
– and the dark days coming on – and enormous
expense among unprincipled people – (I don't
mean Edwin[2] or – Alice – but landladies and
all the tradesmen – and perhaps my di ma
missing me a little too sometimes – poor Donie
very 'samed of himself and very sad. and
wishes his di ma would bid him fot to do

   Evy oos poo poo Donie

The 'Christ's Folk' – in all, will by [L thus]
The King of Italy Rosita
Polissena   The Revenna countefs
Edwige   Francesca herself, and her mother
   And Angeliqa

245. 18 October 1887, [London]

  Brantwood,
   Coniston. Lancashire.
  Tuesday
Sweetest Doanie
 No doctors here yet – but
Edwin and I manage now by
Ourselves very well.
I have your sweet letter about
Dora &c.[1] It is true that when I
came away I thought I should
never see Brantwood more. but my
thoughts are nothing now – and from
day to day new lights – or shades
flicker round me, – throug'h which
there remains now only fixed the hope
not wilfully to give my Joanie or
Francesca ignoble sorrow for me
 Ever your lovingest.
  Di Pa

1. Henry Jowett, Ruskin's printer.
2. Edwin Trice, a local Folkestone man who cared for Ruskin when he was isolated at Folkestone/Sandgate and in a particularly poor mental and physical state (*Later*, pp. 543–45).

Letter 245. 108/170, 1887. Pencil notations: 'Oc. 18:87'.
 1. Dora Lees and her husband Edward, who offered to take Ruskin into their home.

246. 18 October 1887, London

19th Oct 87.

Oh my poo – poo – sweet Pussie, and did'nt oo seep, and was oo misby about oos poo di Pa? Well – he is war-ry misby too himself – feeling more and more foolish and troublesome to every body and most of all to his di ma.
I think the bodily mischief is beginning to be held in better check – but the doctors talk of weeks and weeks before they can get it right – and it has so entirely surprised me by coming on like this at Folkestone, because, while I was at Mrs Slys[1] in the summer I was walking in torrent beds and high above the mines with no feeling of harm
I have the registered packet all safe and will most carefully tell you what I write the cheques for.

I have a nice bright bedroom on the second floor – and every possible comfort. and Edwin[2] is closely and skilfully attentive
I have with your's a beautiful letter from Mr Lees,[3] – explaining the sort of place Thurston Castle is[4] – Which I answer with reserved thanks, but saying that my feeling of being a burden & shadow would be probably, as great there as at Brantwood. and that it seems to me a lodging of my own where Doanie could direct what was done for me if I fell ill, would be the rightest and safest thing.

– Meantime – di wee ma, – me want to 'ite oo booty [mew] etties and to get oo to seep pitty and me's oos ownie poo grateful Di Pa

247. 22 October 1887, [London]

Morley's[1]
22nd Oct 87

Darling Di Ma
It is the best of all comforts and encouragements to me, the hearing of your perfect health and of all the pleasure you have had in the place this autumn. I ought to be thankful every minute of the day that if I can keep only quiet and reasonable, I have so much power in every direction of giving pleasure – but chiefly to my Di Ma

I think she will like Dr Bowles'[2] enclosed letter <u>He</u> is a delightful story teller and evidently enjoyed having me to talk to
Violet's phonetic 8 is quite the loveliest bit of spelling I ever heard of – and Lily's ride round the lake is indeed a triumph.
The two letters from Mammima[3] and Connie enclosed in your's weer also great dites. Now that I can't write books any more, I begin to think letters very pleasant. Connie has been making friends with a dear green parrot, who talks in paroty French to himself,
Que tu es gentille, Coco! – &c.

It is a great comfy to me, that you like those last sentences of

---

Letter 246. 109/170, 1887. Envelope: addressed to 'Mrs Arthur Severn / Brantwood / Coniston / Ambleside'. Postmarked: 'CHARING.CROSS S.W.[?] / A6 / OC18 / 87' (front); 'AMBLESIDE / A / OC 19 / 87' (back). Note that Ruskin wrote '19', but (assuming it is filed with the correct envelope) the letter is postmarked the 18 October 1887.
1. Mrs. Joseph Sly, Landlady of the Waterhead Hotel on Coniston Water. Ruskin had stayed there while in dispute with Joan the previous summer.
2. Edwin Trice.
3. Edward Lees, the husband of Dora (Livesey) Lees. At this point, Ruskin contemplated moving into their home, Thurland Castle.
4. This should be Thurland Castle, O. Wilson, ed., p. 113.

Letter 247. 112/170, 1887.
1. Morley's Hotel, Trafalgar Square.
2. Dr. Bowles was Ruskin's doctor in Folkestone.
3. I assume this to be Lucia Alexander, the mother of his 'Sorella' Francesca Alexander.

Praeterita. There's another little
retouch mentioning ". the Auld House)
that you'll like[4]
– I wish I could fill my paper
But in a London bedroom – the
fancy is'nt lively.
But me's always your lovingest
– penitentest – Di Pa

248. 26 October 1887, London

Wednesday

Darling Di Ma
 Oo says oo've so much to tank
me for; – but me's nevvy tanked
oo and Arfie. for the lovely [care][1] of
the Libers, which it is delightful to me
to hear of. and I am sure I ought
to thank you daily for finding time to
write me these sweet long notes. You
say in one I've been just looking over that
you like doing it; but the regular way
they come now means attentive care.
To day's is a great dite with the account
of the sweet squirrel looking into your eyes
– and enclosed confidential cheque which
relieves my mind about keeping the other –
– But I hope I shall be able to stay
on this side of the water. I've had quite
a delicious walk this morning, not having
ventured out for a week – and really
enjoyed the sunshine, air, and bustle
of the Strand, and walked with more
comfort and security than for years!
The Strand is a wonderful sight to me
now – especially in the perfection of the
etchings and photographs, which
are beyond all I ever believed
pofsible in either art.

Tempting puff and shortbread
pastry cooks! – I walked past Temple
bar and down to the Temple church.
– but felt that my architectural times
were over. and that my interest was
now – all of it that is left – in Francesca's
stories of real people – and in peepies
themselves – my Di ma chiefly
Connie Oldham writes me really quite
diteful letters just now – – so witty and funny
and physiciany and affectionate – She
wants me to sleep in blankets instead
of sheets though – and that's really
more than I can bear.
Another large meeting today and
police on duty by twenties in a group
I see no end to it, unless there
be an order issued that they must
have tickets for the meetings at
a penny for boys and two pence for
adults
I've just had lunch of oysters, brown bread
 [and sherry
and feel that theyre not thrown away on me
Marks[2] called here on Monday, and I let him
 [come
up, and was immensely touched by his
 [affectionateness.
He thought me looking extremely well – –
 [but I'm
greatly subdued by the nice chambermaids
 [always calling
me 'the old gentleman', I really don't look,
 [to myself,
so old, in the glafs, at all!
 Love to you all – and me's oos poo – not
 [so very old
 Di Pa

---

4. Note that the previous letter (not transcribed) includes manuscript material for *Praeterita*.

Letter 248. 117/170, 1887. Envelope: addressed to 'Mrs Arthur Severn / Brantwood / Coniston / Ambleside'. Postmarked: 'CHARING.CROSS / A5 / OC26 / 87' (front); 'AMBLESIDE / A / OC27 / 87' (back). Pencil notations: '26 Oct 87'.
 1. This could be 'case'.
 2. Presumably H. Stacy Marks, R.A.

249. 27 October 1887, London

Thursday

Sweetest honey of a Di Ma

I'm going down to Sandgate then, on Saturday. and hope to stay there without bovying oo till I've got myself right – if I can. I've just signed cheque 65965 carelessly taking the last first, for 25. – the other I shall pay my last bill with when I get away. What a bovy oo has about taxes and evything for your dood for nufin di Pa.
He had a great longing to be inside a theatre once more – and went to the Vaudeville last night to see Thorne once more – but was dreadfuly 'pointed to find 'Sophia' only the old Tom Jones and that Thorne only played Squire Western
which anybody else could have done as well. Allworthy, who might have been extremely interesting in a good actors hands. was a mere [lay] figure – and quantities of time wasted in what an English audience always seems to like, imitations of drunkenness, and the 'spinster aunt' businefs of middleaged women. The Tom was extremely good however – the Sophia beautiful – and the peasant girl Molly extremely pretty and clever.[1]
I <u>never</u> saw such a scene as the Strand when I came out. Three theatres and a 'Hall' were coming out at exactly the same moment – the pavement one crowd all along with the cabs backing into it – and roaring of [carts] from an unbroken line of omnibuses outside

See over page
What marvellous things those selfwinding
[watches
must be, for 12/6.!!! its' enough to make a
[note
of admiration wind up itself to twice the
[length[2]
But my watch does now go beautifully – and strike right to a tick – and is as clean as if it
[were new
Card just sent up by J.P.F. (Chelsea) – I decline
[visit
– sends up again – if he could only see me for
[a moment – he
was begged to call by Mr Fleming.[3] I still
[continue declination
Its time me should get away
– Write still here tomorrow – but on Saturday
[to Kent Hotel, Sandgate
I must see what Wilson's rooms are like before
[venturing there]

Ever your devoted & ovin Di Pa

I allowed a friend to come upstairs since I wrote the third page
Mr Marion H. Spielmann
16 Porchester Terrace
Kensington Gardens. .

He has just been made Editor of Cassell's Magazine of Art – and he is so very nice and gives me such a good report of the way Cassell's are managing, that I want to help him what I can – (this rather than I feel dreadfully shelved and out of the running now). and I want Arfie and you to choose of my small unwanted drawings any one you think would engrave nicely, and send it him for that purpose – I think I shall write him a little letter about my yesterdays walk in the Strand – submitting of course the proof to you that you may judge if its not too weak, for I cant take pains with it.

Letter 249. 119/170, 1887. Pencil notations: '27 Oct 87'; Envelope: red sealingwax; addressed to 'Mrs Arthur Severn / Brantwood / Coniston / Ambleside'; postmarked: 'CHARING.CROSS / A6 / OC27 / 87' (front), 'AMBLESIDE / A / O 28 / 87' (back).
  1. This production of 'Sophia', by Robert Buchanan, a four-act comedy based on *Tom Jones*, opened at the Vaudeville Theatre on 12 April 1886. Fred Thorne played Weston in 1886. [Thanks to Jeffrey Richards for identifying this].
  2. Ruskin has drawn a clockwise swirl.
  3. Albert Fleming.

250. 28 October 1887, [Sandgate]

Friday 28th Oct
87

Sweetest Di Ma
    I don't know if oo ikes
itin to oos Donie, but my chief
pleasure in life is itin to my Di Ma.
I've been sending some mewys letters
to Francesca too, lately which she
says she likes very much – and gets
up in the middle of her breakfast to
answer.
The Harrison Weir book <u>is</u> nice –
and I've sent <u>him</u> a nice ettie,
and said you weer very much 'set up'
by having to acknowledge it
I think its very lovely having you
in the Brantwood 'situation' which
you were clearly meant for – and
relieve me of all tubble wubble in – and
I shall be so glad you have Katie M.[1]
with you – you can't think what a
tearful sort of feeling I have as I fit
the Wigtown and Kikcudbright into my
dissected Scotland.[2]
But I think it would be quite wrong
to take risk of rly[3] and cold merely
to run up to see me. Stay at Brant[d]
till you have quite done there and
are coming up for town life when
if I'm well enough I'll come and
take oo to pantomimes
I'm dited to hear of the wooden huts
being of service for morning and
evening Brant effect – – and that oo
won't bid me seep in bankets.

I've tried to ite some autographs – – but
it is like trying to forge my own signature
my R.[4] long leg is getting gouty – and the
    last iti bone is misby for
    want of its Doanie.

Evy oos poo poo – Di Pa – a little
comforted about the old gentleman and old lady.
Can you tell me how Sir W. Gull[5] is;
and I've always been looking in the
papers for some news of Wilson Barrett[6]
since he lost his wife and the lamp fell
on him – and never see his name.

251a. 8 November 1887, Sandgate

8th Nov. 87

Darlingest Wee Poosmoos.
    I've been daubing at two
leaves of my sketchbook since I
came here – and they're in rather
nice messes – if I do any more I
shall ^ get angry with them and burn
them – so I send them to you
to-day to mount prettily in the
best Baxterian form – and send
to the sorella – <u>any</u>thing does to
amuse her!
    I'm beginning to be curious to know
what you'll send to SPielmann.[1]

Letter 250. 120/170, 1887. Envelope: red sealingwax; addressed to 'M[rs] Arthur Severn / Brantwood / Coniston / <u>Ambleside</u>'; postmarked: 'CHARING.CROSS W. O / [?] / OC29 / 87' (front), 'AMBLESIDE / A / OC30 / 87' (back).
1. Possibly Katie MacDonald, who had formed 'The Friends of Living Creatures' and asked Ruskin to be the group's patron (*Later*, p. 512).
2. During this time, Ruskin occupied himself with puzzle maps.
3. This is shorthand for 'railway'.
4. The tail of the 'R' extends down, which is why the following lines are indented.
5. Sir William Gull, doctor in practice with James Oldham, father of Connie Oldham (*Later*, p. 433).
6. Prominent actor–manager of the Victorian stage (1846–1904).

Letter 251a. 133a/170, 1887. Envelope: red sealingwax; addressed to 'M[rs] Arthur Severn / Brantwood / Coniston / <u>Ambleside</u>'. Postmarked: 'SANDGATE / D / NO 8 / 87' (front); 'CARNFORTH / G / NO 9 / 87' (back). Enclosures: a newspaper cutting entitled 'Hints on Household Management', excerpts transcribed below (133b/170, 1887). Pencil notations: 'A W'; 'newspaper cuttings only' (on the envelope).
1. Marion H. Spielmann, Editor of Cassell's *Magazine of Art*.

The two Mignons have come –
and I'm going to make a point of
reading every word with out skipping
as if it was [Plato].²
Heres the delicious long ettie about
evyting just come: – and oos being
able to send Mignon the last [Praeterita]
– Di wee ma would oo pease
look in drawers of middle
square table in study, those
on the farthest from the fire
if I left the M.S.S. of the
beginning of Vol III, the Grande
Chartreuse – and send the
sheets to me, if there.
And ³ I quite agree about the
bovy of any articles for Mags.
– but Di Ma – sometimes my
own books fall so dead? now
there's the life of Sir Herbert⁴
which I took immense pains
with – nobody ever seems to
know of it – in a magazine
it would have made a sensation
And I do miss the old Fors,⁵
for getting a little bit said of
anything
The enclosed Jowett with its
enclosure gives me great pleasure⁶
I don't think I <u>can</u> be better off than I am,
      [y within
reach of printers and oo and doctors – yet
      [well
out of public reach, & with excellent food
      [and air
and a nice cat, and a Sᵗ Bernard dog, and a
piano, and nice music master – and sorella now
writing me nearly every day like di ma.

 Evy – di wee ma – oos ovinest Donie

251b. Newspaper cutting

HINTS ON HOUSEHOLD MANAGEMENT.
BY A BATCHELOR

I am consumed with a desire to convey a few hints to the British house-wife on the management of her servants, and I find the only way to do this successfully is by a newspaper article; for though I understand all household mysteries and all knowledge, still being a man and a batchelor I am nothing accounted of. [...] Most of my lady friends have studied the subject in the pages of flimsy books on household management with the untoward results that their cooks and housemaids are the burden of their own and their friends' lives. I, on the other hand, have sat at the feet of Plato and Solomon among the ancients and Mr. Ruskin, Gothelf, and Walter Scott among the moderns. [...]

252. 9 November 1887, Sandgate

      9ᵗʰ Nov. 87
Darling Di Ma
 Its so velly coolious and
pity that oo have kept my
Wibbston Pipps for me, and that
I'm just beginning to munch little
bits of apples for dessert – and find
they don't do me any harm, and
I shall so enjoy those wed wibstons.¹
 To put you out of anxiety
about the Art Magazine I wrote
two leaves of the article to-day
it being wet – If I had'nt written
three words twice over it would
have been a nice easy piece of
unaltered M.S.S. – and I hope

---

 2. This could be 'Photo'.
 3. There is a pencil bracket here, the other bracket is at the end of the paragraph, after 'anything'.
 4. *A Knight's Faith*.
 5. *Fors Clavigera*.
 6. There is a pencil bracket here, the other bracket is between 'every day' and 'like di ma.'

Letter 251b. 133b/170, 1887. A newspaper cutting. Ruskin has placed marks in the margin where his own name is mentioned. I have transcribed relevant sections, starting from the beginning.

Letter 252. 134/170, 1887.
 1. This paragraph is about Redstone Pippin apples.

you'll be a little peased with it
Keep it till I send you the rest
and you can send it to Spielmann[2]
altogevy. I'm very sad about
old Mrs Harrison[3] not being
so cheerful – and very grateful
for all that love from her.
I wrote to Susie[4] telling her to ask
you to read about the circus
horses to her. – but am not
quite suree if my account of
them was in a letter to you, or
to Dido.
Dido is paying me not the smallest
attention now, but Francesca and
G. D. write every other day at least!
and the Mignon books give me
plenty to think of. Its nearly
the wettest day I've seen at
the seaside – but I'm really not
at all dull. and am going to
have muttontop for lunch.

    I went downstairs last night
to hear some of the landlords &
landlady's friends sing and play
and I'm <u>very</u> glad I did, for <u>weelly</u> di ma I
                      [nevy
knew what a booty voice oo had, till I heard
                        [that
song you're so fond of – 'just a' something – I
                        [forget what –
– sung by another girl – it was as dead and
                        [dull
as – the harbour when the tides out, every bit of
music dried up! Di wee ma, oo <u>does</u> sing pitty!
    There was an extremely good violinist
                        [player –
one of the regimental band at [Shawcliffe] –
                        [and all that
he did was to confirm me in detestation of
                        [the fiddle
– he played and accompaniment to piano
                        [which was as
if all the mice in Sandgate and Folkestone

                        [were squeaking
togevy. oo would'nt have iked <u>at</u>, Di Ma?
    Di Ma – would oo pease open top drawer
                        [in old
dining room bookcase above wheer the gold
                        [is, and in
the back corner
C, are a lot of   C[5]
F's letters done
up by G. D and
never touched since. me
wants em <u>all</u>, di ma, that
are in that compartment

Me's had mutton top and gass of
serry.   How funny words are
when π one takes pains to
spell 'em quite itely, Di Ma;
    Evy oos poo itie boy
            Donie

253. 11 November 1887, Sandgate

    Sandgate   St Martin's – 1887

Darling wee di Ma.
    The lovely long ettie with MS of
Chartreuse and five fivers, came by
11 post. – two fivers have gone, leaving
me [petty][1] change, on enclosed bill
and I am greatly relieved in mind by
Arfies pleasure on the wave photographs
for having spent some former change
on them. I am going to quote
your account of their impression on you
in my next paper for the Art Magazine
– the two sheets sent to day to finish the
present one are either more carefully
written, , or more carefully corrected,
than the preceding ones: the six will
I think be enough for the present.
Now taking to your letter, I am greatly
set up by your liking the two bits of
colour for Sorel. I began the Abbeville
when I was pining for Abbeville in

---

    2. M. H. Spielmann, Editor of Cassell's *Magazine of Art*.
    3. Possibly Dorothy (Worsdworth) Harrison, a neighbour at Brantwood (*Later*, p. 482).
    4. Susie Beever.
    5. There is a square divided into four quadrants with a 'C' in the top right.

Letter 253. 135/170, 1887. The Feast of St Martin's is 11 November.
    1. This might be 'petty' (meaning small) or 'pretty' (meaning a surprisingly large amount).

Trafalgar Sq. and have finished it
down here – the sky and sea were
those that I saw when last out
walking, about a week since (I had
hoped to get out again to day, but shall not)
I thought the notion of the reflected
glow on the ramparts was nice in the
Abbeville – but it was all blotty
and bunghy – it did come rather bright
by help of scarlet vermilion and Newmans
new Rose Madder, a wonderful colour

My note this morning explains about
the music books – I remember now
giving away my prettily bound one
but I forget to whom. – There are
certainly some plainly bound ones yet
in the old dining room

Your choice of drawings for the
Magazine is admirable

All that you do about Guild
Papers will be right of course
Ill sign any you send

Can you tell me anything about how
Rooke[2] is getting on – left ashore
as I left him?
And. di wee ma, is there a [Boothes]
about the house, or have I lost im too?
I had a present made me before I left the
Paris[3] of an intermediate Folkestone – in the
early days of the Pavilion – rather curious –
I send it with some phots – failures – of Morelle's[4]
done from Turner while I was in London –
[just
to keep the M.S. sheets flat – you may
[perhaps
like to keep them folded in your own way

And pease di ma will you pease send
me all my moosic now out of the squeaking
[little
door in the drawing room?
    Evy Di ma oos poo little squeaking mousie
                    Donie

254. 18 November 1887, Sandgate

          18th ! ?
            Friday
Darling Joanie
   Early post caught, I
hope – just to say I'm going
on all right – though
worried badly yesterday
by Allens[1] folly in letting
the Oxford lectures be
printed without references
to Collie or Wedd-ed-weddie[2]
– with their Greek 'revised'
by – Grace – I suppose – or
the Deuce – and I've to
cancel whole leaves at
the last moment, just when
I'm doing Praeterita – They
been the D's own printing
I think – this time.
– I begin to wish all
printers weer the Devil's
instead of the Devils
all printers.

   Ever your loving
but sometimes short tempered
          Donie

---

2. Thomas Matthews Rooke (1842–1942) 'came to Ruskin from the firm of Morris and Co.' He was hired by Ruskin in 1879 as a painter and copyist and 'was still receiving a monthly wage from St George in 1887' (*Later*, p. 523).
3. This refers to the Paris Hotel, Folkestone, where Ruskin had stayed earlier in the year.
4. Photographer commissioned by Ruskin, see 22 January 1888 [256].

Letter 254. 142/170, 1887. Envelope: red sealingwax; addressed to 'Mrs Arthur Severn / F. Harris Esq, / Lunefield / Kirkby Lonsdale / Westmorland'. Postmarked: 'SANDGATE / B / NO18 / 87' (front); 'KIRKBY-LONSDALE / A / NO 19 / 87' (back). Pencil notations: 'Nov 87'.
1. George Allen, Ruskin's publisher.
2. W. G. Collingwood and Alexander Wedderburn.

255. 25 November 1887, Sandgate

Friday

Darling Doanie

Your long chat from Lunefield gives me intense pleasure – I hope the enclosed to Arfie will be pleasanter than Hotel Bills; – to Lady [Bestive] – please say she ought to have come and nursed me like φίλη and read [Wordsworth][1] on primroses to me – and I should ^have been well in a week instead of being crazy all summer: = to that dear clergyman ^say that it may just make all the difference to me, having such a man for my clergyman – else perhaps I should have asked the Governor of Carlisle castle to take care of me instead of the Lord & Lady of that crook of Lune.[2] To the nymphs of Lune say – with my deeper and more reverent love – that – if – next time shes in a – Wax – (I say I think that's rayther good – & beats Punch?) she wouldn't mind knocking down – I beg her pardon – washing away – most of modern Lancaster and then ~~coming~~ ^running down ^herself quickly just by the windows of our Heysham rooms, ^straight – into Turners bay[3] – I think she'd be happier for it afterwards – and a good many Mortal Nymphs yet unborn, besides ^happier than Yorkshire ones – And thats all the messages ^by Ribble 4 I can send to day, I've lots more to say about home things when you get home.+ Think only of enjoying yourself now (books that I want, &c. next week.)
I've just dined on Sprouts! and chicken Merry thoughts & Gateau

Ever your poo itie dee wee Pa

Letter 255. 146/170, 1887. Envelope: red sealingwax; addressed to 'M[rs] Arthur Severn / Brantwood / Coniston / Ambleside'. Postmarked: 'SANDGATE / E / NO25 / [87]' (front); 'CARNFORTH / G / NO26 / 87' (back). Pencil notations: '? 25 Nov 87'; 'for Joan' (on the envelope).
1. This looks as much like 'Wordewickes' as 'Wordsworth'.
2. The River Lune, which runs through Lancaster and Kirkby Lonsdale.
3. Morecambe Bay.
4. The River Ribble.

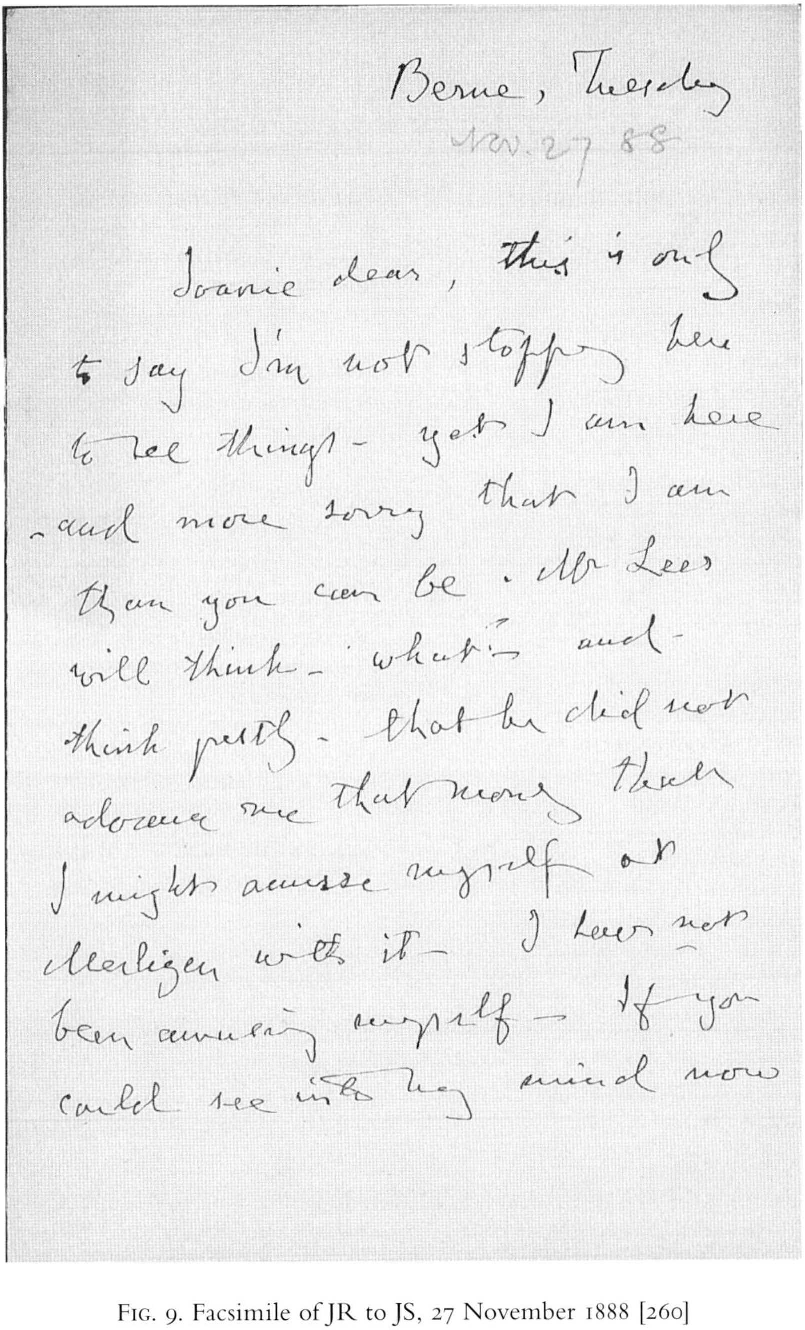
Berne, Tuesday

Nov. 27 88

Joanie dear, this is only to say I'm not stopping here to see things – yet I am here – and more sorry that I am than you can be. Mr Lees will think – what's sad – think pretty – that he did not adore me that much though I might amuse myself at Merligen with it – I have not been amusing myself – If you could see into my mind now

Fig. 9. Facsimile of JR to JS, 27 November 1888 [260]
RF L52, Ruskin Foundation (Ruskin Library, Lancaster University)

1888

R. embarks on a final Continental tour, retracing old haunts, 10 June
J. summoned to Paris to collect him, early December
R. returns home at his Herne Hill Nursery, 8 December

256. 22 January 1888, Sandgate

Sunday, 22nd Jan
.88.

My Doanie
I was in an extremely doleful mood yesterday, and could'nt write. In spite of the kind telegram, – me was anxy, because I thought I was my self the cause of the headache and nose-bleeding. – and well I may be – sorrow on me. And to-day I am little better, thinking over all the years that I have made you wretched in – 1878 – – 1881, 82, – 85–86 – and through all this 87 from May to December. – and now – beginning 88 with no power of doing more the cat does, all day,
Di wee Ma, its ½ past 5 and I've had my tee-wee – And all this blessed day I've done nothing but write one doleful letter to Francesca – and a doleful note to Kate G.[1] How that creature <u>does</u> love me, or the idea she has of me, through any quantity of unkindness or absence.
Oh di wee ma – <u>does</u> oo love me too – through all the hundred fold worse than absence of the pain I've been to oo.? Is oo twite soo me isn't a mere bovy to oo now.
To think of my having oo, and Francesca – and KG and GD – all so good, & loving me so And that me tant be dood – but is always doodfor nufin.
And bad for evyting – Di wee ma, here's [Morelle's account – which I've told him you would [send him cheque for. I'm going to let him sell [impressions from the negatives on his own account – he has had much more trouble than the £15 will pay him for.
And oh my di, wee ma me want some mo cheques please – me's misby to ask for them me's oos poo wee Donie

257. 28 June 1888, Abbeville

Abbeville, Thursday
28th June. 88

My Doanie
I have read your letter over and over, – with bitter sense of the misery I have caused you – and no wish for myself but that I might be spared to you so as to render thees following years – what you can still

---

Autograph letters for 1888 are in 'Bem L 50 / Letters / John Ruskin / to / Joan Severn / Jan-Apl 1888' [letters 1–82]; 'Bem L51 / Letters / John Ruskin / to / Joan Severn / May-June 1888' [letters 83–141]; 'Bem L 52 / Letters / John Ruskin / to / Joan Severn July-Dec 1888' [letters 142–220].

Letter 256. 17/220, 1888. Envelope: red sealingwax; addressed to 'Mrs Arthur Severn / Brantwood / Coniston / Ambleside'. Postmarked: 'SANDGATE / E / JA22 / 88' (front); 'CARNFORTH / [G] / JA23 / 88' (back).
  1. Francesca Alexander and Kate Greenaway.

Letter 257. 138/220, 1888. Envelope: red sealingwax; addressed to 'Mrs Arthur Severn / Brantwood / Monk Coniston / <u>Ambleside</u> / Angleterre'. Postmarked: 'ABBEVILLE / 28 / JUIN / 88 / SOMME' (front). Pencil notations: 'A W'. In response to her letter of 26 June [279].

hope they might be. – and truly if I
come back to Brantwood it would
only be to try to comfort you – in no
state of excitement could I ever again
ask people there against your wish. But
[1]I never before was so conscious of all
that's wrong in me, whether in head
or heart. – never before so unable to
employ myself or interest myself. never
before so unable to determine on anything
– so fearful of every thing when I begin
to consider it. At Broadlands there is the
happy religious & spiritual state
in which I have now no share – I
believe they would see blue lights
flickering round me, – at Brantwood
I recollect too well how I used
to wander – from one room to another
– one field to another – able to rest
nowhere – and in mere sense of
weaknefs – whether in eyes or [strained][2]
in brain. I am far worse now than
I was then. – and entirely helpless to
advise – or beseech you – I will come
to Brantwood if you wish it earnestly –
–. I might say. what else I could
do – if the money question were not
so difficult – for instance [3]I am
strong enough to make my way
with Baxter from here to the Alps
but I don't know how to live cheaply
when I got there – when I have
     thought most earnestly – it always
seems as if Brantwood weer the
only possibility. – but I am so tired
of seeing the leaves fall there – and
I do still cling to the chances of
seeing a little cheerful life. I do like
seeing the French people when I am

the least able to forget myself.

I must not go on [maundering] any
more to day. As it has chanced
this has been one of my worst days.
– [strings], swimming before my eyes – not
so many motes in them as usual – but
     the light dazzling them –
        Oh my Doanie, my poo wee Doanie
          – me's oos poo Di Pa

258. 28 August 1888, Dijon

Dijon. ¼ to 7. morning
Tuesday. – Aug. 28th
1888

Darling Di Ma –
   [1]We had an entirely perfect day
from Paris yesterday – the autumnal
light was exactly like the most intense
golden backgrounds of Van Eyck and
the Flemish purest sacred school.
– Detmar[2] was entirely astonished – he had
never believed such things possible –
I myself was amazed – both at the
clearnefs of my own eyesight – and the
glory of the vine valleys and – most
truly named, Cote dOr, rocks. I never
have felt so well – or so little fatigued
on that journey – we left Paris at ½ past
11 – and got in here at ¼ before six.
having delightfully cushioned large coupé
to ourselves all the way.

– ½ past ten – Above written before
coffee – after coffee, walk for two
glorious hours over all my old haunts
– from the church I drew when I was 14 to
the balconies you know so well
– Its all safe – and lovely and
dicious beyond words. and

---

1. There is a pencil bracket here, the other bracket is after 'wish it earnestly', several lines down the letter.
2. This could be 'stormed'.
3. There is a pencil bracket here, the other bracket is at the end of the letter, after 'dazzling them –'.

Letter 258. 184/220, 1888. Envelope: addressed to 'Mrs Arthur Severn / Sedgwick / Kendal. / Angleterre.' Postmarked: 'DIJON / 5^e 28 / AOUT / [88] / COTE-D'OR' (front); 'KENDAL / A / AU30 / 88' (back). Pencil notations: 'A. W.' This letter is partially reproduced in 37.607.
  1. There is a pencil bracket here, the other bracket is part-way through the letter, after '(introducing Norton)'.
  2. Detmar Blow was a young companion of Ruskin's on this Continental journey (35.xxx-xxxi).

252   LETTERS 1888

I've [come here]³ to write the end
of II Praeterita (introducing
Norton) – and I can't write any
mo Ettie. – but write poste
restante <u>Geneva</u>. I may not
get into Hotel des Bergues.

Tomorrow we take 2 oclock
train to Champagnole. I shall
[sate] three days for the horse,
letting Detmar climb the Dole.
and get to Geneva for Sunday.
and D.V. for once! go to English
Church theer!

    Evy oos own poo wee Di Pa
–I enclose photo⁴ of my little Turk as
she used to [was]. ^ – two years ago – the skirts are
cruelly decorous, <u>now</u>; but the face is
little changed – and if you take a
magnifying glass to it – you will see
the curious decision – She answers
with absolutely the firmness and
              firmness and fineness
of a clever woman of 25. !

Keep it with the greatest care for me.
I find it rather a disturbing element
in my desk– (and I shall be sure to
have another flirt on as soon as I get
to Sallanches.)

Love to my old flames at Sedgwick –
Tell Mary I think it's the awfullest
shame of all thats ever been awful
to me, that she did'nt come to sing to
me when I was ill.

259. 24 November 1888, Thun

    Thun. Saty 24ᵗʰ Nov.
          – 88

My Doanie

    Actually it is Detmar's
21st birthday. – and I should
never have known, but that
a telegram came to him as we
were walking in the market –
– the postman – and everybody in
the town I suppose, knowing his
handsome cheery face by this time.
And now that I do know it
– what are my good wishes worth to [him]
any more than my love has been
to you, my poor Doanie
He talks enough German to be – hail
and well met – with every body he cares
to speak to – and is interested in
every booth in the market and
every house in the town – and has
passed a contended day.

He desires his kindest regards to you
& Arfie –
———

My Doanie – I have nothing to say
but what I have said – of my
selfie – I am your poor Donie

260. 27 November 1888, Berne

        Berne, Tuesday
  Joanie dear, this is only
to say I'm not stopping here
to see things – yet I am here

---

  3. The 'come' is unclear and the 'here' could be 'home'.
  4. This photo is still with the letter. The girl has reddish blond hair. She is dressed in a blue, knee-length skirt and long sailor jacket with a full peplum. The blouse beneath it is red-brown, as are the tights. The boots are black with small heels. She has a scarf or chain and a small cross at her neck. She is seated on a rocky bank, holding a large brown hoop and stick. The back reads 'Photographie / Salons de Pose / au 2me. / G. Blanc / 222 / Rue Sᵗ. Antoine / (Près la Bastille) / Paris'.

Letter 259. 212/220. Envelope: addressed to 'Mʳˢ Arthur Severn / 28. Herne-Hill. / London, S E / Angleterre'. Postmarked: 'TH[UN] / 24.xi.88. – 6' (front); 'LONDON SE / [B 10] / NO26 / [88]' and 'LONDON.S.E. / AN / NO26 / 88' (back).

Letter 260. 213/220. Envelope: addressed to 'Mʳˢ Arthur Severn / 28. Herne-Hill. / London, S E / Angleterre'. Postmarked: 'BERN / 27.XI.88. – 3 / BR.F.EXP. (front); 'LONDON SE / LB / NO28 / [88]'. Pencil notations: 'Nov. 27 88'.

– and more sorry that I am than you can be. Mr Lees[1] will think – what? – and – think justly – that he did not advance me that [money] that I might amuse myself at Merlingen with it – I have <u>not</u> been amusing myself – If you you could see into my mind now – or for weeks back – ! – and yet – I do not know how far you have – I have not signed Di Pa lately – It is only this looking back over all times that I see what the words should have meant – Oh Doanie I am your poor – poor – Di Pa.

1889–90

After 1888, there are no further letters from R. to J.
R. withdraws from society, spending his remaining years in J.s' care at Brantwood
R. dies of influenza, 20 January 1900, and is buried in Coniston churchyard, leaving Brantwood and his estate to the Severns

---

1. Edward Lees, the husband of Dora (Livesey) Lees.

Letters from Joan Agnew (later Severn) 1868–88

261. [1868?] J. to John Ruskin

[I_st_]¹ Thursday

My darling Coz –
First let me say
I am charmed to hear
of your being at Cowley! –
I _know_ you'll enjoy it –
& be happy in the sense
of giving much happiness
to others –
I meant to write to my
wee [Mammy] but I _have_
been so much occupied! –
well – of course its just
like you to be so angelic
& ungrumbling about the
Kingsley visit coming _after_
Windermere – & I feel as if
I could not thank you
enough –
Of course I am wondering
very much whether Arthur
did dine with you last
night – & what the result
was of any talk you had
with him – I think you
pay me a high compliment
in thinking I have neither
said "too much – nor too little" –
I consider _you_ unspeakably
dear & good about the
whole matter – whatever the
consequences may be – "one
never knows"! – truly –
this much I _do_ know
that there never could be
anyone to come up to my
di Pa – or take the same care
of me _he_ has always done –
or be to me what he
has always _been_ – & it is
a great grief to me that
I never have any way of
showing you this thoroughly –
Di Pa I wonder if you
know how much Pussy
loves you; – & how grateful
she is? – & how she can
never repay you except
by just being always
your own wee Pussy –
and she must always be
this; for her chief happiness
in life depends upon it –
whatever happens – or "turns
up" this at least must
be certain –
Now I would like to have
a good cry! –
this is such a horrid
world –
then I am continually think-
-ing of all _you_ have on
your mind – & heart? –
& I shall be oh! _so_
thankful when things are
settled – one way or another –
no I dont mean "or another"
I mean the _one way_ that

Autograph letters from J. to R. are in 'Bem L 55 / Letters / Joan Severn / to / John Ruskin, 1867–87'. This contains a series of sub-folders: 1867, 1 letter; 1868, 8 letters, 1871, 6 letters; 1871 JS to MR [mostly] relating to JR's health, 35 letters; 1872, 1 letter; 1874, 1 letter [AS to JR 9 June 1874]; 1876, 1 fragment; 1880, 1 letter [AS to JR]; 1881, 1 letter; 1882, 1 letter; 1883, 2 letters; 1884, 1 letter; 1885, 2 letters; 1886, 4 letters; 1887, 12 letters. In 'Bem L 56 / Joan Severn – John Ruskin 1888–90' there are 45 letters for 1888. After that point, Ruskin's letters to her dry up, although many more of hers are extant from his last decade.

Letter 261. 1/8, 1868. All but one of the letters in this folder are edged in black and, with the exception of this one, sent from Broadlands (one on Broadlands letterhead is not edged in black). This letter is kept with a blue-green flecked envelope, inscribed in Ruskin's hand with 'Joan. very precious'. Paper one full and a half sheet of black-edged paper; Pencil notations: 'about 1868'.
1. This might be 'Jet'.

is best, & happiest for
my di Pa –
ever your most grateful
and loving – Joan –

Much love to all at Cowley –
please write now care of
T. Richmond Esq.
　　Park Range
　　　　Windermere
to your own Wee Pussie –

262. J. to Margaret Ruskin, April 17 [1867], Harristown

　　　　　Harristown –
　　　　　　April 17th

My dearest Aunt
　I hoped to have
written to you yesterday
but circumstances pre-
vented me which you
shall presently hear –
but before going on any
farther with any of
my news I must first
try as briefly as I can
to make you understand
the great joy and delight
and surprise too, I had
from Mr Ruskin's letter
which came yesterday
telling me that I only
think Aunt dear! that
Joan of all people in
the world was to be
allowed to go abroad
and see things I have
so longed for but never
expected to have any
such longings gratified
and now all words leave
me that ought properly
to express the gratitude
I feel to both you and
my cousin for ever

thinking of, or arranging
such a thing for me –
but I think Aunt dear
if you could fancy
yourself my age, with
such a thing in prospect
you would be better
able to understand
what my feelings are
on the subject only
I must add that I,
and Mamma, Kate, Mary
as well as every body
who takes any interest
in me or my happiness
will feel ever lasting
gratitude to you and
Mr Ruskin for all you
have ever done for me –
as Mr Ruskin cannot un-
-derstand about it, I wish
if it would not trouble
you too much you would
just try to give him
an idea of it – I have
written to him, but then
if you were to say
　　　　　　　2[1]
something of what you
were sure I felt I think
he might be better able
to understand – I hope
I have not tired you
with saying too much
on the subject, only I must
just add that it makes
me twice as light-hearted
knowing I have your app-
-roval of the plan, for
without that – the pain
of leaving you for a
little against your free
will would have over-
balanced the pleasure
I would otherwise have
had, and now have in

Letter 262. 1/6, 1871. Three sheets of paper; The content of this letter feels like 1860s, almost certainly just before the trip to the Continent with Ruskin, Constance Hilliard and the Trevelyans.
　1. Joan has numbered each new leaf of paper.

prospect – as I may have
said perhaps more than
enough on this one topic
now I'll pass on to some-
-thing else – on Monday
M⁻ La Touche took me
with him to see the foun–
-dation stone laid for
a new Presbyterian Church
at [Haas], about seven
miles from Harristown –
I had never seen such
a thing before and
really the ceremony was
both interesting and
impressive and seemed
so to every one present –
M⁻ La Touche laid the
stone and before doing
so made a most earnest
speech very appropriate
for the occasion, other
clergymen offered prayers
and afterwards we had
a nice sermon preached
by a D⁻ Kirkpatrick
from Dublin – but oh
Aunt how you would
delight in M⁻ La Touche
he is the most earnest
Christian in his work
I ever saw, and it seems
his aim to do good to
every one and serve
his heavenly master sure-
-ly his reward will be
great in the next world.
for laying the stone of
the new church M⁻ La
Touche got a very handsome
silver trowel. I believe
it is always customary
on such occasions – –
Rosie and I had a most
delightful day together
   3
yesterday we drove to
beautiful waterfall among
the Wicklow mountains, it
was a great deal more
beautiful than I could

have believed we had
luncheon in a little summer-
-house just opposite, and
really it was very
grand and beautiful, we
had a lovely day for
it – and the whole country
seemed to be rejoicing
and looking it's best
in the bright sunshine –
while we were having
lunch Rosie amused me
by telling me of the
time ~~when~~ M⁻ Ruskin
~~and a large party~~ ˢʰᵉ & some others ∧ had
gone besides. but she took
great pleasure in telling
me of a dangerous part
"St. C." insisted on going
over to try her skill
in [climing], but she was
determined (even at the
risk of her neck being
broken) not to be beaten –
The gong is sounding for
lunch so I must run
& resume my pen
afterwards – "now for it"
again as Lady Delacour
used always to say. well
I'm powerfully refreshed
after having had curried
chops and no end of
pancakes – Rosie and
I walked very leisurᵉly
upstairs to-gether she
carrying in her hand
a missal "St C" had
lent her she suddenly
stopped and began laughing
I wondered what at? –
upon which she declared
that the missal had
grown ever so much
thinner because it's master
had too – it made us both
laugh very much – I so
wished you and "St C" had
both seen the lovely sunset
here last night it really
was <u>quite</u> beautiful with the

reflection in the water – –
and the new moon rising
made the whole scene quite
heavenly – but now good bye
with best love to yourself and
Mr Ruskin ever your
   Very loving
      Joan Agnew – –
Every one here envys me very
much – but express the deepest
regret at my leaving so soon
it <u>is</u> nice to think of seeing
you again in a few days– –

263a J. to John Ruskin, Hawnby 2 May 1871

              Hawnby
              2$^{\underline{nd}}$ May

My preciousest old Pa!
   Me seepy me sink –
me welly ofin seepy
peys, & hungy pung
di Pa! –
Arfies out drawing –
but tums out & in
to see oo's wee Poos-moos –
me welly welly do-o-d
<u>so</u> <u>welly</u> <u>do-o-d</u> di Pa –
me sink me not know
<u>fot</u> to do! –
ere's a cowy now
bo-o-ing oh di Pa
suts an <u>ot</u> of cowy
wows on se wode –
fiten poo wee Poos –
– moos me sink! –
do sink di Pa at sey
gobbie oo's wee Poosie
moosie uppy pup? –
se cowy-wows skeam
boooo! – booo! –
<u>bo-o-o-o-o-o-o-o-o-o-o-o!</u> –
but di Pa <u>me</u> say
<u>pur-r-r-r-r-r-r-r-r!</u> –

miew-ew-w-ew-ew-ew-ew!-
evy oo's own wee
        Pussie
Purr!   <u>Wee 'Amie</u>
            <u>May</u>!

263b. Arthur Severn to Margaret Ruskin, Rivaux, 12 May 1871

       Friday May 12$^{\underline{th}}$
       ¹Rivaux
            Yorkshire.

My dear Mrs Ruskin,
   Joan has told me, that
I may write a line to you
whenever I like! and that
you will like it! So I
sit down now with great
pleasure to do so –
   We have been here
about 3 days and like
the place very much
much more than the
place we have just left
[Hawnby] – The trees there
were <u>not</u> pretty, and
all the best views rather
far away, but here all
the trees are good in
form, and most of them
quite beautiful! the cottage
we are living in also
quite charming for a
picture, well there of
course the Abbey is
a great feature of beauty
so all together we
are quite pleased
with this place, I
have been in so
~~lov~~ ^ ᵐᵃⁿʸ beautiful places
that am not at all
easy to please –
   The weather has
not been quite favourable

Letter 263a. 2/6, 1871. Cream envelope written in Ruskin's hand: 'Arthur & Joanna from / Yorkshire. 1871'. A letter to Margaret Ruskin, dated 27 April, identifies the location as 'Tennant Arms / Hawnby / Helmsley, <u>Yorkshire</u>'.

Letter 263b. The paper is embossed with intertwined 'A J S'.
   1. The paper is printed with an intertwined 'A J S' in blue ink.

to my our of door work.
Yesterday was so very
cold, and to day the
sun was quite burning,
but I have managed
to sit out both days
making drawings of
the Abbey, I could
not help noticing to day
how well built most
of the cottages close
to the Abbey seemed
to be, and how beautifu^lly
the stones were
cut, and then I found
some carved with
ornaments! and then
wondered that so much
of the beautiful Abbey
is left.

Mr Kingsley told me
that a man near here
has built all his stone
walls round his Fields
with stones which once
formed the pillars of the
Abbey. Mr Kingsley
stayed For two nights
at Hemsley and
walked over each
day to see us here
I think him most
agreeable only it is
so tiring to hold a
long conversation with
him! how lucky it
^is that he always has
plenty to say, in Fact,
I have seldom known
a man so ready
to make conversation.

I was often so
amused at Joan
trying to make him
hear, she seems to
be a great favourite
with him, as she is
with every one who
knows here – when
we left Hawnby
Joan walked on

First down the Hill
leaving me to make
some final arrangements
with our Mrs Watson,
but somewhat to my
surprise, M^rs W seemed
only to think of looking
out of the window at
Joan's departing figure,
then I saw her take
up a corner of her
apron! Then she said
"ah! Sir I seem to like
her very much"! she
is the nicest of all the
ladies we have ever
 had here", "I am
sure you have chosen
very well sir!
I was very pleased,
because she did not
know about our having
been so lately married
and so had no reason
beyond the truth for
saying pretty things.

Joan has been every-
-thing that is good
thoughtful and charming
and, I feel, that
with such a partner
to go through life
with! Something
is really very like
success in life, will
be my lot.

I hope you will
not be bored by,
So long a letter, I
had no idea of
writing so much
 and as it is
half past ten, and
Joan has gone to
bed, I must
say good bye
 Hoping you are quite
well, and that you
will give my love to
Mr Ruskin, I am
(Joan says I may

264. [early 1873?], J. to John Ruskin

Ive just been thinking what a horrid bore it will be soon when I'm not able to write to you for a time! – tho' you may be sure the instant I am allowed to hold a pencil I shall use it for your benefit – me <u>pecious</u> – "[M<u>rs</u> Gawp]" comes on Monday or Tuesday, & I've everything in the greatest order, & perfect readiness – & I'm very well – & very happy – & you're to love me <u>all</u> <u>the</u> <u>same</u> di Pa – & me'll be so do-o-d! – & I'll never let <u>it</u> come near you, or bore you, or do anything – unless it can amuse, or help, or comfort my best Cuzzie-Pa – but I think DV – when its able to say "<u>di</u> <u>Pa</u>" quite prettily it <u>may</u> be allowed to give you a kiss? –

 I'm greatly amused with the remarks some people make on the subject – they all conclude as a matter of course that I would prefer a boy to a girl! – & that without doubt we'd call him "John Ruskin" & can't understand why I insist that I never would call a child of mine by that name unless <u>you</u> specially wished it – & I don't know that I would even then – To me, & Arfie too, there is, & never will be, but one John Ruskin – & I don't think (in the sense in which I look upon it) that any other human being is quite worthy of it – & we both feel it would be the utmost presumption in us ever to give a child of ours that name – besides unless he was an angel I could'nt tolerate the creature if he ever by action, or word, or look, did anything the least unworthy of it – so I can't run the risk! – Ever your most devoted & grateful child Jo-<u>an</u>

265. 20 February 1881, J. to John Ruskin

Friday evening –

Herne Hill
S.E.

My darling di Pa –
 That <u>owl</u> is <u>the</u> most horrible nuissance – it's hooting now with all it's might in our garden! – & goes on for hours – Arthur says <u>he</u> thinks it's quite a reason for renewing our lease – & that he'd love seeing the dear thing – the entire Herne Hillers are up in arms – & can't sleep – & yet

Letter 264. 1/1, 1872. Probably a fragment as there is no salutation. Pencil notations: '1872?'. The contents suggest this was written shortly before the birth of her first child.

Letter 265. 1/1, 1881. Paper: blue letterhead. Envelope addressed to 'Professor Ruskin / Brantwood / Coniston / Lancashire'. Postmarked: 'AMBLESIDE / A / 21FE / 81' (back). Pencil notations: '20 Feb 81'.

dare'nt molest it – owing
to the new "Bird
preservation act"! – & I
think the brute knows
this – I feel very
strongly at this minute
when I'm sitting alone
& the owl almost I
believe perched on the
window railing! – the
night I arrived it
began at once – & has
never missed a night
or morning since! – it's
a proud possession
no doubt – & very
soft to stroke – but –
"a norrible noise" as
Laurie would say –
when it first came –
Lily at once said (in
the night) to M^{rs} [Harvey]
that's an owl – to
which as she assures
me she said "no,
it ain't a howl child!
it's a noise on the
railway" – oh! if it
only would stop! –
no louder & louder! –

It was by the
merest chance yesterday
when we went ~~yesterday~~
to the "Fine Art Society"
that Arthur mentioned
to Ward who happened
to be there – that
your "Bible of Amiens"
was delayed owing to
the missing parcels – upon
which he said, he had
had them for more
than a month – & that
directly he got them
he wrote to you telling
minutely what the things
were, & asking what
to do with them – whether

to send them on, or
what? – & never got
an answer. Arthur inferred
to Ward that he must be
a fool – & said to
me afterwards he
certainly was one! – & ought
after not hearing from you
to have written again
with every detail in writing
an inch high ! ! –
Your lovely letter to
Lily to-day about the
silk-worms[2] is quite a
possession – & has filled
her with interest – I
took her yesterday to
see Miss Rudkin[3] – with
all the things on en
suite – & she was charmed
& on our own little
book – & our sale of
pickies. Arfie ordered me
a bonnet – cloak – & a
dress to be made! –
we lunched with the
Tylors who were all
very gushing & tea'd with
with the Hope's who
have a lovely corner
house facing the Park
in St Cumberland Street –
& between these places I
took Lily & her doll
to see Aunt Margaret
who became quite young
with the interest or
pleasure in short at
each place everybody
was filled with admiration
& Lily beamed – tho'
never with an atom of
self consciousness – only
real joy that the things
themselves which she thinks
lovely should be admired
by every body else – & the
pretty way she told at

2[1]

1. The letter spans three sheets of paper, Severn has numbered each in the top right corner.
2. See Ruskin's letter of 17 February 1881 [173].
3. See 28. 559 and 610.

each place "they were her
di Pa's birthday present –
& <u>wasn't</u> it kind &c! – Arthur
brimming over with pride
in his daughter – & so was
I – Aunt M. declared Lily
to be exactly <u>my</u> image
at that age – & that she could
never have believed two
children could ever be <u>so</u>
<u>exactly</u> alike – as Lily & me! –
It is <u>so</u> sweet of you
to let me stay a little
& settle things here – it
<u>is</u> really important – &
I came just at a climax,
& will be able very
soon to put everything
straight – & in good
working order – & then
I can come off much
more settled & comfy
in every way – Please
don't trouble to write
darling – it's enough to
know from Mat that
all is well with you my Darling –
always your
    devoted
        <u>wee Doanie</u>
Begun Friday night
    finished Saturday

266. 3 March 1885, J. to John Ruskin

H. Hill. 3rd March 1885.

Darling pecious di Pa –
   What a lovely
sweet little letter you've
sent me – it's <u>such</u>
a cosy thing to keep
in my pocket – & to
have safe there to
feast on all day
tomorrow – besides the

3.

little taste of it's
sweetness that I've
had a day in advance! –
But <u>if</u> there's a
<u>pise</u> – fot sall it
be? – me sant
be pised if there
is'n't' any – so
oo mut mind at –
   my chief gratitude
is all I owe to my
di Pa of infinite
blessing – & happiness,
in the past & present –
& my chief hope <u>is</u>,
that he may be
long spared to me
in the future – that
is if his Doanie
wont get too old
or uggy for him,
if she's spared to
hive, & love him too.
as she <u>did</u>, & <u>does</u>,
& <u>will</u>, always! –
   His very own most
grateful – & loving
wee Ma D-o-anie

267. 23 June 1886, J. to John Ruskin

Herne Hill.
   S. E.   23rd June –
Darling Pwesh[1]
   Your mother's age in
1844 was 63. this is
accurate supposing her, as
I always understood to be
90 when she died – and
38 in the year you were
born 1819 – for I always
understood she was 37 when
she was married – & that
you were born the year after
when she was 38 –
I am <u>so</u> <u>very</u> <u>sorry</u>
not to have answered

Letter 266. 1/2, 1885.

Letter 267. 1/4, 1886. Pencil notations: '1886?'.
   1. This seems to be baby-talk on her part, possibly meaning 'precious'.

this most important
question – but it quite
escaped my mind – &
I remember at the time
thinking oo would know,
better than the Doanie! –

Arthur has answered
the Rawlinson letter very
carefully, about portrait
of Dean of Durham –
recommending a Mr Walker,
& also himself ! – & evidently
hopes the latter will be
chosen! . – . He is anxious
to hear farther about
your "O-ur Father's" mezzo
-tint work? –

I hope the Chapman
nuisance – won't bother you
too much. I am very
sorry about it – &
feel so grieved he should
blunder himself into such
a position – What a very
nice, manly, sweet letter
that is from Frank Dillon –
How I wish you could
have seen the excitement
& joy, when I told the
children to-day, there was
a letter from Di Pa to
each of them – we all
sat round the table – &
I doled each one out –
but the excitement – &
trembling of fingers – excited
my offer to open the
envelo-pes carefully with
a silver knife – Clennie
actually said. to them "you'll
think these letters very
precious some day"! –
  Herne Hill.
   S. E.
then the shrieks of "Oh!" –
when they pulled out
those lovely Lambie photos –
& "Baby Himself" (how that
address delights us!) –

gave me the Kitty one –
with rather a grudge
I fancy! – your precious
letters – & the lovely
Lambies are indeed
treasures – & we are
all so grateful for the
great pleasure you've given
such a shower of good
things! & what a
too kind Di Pa –
I shall be able to fill
Jean Ingelow's soul
with joy tonight about
coming – Poor Jowett! –
he's quite the sensitive
plant! – I return the
cutting! – Lily will write
to you herself – ever
your most grateful devoted
How about wee Doanie
that watch?

268. 22 January 1887, J. to John Ruskin

     22nd Jany
     1887
  Herne Hill.
   S. E.

Darling Di Pa
 It was very
sweet of you to throw
a maternal eye over
Baby & have him, &
Violet seen to by D^r
Parsons – he has very
kindly written to assure
me that there is little,
if anything the matter –
so I am grateful to you,
  & comforted –
I took our Boys back
to school last night,
with a pang of course –
& they were very
tearful at parting – but
I had a nice time with
Connie, Harry – & their

Letter 268. 1/13, 1887.

chicks – the latter such
sweet loves in bed.
& gave me some cuddly
kisses – I came back
from London Bridge to the
Denmark Hill Station, & it
was fine, & I walked
up to the old house to
meet Arthur & walk home
with him – as the little
gate clicked – & I walked
up the drive in the
darkness – with the old
cedar just the same –
such a rush of old
memories came to me! –
& I thought of the
beginning when my
"week's visit" came to the
end, & I said so regretfully
"Oh Mrs Ruskin it is time
now for me to go
back to my Uncle's" –
& she flung down her
netting, & said rather
sharply "Are you unhappy
child"? – Oh dear no,
said I – I never was
happier! –" 'Then, said
she, never let me hear
you again say you wish
to go – if you are happy
here, & call me "Aunt" – <u>not</u>
Mrs Ruskin" – & so my
week rolled itself out into
seven years! – & I only left
her to go home on visits to
Scotland – but she always
expressed so much longing
to have me back – I
never had the heart
to stay away much over
a month at a time – &

my mother felt Auntie
was so old! it was cruel
not to give her all
the pleasure I could, ^while
she lived – then, as you
know, when my seven
years were up – & I married ^in April 1871
it was a year of both
happiness, & great trouble –
for first came my
rheumatic fever in Scotland –
then <u>your</u> illness at
Matlock! – & Auntie's
death in ^ beginning of December –
why I should drift into
these details – but I thought
perhaps some of the
dates might help you
in reflecting over that
time – At last A.D.O.W.
who gave you the original
"Optic Marvel" has got me
another for you, which I
send to-day, the address is on
the bottom of the box –
where you can get extra
subjects if you want them.
the "subjects" are in the
little drawer at bottom
of box – made of [tin. &c.,]
to fix on, before blowing
through the tube –
now I <u>must</u> stop
ever your devoted
   Doanie
The May Queen dress
must be made to
enlarge in length – &
width to suit the
sizes of varying Queens! –
Arthur has gone off to the
Fine Art So<u>c</u>ty about your
  Father's portrait –

269. 5 March 1887, J. to John Ruskin

You may
like to see second
page of this[1]   March 5th –
                              Saty
     Herne Hill.
        S. E.

Darling Di Pa
    You can't think
<u>how</u> delighted Lockie
will be with the
portraits of [Jowetts][2] –
they are v<u>e</u>ry like – &
I've sent them instantly
with your sweet message –
tho' I <u>devoutly</u> hope you
never will again want
<u>any</u> nursing you Pwesh –
& I believe Hospital nurses
are not allowed to <u>go
out</u> ever – I asked her
once if she could
come to us if we
wanted her – & she then
said no –
    Its' joyous to hear
oo say oos a bit bitty
bettie. of course oo will
be all the betty-er for
being dood for nufin –
I wish you could
have seen us last
night dancing in the
Hut in the garden –
each playing the
children's organ in turn –
Baby was our only
gentleman – Lily – Bow
Violet – myself – Hannah
Susan & [Winn] – & Baby
who was <u>quite</u> the
partner – & asked us

all to dance with him
with quite an air –
& I found was called
"Col. Herbert!" – "can I
have the pleasure of
this dance" from him
had to be borne with
gravity – for had we
laughed! he'd have felt
it keenly – & sometimes
he said "Beg your pardon
miss! will you dance this
dance with me? – don't
be in a hurry miss" –
was generally said to
Bow whom it almost
convulsed – quite the
birthday ball! – Lily laid
out a table with light
refreshments at a time
of a cherry! or bit
of nougat, – & the
maids had an apple[3]
& orange in leaving –
    Poor K. G. is
       coming this afternoon
to tea –
    Tomorrow I lunch
at the Tylors – (who
now live at Kensington)
& dine at the Simons –
ever your most devoted
    wee Doanie

[4]<u>Fot</u> a tuk up Doanie she'll
be if her Venetian photo
is put in the Præterita! –
the original negative got
broken – but Barrand has
just made an excellent
copy from one of the
ovey photos I had – &
when I get them, I'll
send them on to oo –

Letter 269. 2/13, 1887. Envelope: Ink notation: 'D. Doanie on Col^l Herbert 1887' (on envelope in Ruskin's hand), addressed (typed) to '*MISS ALEXANDER, / Banca Fenzi, / Piazza della Signoria, / Florence, / ITALY.*' Pencil notations: '1887';
1. This postscript is in Ruskin's hand.
2. This could be 'Touttes'.
3. As Ruskin sometimes did, Joan here emphasises the word and a sense of playfulness by putting a long, curling tail on the 'e'.
4. The rest of this letter is in Ruskin's hand.

would you prefer them, (not that I shall ever be pointed if oo don't want anything for such & too – honoured purpose for me) to the portrait Arfie did, if any illustration of the little Scotch cousin <u>is</u> wanted! –[5]

270. 11 June 1887, J. to John Ruskin

11th June
1887 –

Herne Hill.
S.E.

My <u>Di Pa</u>
My conscience is clear of ~~ever~~ having ^{ever} done anything to lose <u>that</u> name, or <u>you</u>! –
We are <u>absolutely innocent</u> of any Paragraph in the papers – & have neither seen it, nor know to what you allude?
It has always been our chief care, if ever you have been ill, to guard the fact, to the uttermost from being made public.[1]
The only outside friend I saw during this last visit to Brantwood was Mr Fleming – and conditionally, that it was <u>in confidence</u> – I answered his questions – & told him then, a month ago, of my anxiety about you – and anything <u>he</u> may have said about my

gossiping about you is untrue –
Since our return here, Arthur, who has been asked dozens of times about you, at his Institute, & elsewhere, has invariably answered, that "you are <u>very well</u>. & at home" –
as ever, your faithful
<u>Jo-an</u>

271. 14 June 1887, J. to John Ruskin

Herne Hill.
S.E.   14th June –
1887.

My Di Pa,
Indeed I have suffered too cruelly to wish ever to speak more of the past – & wish it could be, as though it never had been –
I hope you are having the same lovely weather we have here now – the wisteria is a purple blaze all over the front, & back of the house – & the smell of it delicious – & I lie on a nice little basket sofa in the garden – – & make chains for Violet & Baby of the daisies they pick – & find this <u>goo-d</u> work! –
The Bishop of Carlisle came our on Saturday with Ellen[1] – they sat with me nearly 2 hours –

---

5. Ruskin's comments end here. The other half of the page has been torn away; it was clearly torn after composition for the letters on this side bleed across to nothing.

Letter 270. 7/13, 1887.
1. The following paragraph has been struck through with two long lines of ink, from 'The only' to 'is untrue'.

Letter 271. 8/13, 1887. Envelope: addressed to 'Professor Ruskin / Brantwood / Coniston / Lancashire'. Postmarked: 'LONDON.S.E. / 3 / AP14 / 87' (front); 'AMBLESIDE / A / AP15 / 87' (back).
1. Ellen Goodwin.

he begged his special
love to be given to you –
and Ellen seems very
happy about her intended
wedding on the 29th to the
Vicar of Kirkby Lonsdale
    ever your Jo-anie

272a. 30 June 1887, J. to John Ruskin

30th June
1887.

Herne Hill.
S.E.

Darling Di Pa
    I am indeed grateful
to you for sending to
Dr Parsons – it will be
new life to him – &
it gives me such pleasure
too –
    I am quite hopeful
now – that all will
soon be well – Life
to me, is now a new
thing! – and I'm going
tonight to the R.G. conversazione,
& mean to enjoy it! –
    We went yesterday to
Ellen Goodwin's wedding,
& from the Bishop down,
there were tenderest enquiries
& much love sent to you.
    I think of going
next Monday for a
few days to Brighton,
to see my Aunt Susan,
who was lately very
ill – & also to get
rid of my cough if I
can – & leave it behind! –
soon I hope for
brighter news of you –
ever your grateful
    loving Do-anie

272b Lockie to Ruskin

S. George's Hospital
    June 29.th
My dear Mr Ruskin –
Many thanks for
your sweet little
note. If I ever
wrote any thing
pretty or wise it
must have been
your influence
produced it!
It always seems to
me that neither
my tongue or pen
can ever give any
idea of the love
& gratitude that
is in every breath –
for oo & all the dear
Brantwood friends
Hoping you are feeling
well and strong &
enjoying this lovely summer
weather
    From your
        devoted & very busy
            Lockie.

273. 2 July 1887, J. to John Ruskin

28 *Herne Hill.*
    S.E.   2nd July –
        1887.
My Di Pa,
    I do hope you feel
better now –
    I enclose you a
cheque that was never
used – you need have
no concern about money
matters – yo-ur books are
selling splendidly – & always
will – and as I proved
to you the keeping up
of Brantwood, with all its'
wages &c does'nt amount

Letter 272a. 10/13, 1887. Enclosure: a letter from Lockie, the Severns' former governess.

Letter 273. 11/13, 1887. Enclosures: an uncancelled cheque from Ruskin to Joan for £10.
    1. This could be 'Hove'.

to half your income –
   Be assured of this –
You know you can trust
to my telling you the
truth – I say this
hearing you were disturbed
(<u>quite</u> unn<u>ec</u>essarily) about money
matters – I am <u>much</u>
<u>better</u>. and ever your own
    loving <u>Jo-anie</u>
a letter tomorrow Sunday
had better be sent here
to Herne Hill –
& on Monday, or Tuesday to
   16 Norton Road
     [Horne]¹
      West Brighton
       Sussex
where I shall probably be
till Thursday, & then
return here–

274. 9 September 1887, J. to John Ruskin

       Friday 9th S'eptr
          1887
     Rose Castle,
      Carlisle

My Di Pa,
   I am distressed by the
tone of your letter to-day –
   After nursing you into
life as I did lately, and
after the gratitude you
expressed – I <u>did</u> think
you would try and spare
me such a letter as your's
of to-day – but it can't
be helped I suppose! –
In much sorrow of heart,
   Believe me
     Your loving <u>Joan</u>

275. [Autumn] 1887, J. to John Ruskin (fragment)

<u>have</u> expressed your gratitude,
to me for having done
so – & I have <u>never</u>
Di Pa set myself up
as "directress general" of
your affairs – & cannot
think what you mean
I have done what
you asked me – nothing
more – & it is deep
pain to me you should
think I have done
otherwise – God only knows
what a heart breaking ^{sorrow}
it is ever to have you ill.
for it is then only such
cruel misunderstandings come.
may it please Heaven
for your sake, & mine –
that such cannot happen
again –
   If I took no notice
of what you say – it
might seem as if I
disregarded it –

276. Easter Sunday 1888, J. to John Ruskin

      Easter Sunday
        1888
     HERNE HILL.
      S.E.
Darling Di Pa
   You have hardly
been out of my thoughts
all day –
at a quarter to ten
Lily & I started – weather
lovely – down past the
Queen's Hotel – with all
it's old past memories of
Auntie, & Rose,¹ fresh in

Letter 274. 12/13, 1887. Paper: half a leaf of paper.

Letter 275. 13/13, 1887. Paper: half a leaf of paper, forming the final two pages of a letter.

Letter 276. 4/45, 1888. Pencil notations: '88'
   1. Rose had stayed at the Queen's Hotel, Norwood 1874, and Margaret Ruskin had done so a decade earlier (*Later*, p. 269).

my mind! – then we
drove on to Shirley &
got there in excellent time
about a quarter to eleven –
I went straight to
Auntie's grave – all beautifully
in order, & well kept; –
I had time to pray for
forgiveness in the past
if I had ever done you
wrong – & for help and
guidance in the future
(& by the grave of your
Father & Mother) to do
what is indeed best for
their son – & nothing that
can every dishonour their
memory, or your fame –
The church was beautifully
decorated – with <u>such</u> <u>flowers</u>! –
the singing was grand –
& the whole service
impressive about the
Resurrection – & it went
straighter to my heart
in thinking of dear
Auntie there – & all she
had been to me – oh
how I wish she had
never left us! –
I took the Sacrament –
& then went straight
back to kneel & have
a parting prayer on that
most sacred bit of ground –
I feel assured neither Auntie,
nor Rose, will meet me,
but as feeling I <u>have</u>
done the best, as far
as a human mortal can,
praying each day for
spiritual guidance to do
what is right for you–
& that you may be
blesssed & kept free from
all evil here – and my

heart found sweet rest –
as I trust your's <u>will</u> in
living a life, such as will
bring <u>them</u> peace – & <u>you</u>,
divine help & blessing –
ever your devoted grateful
      Jo-an

277. 28 May 1888, J. to John Ruskin

      Monday
        28th May
    Brantwood, 1888
     Coniston. Lancashire.

Darling Di Pa
  Just starting for
the joy of seeing
oo! –
  Your most devoted
  Ownie Do-anie

<u>purr</u>[1]

278. 21 June 1888, J. to John Ruskin

    Brantwood,
     Coniston. Lancashire.

Beloved Di Pa –
  Such a sweetie
letter of the 19th – &
it came so quickly too –
here on the evening of
the next day! –
quicker really than
from Sandgate! –
  Fot a tebby – & fite<u>ful</u>
sing – my Di Pa – &
[Nyache] being marched
off by gendarmes to the
Police Office! – & their
crime being – to have
been seen drawing! –
Arfie sent me a thrilling
account! –
  But has it really
come to this! that
my Di Pa find a Railway

Letter 277. 6/45, 1888. Half a sheet of letterhead.
  1. This entire letter is written in a relatively large hand culminating in the '<u>purr</u>', which measures 11cm wide by 4.5 cm high.

Letter 278. 11/45, 1888. Pencil notations: 'JR abroad 1888', '21 June'

carriage a comfy place! –
what next I wonder! –
& what is the world
coming to – if that's
what it's about already
wif oo – my pecious Di Pa! –
It must indeed too
be a new sensation
if oo thinks, & thinks,
with no result –
but it's good really
& restful to be in
such a state for a
while –
weather here lovely
& I'm just going
off to tea at
Susie's with Emmie W.[1]
ever your own devoted
   wee Do-anie

21st June 1888
    Thursday

279. 26 June 1888, J. to John Ruskin

Brantwood,
   Coniston. Lancashire.

Beloved one –
  I wonder what
the [move] will be –
or if Arfie has aired
his Hampshire plan.
  I wish you'd open
your blessed heart
& tell me just why
you dread coming
here so? – There
is yet so much possibility
of happiness for us
both – God will I
trust be gracious, &
keep you well – &
then there is nothing
to fear. It is only
these most cruel
illnesses that have
ever distorted your
mind, & caused me the

misery I've had! –
but you have been
so dear & precious to
me lately that the
wounds are healed – no
scar even left – & I
want to dispel all
the unhappy associations
you have with the
place – & I don't
think you'd put me
to the pain of
asking Albert Fleming
here! – for quite ^{apart}
from you – he has
said & done things ^{which}
have caused me deep
suffering – & has been
quite untruthful in his
statements – & I'm sure
there is much of real
happiness & enjoyment
possible without the
discord that a renewal
of those "classes", ^{might}
bring between us –
Indeed not from any
jealousy of mine – It
is better to speak out –
It made me furious
I grant you, those girls
not understanding your
great goo-dness – laughing
at it! – & behaving ^{insolently}
to me – I can't bear
to speak of it at all
for the pain it may
give both of us –
but almost a year
has gone! – & the gossip
  has died out! –
and we can [start]
happily afresh – &
you would have the
dearest welcome from
everyone when you
come! – & the respect
& devotion you deserve –

  1. Emmie Warren.

Letter 279. 14/45, 1888. Pencil notations: '88'

& your Do-anie would
make your happiness
& comfort in all
ways a study –
you can see, & talk
as much as you like
to any children – in
the ordinary way – as
other people would – not
in an <u>unusual</u> way! –
you will forgive me
darling if I have
said a word to pain
you – but I don't
want you to "<u>dread</u>"
coming to your own
beautiful Brantwood –
& I thought it might
be on account of what
I have said – tho'
I can't bear saying a
word about it all now –
only I feared some of
these thoughts might be
the cause – ever you
own devoted & ever grateful
Wee Do-anie

280. 30th June 1888, J. to John Ruskin

30th June
Brantwood, 1888.
Coniston. Lancashire.

My beloved Di Pa –
  I'm afraid I oughtn't
to let you do such
finks about plans ! – &
yet I have been anxious
you should do what is
best – & if possible what
you <u>like</u>, my precious one –
but if you have no di<u>stinct</u>
w<u>ishes</u>, then I feel perhaps
for a time at least your
own home would be best –
& I could be here to
be all the comfort in
my power – & if after

a little time you wanted
to go somewhere else we
could – as regards the
money question – with
care, you need have no
anxieties – & in Octr or
Nov^r, you will have ^{made}
considerable profits from
your new edition of Modern
Painters – that you will
have a good Balance to
go anywhere you like
next Spring, or Summer
Lily rides round to
Coniston alone every
afternoon on Norway
(who goes beautifully
now) to the Post Office
to get your letters &
Arfie's – that always come
in by the 3–35 train,
& she gets back with
them in time for me
if necessary to add
anything before Tom
goes with the bag at
4–30.
  I have told Arfie
to ask you about the ice
lasting longer, when frozen
in a colder temperature –
can aliatico be a yellow
wine that fizzes? – or
is it dark? – I ask
because two days ago, in
putting the cellar tidy
I observed a bottle with
the wine oozing out – &
"<u>chablis</u>" was written on a
paper on the shelf – I
thought I'd better drink [this]
leaking bottle – so today Alice
suggested it's being drawn –
& it fi<u>zz</u>ed to my joy – &
was qu<u>ite</u> <u>delicious</u> & [u<u>yumy</u>] –
& a yellow colour – Mary
says it was sent as a present
to you – & thinks it's "aliatico" –
It's more like mosell, than anything

Letter 280. 17/45, 1888.

I know. tho' nicer – there are about
9 bottles of it – & I'll have
them re-sealed in case
they take to leaking too! –
Froude writes <u>if</u> Lord
Ducie came home, the
yacht would be at <u>Cowes</u>
for Arfie to join it there,
perhaps for a trip to the
coast of Ireland ^ ᴷᵉʳʳʸ – Do
you ever fancy a little
being <u>on</u> the sea? – if
so – & this vacancy came,
perhaps that would be
a good thing for you to
join Froude instead of Arfie.
Froude tells me to write
to Yacht Monarch R. g.S'.
    Earl of Ducie
       Floëo
          Norway –

& I can find no such place
as "Floeo" in the map in Norway
                   or elsewhere
He's to telegraph if they
come back –
I can't bear that my
pecious Di Pa should
be saddened with his thoughts.
soon I trust they will vanish –
I'm sure to me you have
said all & more, of
sweet comfort – & tenderness –
your own most grateful
            We<u>e Do-anie</u>
I'll just go on writing to
Abbeville till farther orders.
& if you leave, direct that
any letters may be forwarded
after you –

APPENDICES

❖

Appendix A: An Idiolectical Glossary   274
Appendix B: Baby-talk Names   281
Appendix C: Chronology   283
Appendix D: Names Identified in this Edition   287

APPENDIX A
An Idiolectical Glossary

❖

This glossary lists baby-talk terms used in the letters transcribed. For contextual reference, I have included a date of use, usually the first occurrence in this edition. Note that this is not necessarily the first occurrence of the word within the idiolect; for example, 'ownie' for 'own' was in use by November 1869, yet first occurrence in this volume is in November 1884. Words from the 'Tottish' and 'Mexican' idiolects are identified as such in square brackets.

a fa o. all full of [Tottish](13/07/69)
a stickin. all sticking [Tottish] (29/07/69)
aboot. about [Tottish](13/07/69)
Acad. Tickwickets. Academy tickets (20/04/86)
aden. again (12/11/69)
ae. all [Tottish] (29/07/69)
agen. again (28/11/72)
alltogevy. altogether (28/11/72)
amie. Joan (Agnew) Severn; originally short for 'lamb', also French for 'friend' and short for 'mamie' (02/07/67)
an. and (13/07/69)
andthoughtoowoodnt. and thought you would not (02/06/86)
angy. angry (12/11/69)
anowy. another (30/01/73)
anxy. anxious (?/01/85) [205]
applepappies. apple-blossoms (27/05/86)
are all gote. have all become [Tottish] (13/07/69)
Arfie-fied. affected by and filled with Arthur(s) (12/07/73)
at. that (13/07/69)
aughty. naughty (12/11/69)
auld. old [Tottish] (13/07/69)
awa. away [Tottish] (13/07/69)
awainy. rainy (??/07/71) [91]

babes. babies; small children (07/01/73)
back. black (13/07/69)
badd. very bad (29/04/71)
bairnies. children [Tottish] (13/07/69)
beadies. beads (17–18/08/69)
beauty. beautiful (03/06/69)
bedgowny. nightgown (27/0769)

bedient. obedient (19/03/73)
bein. being (29/07/69)
bery. very (15/09/68)
betause. because (03/09/68)
bettering. getting better (09/05/86)
bettie. better (17–18/08/69)
betty. better (24/11/69)
beezy bo. [possibly 'bed'] (12/07/82)
biged. begged (27/0769)
biggit. biggest (13/07/69)
birdie. bird [Tottish] (30/10/72)
bit. little [Tottish] (29/07/69)
bit-bit-bit bit-bitin. making small corrections (27/05/86)
bite. bright (29/04/71)
bof. both (04/06/82)
bofes. both of yours (?/01/73) [120]
bonnie. pretty [Tottish] (13/07/69)
boo. blue; beautiful (27/0769)
boobells. bluebells (26/04/71)
booful. beautifully (20/04/86)
bookies. books (30/01/73)
bookies. brooks (13/07/69)
booty. beautiful (24/11/72)
bothy wothy. bother (06/11/72)
botted. blotched or blotted (29/07/69)
bout. about (07/01/73)
bovyed. bothered (13/01/78)
bovyin. bothering (?/85) [205]
bovying. bothering (27/10/87)
bown. brown [here for the surname 'Brown'] (14/08/69)
bown. blown (24/11/69)
bow-wow. whine or complain (like 'mew' but less common) (24/04/71)
brigs. bridges [Tottish] (29/07/69)

buful. beautiful (12/02/73)
bushes. brushes (12/11/69)
busywifinefs. business + wifely: efficiently housewifely (?/05/82) [177]

ca. call [Tottish] (13/07/69)
cabbies. cabinets (24/11/72)
ca'd. called [Tottish] (13/07/69)
canna. cannot [Tottish] (29/07/69)
Cat-licks. Catholics (16/08/69)
-ceive. receive (28/11/72)
cept. except (?/01/73) [120]
Charlie. man [Tottish] (30/10/72)
charywars. char [fish] (02/06/86)
chicks. children (26/02/83)
choppy pop. chopping wood (12/02/78)
cited. excited (?/06/71) [90]
cock. clock (?/02/76) [156]
comfy. comfort (27/07/69)
comfy. comfortable (27/12/72)
comfying. comforting (22/06/71)
comfy-wumfy. comfort (?/11/73) [149a]
conomical. economical (6/07/82)
coo-el. cruel (19/03/73)
cooky. cookery, cooking (30/01/73)
coolious. [courteous?] (09/11/87)
coont. count [Tottish] (29/07/69)
cos. because (16/08/69)
coss. cross (03/09/68)
coss and woss. cross (27/05/86)
Cote-Rotie. Cote du Rhone wine (19/08/82)
Crawleywawlian. means of communication with Crawley (?/11/73)
curly wirlies. curls (29/07/69)
cutit. cut (27/01/73)
cutited. cut (13/09/71)
cuttitet. cut (n.d.) [169]

darky. dark (12/07/82)
darlin. darling (?/10?/72?) [101]
dat. that (13/07/69)
dauties. daughters (07/12/72)
daw. draw (07/07/69)
dawing. drawig (13/08/69)
dearie. dear (17/08/69)
dectly. directly, meaning immediately (12/09/71)
dedfu. dreadfully (24/11/72)
dedful. dreadful (17/08/67)

dedfully. dreadfully (15/12/69)
dee. dear (07/07/69)
dee-est. dearest (27/07/69)
dee wee. dear little (09/07/69)
den. then (07/07/69)
det. has, derived from 'gets' (07/07/69)
det. get (15/09/68)
di. dear (13/07/69)
dicious. delicious, meaning delightful, wonderful or charming (17/08/69)
diffy. different (10/03/73)
dinin. dining (31/10/72)
dinna. do not [Tottish] (13/07/69)
dinnie. dinner (?/71) [95]
dinnywin. dinner (28/11/72)
dir. dear (07/01/73)
dis. this (30/01/73)
dismy. dismal (21/02/86)
dited. delighted (27/12/72)
diteful. delightful (31/07/78)
ditefullest. most delightful (14/03/73)
dites. delights (07/02/73)
do. go (12/11/69)
doggy poggy. dog (03/06/86)
doin'. going (?/10/72) [101]
doin. doing (16/08/69)
don. down (24/11/72)
dood. good (27/07/69)
doon. down [Tottish] (29/07/69)
doons. downs [Tottish] (29/07/69)
dooties. duties (28/11/82)
dop. drop (07/07/69)
dos'nt. does not (27/07/69)
do't. do it [Tottish] (29/07/69)
dot. got (17/08/69)
dot. have, or received, derived from 'have got' (30/09/69)
dovsy. dozen (27/05/86)
dressy wess. dress (21/02/86)
drinkie. drinking (19/08/82)
dump. jump (07/07/69)
dumpy-dump. plump woman (13/05/82)
dune. done [Tottish] (30/10/72)
dust. just (07/07/69)

''eally. really (15/12/69)
ecococomical. economical (21/02/86)
eccocomical. economical (02/06/86)
ecties. lectures (28/11/72)
ed. red (17/08/69)

eddies. ladies [Tottish] (13/07/69)
een. own [Tottish] (30/10/72)
eerie. weary (13/07/69)
eevies. leaves (14/08/69)
eggie pegs. legs (6/07/82)
em. them (??/02/76) [156]
emselves. themselves (16/08/69)
en. then (13/07/69)
Eng-ish. English (12/11/69)
envy. envelope (06/11/72)
eopold. Leopold, Prince (25/11/72)
'Eptember. September (15/09/68)
esson. lesson (30/01/73)
est. superlative, as in 'deewee est' (27/05/86)
etched. wretched (30/10/72)
etties. letters (7/07/69)
ey. they (13/07/69)
evie. ever (24/11/72)
evy. ever (07/07/69)
evything. everything (??/01/73) [120]
evy. every (??/03/69) [158]
evybody. everybody (16/08/69)

facie. face (29/07/69)
fawcktories. factories [Tottish] (13/07/69)
feeves. thieves (03/06/73)
Fench. French (03/09/68)
Fessy. Professor (8/11/73?)
Fessyship. Professorship (??/??/85) [205]
fetchment dinnywin. refreshingdinner (??/02/76) [156]
fevys. feathers (10/03/73)
Fifle. Thistle [pet name for Joan's unborn child] (14/03/73)
fightened. frightened (13/07/69)
fightin. fighting (17/08/69)
fillos — sofical. philosophical (?/06/71) [90]
fingys. fingers (14/08/69)
firt. flirt [usually verb] (17/08/69)
firtie. flirt (usually noun) (17/08/69)
firtin. flirting (13/07/69)
fiswis. fish (04/06/82)
fitened. frightened (03/09/68)
fitie. thistle [esp. 'iti Fitie', a pet-name for Joan] (17/08/67)
fizziditt. sizzled ([??78]) [169]
fost. frost (30/01/73)
fot. what (24/03/69)

fowies. flowers (14/08/69)
Fowl-rotie. roast fowl (19/08/82)
fringy. hair cut with a fringe [bangs] (15/11/84)
fsimpacy. sympathy (?/82) [182]
fu o. full of [Tottish] (13/07/69)
fwesh and pwesh. refresh and precious; effect of Joan's letters (?/01/85) [20]

gae. go [Tottish] (30/10/72)
gaein. going [Tottish] (13/07/69)
gavy. gravy (13/09/71)
geen. green [sometimes Tottish] (13/07/69)
gen. again (28/11/72)
gettin. getting (16/08/69)
gey. grey [poss. + gay] (17/08/69)
gin. given [Tottish] (30/10/72)
girlies. girls (27/07/69)
goin. going (15/12/69)
gowden. golden [Tottish] (13/07/69)
growly wowly. in a bad mood (?/05/82) [179]

hae. have [Tottish] (13/07/69)
happie. happy (07/01/73)
hav. have (12/10/84)
he. [third person for himself] I (?/10/72) [102]
hearin. hearing (20/03/73)
hersell. herself [Tottish] (29/07/69)
him. [third person for himself] I (?/10/72) [102]
hoose. house [Tottish] (30/10/72)
housie. house (07/01/73)
hug and snuggywug. comfortable and warm (31/12/84)

ibbon. ribbon (17/08/69)
'ice. nice (15/09/68)
ike. like (15/09/68)
ilie-willie. lily [here Ilie-willie for Lily Armstrong] (??/10/72) [101]
illie. lily [here 'Illie' for Joan's daughter] (19/03/73)
illywistible. irresistible (12/10/84)
im. him (11/11/87)
ime. rhyme (17/08/69)
incerely. sincerely (12/11/69)
inks. thinks (12/11/69)
intil't. into it [Tottish] (13/07/69)

intyecting. interesting (13/05/82)
ired. tired (13/07/69)
istyday. yesterday (29/04/71)
ite. write (03/09/68)
ite. right (27/07/69)
ither. other [Tottish] (29/07/69)
itie. little (02/07/67)
itinged. affected by lightening (02/06/86)
ive. alive (27/0769)
'ixty-ate. sixty-eight (15/09/68)
'ixty-ine. sixty-nine (10/11/69)

Jeans and Joanies. Scottish girls [Tottish] (13/07/69)
jes. just [Tottish] (29/07/69)
jeust. just [Tottish] (13/07/69)
'joy. enjoy (?/09/72) [100]
joyed. enjoyed (?/09/72) [100]

keem. scream [Tottish] (06/04/73)
ken. know [Tottish] (13/07/69)
Kev. clever person [noun] (25/02/86)
kevy. clever [??] [169]
kevvy. clever (??/03/76) [158]
Kiss-me-Alices. girls (08/10/82)
Kistial palaces. crystal palaces (08/10/82)
Kisty Mins. Christy Minstrels (12/01/73)
ky. cry (31/10/72)

lassies. girls [Tottish] (30/10/72)
leavin. leaving (16/08/69)
letty. letter (?/03/72) [158]
lins. lines [Tottish] (for dancing) (30/10/72)
loup. leap [Tottish] (30/10/72)
loveletters. letters from girls, young women, and close female friends (12/02/78)
lovingest. most loving (13/04/71)
lunchy punchy. lunch (??/71) [95]
luve. love [Tottish] (13/07/69)

mair. more [Tottish] (13/07/69)
me. I am (28/11/72)
memby. remember (16/08/69)
mes. I am (?/02/76) [156]
me's. I have (28/11/72)
mew. whine or complain, also means baby-talk (10/05/71)
minie. mine (04/03/85)
minnies. minerals (24/11/72)

misby. miserable (24/04/69)
misby dismy. miserable and dismal (21/02/86)
misbinefs. miserable business (31/10/72)
misby-thisby-misby. very miserable (25/04/71)
missiby. miserable + missing (6/11/72)
missin. missing (27/05/86)
mo. more (27/07/69)
monin. morning (28/11/72)
moos. [second half of poos moos, possibly mouse] (03/09/68)
moos. amuse (25/05/86) [217]
moofsie. music (27/05/86)
moosie. [second half of poos moosie, possibly mouse] (14/08/69); music (04/06/82)
mornin. morning (30/01/73)
mouthie. mouth (??/03/73) [132]
mowy. tomorrow (28/11/72) [derived from 'to mowy' (29/07/69)]
munchy-unchy-punchy. lunch (?/71) [95]
munny. money (31/12/84)
mut. much (15/09/68)
mut. must (27/07/69)
munt-nt. must not (30/10/72)

nae. no [Tottish] (13/07/69)
naethin'. nothing [Tottish] (29/07/69)
naughty. misbehaving (03/09/68)
neebody. nobody [Tottish] (30/10/72)
nevy. never (16/08/69)
nevvy. never (?/01/73) [120]
ni-mits-tsika-waka-thasolta. I love you [Mexican] (??/ 02/76) [155]
no. not [Tottish] (29/07/69)
no. don't [as in 'no be angy'] (28/01/73)
no. know (26/04/71)
noo. now [Tottish] (13/07/69)
nothin. nothing (16/08/69)
notie. note (01/01/68)
nufin. nothing (04/01/82)

o'. of [Tottish](13/07/69)
'obbin. robin (08/03/73)
'oetry. poetry (15/09/68)
ometimes. sometimes (15/09/68)
ong. long (29/07/69)
onie. only (13/07/69)
'ony. only (15/09/68)
oo. you (03/09/68)

ood. good (15/09/68)
ood. you would (27/05/86)
ook ite. look right (27/0769)
ool. you will (31/12/84)
oom. room (??/82) [182]
oos. your (13/07/69)
oos. use (26/04/71)
oos. you are (07/01/73)
oosed. used to (15/09/68)
oosed. used (13/07/69)
oot. out [Tottish] (29/07/69)
oot. ghost [Tottish] (30/10/72)
ose. those (16/08/69)
ot. hot (10/07/69)
ot. of it [Tottish] (30/10/72)
'ote. wrote (15/09/68)
othie. other (12/11/69)
'ought. thought (15/09/68)
'oup. soup (15/09/68)
ove. love (30/10/69)
ovies. others (?/01/73) [120]
oviest. most loving (?/71) [95]
oving. loving (30/10.69)
ovy. over (??/09/72) [100]
ovy. other (06/12/72)
owange. orange (14/08/69)
ower. over [Tottish] (30/10/72)
ownie. own (12/11/69)
owre. over [Tottish] (13/07/69)

paces. places [Tottish] (13/07/69)
pagues and pagues. plagues (27/05/86)
paidlin. paddling [Tottish] (13/07/69)
pairties. parties [Tottish] (13/07/69)
paps. perhaps (07/07/69)
pashing. splashing (13/07/69)
pay. play (13/07/69)
peached. preached (16/08/69)
peachweechies. peach blossoms (27/05/86)
pease. peas (25/07/67)
pease. please (03/09/68)
peased. pleased (12/11/69)
pected. expected (03/06/1886)
pects. expect (27/02/86)
pectin. expecting (15/12/69)
peepies. people (13/07/69)
peeps. children [and people generally?] (?/05/82) [179]
peeps. looks (7/02/73)

Pefsor. professor (?/10/72) [101]
pell. spell (24/11/72)
pesent. present (?/01/73) [120]
pensy. pencil (14/08/69)
Pessy. Professor (24/12/72)
Pesssy-wessorial. baby-talk means of communication (?/11/73)
Pfessy. Professor (31/10/72)
physiciany. healing like a doctor (26/10/87)
piccolocomical. small (piccolo) + economical +comical (04/06/82)
pickarly-tickarly. particularly (30/10/72)
picties. pictures (24/11/72)
pince. prince (25/11/72)
pickular. particular (08/10/82)
pinie-winie. pinafore (31/07/78)
pinky winky. pink (26/06/82)
pise. surprise and/or prize [meaning present] (04/03/85)
pised. surprised (?/03/876) [158]
pît. pretty (27/0769)
pittier. more pretty (12/11/69)
pitty. pretty (03/09/68),
pittyest. prettiest (17/07/82)
poking. provoking (25/04/71)
pointed. disappointed (31/01/73)
poo. poor (03/09/68)
pooest. poorest (24/11/69)
popy. proper or appropriate (16/08/69)
pose. suppose (13/07/69)
possiby. possibly (27/04/71)
Pot land. Italy (land of pottage) [Tottish] (13/07/69)
potted. spotted (29/07/69)
poud. proud (04/03/85)
pro-fess. be a professor (16/08/69)
Professorial. communication as a lecturer (?/11/73) [149]
puîr. poor [Tottish] (30/10/72)
pussy-mussied. affected by Joan Severn (10/03/73)
puzzywuzzied. puzzled (10/03/73)
puzzywuzzled. puzzled (12/01/73)
pwimwoses. primroses (27/05/86)

ribb. rib (13/09/71)
rollditit. rolled it (??) [169]
rolled it-it. rolled it (??) [169]
roomie. room (17/08/69)

Rosie-Posiefied. affected by Rose La Touche (?/10/72) [102]
ruinnin. running [Tottish] (29/07/69)

sae. so [Tottish] (13/07/69)
save. shaved (10/03/73)
sal. shall (17–18/08/69)
sall. shall (28/11/72)
Sat-day. Saturday (25/04/71)
sayin. saying (30/10/72)
sciptions. description (08/10/82)
Scôtch. Scottish (17/06/86)
se. she (16/08/69)
seep. sleep (27/0769)
seepy. sleepy (04/10/68)
seety. sheet (27/0769)
selfie. self (17–18/08/69)
sept. except (16/08/69)
ses. she is (24/11/72)
sey. they (16/09/68)
shellywells. shells (08/03/73)
sic. such [Tottish] (13/07/69)
sîgned. signed (02/07/78)
sings. things (28/11/72)
sipped. slipped (30/01/73)
sippies. slippers (30/01/73)
sippy. slippery (30/01/73)
sist. exist (13/07/69)
sist. insist (13/07/69)
sistence. exist + distance (13/07/69)
so. such [Tottish] (29/07/69)
socked. shocked (24/11/72)
sometin. something (27/0769)
sood. should (15/03/73)
sow. show (27/07/69)
sowy. sorry (12/11/69)
spelt. spelled (15/09/68)
spoted. spotted (29/07/69)
squealin. squealing (17–18/08/69)
squincy deary. fortuitous coincidence (??/87) [230]
stainin. straining (17/08/69)
standin. standing (24/11/72)
stomachically. experiencing stomach ache (08/07/82)
straity wait. straight away (28/05/86)
sud. should (13/07/69)
sud'nt. should not (30/10/69)
sulk and wulk. very sulky [+ weak?] (27/05/86)

Sun-day. Sunday (25/04/71)
sut. such (17–18/08/69)
sweeties sweet. very sweet (30/01/73)
sy. shy (28/11/72)

tafe. safe (03/09/68)
tan. can (12/11/69)
tank. thank (26/10/87)
tan't. cant' (17–18/08/69)
tant. can't (9–10/07/6)
tatues. statues (27/0769)
teep. keep (03/09/68)
tee-wee. tea (19/05/84)
tebby. terribly (13/07/69)
tebby. terrible (01/01/78)
teep. keep (03/09/68)
tellin. telling (06/11/72)
tetches. sketches (07/01/73)
tetenamiquilitzli. kiss. [Mexican] (??/02/76) [155]
tick. stick (03/09/68)
tick. sick (13/07/69)
tied. tried (30/01/73)
till. to [Tottish] (13/07/69)
tings. thing (16/08/69)
tink. think (03/09/68)
tinys. small children (07/01/73)
tipsywipsy. drunk (19/08/82)
tome. come (07/07/69)
to mowy. tomorrow (29/07/69)
tonish. astonish (6/07/82)
tood. could (17–18/08/69)
tood'nt. could not (?/03/76) [158]
tooktitit. took (25/11/72)
tolld. told (03/06/86)
toon. town [Tottish] (29/07/69)
toopid. stupid (20/06/86)
top. stop (?/10/72) [101]
Totland. Scotland + tot for children (13/07/69)
tots. children [Tottish](13/07/69)
tould'nt. could not (30/01/73)
tout. trout (17–18/08/69)
toutywouts. trout (02/06/86)
trooties. trout [Tottish] (13/07/69)
tubby wubby. trouble (12/10/84)
Tuck up. vain, stuck up woman [pet-name for Rose La Touche] (??/06/71) [90]
tuffed. stuffed (08/03/73)

Tukup. vain, stuck up woman [pet-name for Rose La Touche] (30/10/69)
tuk ups. vain, stuck up woman in general (31/01/73)
tuck up. stuck up, vain (08/10/82)
tum. come (??/71) [95]
tumfy. comfort (16/08/69)
tumin. coming (??/73) [156]
tummer. summer (27/0769)
tummy. to comfort (13/07/69)
twa. to (27/0769)
twa. two [Tottish] (29/07/69)
twit. quickly, derived from quick (?/06/71) [90]
twite. quite (16/08/69)
twolips. tulips (27/05/86)
Two's day. Tuesday (25/04/71)

ubby. lovely (19/08/82)
uggie. ugly (09/10/87)
ugy. ugly (13/07/69)
un. and [Tottish] (29/07/69)
un. run (17–1808/69)
uncomfy. uncomfortable (04/06/82)
'under twenty'. women aged under twenty (17/05/86)
'uvin'. loving (18/08/69)

ve. we (12/10/84)
vee'd. we had (12/10/84)
velly. very (27/05/71)
vely. very (?/82) [182]
vetly. very (25/10/72)
vewy. very (27/07/69)
Vi-mits-tsibāwakā-thosolta. [term of endearment?] [Mexican] (??/02/76) [157]
voted. devoted (02/06/71)
votedest. most devoted (??/05/71) [79]

wain. rain (27/05/86)
waisty. waist (27/0769)
wam. woman / mother (07/06/86)
war-ry. worry + very (18/10/87)

wed. red (09/11/87)
wee. little (02/07/67)
weelly. really (12/10/84)
welly. very (02/06/71)
wes. we are (04/06/82)
wha. which [Tottish] (13/07/69)
wha. who (from which) [Tottish] (30/10/72)
what at?. what's that, meaning to flirt (13/07/69)
whilk. which [Tottish] (13/07/69)
wi. with (13/07/69)
wi. little (29/07/69)
Wibbston Pipps. Ribston Pippins, a type of apple (09/11/87)
wick. wicked 06/10/82)
wick. man, from 'wicked' (07/06/86)
wicked. flirtatious (12/02/78)
windys. windows (27/0769)
winna. will not [Tottish] (30/10/72)
wis. wish (15/12/69)
wisky-punch. whiskey punch (12/01/73)
wite. write (10/08/78)
wobbin. robin (not baby-talk, but mimicking his own speech impediment) (??/03/73) [132]
wody dendys. rhododendrons (07/06/86)
worrited. worried (28/11/72)
wotedit. wrote (27/05/86)
wust. worst (30/10/72)

y. the (12/02/73)
ye. you [Tottish] (13/07/69)

Zips and Tips. girls; Zip is short for 'Zipporah', initially derived from Boticelli's 'Zipporah', the term came to be associated with Rose La Touche and, when pluralised, with girls in general, while 'Tips' may be derived from Tiny White. (08/10/82)

APPENDIX B
Baby-Talk Names

❖

This chronological listing of pet-names is in three parts. First, Ruskin's names for Joan. Second, Ruskin's names for himself. Third, terms used specifically to describe the baby-talk letters. Because there are so many slight variations in such names, these lists are indicative rather than complete, offering a sense of how the personae evolved.

1. Names for Joan Severn

pussy	08/05/65	Pussky Mussky	24/06/71
Cuzzie	28/09/66	Pussie, pussie dearie	?/06/71 [90]
wee 'amie	02/07/67	Pussky	?/06/71 [91]
wee piggie	02/07/67	Pufs	12/09/71
wee Doanie	22/07/67	Pussky (Puss of the Sky)	(?/71) [95]
Wee Pussy	23/07/67	Darlingest of Dauties	07/12/72
wee Fernie	15/08/67	Di wee Dautie	07/12/72
itie Fitie	17–19/08/67	his amie	?/09/72 [100]
pussie	17–19/08/67	Joanie Ponie	?/?/72 [101]
Doanie	01/01/68	Pufsie-Amie	01/11/72
wee Pussie	05/06/68	Poos	24/11/72
pussie moos	03/09/68	Mamie di	08/03/73
wee ittie Fittie	26/09/68	my di-di di Joanie	25/03/73
'amie	21/10/68	my Di, wee, Di-wee wee-Di didima	
dee mamie	07/07/69		30/03/73
di pussie	13/07/69	Di wiema	??/02/76 [155]
di mammy	27/07/69	Pusswoosky.	02/07/78
wi mamie	29/07/69	Doanikie-Poanikie	26/02/79
wee pussiky	13/08/69	Doaneyky <u>Pone</u>yky	26/02/79
pussiky	13/08/69	Pugwagsie	02/07/82
Dee-est of wee (piggie)-pussies	17–18/08/69	Sweetest di wee mawa	06/10/82
dee wee piggie	17–18/08/69	Dee-est wee Ma wa	08/10/84
piggie dearie	17–18/08/69	Doanie Poanie	19/11/84
Di ma	15/12/69	Doanie minie	04/03/85
Pufskins	19/04/71	My deedy dïest-Weedy — I mean,	
Pufsie Amie Agnew	19/04/71	Flowery-weest-Doanie Poanie	03/03/86
Poos. moos	24/04/71	My poo woo di ma	02/06/86
Poos-moos	24/04/71	My poor Doanie	29/06/87
Poosmoos	24/04/71	my poo — poo — sweet Pussie	18/10/87

2. Names for John Ruskin

Cuzzie	28/09/66	Donie the Martyr	30/01/73
cuzzie-piggie.	02/07/67	oos wee Robin-Donie	31/01/73
St C.	25/07/67	Fisy's di Gan Pa	11/02/73
Mr Pencil	13/08/68	oos own ovin-ovin-ovin Donie	12/02/73
poo tuzzie	03/09/68	oos <u>own</u> old poo Donie	17/02/73
itie Pig	09/09/68	your lovingest Old Fessy	08/11/73
wee Donnie	07/07/69	oos poopoopoomisby Dipa.	01/01/78
Donie	07/07/69	oos poo old wicked Di Pa	12/02/78
di pa	13/07/69	oos own poo itie Donie	04/07/78
dood itie Donnie	27/07/69	Donikie-Ponikie	26/02/79
wee donie	29/07/69	Donkey Ponky	26/02/79
poo, wee, itie, piggie, Donie	17–18/08/69	Gobble Johnnie	04/06/82
St Donie.	?/?/72 [101]	os poo old wick of a Di Pa	06/10/82
Pefsor	?/?/72 [101]	oos own wee <u>real</u> Fessy Donie	
so velly, bad boy	01/11/72	Ponnie	09/03/83
missiby Donie	06/11/72	oos <u>little</u> Donie	12/10/84
Pessy	24/11/72	Duncie Donie	04/03/85
oos pessy	25/11/72	oos own good itie boy Donie	02/06/86
oos dood donie	05/12/72	oos poo little squeaking mousie	
oos bofes ovin Donie	?/01/73 [120]	Donie	11/11/87
oos poo — poo poo fitened wee Donie	28/01/73	you poo itie dee wee Pa	25/11/87

3. Names for baby-talk

play-letters	18/09/68	wee etties	?/09/72 [100]
nonsense	02/07/69	moosin etties	12/02/73
<u>our</u> baby letters	13/07/69	Mexican	?/02/76 [155]
nonsense letters	13/07/69	baby talk	??/02/76 [156]
pussy talk,	16/08/69	baby tawk	12/10/84
our wee English Eng-ish	12/11/69	booty [mew] etties	18/10/87
baby misbinefs	31/10/72	mewys letters	28/10/87

APPENDIX C
Chronology

❖

This chronology lists some events which affect the narrative of Ruskin's correspondence with Joan. It is permeated with references to Rose because she so haunts these letters.

1781	Birth of Margaret Cock (later Cox), 2 September
1785	Birth of John James Ruskin, 10 May
1817	John James and Margaret marry, 2 February
1819	Birth of John Ruskin, 8 February, to Margaret and John James Ruskin at the family home, 54 Hunter Street, Brunswick Square, London
	His Nurse, Ann[e] Strachan had joined the household in 1814
1822	First holiday in Scotland, visiting relatives in Perth
1823	Ruskin family move to 26 Herne Hill
	Painted by James Northcote, RA
	First tour of the South and Southwest of England
1824	First tour of the Lakes (then on to Scotland)
1825	First Continental journey 11 May to 13 June
1828	Mary Richardson (fourteen-year-old Scottish cousin) joins the Ruskin's household until 1848
1829	First tutor hired: John Rowbotham (mathematics)
1830	First publication: 'On Skiddaw and Derwent Water' in *The Spiritual Times: A Monthly Magazine*
	Extended tour North and into the Lakes
1831	Compiles a dictionary of minerals
1832	Given Samuel Rogers's *Italy*, illustrated by Turner
1833	Meets Adèle Domecq
1836	Matriculates as a gentleman-commoner at Christ Church, Oxford
1837	Moves to Oxford with his mother; his father joins them at weekends
	Poetry of Architecture in *Architectural Magazine* as 'Kata Phusin' (according to nature)
1839	Wins Newdigate Prize for English verse at Oxford
1840	Becomes a Fellow of the Geological Society
	Rejected by Adèle Domecq
	Meets Turner
	Euphemia Chalmers Gray (Effie) visits the Ruskins, age twelve
	King of the Golden River written for Effie
1842	Ruskin family move from Herne Hill to Denmark Hill (lease to 1878), keeping the former house at Herne Hill
1843	*Modern Painters I* (four volumes to 1860)
1845	First Continental tour without his parents
1846	Birth of Joan Agnew, 4 March
1847	Meets Sir Walter and Lady Pauline Trevelyan
	Visits Folkestone to relax, mid-November to mid-December
1848	Birth of Rose La Touche, 3 January

	Marriage to Euphemia Chalmers Gray, 10 April
1849	*The Seven Lamps of Architecture*
1851	*The Stones of Venice I* (three volumes to 1853)
	Pre-Rapahelitism
1854	Annulment of marriage to Euphemia Chalmers Gray Ruskin
1857	*The Elements of Drawing*
1858	'Unconversion' in Turin
	Meets Rose La Touche
1859	First visit to Winnington Hall, March
	Final Continental tour with his parents
	The Elements of Perspective
1860	Rose becomes a dominant force in Ruskin's life
	Unto this Last in *Cornhill Magazine* (published as a book in 1862)
1861	Visits the La Touche family at Harristown, August to September
	Receives Rose's 'Star-letter' from 'Posie-Rosie-Posie' to 'St Crumpet' on 26 December
1862	Rose taken away by her parents, April
1863	Rose falls ill, 12 October
1864	Death of John James Ruskin, 3 March
	Joan Agnew joins the Ruskin household, 19 April
	Repeatedly visits Winnington
1865	*Sesame and Lilies* (lectures given in 1864)
	Ethics of the Dust (although dated 1866)
	Sees Rose again on 10 December and she visits on 21 December
1866	Rose's 18th birthday celebrated at Denmark Hill, 3 January
	Rose asks him to wait three years for her on 2 February; Ruskin had proposed on or previous to that day
	Joan travels to Ireland with the La Touches to visit them at Harristown, mid-April
	Continental tour with Joan, Constance Hilliard and Trevelyans, 24 April to 12 July
	Lady Trevelyan dies at Neuchâtel, 13 May
	While staying at Hotel Giessbach, meets Marie Schmidlin, 5 June
1867	Joan Agnew engaged to Percy La Touche but Ruskin is barred from contact with Rose
	Tour of the North, especially the Lake District, 28 June to 25 August
1868	Joan's engagement to Percy broken off
	Final stay at Winnington
	Visits France with C. E. Norton, October
1869	*Queen of the Air*
	Continental tour 27 April to 31 August
	Elected first Slade Professor of Fine Art at Oxford, August
1870	Gives inaugural Slade Lecture at Oxford, 8 February
	Continental tour with Joan, as well as Mary and Constance Hilliard, 27 April to July 29
1871	*Fors Clavigera* begins
	George Allen becomes his agent, then publisher (up to then Smith, Elder & Co.)
	Ann Strachan dies, 30 March
	Marriage of Joan Agnew to Arthur Severn, 20 April

	Arrives in Matlock for a holiday on 26 June, suffers a breakdown in July and is cared for by the Severns, Acland and Mrs Cowper-Temple.
	Purchases Brantwood in the Lake District, which he first visits on 11 September
	Death of Margaret Ruskin, 5 December
1872	Continental tour with Severns, Albert Goodwin, Mary Hilliard and Constance Hilliard, 1 April to 27 July; returns to see Rose (then staying with George MacDonald). Ruskin and Rose meet for the first time in six years; he again suggests the possibility of marriage and she becomes hysterical
	September and October at Waterhead Hotel Coniston to arrange Brantwood matters
	Lectures at Oxford, November and December
1873	Lily Severn born to Joan and Arthur (d. 1920)
	Settles at Brantwood, where he spends as much time as possible
	Begins lectures on birds in March, later published at *Love's Meinie*; Robin lecture 15 March
	Severns, with young Lily, arrive at Brantwood on 2 July
	October and November, gives next set of Oxford lectures, later published as *Val d'Orno: Ten Lectures on Tuscan Art*
1874	Arthur Severn Jr. born to Joan and Arthur (d. 1949)
	Ferry Hinksey road-digging experiment with undergraduates of Oxford
	Continental tour 30 March to 23 October
	Spends much of May copying Botticelli's *Zipporah*
	Receives letters from Rose, September and October
	Sees Rose on return from Continent
	Divides time between Oxford, where lecturing and London, where Rose was staying
	Rose stayed at the Queen's Hotel, Norwood, returning to Ireland on 15 December
	Ruskin goes to Brantwood for turn of New Year
1875	Agnew Severn born to Joan and Arthur (d. 1929)
	At Brantwood into January, then Dales tour
	Death of Rose La Touche, 25 May
	Ruskin receives telegram, informing him of Rose's death on 28 May
	October and December, extended visits to Cowley (Hilliards) and Broadlands (Cowper-Temples). At the latter he attends séances; feels Rose's presence.
1876	Continental tour 24 August to 16 June of the following year; spent mostly at Venice from where he became obsessed with Carpaccio's *Dream of St Ursula* (see Burd's *Christmas Letters* for his important correspondence to Joan during this period)
1877	Returns from Continent, 16 June
	Attacks Whistler in *Fors* 79
1878	Breakdown, February to April
	Whistler libel suit called for 25 November
	Resigns Slade Professorship
1879	Mental state remains to be precarious, but he continues work
	Spends most of the year at Brantwood
1880	Violet Severn born to Joan and Arthur (d. 1940)
	Spends half the year at Brantwood, leaving only to give public lectures
	France 21 August to 5 November

1881	All but one week spent at Brantwood
	Breakdown on 20 February
1882	Herbert Severn born to Joan and Arthur (d. 1935)
	Severe breakdown in March, improving by April
	Continental tour 10 August to 2 December
	Meets Francesca Alexander in Florence, 8 October
1883	Resumes Slade Professorship
	Gives *The Art of England* lectures
	Kate Greenaway spends a month at Brantwood, 10 April to 7 May
1884	Much of the year until September at Brantwood with Joan and her children, Ruskin teetering on edge of breakdown
	First two weeks of October at Euston Hotel, London, then begins erratic lectures at Oxford
1885	Mostly spent at Brantwood with Joan
	Resigns Slade Professorship, 22 March
	Major breakdown in July, diary ceases on 20 July until sparse entries on 18 October
	Praeterita begins ('completed' in 1889)
1886	Mostly spent at Brantwood
	Major argument with Joan, 8 April; such severe arguments recur throughout the next year, tempered by periods of penitence
1887	In May, Ruskin becomes violent towards Joan; the Severns leave Brantwood for London
	Moves to Folkestone in October, then to Sandgate
1888	Final Continental tour, retracing old haunts from 10 June to early December when Joan summoned to Paris to collect him; home at his Herne Hill Nursery by 8 December
1889	Withdraws from society, spending his remaining years in Joan's care at Brantwood
1900	Dies of influenza, 20 January

APPENDIX D
Names Identified in the Edition

❖

Entries are arranged by Ruskin's preferred usage; the date at the end of each entry is the first occurrence in this edition.

φίλη: 'Filē', Ruskin's pet name for Georgiana Mount-Temple. At this time (1868) her surname was Cowper. She later became Cowper-Temple then Mount-Temple. Ruskin also referred to her as 'grannie' (see [156]). Note that I use the Greek letters which match Ruskin's choice of letters, rather than Φιλη, as it is generally transcribed by Ruskin scholars.

Ac, Dr: Henry Acland (1815–1900), a life-long friend whom Ruskin met while both were students at Oxford. Van Akin Burd, ed., *The Ruskin Family Letters: The Correspondence of John James Ruskin, his Wife, and their Son, John 1801–1843*, 2 vols (New York: Cornell UP, 1973), 1, 478–80.

Adèle: Adèle Domecq, daughter of John James Ruskin's partner in the sherry business and Ruskin's first intense infatuation. (68)

Aggie Marks: the context implies she was the daughter of artist H. Stacy Marks. (86)

Agnew: Joan and Arthur's son (1875–1929). (82)

Allen: George Allen, Ruskin's publisher. (87)

Alice: Alice Liddell of *Wonderland* fame, daughter of Henry George Liddell, Dean of Christ Church, and Lorina (Ina) Liddell. (71)

Angie: Sarah Angelina Acland (b. 1849), daughter of Henry Acland, generally referred to as 'Angie' (*Later*, p. 195). (72)

Ann: Anne Strachan, Ruskin's old nurse. (64)

Arbuthnot: Arbuthnot Simson, who married Joan's sister Kate in 1867.

Arfie: Arthur Severn, who married Joan on 20 April 1871. (71)

Arthur/Baby: Arthur Severn, Jr, oldest son of Joan and Arthur (1874–1949).

Baker, Mr.: George Baker, Mayor of Birmingham who 'look[ed] after the Guild's affairs' (*Later*, pp. 357 and 437). (82)

Baron: Frederick, Grand-Duke of Hesse-Darmstadt (*Later*, p. 305). (73)

Barrington, Mrs.: Perhaps the Mrs. Russell Barrington mentioned on 37.715. (73)

Baxter: Peter Baxter, Ruskin's valet. (86)

Bell, Miss: Margaret Alexis Bell, head of Winnington Hall, Chester, a school for girls. Ruskin first visited the school in February 1859 and by April of that year he had lent the school £500; 'by 1867 he had paid out £1,130 15s 4d to Miss Bell' (Batchelor, pp. 200–01). (67)

Bells: a Coniston family. (86)

Bibsy: Lily Severn (1873–1920) (73); note that the other Severn children also are referred to as 'Bibsy' and 'Baby' when they are the youngest.

Bowles: Dr. Bowles was Ruskin's doctor in Folkestone. (87)

Bramble: Ruskin's dog. (86)

Brayshay: 20 March 1873 for a letter fragment from a 'Brayshay' who lived in Malham;

this may be the same person. This may also be the W. H. Brayshay identified as the source of Record Office information on the derivation of 'Ruskin' (see 35.lx n), also identified as W. Hutton Brayshay of Wharfedale, Yorkshire, a letter to whom (of 18 November 1865) is reproduced in 36.498. (67)

Brett: John Brett, A.R.A., Ruskin owned works by him. (39.86) (82)
Bridge, Mr: Rev. S. F. Bridge of St. Matthew's, Camberwell (36.141n). (67)
Burgefs: Arthur Burgess, engraver and artist employed by Ruskin (39.92). (81)
Buth: Arbuthnot Simson, see above. (68)
Carlyle, Mr: Thomas Carlyle, author whom Ruskin referred to as 'papa.' (65)
['company'] = Frederic Shields and Mrs. Alexander Scott (Burd, *Winnington*, p. 545n).
Chesneau: Ernest Chesneau, a French writer on English art who had corresponded with Ruskin since 1867 (*Later*, p. 490). (84)
'Clennie' McClelland: governess to the Severn children. She was from the Isle of Skye (*Later*, p. 485). (86)
Collie Woll: William Gershom Collingwood, one of Ruskin's secretaries. (82)
Collie: W. G. Collingwood. (86)
Connie: Constance Hilliard, who had joined the Trevelyans (a maternal aunt and uncle), Ruskin, and Joan Agnew for a Continental journey earlier that year. (66)
Connie: Constance Oldham, a pupil at Winnington who was also a neighbour at Denmark Hill and one of Ruskin's goddaughters. (66)
Conrad: Conrad Dressler, a sculptor (*Later*, p. 489). (84)
Coward: Mr. Coward seems to have been employed at Brantwood (38.331). (82)
Crawley: Frederick Crawley, Ruskin's valet. (65)
Dane Anne: Jane Anne Wilkinson. (86)
David: David Fudge, the coachman at Denmark Hill. (65)
David: David Downes, the head gardener at Denmark Hill and, later, Brantwood. (66)
Detmar: Detmar Blow was a young companion of Ruskin's on this Continental journey, see 35.xxx–xxi. (88)
Diddie: Sara Anderson, one of Ruskin's secretaries. (78)
Dilke, C.: Sir Charles Dilke; see 36.332 and 37.588 for letters from Ruskin to Lady Dilke, see also 20.7n.
Dixon, Mr.: Presumably the cork cutter Thomas Dixon of Sunderland, the recipient of Ruskin's 1867 letters published as *Time and Tide, By Wear and Tyne*. (73)
Doadie: Dorothy Livesey (Burd, *Winnington*, p. 671n). (72)
Dora: Dorothy Livesey, later Lees, a student at Winnington. She was also given the pet name 'Doadie' by the cousins. (68)
Downes: David Downes, gardener.
Dudley, The: The Dudley Gallery (14.264).
Edith: Edith Liddell, Ruskin's favourite of the Liddell sisters ('the three Graces'). They were daughters of Henry George Liddell, Dean of Christ Church, and Lorina (Ina) Liddell. (71)
Edwin: Edwin Trice, a local Folkestone man who cared for Ruskin when he was isolated at Folkestone/Sandgate and in a particularly poor mental and physical state (*Later*, pp. 543–45). (87)
Ettie: Ethel Hilliard, sister of Connie. (68)
Fall, Mifs: Eliza Fall, identified by Burd as 'the younger sister of Ruskin's boyhood friend at Herne Hill, Richard Whiteman Fall' (Burd, *Winnington*, p. 554n.). (65)
Faunthorpe: Rev. John Faunthorpe, Principal of Whitelands College, Chelsea. (86)
Fisy: 'thistle', pet-name for the unborn Lily Seven. (73)

Fleming, Albert: Fleming was a lawyer and Companion of the Guild of St. George. With Marion Twelves, Fleming founded the Langdale Linen Industry and revived the local traditions of spinning and weaving and was editor of *Hortus Inclusus*; see Jennie Brunton, 'The late nineteenth-century revival of the Langdale linen industry' in *A History of Linen in the North West*, ed. by Elizabeth Roberts (Lancaster: Centre for North West Regional Studies, 1998), pp. 93–118. Joan did not trust him, see her letter of 26 June 1888 [279].
Fletcher, Mr.: Lazarus Fletcher, Keeper of the British Museum Mineral Collection from 1880 and a friend of Ruskin's (see 26.1 and 34.199). (82)
Fletcher, Mrs.: may have been the wife of Lazarus Fletcher, as above. (64)
Froude: James Anthony Froude (1818–94), a historian and biographer whose correspondence with Ruskin began in 1862; Viljoen, *The Froude–Ruskin Friendship, as Represented through Letters* (New York: Pageant, 1966). (68)
Gladstones: The family of Rt. Hon. William Ewart Gladstone. Ruskin occasionally visited them and became a good friend to his daughter Mary, although he was sometimes very critical of her father.
Gladys: daughter of William Holman Hunt. (82)
Goodwin: Albert Goodwin (1845–1932) was a 'widely-travelled oil and watercolour artist' commissioned by Ruskin (Bradley and Ousby, p. 261n). (71)
Gooseberry: a Brantwood cook or kitchen maid. (86)
Grannie: probably Mrs. Cowper-Temple. (86)
Green-away, Miss: Kate Greenaway, artist and good friend of Ruskin. (82)
Gull: Sir William Gull, doctor in practice with James Oldham, father of Connie Oldham (*Later*, p. 433).
Herbert: Herbert Severn, Joan and Arthur's youngest (1882–1935).
H, Sir: Sir Herbert: '[t]he lecture on Sir Herbert Edwardes had been given at Coniston on December 22, 1883, and was afterwards expanded into *A Knight's Faith* (Vol. XXXI.). The proposed lectures in London [...] were not delivered.' (37.499). (84)
Harrison, Old Mrs: Possibly Dorothy (Wordsworth) Harrison, a neighbour at Brantwood (*Later*, p. 482).
Harry Acland: Ruskin's godson, son of Henry Acland (*Early*, p. 206). (71)
Haxton: Hilton transcribes this as 'Hackstoun' (*Later*, p. 429). W. Hackstoun was an artist and copyist for Ruskin (39.253). (81)
Herdson: Dawson Herdson was Ruskin's gardener (27.lxxii). (82)
Hill, Miss: Octavia Hill, aspiring artist, social reformer and a founder of the National Trust.
Hilliard, Mrs: Mrs [J. C.] Hilliard is Mary (1827–82), the sister of Pauline Trevelyan and wife of Rev. J. C. Hilliard of Cowley Rectory (Bradley and Ousby, 195n). (67)
Holman Hunt: William Holman Hunt, Pre-Raphaelite artist. (82)
Holyoake: George Jacob Holyoake, mentioned in 17.415, where he is identified in a note as a 'reformer' and 'agitator in popular causes'. (78)
Howell: Charles Augustus Howell, Ruskin's secretary. (68)
Huish: Marcus Huish, a director of the Fine Art Society. See Hilton for a discussion of Huish and the Turner Catalogue (*Later*, pp. 373–75). (78)
Ina: Lorina Liddell, wife of Henry George Liddell, Dean of Christ Church. (71)
Ingelow, Miss: Jean Ingelow, a popular Victorian poetess (1820–97). (78)
Irving: the actor–manager Henry Irving (1838–1905). (86)
James Knowles: an architect, a founder of the Metaphysical Society, and the Editor of the *Contemporary Review* and *Nineteenth Century* (*Later*, pp. 252, 396). (78)

Jamie Anderson: James Reddie Anderson, one of Ruskin's pupils and assistants at Oxford. (72)
Joe: Joe Wilkinson, one of the Ruskin servants, see Evans and Whitehouse, 1135n. (86)
John Ruskin Tweddale: uncle of Joan Agnew with whom she was staying before she joined the Ruskin household. (64)
John Simson, Esq.: The mention of 'Wigtown' implies this is part of the extended Scottish family in Wigtown, possibly John Simson the father of Arbuthnot Simson who was, in turn, the widower of Joan's sister Kate. (78)
Joneses: The artist Edward Burne-Jones and his wife Georgiana, with whom Ruskin travelled to the Continent in 1862.
Jowett: Henry Jowett, Ruskin's printer. (82)
Julia: Possibly Julia Richmond, the wife of George Richmond. (68)
Julia Tylor: Juliet Tylor, daughter of Alfred Tylor of Carshalton, Surrey (*Later*, p. 222). (73)
Kate: Kate Agnew, who married Arbuthnot Simson in 1867. She died two years later, in childbirth; see 13 November 1869. (65)
Kate Smith, who became the 'Indoor Stewardess at Brantwood' (*Fors* (28. 520, 531) L. 62, February 1876), later Kate Raven. (68)
Katie M.: Possibly Katie MacDonald, who had formed 'The Friends of Living Creatures' and asked Ruskin to be the group's patron (*Later*, p. 512).
Kingsley, Mr.: Rev. William Kingsley of South Kilverton, Yorkshire. He was a Turner expert (*Later*, p. 205).
Lacerta: Maria La Touche. (87)
Lewis: the artist John Frederick Lewis, R.A.; Ruskin owned works by him (39.310). (82)
Liddell: Henry George Liddell, Dean of Christ Church. (71)
Lilias: Lilias Trotter, artist and, later, missionary. (83)
Lily: Lily Armstrong (1852–1931), a friend from Winnington and daughter of Sargeant Armstrong, MP for Sligo (Bradley and Ousby, p. 110n). Ruskin referred to her as 'Bear' or 'Little Bear', a name which also occasionally applied both to himself and to Rose La Touche.
Lily: Lily Severn, daughter of Joan and Arthur (1873–1920).
Lily: Lilias Trotter.
Lizzie: Lizzie White. Burd identifies her as Sarah Elizabeth White, a pupil at Winnington who lived in Liverpool. He adds that, anecdotally, she 'never married because she "gave her heart to Ruskin"' (Burd, *Winnington*, p. 461n.). (69)
Lizzie: a Brantwood servant. (86)
Locker: Frederick Locker-Lampson who had written Ruskin the enclosed letter from the Giessbach, which he visited with Tennyson in June 1869. See Hallam Tennyson, *Alfred Lord Tennyson: A Memoir by His Son*, 2 vols (New York: Greenwood, 1969), II, 66.
Lockie: The Severn's governess. (82)
Lollie: Laurence Hilliard. (78)
Longfellow: Henry Wadsworth Longfellow, the American poet. (68)
Loudon: Mrs. J. C. Loudon. Plates from her *Flower Garden of Bulbous Plants* are referred to in 21.229, 235 and 243. (82)
Lucy: Lucy Tovey, the Ruskin's parlour-maid from 1829 to 1875 (Burd, *Winnington*, p. 326n). (65)
Mama, and Kate & Mary, and Arbuthnot.: members of Joan's family (mother, sisters and brother-in-law). (67)

Mamie/Mama: Ruskin referred to many women with variations on this name, including his own mother, Joan's mother, Joan and Mary Hilliard. (71)
Mammima: I take this to be Lucia Alexander, the mother of his 'Sorella' Francesca Alexander. (87)
Morelle: Photographer commissioned by Ruskin, see 22 January 1888 [256]. (87)
Newman: Cardinal Henry Newman (1808–92), see Bradley and Ousby, p. 214n.
Maria: one of Ruskin's housemaids. (68)
Marks: H. Stacy Marks, R.A, a friend of Ruskins, 36.lxxi–ii. (72)
Margaret: Margaret Burne-Jones. (73)
Marshall, Professor: Professor Alfred Marshall. (84)
Mary: Mary Milroy, Joan's sister (67)
Mary: Mary Newton, Arthur's sister.
Mary: a Brantwood servant. (86)
Maude: The Brantwood cook's dog, which Ruskin seems to have appropriated. (73)
Max Muller: Frederick Max Müller (1823–1900), Professor of Comparative Philology (Evans and Whitehouse, p. 769n).
Millais: The artist John Everett Millais, who had married Effie, the former Mrs. John Ruskin, in 1855. (71)
Moore, Mr.: Probably Professor Charles H. Moor of Harvard University (Evans and Whitehouse, p. 1128n). (86)
Morris: William Morris. (82)
Ned: Edward Burne-Jones (1833–98), artist and good friend of Ruskin. (72)
Newton: Charles Newton, Keeper of Greek and Roman Antiquities at the British Museum (Burd, *Winnington*, p. 392n); married to Arthur Severn's sister Mary (*Later*, p. 130). (68)
Norton: Charles Eliot Norton (1827–1908), an American friend and one of Ruskin's executors, see Bradley and Ousby. (68)
Oscar: Oscar Wilde was an undergraduate at Oxford in the early 1870s, becoming friends with Ruskin who was then Slade Professor of Fine Art; surprisingly, Wilde took part in Ruskin's Hinksey Road building project in 1874. (82)
Owl: Charles Augustus Howell, see above.
Parsons, Dr.: Dr. George Parsons, whose practice was 'at Hawkshead, some five miles from Brantwood'; he 'first treated Ruskin in 1873' (*Later*, p. 387). (87)
Patmore: Coventry Patmore, poet. (68)
Peggy: Peggy Webling, sister of Rosalind; they were child performers specialising in recitation (*Later*, pp. 426–28). (82)
Phil: Philip Burne-Jones, son of Edward and Georgiana. (82)
Pigwiggina: Jane Anne Wilkinson. (86)
Prince Leopold: Prince Leopold, Duke of Albany (1853–84), youngest son of Queen Victoria. For his friendship with Ruskin see 20.xxxv–vi. (72)
Randal: Frank Randal, an artist employed by Ruskin (39.438). (81)
Rhoda: Rhoda Liddell one of 'the three Graces', the daughters of Henry George Liddell, Dean of Christ Church, and Lorina (Ina) Liddell. (71)
Richmond, Mr: George Richmond (1809–96), a painter and good friend of Ruskin from 1840 (Bradley and Ousby, p. 29n). (67)
Roch, Madame: Madame Roch of Geneva. See 34.509. (66)
Rooke: Thomas Matthews Rooke (1842–1942) 'came to Ruskin from the firm of Morris and Co.' He was hired by Ruskin in 1879 as a painter and copyist and 'was still receiving a monthly wage from St George in 1887' (*Later*, p. 523).

Rosalind: Rosalind Webling, sister of Peggy; they were child performers specialising in recitation (*Later*, 426–28). (82)
Schmidt, Mr: Given the context of Mr West (Ruskin's music teacher), this might possibly be J. H. H. Schmidt, who developed a musical notation for prosody (31.xxxiii). (82)
Simon, Mrs: Probably Jane Simon, wife of Dr (Sir) John Simon, good friends of Ruskin. (68)
Simon, John: one of Ruskin's doctors and a friend. (71)
Snell: Snell & Son's (William and Edwin Snell), London cabinet makers favoured by John James Ruskin. (68)
Sor: Sorella, Francesca Alexander. (85)
Sowerby: James Sowerby, illustrator of *English Botany* (39.573) (82)
Spielmann: Marion H. Spielmann, Editor of Cassell's *Magazine of Art*. (87)
Stalker, Mrs.: A shepherd's wife; the family lived in 'Lawson Park' above Brantwood (*Later*, p. 320).
Strode, Louisa: '[a]n Edinburgh friend, daughter of a naval officer', (Evans and Whitehouse, p. 1129). (86)
Susie and Mary: Beever sisters, neighbours at Coniston, see *Hortus Inclusus*. (78)
Talbot, Mrs.: Fanny Talbot, a widow who made a gift of land to the Guild of St. George. Ruskin referred to her as 'Mama', see *Dearest Mama Talbot: A Selection of Letters from John Ruskin to Mrs Fanny Talbot* (Manchester: Bulletin of the John Rylands Library, 1966).
Talling, Mr.: Talling of Lostwithiel, Cornwall 'from whom Ruskin purchased many minerals' (36.499). See also 26.449–51.
T. and Mackrells: Tarrant & Mackrell, solicitors. (82)
Tiny: Tiny White was a child actress. Ruskin had met her through the Webling sisters, Rosalind and Peggy, who were child performers specialising in recitation (*Later*, pp. 426–28 and 438–39). (82)
Tylors: The family of Alfred Tylor, who had three daughters, see *Fors* 54 (June 1875), 28.353.
Tyrwhitt, Mr: Rev. Richard St. John Tyrwhitt. (72)
Violet: Violet Severn (1880–1940), daughter of Joan and Arthur.
Walter: Walter Severn, an artist and brother to Arthur Seven. (68)
Ward, Mr: William Ward, one of Ruskin's assistants on the 1868 journey. (68)
Watson, Miss: Marion 'Tenzo' and her sister Lizzie Watson were then visiting Ruskin (*Later*, p. 534). (87)
W. B.: Wilson Barrett, actor–manager (1846–1904). (86)
Wedd-ed-weddie: Alexander Wedderburn. (87)
WHH: William Holman Hunt. (78)
Whistler, Mr: James Abbott MacNeill Whistler. For the Whistler v. Ruskin libel trial, see *Later*, pp. 356–57, 396–98.
William and Mary Milroy of Kirkcudbright: Mary was Joan's sister. (71)
Wilkinsons: shepherd family living in 'Lawson Park' in the 1880s, the home inhabited by the Stalkers when Ruskin first moved to Brantwood. Young Jane Anne Wilkinson became a special friend of Ruskin's. (83)
Woodhouse, Mr: Ruskin's dentist, who was also Rose's dentist when she was in London. (71)
Venice: Venice Hunt, the eight-year-old daughter of William Henry Hunt, and one of Ruskin's goddaughters (*Later*, p. 259). (73)
Violet: Violet Severn, daughter of Joan and Arthur (1880–1940).
Yewdale, Miss: the local schoolmistress at Coniston. (84)

WORKS CITED

❖

Primary Manuscript Sources

Ruskin Library, L 33–54, Ruskin to Joan Severn (1864–88)
Ruskin Library, L55 and 56, Joan Severn to Ruskin (1867–87 and 1888–90)
Ruskin Library, L 64 (misc. correspondence to Joan Ruskin Severn)
Ruskin Library, MS 16 (diary 1869, 1870, 1871, 1873, 1874)
Ruskin Library, MS 18 (diary 1871–73)

Primary Published Sources

The Works of John Ruskin ('Library Edition'), ed. by E. T. Cook and Alexander Wedderburn, 39 vols (London: George Allen, 1903–12)
BIRKENHEAD, SHEILA, ed., *Illustrious Friends: The Story of Joseph Severn and His Son Arthur* (London: Hamish Hamilton, 1965)
BRADLEY, JOHN and IAN OUSBY, eds, *The Correspondence of John Ruskin and Charles Eliot Norton* (Cambridge: Cambridge University Press, 1987)
BRADLEY, JOHN LEWIS, ed., *The Letters of John Ruskin to Lord and Lady Mount-Temple* (Columbus: Ohio State University Press, 1964)
BURD, VAN AKIN, ed., *Christmas Story: John Ruskin's Venetian Letters of 1876–1877* (Newark: University of Delaware Press; London and Toronto: Associated University Presses, 1990)
—— *John Ruskin and Rose La Touche* (Oxford: Clarendon, 1980)
—— *The Ruskin Family Letters: The Correspondence of John James Ruskin, his Wife, and their Son, John, 1801–1843*, 2 vols (New York: Cornell University Press, 1973)
—— *The Winnington Letters: John Ruskin's Correspondence with Margaret Alexis Bell and the Children at Winnington Hall* (London: George Allen & Unwin, 1969)
CLAIBORNE, JAY WOOD, ed., 'Two Secretaries: The Letters of John Ruskin to Charles Augustus Howell and the Rev. Richard St. John Tyrwhitt' (unpublished doctoral dissertation, The University of Texas at Austin, 1969, copyright 1970)
DEARDEN, JAMES S., ed. *The Pigwiggian Chaunts of John Ruskin* ([n.p.]: privately printed, 1960)
—— , ed., *The Professor: Arthur Severn's Memoir of John Ruskin* (London: Allen and Unwin, 1967)
EVANS, JOAN and JOHN HOWARD WHITEHOUSE, eds, *The Diaries of John Ruskin*, 3 vols (Oxford: Clarendon Press, 1956–59)
LUTYENS, MARY, ed., *Young Mrs. Ruskin in Venice: Her Picture of Society and Life with John Ruskin, 1849–1852* (New York: Vanguard Press, 1965)
MEYNELL, VIOLA, ed., *Friends of a Lifetime: Letters to Sidney Carlyle Cockerell* (London: Jonathan Cape, 1940)
SPENCE, MARGARET, ed., *Dearest Mama Talbot: A Selection of Letters from John Ruskin to Mrs Fanny Talbot* (Manchester: Bulletin of the John Rylands Library, 1966).
SURTEES, VIRGINIA, ed., *Reflections of a Friendship: John Ruskin's Letters to Pauline Trevelyan, 1848–1866* (London: George Allen & Unwin, 1979)

——— *Sublime & Instructive: Letters from John Ruskin to Louisa Marchioness of Waterford, Anna Blunden and Ellen Heaton* (London: Michael Joseph, 1972)
VILJOEN, HELEN GILL, ed., *The Brantwood Diary of John Ruskin* (New Haven, CT: Yale University Press, 1971)
——— *The Froude–Ruskin Friendship, as Represented through Letters* (New York: Pageant, 1966)
WILSON, OLIVE, ed., *My Dearest Dora: Letters to Dora Livesey, Her Family and Friends 1860–1900 from John Ruskin* (Kendal: Frank Peters, [n.d.])

Secondary

ATTFIELD, JUDY and PAT KIRKHAM, eds, *A View from the Interior: Feminism, Women and Design* (London: Women's Press, 1989)
AUSTIN, LINDA, *The Practical Ruskin: Economics and Audience in the Late Work* (Baltimore, MD: Johns Hopkins University Press, 1991)
BALIA, MIMMA and MICHELLE LOVRIC, *Ruskin's Rose: A Venetian Love Story 'A True Tale by Mimma Balia with Michelle Lovric'* (New York: Artisan, 2000)
BATCHELOR, JOHN, *John Ruskin: No Wealth but Life* (London: Chatto & Windus, 2000)
BIRCH, DINAH, *Ruskin's Myths* (Oxford: Clarendon Press, 1988)
———ed., *Ruskin and the Dawn of the Modern* (Oxford: Oxford University Press, 1999)
———'Ruskin's "Womanly Mind"', in *Ruskin and Gender* [as below], pp. 107–20
———and FRANCIS O'GORMAN, eds, *Ruskin and Gender* (Basingstoke: Palgrave, 2002)
BRADLEY, J. L., *A Ruskin Chronology* (Basingstoke: Macmillan, 1997)
BULLEN, J. B., 'Ruskin, Gautier, and the Feminization of Venice', in *Ruskin and Gender*, ed. by Birch and O'Gorman (Basingstoke: Palgrave, 2002), pp. 64–85
BURD, VAN AKIN, *John Ruskin and Rose La Touche* (Oxford: Clarendon Press, 1980)
BRUNTON, JENNIE, 'The Late Nineteenth-century Revival of the Langdale Linen Industry', in *A History of Linen in the North West*, ed. by Elizabeth Roberts (Lancaster: Centre for North West Regional Studies, 1998), pp. 93–118
COLLINGWOOD, W. G., *The Life of John Ruskin*, 2 vols, 2nd edn (London: Methuen, 1900)
COLVIN, SIDNEY, *Memoires and Notes* (London: Edwin Arnold, 1921)
CORREA, DELIA DE SOUSA, 'Goddesses of Instruction and Desire: Ruskin and Music', in *Ruskin and the Dawn of the Modern*, ed. by Dinah Birch (Oxford: Oxford University Press, 1999), pp. 111–30
CULLEN, ANTHEA, 'Sexual Division of Labour in the Arts and Crafts Movement', in *A View from the Interior: Feminism, Women and Design*, ed. by Judy Attfield and Pat Kirkham (London: Women's Press, 1989), pp. 151–64
DEARDEN, JAMES S., 'Dating of Ruskin letters: by note-paper styles' (self-published pamphlet)
———'John Ruskin's Dogs' (Bembridge, Isle of Wight: Desktop Studio, 2003)
———*John Ruskin: A Life in Pictures* (Sheffield: Sheffield Academic Press, 1999)
DICKERSON, VANESSA D., ed., *Keeping the Victorian House: A Collection of Essays* (New York and London: Garland, 1995)
DICKINSON, RACHEL, 'Terms of Empowerment: John Ruskin's Correspondence with Joan Severn' (unpublished doctoral dissertation, Lancaster University, 2005)
———'Theatre's Heroines and Ruskinian Morality', in *Ruskin, the Theatre and Victorian Visual Culture*, ed. by Anselm Heinrich, Kate Newey and Jeffrey Richards (Houndmills: Palgrave, forthcoming 2008)
———and KEITH HANLEY, eds, *Ruskin's Struggle for Coherence: Self-Representation through Art, Place and Society* (Newcastle: Cambridge Scholars Press, 2006)

GERRARD, JESSICA, 'The Chatelaine: Women of the Victorian Landed Classes and the Country House', in *Keeping the Victorian House: A Collection of Essays*, ed. by Vanessa D. Dickerson (New York and London: Garland, 1995), pp. 175–206
GORDON, BEVERLY, 'Woman's Domestic Body: The Conceptual Conflation of Women and Interiors in the Industrial Age', *Winterthur Portfolio*, 31 (1996), 281–301
HILTON, TIM, *John Ruskin: The Early Years 1819–1859* (New Haven, CT: Yale University Press, 1985) [reissued as paperback, 2000]
—— *John Ruskin: The Later Years* (New Haven, CT: Yale University Press, 2000)
HOWITT, DENNIS, *Paedophiles and Sexual Offences against Children* (Chichester: John Wiley & Sons, 1995)
HUNT, JOHN DIXON and FAITH M. HOLLAND, eds, *The Ruskin Polygon: Essays on the Imagination of John Ruskin* (Manchester: Manchester University Press, 1982)
MARSH, JAN, *Pre-Raphaelite Women: Images of Femininity in Pre-Raphaelite Art* (London: Artus, 1987)
MILBANK, ALISON, 'A Fine Grotesque or a Pathetic Fallacy? The Role of Objects in the Autobiographical Writing of Ruskin and Proust', in *Ruskin's Struggle for Coherence: Self-Representation through Art, Place and Society*, ed. by Rachel Dickinson and Keith Hanley (Newcastle: Cambridge Scholars Press, 2006), pp. 90–105
MILLETT, KATE, *Sexual Politics* (New York: Doubleday, 1970)
O'GORMAN, FRANCIS, *John Ruskin* (Stroud: Sutton, 1999)
ROBSON, CATHERINE, *Men in Wonderland: The Lost Girlhood of the Victorian Gentleman* (Princeton, NJ: Princeton University Press, 2001)
—— 'The Stones of Childhood: Ruskin's "Lost Jewels"', in *Ruskin and Gender*, ed. by Dinah Birch and Francis O'Gorman (Basingstoke: Palgrave, 2002), pp. 29–46
ROSSETTI, CHRISTINA, 'In an Artist's Studio', in *New Poems by Christina Rossetti*, ed. by William Michael Rossetti (London: MacMillan, 1896)
—— *Sing-Song: A Nursery Rhyme Book, with One Hundred and Twenty Illustrations*, illus. by Arthur Hughes (London: Routledge, 1872)
SMITH, LINDSAY, 'The Foxglove and the Rose: Ruskin's Involute of Childhood', in *Ruskin and Gender*, ed. by Dinah Birch and Francis O'Gorman (Basingstoke: Palgrave, 2002), pp. 47–63
SIMPSON, MARK, 'The Dream of the Dragon: Ruskin's Serpent Imagery' in *The Ruskin Polygon: Essays on the Imagination of John Ruskin*, ed. by John Dixon Hunt and Faith M. Holland (Manchester: Manchester University Press, 1982), pp. 21–43
SPIELMANN, MARION H., *John Ruskin* (London: Cassell, 1900)
—— and G. S. LAYARD, *The Life and Work of Kate Greenaway* (London: A. C. Black, 1905; repr. London: Bracken Books, 1986)
TENNYSON, HALLAM, *Alfred Lord Tennyson: A Memoir by His Son*, 2 vols (New York: Greenwood, 1969) [first pub. 1897]
VILJOEN, HELEN GILL, *Ruskin's Scottish Heritage: A Prelude* (Urbana: University of Illinois Press, 1956)
WELTMAN, SHARON ARONOFSKY, 'Myth and Gender in Ruskin's Science', in *Ruskin and the Dawn of the Modern*, ed. by Dinah Birch (Oxford: Oxford University Press, 1999), pp. 153–73
—— *Performing the Victorian: John Ruskin and Identity in Theatre, Science, and Education* (Columbus: Ohio State University Press, 2007)
—— *Ruskin's Mythic Queen: Gender Subversion in Victorian Culture* (Athens, OH: Ohio University Press, 1998)
WILSON, A. N., *The Victorians* (London: Hutchinson, 2002)

INDEX

❖

Abbeville 95-104, 106, 131, 250, 271
Abingdon 132, 134, 135, 186
Acland, Harry 140
Acland, Henry 131n, 132, 152, 169, 178-79, 210
Agnew, Joan *see* Severn, Joan
Agnew, Kate *see* Simson, Kate
Agnew, Mary, *see* Milroy, Mary
Alexander, Francesca (Sorella) 27-28, 34, 49, 55, 221, 224, 236, 239-42, 244, 246, 250, 264 L269n
Alexander, Lucia (Mammima) 241
Alighieri, Dante 16, 64 n. 235, 112, 139
Alison, Archibald 223
Allen, George 29, 202, 216, 247
American Civil War 124
Amiens 102, 195
Anderson, James Reddie (Jamie) 16, 147, 174
Anderson, Sara (Diddie) 16, 146, 155, 189-90, 233
Angelico, Fra 160
architecture 103, 105, 119-20, 140, 242
Armstrong, Lily (Bear) 61 n. 91, 74, 95
Arras 105
art criticism 115, 120-21, 125, 133-34, 151, 204, 224, 251
art supplies 134, 247
Athenaeum Club 137-38
Audran, Edmond, 203-05
Austin, Linda 65 n. 247
Avallon 206

Bach, Johann Sebastian 170, 177
Baker, George 196
Barrett, Wilson 222, 244
Batchelor, John 7, 16, 25, 34, 36, 50, 56
Baveno 110
Baxter, Peter 187, 209, 224, 229, 237-38, 244, 251
Beever, Mary 27, 191
Beever, Susie 21, 27, 188, 191, 197, 201, 212, 225-27, 234-35, 246, 269
Bell, Margaret Alexis 90
Berne 252
Bible 64 n. 235, 66 n. 301, 81, 88-90, 165, 172
Birch, Dinah 23, 49-50
birds 30-31, 44-45, 85, 105, 112, 135, 140, 162, 165-67, 191, 199, 211, 213, 222, 224, 227, 229, 260
Blencathra (Saddleback) 82
Blow, Detmar 55, 251
Borromeo, Count 113, 120, 123

botany 18, 76-77, 85, 98, 111, 122 127, 133, 140, 193, 198, 201, 204, 206-07, 216, 229-30
Botticelli 38, 152, 184 n. 1, 206, 207 n. 1
Boulogne 95, 132, 182
Bowles (Dr) 241
Bradford, Mary Frances 33
Bradley, J. L. 49, 60 n. 60, 66 n. 305
Brantwood xii, 1, 4, 6-7, 11, 13-14, 21, 24-25, 29-31, 39-40, 43, 52-57, 140-41, 147, 150, 155, 158-68, 171-76, 181, 188-89, 192-94, 198, 209, 211-37, 240-41, 244, 251, 265-66, 268-70
Brescia 115
Brett, John 198
Bridge, S. F. 90
Brientz 107, 122
British Museum 72 n.2, 91 n. 2, 156, 167, 169, 186, 196, 199, 203, 205-06
Broadlands 126, 251
Brown, Rawdon 113, 118, 122 n. 6, 132, 184
Burd, Van Akin 26, 49, 71
Burgess, Arthur 16, 61 n. 105, 103, 115, 195, 225
Burne-Jones, Edward (Ned) 5, 12, 15, 36, 104, 151, 160, 167, 176, 201-02, 212
Burne-Jones, Georgiana (Georgie) 36, 104, 158-60, 201-02
Burne-Jones, Margaret 36, 158-59, 201-02
Burne-Jones, Philip (Phil) 202

Calais 238
Carlisle 140, 191, 267
Carlyle, Thomas 5, 14, 48-49, 74, 170
Carré, Louis 236
Carroll, Lewis *see* Dodgson, Charles
Castle Crag 88
Catholicism 92, 120
Causey Pike 82
Champagnole 252
Chartres 104
Chesneau, Ernest 212-13
chess 51, 92-93, 152, 161-62, 164 L127n, 196, 199-200, 223
chopping wood 48, 51, 141, 188, 222
Christie's Auction House 6, 198, 200-03
Christy Minstrels 159, 195
Collingwood, William Gershom (Collie) 7, 16, 18, 196, 198-99, 201, 205, 207, 223, 247

Index

Colwith 229-30
Como 115, 118
Coniston Old Man 65 n. 248, 162
Cook, E. T. xi, 21-22, 24, 46, 88 n. 5
cooking 3, 8, 24-25, 51, 82, 101, 102, 106, 110, 153, 161, 178
Coniston 140-41, 146, 181
Cowley 82 n. 8, 91-93, 125, 156, 254-55
Cowper-Temple, Georgiana (φίλη or filē) 49, 66 n. 305, 101, 110-11, 113, 126, 129, 137, 183, 204, 222, 248
Crawley, Frederick 30, 75, 81, 86-87, 102, 154, 163, 167, 175, 177
crossing sweepers 92
Croyden 136

Dante, *see* Alighieri, Dante
Dearden, James S. 8, 43, 70
Denmark Hill 74-77, 79, 91-94, 106, 110, 125-38, 141, 144, 224
Derwentwater 82
Dickens, Charles 29, 110
Dijon 104, 206, 208, 251
Dilke, Charles 197
Dixon, Thomas 173
Dodgson, Charles (Lewis Carroll) 35-36, 134 n. 2, 170
Doré, Gustave 151
Domecq, Adèle 9, 14, 36-37, 104
Dover 140
Downes, David 80-81, 102-03, 111, 113, 127, 153, 171-72
dreams 12, 82, 92, 97, 99, 119, 155, 194, 209
Drewitt, Dawtrey 178
Drury Lane Theatre 239
Dudley Gallery 202, 217
Durham 228

education 8- 9, 41, 49-50, 60 n. 71, 62 n. 135, 174, 194, 213-14, 228
Edwardes, Herbert 216, 245
Ètaples 105

Faunthorpe, John 21, 226
Fine Art Society 189 n. 3, 212, 260
Fleming, Albert 226, 234, 243, 265, 269
Florence 206-07
Folkestone 51, 106, 238-39, 241, 246-47
Frère, Edouard 149
Froude, James Anthony 97-98, 196, 271

Gainsborough, Thomas 160
gardening *see* botany
geology 18, 42, 72 n.2, 75-77, 80, 83-84, 86-87, 90, 99-101, 140, 149, 154 n. 2, 156, 171, 182, 196-97, 202-03, 205-06, 212
George, Prince of Auhalt 210
Geneva 208

Gibbon, Edward 213
Giessbach 113-15, 122-24, 141
Gilchrist, Connie 239
Gladstone, Mary 188
Gladstone, William Ewart 5, 96, 187-88, 203
Goodwin, Albert 134
Goodwin, Ellen 265-66
Gordon, Osborne 73
Gray, Effie *see* Millais, Euphemia
Greenaway, Kate 21, 32, 46, 209, 224, 250, 264
Guild of St George 6, 17, 22, 29-30, 66 n. 275, 177, 196 n. 2, 201 n. 1, 226 n. 5, 247 n. 2
    The 'Order' and 'our Society' 44, 112, 127
    Sheffield Museum 205 n. 1
Gull, William 244

Harrison, W. H. 73, 244
Harristown 101, 182, 256
Hawarden Castle 187 n. 3, 188
Hawnby 257
Helvellyan 86
Herdson, Dawson 200, 230
Herne Hill 100-01, 154, 184, 197-205, 223, 259, 261, 264-66
Hill, Octavia 95
Hilliard, Constance (Connie) 44, 61 n. 84, 80, 82, 91, 93, 105, 108, 110, 113, 116, 120, 122-23, 125, 127, 129-30, 135 n. 3, 146, 158, 162-63, 168, 232
Hilliard, Ethel (Ettie) 91, 93, 127
Hilliard, Mary 82, 84, 135, 206
Hilliard, Laurence (Lollie) 16, 61 n. 84, 192, 216, 218, 260,
Hilton, Tim 12, 14, 16, 22-25, 34-35, 40, 43, 50, 158 n. 2, 184 n. 1, 189 n. 3
Holyoake, George Jacob 190
Howell, Charles Augustus (Owl) 15-18, 40, 61 n. 93, 100-01
Hughes, Arthur 158, 159
Huish, Marcus 189, 198
Hunt, Gladys 24, 204
Hunt, William Henry 174 n. 1, 175
Hunt, William Holman 24, 149, 160, 189, 204, 235
Hunt, Venice 174-75
hunting 105

Ingelow, Jean 188, 262
Interlaken 107
Irving, Henry 222
Isle of Man 145

Jackson (servant) 166
Jowett, Benjamin 66 n. 290, 209, 214
Jowett, Henry 199, 239, 245, 262

Keswick 80-90, 140
Kingsley, William, 13, 131-32, 254, 258
Kirkby Lonsdale 266

Kirkcudbright 244
Knowles, James 190

Lago Maggiore 110, 115, 140
Lancaster 139, 154, 248
Langdale 90
La Touche, John 256
La Touche, Maria (Lacerta) 12, 61 n. 95, 92 n. 5, 137-38, 195, 196 n. 6, 232
La Touche, Percy 5, 10, 12, 102
La Touche, Rose (Rosie and Tuk Up) 7-14, 16, 25-26, 33-39, 43, 45, 52, 56, 59 n. 35, 59 n. 38, 60 n. 81, 64 n. 234, 74 n. 1, 83, 84, 85 n. 7, 87-88, 90-92, 95, 101 n. 1, 102, 105 n. 7, 125, 134, 136-38, 146, 155 n. 1, 162 n. 1, 169, 176 n. 1, 181-82, 184, 207 n. 1, 232-33, 256, 267-68
Leech, John 29, 125, 147 L104n, 236
Lees, Dorothy (Doadie, Dora) 44, 66 n. 275, 100, 144, 240-41
Lees, Edward 240-41, 253
Leopold, Prince, Duke of Albany 68 n. 344, 150-52, 169-70, 177-79, 186-88
Lewis, John Frederick 198
Lichfield 168
Liddell, Alice 35, 134, 150-51, 169-70, 174, 179
Liddell, Edith 134 n. 2, 150-51, 177, 179
Liddell, Henry George 134 n. 2, 178
Liddell, Lorina (Ina) 134 n. 2, 169, 234
Liddell, Rhoda 134, 150-51, 179
Linton, William James 140-41
Livesey, Dorothy *see* Lees, Dorothy
Locker-Lampson, Frederick 113-14
Lockie 38-39, 197, 199, 202, 206, 207, 212, 224, 264, 266
London 148, 164, 190, 196, 198, 225, 240-43
London Institute 183, 184 n. 1
Longfellow, Henry Wadsworth 105, 106 n. 1, 114, 119
Loudon, J. C. 18, 201
Louis, Prince of [Hesse] 178-79
Louise, Princess 169-70, 179
Louise, Princess of Dessau 210
Louvre 104
Lucca 204, 207
Lucerne 120, 151, 182
Lugano 115
Luini 120

Magazine of Art (Cassell's) 6, 243-47
Malham 190-91
Manning, Cardinal 188
Mantegn, Andrea 178
Marks, H. Stacy 145, 186, 187, 225-26, 242
Marshall, Alfred 214
Marshalls (of Monk Coniston) 39, 195, 219 n. 2
Matlock 8, 14-15, 137-38, 141, 263
McClelland, 'Clennie' 219, 221-23, 225, 228, 231, 262
Meissonier, Jean-Louis-Ernest 124, 198-200

Melrose 140
Metaphysical Society 190 n. 3
Meyringen 113, 253
Michaelangelo 152
Milan 113, 115
Milbank, Alison 64 n. 235
Millais, John Everett 134, 204
Millais, Euphemia, (Effie) 9, 11-12, 36-37, 40, 134 n. 2
Millett, Kate 50
Milroy, Mary *née* Agnew 83, 138, 255
Milroy, William 113, 136, 138, 148-50, 176
Milton, John 234
minerals *see* geology
Monk Coniston *see* Marshalls
Moore, Charles H. 228
Morelle (photographer) 247, 250
Morning Post 66 n. 290, 197,
Morris, William 202, 212, 247 n. 2
Mount-Temple, Georgiana *see* Cowper-Temple, Georgiana
Mozart, Wolfgang Amadeus 202
Müller, Friederich Max 178-79
music 21, 62 n. 135, 82, 89, 122, 124, 126, 150, 154, 159, 170, 177, 179, 198-200, 202, 214, 218-19, 225-26, 231, 245-47, 264
Myers, F. W. 152

Neuchâtel 104, 110
Newman, John Henry (Cardinal) 188
Newman (painter) 204
Newton, Charles 91, 148
Norton, Charles Eliot 21-22, 61 n. 117, 103-06, 111, 113, 119, 121 n. 2, 123, 149, 151, 161 n. 5, 252

O'Gorman, Francis 49-50
Oldham, Constance (Connie) 80, 146, 242
opera 201, 202, 204-05
Oxford 120, 127, 131, 134, 136, 146, 148, 182, 208-09, 213
Oxford University:
  Balliol College 147, 214
  Christ Church College 68 n. 144, 134 n. 2, 198, 244
  Corpus Christi College 144-53, 166, 168-70, 173, 176-79, 181, 183-84, 186-87, 198
  Magdalen College 215
  Oxford Museum 187 n. 5-6
  Oxford Union 187 n. 6
  Ruskin's gifts to 126
  Ruskin's lectures at 2, 17, 28-29, 30-31, 57, 120, 127-29, 134, 145, 152, 165-66, 169, 173, 177, 182, 208-10, 213-14, 247
  Ruskin as student at 14, 131 n. 2
  Ruskin teaching at 134, 147
  vivisection debate 57, 218

Pallmall Gazette 149
Paradise Row 95

Paris 104, 115, 129, 132, 208, 251
Parsons, George (Dr.) 232, 237, 262, 266
Patmore, Coventry 92, 93 n. 1, 144
Punch 125 n. 2, 141, 212, 248
peasants 96, 110-11, 115
penmanship 7, 72, 77, 99, 244
pets:
  Bramble (dog) 224
  cats 164, 174-75, 245
  Maude (dog) 159 n. 1, 163-64, 167-68, 174, 176
  Norway (horse) 231, 270
photographs xii, 1, 21, 27-28, 31, 34, 37-38, 58 n. 1, 83, 123, 158, 190, 197, 205, 233, 242, 246-47, 252, 262, 264
politics 129-30, 141, 176, 188
post card 221, 223
postal system 13, 29, 79, 96, 101, 112, 123, 168-69, 174, 176, 191, 206, 213, 246, 247, 252, 270
Protestantism 120, 213
Prout, Samuel 160

Randal, Frank 195
Raphael 149, 179, 186
railway *see* transport
Rathbone, Philip 144 n. 000
Raven, Kate 15, 101, 138, 159, 161, 167
Reynolds, Joshua 149
Richardson, Jessie 8-9, 25, 45
Richardson, Mary 8-9
Richmond, George 14, 22, 89, 108 n. 1
Richmond, Julia 14, 108
Richmond, Thomas 255
Robbia, Lucca della 204
Robbespierre 105
Robson, Catherine 26, 36, 41-44, 50
Roch (Mme) 80
rocks *see* geology
Rome 152
Rooke, Thomas Matthews 235, 247
Rossetti, Christina 158
Rossetti, Dante Gabriel 46, 187
rowing 90, 140-41, 229
Royal Institution 92
Ruskin, Effie *see* Millais, Euphemia
Ruskin, John:
  Bible of Amiens 260, 262
  Christ's Folk in the Apennines 236, 239-40
  Dilecta 234
  Ethics of the Dust 42, 49
  Fors Clavigera 4, 9, 16, 18, 64 n. 200, 141, 163 n. 4, 245
  Hortus Inclusus 27, 191 n. 1, 226 n. 5
  King of the Golden River 204
  Modern Painters 1, 9, 50, 62 n. 117, 270
  Praeterita 2, 3, 5, 8-9, 11, 15, 17, 19, 23, 25, 27-28, 34-37,39, 42-43, 53, 59 n. 17, 59 n.44, 64 n. 233, 66 n. 301, 140 n. 2, 224-25, 233, 242, 245-47, 252, 264

Sesame and Lilies 29, 49
babytalk 19-32, 40, 46, 55-58, 115, 120, 214
  Pig-wiggian 3-4, 23, 25, 62 n. 140, 62 n. 146, 81, 82, 85, 97, 98, 101, 103, 105, 121-24,
financial worries 6-7, 17, 22, 24, 57, 216, 221, 227, 234, 243, 266-67
and girls 8-9, 24-25, 27, 33-51, 74, 76, 91, 117, 127, 179, 197, 202-05, 207, 211-14, 216, 219, 223-25, 229-30, 239, 252, 260-61
illnesses 7, 13-14, 41, 51-52, 61 n. 84, 231-37, 240, 250, 263, 267, 269
painting and drawing 85, 92, 95, 104, 149, 153, 159-60, 167-68, 173, 188, 191, 196, 201, 204, 206-08, 215, 230, 238, 244
Ruskin, John James 8, 11, 12, 23, 33, 49, 50, 101 n. 7, 104 n. 1, 149, 173, 182, 187, 196, 263, 268
Ruskin, Margaret (Auntie) 8, 12, 15, 88, 93, 105-07, 138, 150, 182, 227, 232, 255-59, 261, 263, 267-68

Saint Gotthard 115, 118
Sandgate 6, 51, 243-50, 268
Scawfell 86
Schmidlin, Marie (of the Giessbach) 33-34, 64 n. 200, 113-14, 121-24
Scott, Walter 151, 187, 195, 245
Sens 104, 206
Settle 190
Severn, Agnew (boys) 198, 199, 201, 218, 230, 236, 262
Severn, Arthur (Arfie) 5, 8, 9-16, 27, 30-31, 45, 60 n. 53, 64 n. 204, 97 n. 3, 102 n. 3, 130, 132, 134, 136-40, 142, 144-48, 150, 152-54, 156, 158-60, 163-65, 169-73, 175, 177-78, 180-82, 189-92, 196-202, 205, 207, 211, 213-14, 217-18, 222-24, 227, 230, 234, 238, 242-43, 246, 248, 252, 254, 257-63, 265, 268-71
Severn, Arthur Jr. (boys) 199, 207, 262
Severn, Herbert 28, 269
Severn, Joan:
  assistant to Ruskin 15-18, 22, 29-30, 74-75, 77, 94, 99, 101, 107, 233, 243, 261
  care of Ruskin 7, 14-15, 28, 31-32, 46, 56-58, 192-93, 203, 208, 214, 232, 235-36, 238, 241, 250, 265, 268-70
  honeymoon of 13-14, 59 n. 16, 60 n. 80, 131-39, 257-59
  marriage of 5, 9-13, 130-31, 153
  pregnancy and problems breastfeeding 163 L125n, 164, 166, 168-69, 172, 259
Severn, Lily (Fisy and Bibsy) 58 n.2, 160 n. 1, 163 n. 164, 166, 168-69, 171, 177, 188-89, 193-94, 216, 222-23, 231, 241, 260-62, 264, 270
Severn, Violet 52, 214, 223-24, 227, 231, 233, 235-36, 241, 262, 264-65
Severn, Walter 91, 202
Shakespeare, William 133
Sharpe, Edmund 139

Simon, John 91, 137, 264
Simson, Arbuthnot 75 n. 1, 83, 103, 106, 125-28
Simson, Kate 31, 67 n. 320, 75-77, 83-85, 94-95, 103, 106, 122-23, 125 n. 1, 126, 160 n. 1, 190 n. 1, 255
Skiddaw 85-87, 90, 124
Smith, George 163
Smith, Kate *see* Raven, Kate
Snell & Sons 101
Society for the Employment of the Poor 106 n. 3, 108 L42n
Sowerby, James 18, 198, 201
Spielmann, Marion H. 6, 46, 243-46,
Stalker, [Hannah ?] 159 n. 1, 163, 211 n. 1
Staunton, Howard 223
Strachan, Ann 34, 72, 145, 182
Strode, Louisa 41, 43, 227-28, 232, 234

Talbot, Fanny (Mama) 49, 201, 209, 225-27
Tarrant & Mackrell 196, 202, 217
Taylor Gallery 179
theatre 7, 33, 51, 65 n. 254, 104, 129, 144, 239, 243, 245
Thun 123, 252
Thurland Castle 241
Tintoretto 149
Titian 114, 149, 178
transport:
    carriage 47, 74, 77, 93, 96, 205, 228
    coupé 251
    post 140
    rail 77, 93, 95, 140, 154, 162, 169-70, 175-76, 188, 205, 206, 228, 252, 268-70
Trevelyan, Pauline (Lady) 61 n. 84, 80 n. 4, 104, 110, 206, 208, 232 n. 4, 255 L262n
Trotter, Lilias 209
Turner, J. M. W. 6, 100, 107, 108, 118, 126, 131 n. 3, 149, 150, 160, 175, 178, 179, 189 n. 3, 198, 199, 201, 203, 209, 235, 240, 242, 247, 248
Tweddale, John Ruskin 5, 73

Twelves, Marion 226 n. 5
Tyrwhitt, Richard St. John 15, 18, 128, 151

Van Eyck, Jan 251
Vaudeville Theatre 245
Venice 26, 35, 44, 50, 113, 115, 117, 120, 212
Verona 43, 110-19, 120 n. 2
Vevay 113
Victoria, Queen 150 n. 1, 151
Viljoen, Helen Gill 19

Ward, William 102, 26
Warren, Emily 269
war 129
Watson, Marion (Tenzo) 233
Webling, Peggy 203 n. 3
Webling, Rosalind 24, 203, 205
Wedderburn, Alexander xi, 16, 21, 22, 24, 46, 70, 88 n. 5, 247
Weir, Harrison 244
Weltman, Sharon Aronofsky 36, 50
Whistler, James Abbott MacNeill 62 n. 128, 192
White, Sarah Elizabeth (Lizzie) 110, 127, 154
White, Tiny 24, 202 n., 203, 205
Whitelands 226 n. 2, 263
Wigtown 110, 123, 244
Wilde, Oscar 203
Wilde, Jane 203
Wilkinson, Jane Anne 25, 211, 213, 221-24, 231
Wilson, A. N. 25-26, 35-36, 63 n. 164
Wilson, Olive 66 n.275, 241 n. 4
Windermere 123, 228, 254-55
Windsor Castle 186-87
Winnington Hall 33-34, 37, 47, 48, 49, 74, 80 n. 4, 90, 100 n. 5, 110 n. 2
Woodhouse (dentist) 137
Woodward, Benjamin 187
Woolwich 127
Wordsworth, William 35, 153, 248